# Dominant Algorithms to Evaluate Artificial Intelligence: From the View of Throughput Model

Authored by

**Waymond Rodgers**
*University of Hull*
*University of Texas*
*El Paso*
*USA*

**Dominant Algorithms to Evaluate Artificial Intelligence: From the View of Throughput Model**

Author: Waymond Rodgers

ISBN (Online): 978-981-5049-54-1

ISBN (Print): 978-981-5049-55-8

ISBN (Paperback): 978-981-5049-56-5

need for a court order if at any point you breach any terms of this License Agreement. In no event will any delay or failure by Bentham Science Publishers in enforcing your compliance with this License Agreement constitute a waiver of any of its rights.

3. You acknowledge that you have read this License Agreement, and agree to be bound by its terms and conditions. To the extent that any other terms and conditions presented on any website of Bentham Science Publishers conflict with, or are inconsistent with, the terms and conditions set out in this License Agreement, you acknowledge that the terms and conditions set out in this License Agreement shall prevail.

**Bentham Science Publishers Pte. Ltd.**
80 Robinson Road #02-00
Singapore 068898
Singapore
Email: subscriptions@benthamscience.net

BENTHAM
SCIENCE

# CONTENTS

# PREFACE

*"Artificial intelligence would be the ultimate version of Google. The ultimate search engine that would understand everything on the web. It would understand exactly what you wanted, and it would give you the right thing. We're nowhere near doing that now. However, we can get incrementally closer to that, and that is basically what we work on."* —Larry Page

I think we're going to need artificial assistance to make the breakthroughs that society wants. Climate, economics, disease -- they're just tremendously complicated interacting systems. It's just hard for humans to analyze all that data and make sense of it.

Artificial intelligence (AI) systems are already transforming individuals and organizations manner of functioning in today's world. AI can automate repetitive tasks, analyze large volumes of data, recommend content, translate languages, and even play games. Further, AI and related technologies are progressively ubiquitous in business and society. For example, AI increasingly find their way into everything from advanced quantum computing systems, automobiles, household appliances, and leading-edge medical diagnostic systems to consumer electronics and "smart" personal assistants. AI tools are also employed virtual reality, augmented reality as well as making IoT devices and services smarter and more secure.

Nonetheless, the current scope of things that AI can accomplish is relatively narrow. Some experts say the technology is far from becoming so-called artificial general intelligence, or AGI. That is, AGI is the capability to understand or learn any intellectual task that a human being can.

Furthermore, others have noted that even in its current, narrow proficiencies, AI provokes a series of ethical and trustworthiness questions. These questions represent issues such as whether the data fed into AI programs are without bias, and whether AI can be held accountable if something goes wrong.

To construct ethical and trusted AI systems, there needs to be cooperation among nations and various stakeholders. Experts have previously warned that inherently biased AI programs can present momentous problems and it may get in the way people's trust in those systems. For example, facial recognition software, for example, may incorporate accidental racial and gender bias, which may pose a threat to a particular group of individuals.

Therefore, this book provides a methodology described as the Throughput Model that can enable individuals and organizations to better identify, understand, and use algorithms to solve daily problems. Moreover, the Throughput Model can further the AI field since it represents symbol manipulation in six algorithmic pathways that seems to be essential for *human* cognition, namely, perception, information, judgment, and decision choice. Finally, The Throughput Model provides the first steps towards building architectures that combine the strengths of the symbolic approaches that can be adapted for machine learning/deep learning, and to develop better techniques for extracting and generalizing abstract knowledge from large, often noisy data sets.

As AI is employed more and more for applications where decisions require explanations, the Throughput Model offers the means to look under the hood of AI and comprehend how those decisions are attained by organizations. This is, particularly important for employing ethical and trustworthiness systems. Hence, Throughput Modelling ought to be considered from the start as it will inform the design of an AI system. Building trusted and ethical AI systems and the governance around them may potentially become a competitive strength for organizations.

## CONSENT FOR PUBLICATION

Not applicable.

## CONFLICT OF INTEREST

The authors declare no conflict of interest, financial or otherwise.

**Waymond Rodgers**
University of Hull
University of Texas
El Paso
USA

# ACKNOWLEDGEMENTS

I would like to express my gratitude to the many people who saw me through this book; to all those who provided support, talked things over, read, wrote, offered comments, allowed me to quote their remarks and assisted in the editing, proofreading and design of the book. Further, I would like to thank those for using artificial intelligence figures in the book.

Further, I would like to thank my students. Learning is a collaborative activity when it is happening at its best. We work together using each other's strengths to build our own challenges, developing our thinking and problem-solving skills. Therefore, the relationship we develop with our students at every age is one that is to be respected, nurtured, and admired.

Last and not least: I request forgiveness of individuals who have been with me over the course of the years and whose names I have failed to mention.

# CHAPTER 1

# Introduction to Artificial Intelligence and Algorithms

*"We have seen AI providing conversation and comfort to the lonely; we have also seen AI engaging in racial discrimination. Yet the biggest harm that AI is likely to do to individuals in the short term is job displacement, as the amount of work we can automate with AI is vastly larger than before. As leaders, it is incumbent on all of us to make sure we are building a world in which every individual has an opportunity to thrive".*

---Andrew Ng, Co-founder and lead of Google Brain

*The AI of the past used brute-force computing to analyze data and present them in a way that seemed human. The programmer supplied the intelligence in the form of decision trees and algorithms. Imagine that you were trying to build a machine that could play tic-tac-toe. You would give it specific rules on what move to make, and it would follow them. Today's AI uses machine learning in which you give it examples of previous games and let it learn from the examples. The computer is taught what to learn and how to learn and makes its decisions. What's more, the new AIs are modeling the human mind itself using techniques similar to our learning processes.*

---Vivek Wadhwa

*Google's work in artificial intelligence ... includes deep neural networks, networks of hardware and software that approximate the web of neurons in the human brain. By analyzing vast amounts of digital data, these neural nets can learn all sorts of useful tasks, like identifying photos, recognizing commands spoken into a smartphone, and, as it turns out, responding to Internet search queries. In some cases, they can learn a task so well that they outperform humans. They can do it better. They can do it faster. And they can do it at a much larger scale.*

---Cade Metz

**Abstract**

The Fourth Industrial Revolution generation has ushered in extremely sophisticated digital apparatuses that have taken the place of manual processing to ensure higher automation and sophistication. Artificial Intelligence (AI) provides the tools to exhibit human-like behaviors while adjusting to the newly given inputs and accommodating change in the environment. Moreover, the tech-giants such as Amazon, Apple, IBM, Facebook, Google, Microsoft, and many others are investing in generating AI-driven products to facilitate the market demands for sophisticated automation. AI will continually influence areas such as job opportunities, environmental protection, healthcare, and other areas in economic and social systems.

**Keywords:** Algorithms, Artificial intelligence.(AI), Audit, Bias, Big data, Cognitive automation, Decision choice, Deep learning, Digital workforce, Financial robots, Information, Judgment, Machine learning, Natural language processing (NLP), Neural networks, Perception, Robotic process automation (RPA), Throughput Model, Transparency.

## INTRODUCTION

The development of artificial intelligence (AI) has transformed our economic, social, and political way of life. Tedious and time-consuming tasks can now be delegated to AI tools that can complete the work in a matter of minutes, if not seconds. Within the world of business, this have significantly decreased the time required to conclude transactions. Nonetheless, there is always the fear of a person being replaced by AI tools for the sake of cost and time efficiency. Although these fears are valid in some arenas, AI is not developed enough to completely replace a human's judgment or expertise in a variety of situations. Moreover, AI can be considered as a tool that should be fully embraced to improve an individual or organization efficiency and effectiveness when performing a task. Within the human resource department, machines can be used throughout the entire process.

This book presents a decision-making model described as the "Throughput Model," which houses six dominant algorithmic pathways for AI use. This modeling process may better guide individuals, organizations, and society in general to assess the overall algorithmic architect that is guiding AI systems. Moreover, the Throughput Modeling approach can address values and ethics that are often not baked into the digital systems, which assembles individuals' decisions for them. Finally, the Throughput Model specified six major algorithms (to be discussed later) that may augment human capacities by countering people's deepening dependence on machine-driven networks that can erode their abilities to think for themselves, act independent of automated systems and interact effectively with others [1]. The Throughput Model dominant six algorithms can be utilized as a platform for an enhanced understanding of the erosion of traditional sociopolitical structures and the possibility of great loss of lives due to accelerated growth of autonomous military applications. Further, the model may assist in the understanding of the use of weaponized information, lies and propaganda to dangerously destabilize human groups.

AI is the ability of a computer, machine or a robot controlled by software to do tasks that are typically performed by humans since they require human intelligence and discernment. In other words, AI can simulate humans' style of living and work rules, as well as transform people thinking and actions into systematized operations. Scientists have discovered more about the brain in the last 10 years than in all prior centuries due to the accelerating pace of research in neurological and behavioral science and the development of new research digital techniques [2].

In addition, neurological brain research experts have found that the human brain has approximately 86 billion neurons, and each neuron is divided into multiple layers [2]. There are more than 100 synapses on each neuron, and the connections between each neuron are communicated by synapses, and this transmission mode establishes a complex neural network [3]. AI mimics the brain nerve to operate, analyze and calculate things, and distribute them in the neural network like a picture by picture, completing various activities. This immensely augments people work efficiency and saves the corresponding labor force, thus reducing many labor costs and helping enterprises to have a better development [1].

Furthermore, digital life is augmenting human capacities and disrupting eons-old human activities. Algorithmic driven systems have spread to more than half of the world's inhabitants in encompassing information and connectivity, proffering previously unimagined opportunities. AI programs are adept of mimicking and even do better than human brains in many tasks [1]. The rise of AI will make most individuals and organizations better off over the years to come. AI will become dominant in most, if not all, aspects of decision-making in the foreseeable future. The utilization of algorithms is rapidly rising as substantial amounts of data are being created, captured, and analyzed by government, businesses, and public bodies. The opportunities and risks accompanying with the utilization of algorithms in decision-making depend on the kind of algorithm; and understanding of the context in which an algorithm functions will be essential for public acceptance and trust [1]. Likewise, whether an AI system acts as a primary decision maker, or as an important decision aid and support to an individual decision maker, will suggest different regulatory approaches.

Fundamentally, the goal of an algorithm is to solve a specific problem, usually defined by someone as a sequence of steps. In machine learning or deep learning, an algorithm is a set of rules given to an AI program to help it learn on its own. Whereby machine learning is a set of algorithms that enable the software to update and "learn" from prior results without the requirement for programmer intervention. In addition, machine learning can get better at completing tasks over time based on the labeled data it ingests. Also, deep learning can be depicted as a related field to machine learning that is concerned with algorithms stimulated by the structure and function of the human brain called artificial neural networks [1].

## AI SUB AREAS: NATURAL LANGUAGE PROCESSING, MACHINE LEARNING AND DEEP LEARNING

For many years ago, AI was housed in data centers, where there was satisfactory computing power to achieve processor-demanding cognitive chores. Today, AI has made its way into software, where predictive algorithms have changed the nature of how these systems support organizations. AI technologies, from machine learning and deep learning to natural language processingnatural language processing *See* (NLP) and computer vision, are precipitously spreading throughout the world. NLP is a subfield of linguistics, computer science, and AI that is concerned with the interfaces between computers and human language. In addition, it involves program computers to process and analyze large amounts of natural language data. Whereas computer vision is an interdisciplinary scientific field that deals with how computers can access elevate its understanding from digital images or videos. From the viewpoint of engineering and computer scientists, it pursues to understand and automate tasks that the human visual system can do.

NLP applications are in use at least hundreds of times per day. For example, predictive text on mobile phones typically implements NLP. Furthermore, searching for something on Google utilizes NLP. Finally, a voice assistant application such as Alexa or Siri utilizes NLP when asking a question.

Machine learning is a branch of AI that enables computers to self-learn from data and harness that learning without human intervention. When confronted with a circumstance in which a solution is hidden in a large data set, machine learning performs admirably well [1]. Furthermore, machine learning does extremely well at processing that data, extracting patterns from it in a fraction of the time a human would take, and generating otherwise unattainable insight.

Deep learning is a tool for classifying information through layered neural networks, a rudimentary replication of how the human brain works. Neural networks have a set of input units, where raw data is supplied. This can be from pictures, or sensible samples, or written text. The inputs are then mapped to the output nodes, which determine the category to which the input information belongs. For instance, it can determine that the fed picture comprises a dog, or that the small sound sample was the word "Goodbye".

Deep learning can be depicted as a subset of machine learning, and machine learning is a subset of AI, which is an umbrella term for any computer program that does something intelligent [1]. Deep learning models operate in a manner that draws from the pattern recognition capabilities of neural networks (Fig. **1.1**). These so-called "narrow" AIs are ubiquitous, that are embedded in people's GPS systems and Amazon recommendations. Nevertheless, the goal is artificial general intelligence, a self-teaching system that can outperform humans across a wide range of disciplines [1].

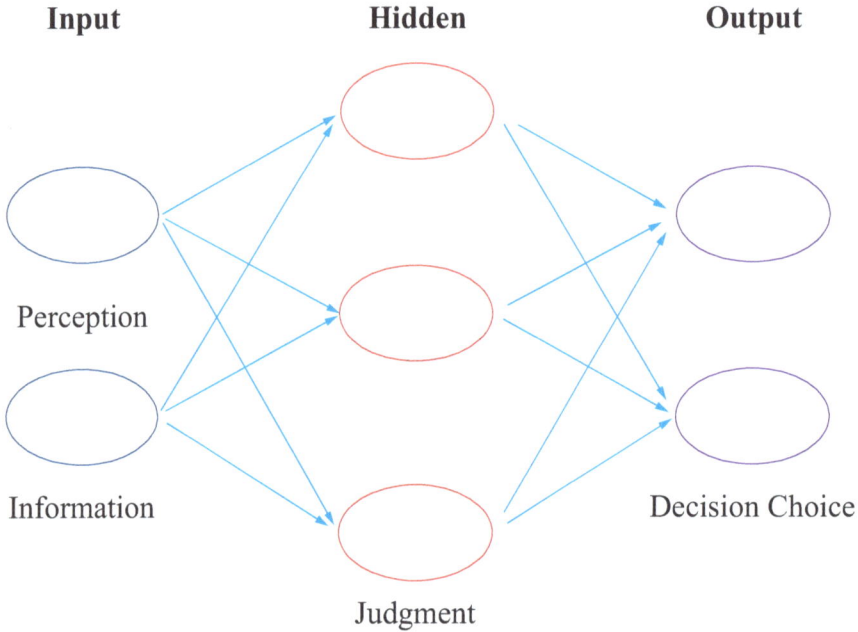

**Fig. (1.1).** Artificial single layer neural network. Source: Adopted by author.

The enormous data digitization as well as the emerging technologies that implement them are disrupting most economic sectors, comprising of transportation, retail, advertising, energy, and other areas [4]. Further, AI is also having an influence on democracy and governance as computerized systems are being adopted to enhance accuracy and drive objectivity in government operations. Nonetheless, the risks are also considerable and conceivably present tremendous governance challenges. These consist of labor displacement, inequality, an oligopolistic global market structure, reinforced totalitarianism, shifts and volatility in national power, strategic instability, and an AI race that sacrifices safety and other values.

AI tools are progressively expanding and elevating decision-making capabilities through such means as coordinating data delivery, analyzing data trends, providing forecasts, developing data consistency, quantifying uncertainty, anticipating the user's data needs, and delivering timely information to the decision makers. Moreover, decision-making is essential to individuals and organizations, and AI algorithms are progressively being utilized in our daily decision choices. AI can be depicted as a group of technologies used to solve specific problems [1]. AI is typically pitched around delivering a data-based answer or offering a data-fueled prediction. Then features and elements begin to diverge. For instance, natural language processing (NLP) may be used to automate incoming emails, machine vision to assess quality on the product line, or advanced analytics to predict a failure of an organization network [5].

Computer algorithms are widely employed throughout our economy and society to make decisions that have far-reaching impacts, including their applications for education, access to credit, healthcare, and employment. The ubiquity of algorithms in our everyday lives is an important reason to focus on addressing challenges associated with the design and technical aspects of algorithms and preventing bias from the onset. That is, algorithms gradually mold our news, economic options, and educational trajectories.

Traditional algorithms are rule-based, which represents a set of logical rules that are created based on expected inputs and outputs. Algorithms often depend upon the analysis of considerable amounts of personal and non-personal data to infer correlations or, more generally, to derive information regarded beneficial to make decisions. Moreover, the decision-making processes for such algorithms can easily be explained and the process is typically transparent. Nonetheless, AI generated machine learning and/or deep learning algorithms create rules internally; therefore, are very difficult to make transparent. This also implies that the utilization of some machine learning and deep learning algorithms are encapsulated in a so-called "black box". Hence, AI produced algorithms are problematic, since how the black boxes arrive to their decision choices are irresolvable to explain.

In other words, decision-making on the quintessential characteristics of digital life is automatically relinquished to code-driven, black box tools. Individuals lack input and do not learn the context about how the technology operates in practice. Further, society sacrifice independence, privacy and power over choice and there is no control over these processes. This effect may expand as automated systems become more prevalent and complex.

In addition, human involvement in the decision-making may diverge, and maybe entirely out of the loop in operating systems. For example, the influence of the decision on individuals can be sizeable, such as access to credit, employment, medical treatment, or judicial sentences, among other issues. Entrusting algorithms to make or to sway such decisions produces an assortment of ethical, political, legal, or technical issues. where careful consideration must be taken to study and address them properly. If they are ignored, the anticipated benefits of these algorithms may be invalidated by an array of various risks for individuals (*e.g.*, discrimination, unfair practices, loss of autonomy, *etc.*), the economy (*e.g.*, unfair practices, limited access to markets, *etc.*), and society (*e.g.*, manipulation, threat to democracy, *etc.*). These systems are globally networked and not easy to regulate or rein in.

In sum, AI's foremost improvement over humans sits in its capability to detect faint patterns within large quantities of data and to learn from them. While a commercial loan officer will look at several measures when deciding whether to grant an organization a loan (*i.e.*, liquidity, profitability, and risk factors), an AI algorithm will learn from thousands of minor variables (*e.g.*, factors covering character dispositions, social media, *etc.*). Taken alone, the predictive power of each of these is small, but taken together, they can produce a far more accurate prediction than the most discerning loan officers are capable of comprehending.

## AI ALGORITHMS IMPACT ON SOCIETY

An algorithm is only as suitable as the data it works with in a system. Data is often imperfect in ways that permit these algorithms to inherit the predispositions of previous decision makers. In other cases, data may merely replicate the pervasive biases that persevere in society at large. In other applications of algorithms, data mining can uncover unexpectedly advantageous regularities that are just preexisting patterns of exclusion and inequality. The arena of data mining is somewhat contemporary and in a state of evolution. Data mining is the study of collecting, cleaning, processing, analyzing, and gaining useful insights from data [6].

Further, data mining is the process of extricating beneficial information from huge amounts of data. In addition, data mining is the technique of uncovering meaningful correlations, patterns and trends by filtering through substantial amounts of data gathered in repositories. Data mining utilizes pattern recognition technologies, as well as statistical and mathematical techniques.

For example, e-mail spam filter depends on, in part, rules that a data mining algorithm has learned from scrutinizing millions of e-mail messages that have been catalogued as spam or not spam. Moreover, real-time data mining techniques facilitate Web-based merchants to instruct "customers who purchased product "A" are also likely to purchase product "B". In addition, data mining assists banks to ascertain applicants' types that are more likely to default on loans, supports tax authorities to pinpoint the type of tax returns that are most likely to be duplicitous, and aids catalog merchants to pursue those customers that are most likely to purchase [7].

Flourishing organizations are constructing effective use of the abundance of data, whereby they have access to make better forecasts, enhanced strategies, and improved decision choices. Nevertheless, in a world where algorithms are fixtures of organizations and by extension, peoples' lives, the issue of biased training data is increasingly consequential. Nevertheless, AI insurance could emerge as a new revenue stream for insurance companies indemnifying organizations.

Gradually more, AI systems acknowledged as deep learning neural networks are relished to inform decisions essential to human health and safety, such as in autonomous driving or medical diagnosis. These networks are respectable at identifying patterns in large, complex datasets to facilitate in decision-making.

Moreover, AI algorithms and robotics are digital technologies that will have momentous influence on the development of humanity in the near future. Ethical issues have been raised regarding what we should do with these systems, what the systems themselves should do, what risks they involve, and how we can control these apparatuses.

The focus comes as AI research progressively deals more with controversies surrounding the application of its technologies. This is especially the case in the use of biometrics such as iris and facial recognition. Issues pertain to grasping and understanding biases in algorithms may reflect existing patterns of perceptual framing in data. There is no such thing as a neutral technological platform since algorithms can influence human beliefs.

AI is the leading technology in "Fourth Industrial RevolutionFourth Industrial Revolution *See* Fourth Industrial Revolution". AI denotes technological advances from biotechnology to big data, which are precipitously reshaping the global community. The First Industrial Revolution utilized water and steam power to industrialize production. Next, the Second Industrial Revolution employed electric power to produce mass production. Thereafter, the Third Industrial Revolution exercised electronics and information technology to computerize production. The Fourth Industrial Revolution is assembled on the Third. That is, the digital revolution has been transpiring since the middle of the last century. It is characterized by a merging of technologies that has obscured the lines between the physical, digital, and biological spheres.

Furthermore, AI represents a family of tools where algorithms uncover or learn associations of predictive power from data. An algorithm is depicted as a step-b--step procedure for solving a problem. The most palpable form of AI is machine learning, which comprises a family of techniques called deep learning that bank on multiple layers of representation of data and are therefore able to embody complex relationships between inputs and outputs. Nonetheless, learned representations are difficult for humans to interpret, which is one of the advantages of deep learning neural networks.

Algorithms have been cultivated into more complex structures; however, certain challenges still emerge. That is, AI can aid in identifying and reducing the influence of human biases. Nonetheless, it can also make the problem worse by intertwining in and positioning biases in sensitive application areas, such as profiling people in facial recognition apparatus. It is not the machines that have biases. An AI tool does not 'want' something to be true or false for reasons that cannot be explained through logic. Unfortunately, human bias exists in machine learning from the creation of an algorithm to the interpretation of data. Further, until now hardly anyone has tried to solve this huge problem.

The potential of AI stands on the transition of AI that differentiates the past, grounded on symbol processing and syntax, from the future, constructed on learning and semantics grounded in sensory experience.

## THE ROOTS OF MACHINE LEARNING BIAS

Machine learning is the field most frequently related with the current explosion of AI. Machine learning is a set of techniques and algorithms that can be implemented to "train" a computer program to routinely identify patterns in a set of data.

Machine learning can be encapsulated as a research field that is proficient of recognizing patterns in data and developing systems that will learn from those. More specifically, *supervised* machine learning guides systems using examples classified (labelled) by individuals. For example, these transactions are deceptive; those transactions are not deceptive. Grounded on the features of that classified data, the system learns what the underlying patterns of those kinds are, and then can predict which new transactions are decidedly likely to be duplicitous. Whereas *unsupervised* machine learning can uncover patterns in large quantities of unlabeled data. This procedure endeavors to unearth a fundamental structure of its own accord, such as by clustering cases that is similar to one another and formulating associations [1].

Many diverse tools fall under the umbrella of "machine learning". Typically, machine learning utilized "features" or "variables" (*e.g.*, the location of fire departments in a city, data from surveillance cameras, attributes of criminal defendants) procured from a set of "training data" to learn these patterns without explicitly being told what those patterns are by humans. Machine learning has come to comprise of items that have historically been more basically described as "statistics". Machine learning is the tool at the heart of new automated AI systems, making it challenging for people to comprehend the logic behind those systems.

There is typically a trade-off between performance and explainability for machine learning, deep learning, or neural networks. Machine learning will often be more advantageous when the situation is depicts a black box scenario due to multifaceted elements with many intermingling influences. As a result, these systems will more than likely be accountable *via* post hoc monitoring and evaluation. For example, if the machine learning algorithm's decision choices are significantly biased, then something regarding the system or the data it is trained on may need to change.

Algorithms are not inherently biased. In other words, algorithmic decision choices are predicated on several aspects, including how the software is deployed, and the quality and representativeness of the underlying data. Further, it is important to ensure that data transparency, review and remediation is considered throughout algorithmic engineering processes. Yet, the increasing use of algorithms in decision-making also brings to light important issues about governance, accountability, and ethics.

While organizations today employ widespread utilization of complex algorithms, the viewpoint of algorithmic accountability persists as an elusive ideal because of the opacity and fluidity of algorithms. Machines may not suffer from the same biases that we humans have, but they have their own problems. Machine learning procedures may aggravate bias in decision-making due to poorly conceived models. Moreover, the occurrence of unrecognized biases in training data or because of disparate sample sizes across subgroup can cause problems.

## PROPERTIES OF ALGORITHMS

A common principle of AI ethics is explainability [8]. The risk of producing AI that reinforces societal biases has stimulated calls for greater transparency about algorithmic or machine learning decision processes, and for means to understand and audit how an AI agent arrives at its decision choices or classifications. As the utilization of AI systems flourishes, being able to explain how a given model or system works will be imperative, particularly for those used by industry, governments, or public sector agencies.

AI algorithms entail a computational process, comprising one derived from machine learning, deep learning, statistics, data processing or related tools, that makes a decision choice or contributes to human decision making, that influences users such as consumers. Abused Employed across industries, AI algorithms can open smartphones utilizing facial recognition, make driving decisions in autonomous vehicles, endorse entertainment assortments grounded on user preferences. Further, AI applications can support the process of pharmaceutical advancement, ascertain the creditworthiness of potential homebuyers, and screen applicants for job interviews. In addition, AI automates, accelerates, and make better data processing by locating patterns in the data, acclimating to new data, and learning from experience.

Algorithmic accountability appeal to the following related remedies.

a. *Transparency*. Decision makers cannot utilize the intricacies and proprietary nature of many algorithmic models as a shield against inquiry.
b. *Explanation*. Certify those algorithmic decisions as well as any data driving those decisions can be interpreted to end-users and other stakeholders in non-technical terms. At a minimum, there is the "right to explanation" the nature and construction of algorithms.
c. *Audits*. Algorithmic techniques should be examined by some internal auditor and/or independent third party. In addition, interested third parties can inquire, understand, and check the nature of the algorithm through disclosure of information that facilitates monitoring, checking, or criticism, integrating through provision of detailed documentation, technically suitable, and accommodating terms of use. In other words, make available externally discernable avenues of redress for adverse individual or societal effects of an algorithmic system.
d. *Fairness*. Verify that algorithmic decision choices do not produce discriminatory or unjust influences when differentiating transversely different demographics (*e.g.*, race, sex, *etc.*). The issues of unfairness and bias may be confronted with by constructing fairness requirements into the algorithms themselves.

To reduce the risks in algorithms, issues pertaining to intrinsic and extrinsic requirements can apply to any algorithmic properties, such as safety, security, or privacy [9]. Intrinsic prerequisites, such as fairness, absence of bias or non-discrimination, can be articulated as properties of the algorithm itself in its application framework. 'Fairness' can be construed with 'absence of undesirable bias.' In addition, 'discrimination' can be depicted as a particular type of unfairness associated to the utilization of distinctive types of data (such as ethnic origin, political opinions, gender, *etc.*) [8]. Extrinsic requirements are related to 'understandability,' which is the possibility to provide understandable information about the connection between the input and the output of the algorithms. The two foremost forms of understandability are deemed to be "transparency" and "explainability" [9].

Algorithmic *transparency* is openness about the purpose, structure and fundamental actions of the algorithms employed to search for, process and deliver information. Transparency is delineated as the availability of the algorithmic code with its design documentation, parameters, and the learning dataset. When the algorithm relies on machine learning or deep learning tools. Transparency does not necessarily imply availability to the public. It also embodies situations in which the code is made known only to actors, for example for audit or certification. For example, a common method utilized to offer transparency and ensure algorithmic accountability is the use of third-party audits.

Decision choices formulated by algorithms can be opaque due to technical and social reasons. Furthermore, algorithms maybe deliberately opaque to protect intellectual property. For example, the algorithms may be too multifaceted to explain or efforts to illuminate the algorithms might necessitate the utilization of data that infringes a country's privacy regulations.

*Explainability* is described as the availability of explanations about AI algorithms. In contrast to transparency, explainability necessitates the delivery of information beyond the AI algorithms [9]. Explanations can be of diverse kinds (*i.e.*, operational, logical, or causal). Further, they can be either global (about the whole algorithm) or local (about specific results); and they can take distinctive forms (decision trees, histograms, picture or text highlights, examples, counterexamples, *etc.*). The strengths and weaknesses of each explanation method should be evaluated in relation to the recipients of the explanation (*e.g.*, professional or employee prospect), their level of expertise, and their objectives (to challenge a decision, take actions to obtain a decision, verify compliance with legal obligations, *etc.*).

The next section highlights explainability in terms of a model described as the Throughput Model [10]. This model emphasizes "explainability" by considering stages of AI development, namely, pre-modelling, model development, and post-modelling. The majority of AI explainability literature targets illuminating a black-box model that is already developed, namely, post-modelling explainability. The Throughput Model theory is suggested to resolve these issues.

## THROUGHPUT MODEL

The centrality and concerns about algorithmic decision-making is increasing daily. Issues link to addressing legal, policy and ethical challenges indicates that algorithmic power in media production and consumption, commerce, and education. Moreover, a case is often made that we are looking to a future in which decision-making will be based on automated processing of large datasets becomes increasingly common. Big data, machine learning, algorithmic decision-making and similar technologies have the capacity to bring substantial advantage to individuals, groups, and society. They could also produce new injustices and entrench old ones in manners that permit them to be strongly reproduced across national and international networks. The Throughput Model allows us to view the design of the algorithms, which in effect is looking inside of the black box (see Fig. **1.2**).

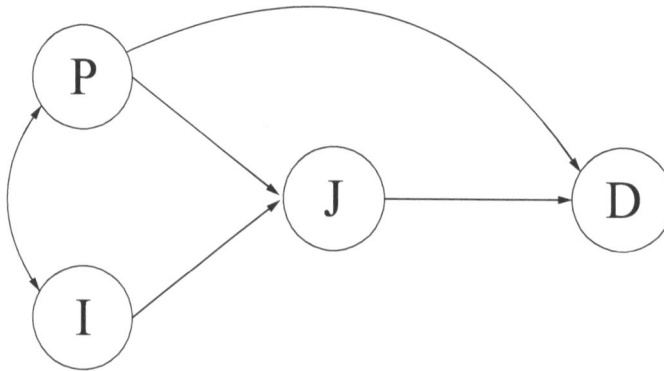

*Where P = perception, I = information, J = judgment, and D = decision choice*

**Fig. (1.2).** Throughput Modelling Diagram. *Where P= perception, I= information, J= judgment, and D= decision choice.* Source [11].

Further, the Throughput Model outlines the steps and strategies that decision makers need to determine before making decision. The daily decision-making process depicted in the Throughput Model that affects the activities of individuals and organizations involves different algorithmic paths among four factors, which are "perception (P)", "information (I)", "judgment (J)" and "decision choice (D)".

As shown in Fig. (**1.2**), these four components link to six algorithmic decision-making routes. The first of these components is "perception" of the environment and framework within an individual or organization operates, and how relevant "information," specifically facts or details related to the issue under review, should be considered for use. Perception can be influenced by biases and heuristics on the part of decision makers, their previous experience, and other external and internal factors, all of which will affect the way information is processed. Among these, the double arrows in Fig. (**1.2**) indicate the consistency between perception and information Also, this relationship is like a neural network in that information updates perception; and perception influences the selection of information [12]. "Information" affects and reshapes individuals' or organizations' perception and decision choice. Rodgers [13] concluded that a lack of coherence between perception and information by decision makers will lead to a loss of cognition. The process of "judgment" includes weighing existing information and making an objective assessment, while decision-making is the final element of an executive's action plan. In the Throughput Model, the six algorithmic different paths available to decision makers are:

1. P→D,
2. P→J→D,
3. I→J→D,
4. I→P→D,
5. P→I→J→D, and
6. I→P→J→D.

As contrast to the Throughput Model approach, the black box approach analyses the behavior of systems without 'opening the hood' of the vehicle. That is, without any knowledge of the system codes. Explanations are constructed from observations of the relationships between the inputs and outputs of the system. This is the only possible approach when the operator or provider of the system is uncollaborative (does not agree to disclose the code).

The Throughput Modelling approach in contrast to the black box approach assumes that analysis of a system code is possible. Further, this approach in contrast with the black box approach, provides a design for systems by designing dominant algorithms that assist in explainability. This is possible by (1) relying on six dominant algorithmic pathways, which by design, provides sufficient accuracy, and (2) enhances precise algorithms with explanation whereby that it can generate, in addition to its nominal results (*e.g.*, classification), a faithful and intelligible explanation for these results.

In addition, the Throughput Model and its algorithmic pathways uncovers strategies used by individuals or organizations in arriving at a problem [14]. This model is useful since AI systems are primed by human intelligence. Moreover, interesting enough, the Throughput Model is closely related to Machine Learning. Machine learning relates to computer systems that can perform autonomous learning programs without specific programming. For example, in cloud computing and cloud storage, the calculator can automatically insert massive data in the original function with the help of the Throughput Model, which can reduce the data reserve [1]. At the same time, it can enhance the computing power to automatically improve itself. The Throughput Model can be depicted as a theoretical system to address the adoption of up-and-coming tools and technologies (such as deep learning components, digitization, neural networks, *etc.*) and to describe the development capabilities needed to effectively address the challenges of this century.

The Throughput Model alerts our attention that for cognitive tasks, it depicts the process steps that individuals or organizations make to arrive at a decision choice. This algorithmic model highlights that they can continuously learn from new data and perform better depending upon the selected algorithmic pathway. In its entirety, the Throughput Model suggests that not only one algorithmic pathway is considered, but also parallel algorithmic paths can be considered based on the perceptual and information sets that are processed through the algorithms. Together, this allows the Throughput Model to place into algorithmic format over countless tasks across society. Such as driving a car, diagnosing a disease, or providing customer support.

## FUTURE AI OPPORTUNITIES FOR SOCIETY

The coming of AI will eventually produce occupations and positions, we cannot even elaborate at the present time. Examples today comprise AI engineers, data scientists, data-labelers, and robot mechanics. Integrating AI optimization and the human cognitive theories (*i.e.*, decision-making) may reinvent many occupations and generate even more opportunities. AI will handle routine tasks in in concert with people, who will perform the tasks that necessitate, consideration and compassion is specific cases. For example, future doctors will still lead as a patient's primary overseer; however, they can depend on AI diagnostic tools to determine the best treatment. This can enable the doctor's responsibility into that of a supportive caregiver, providing them more time with their patients.

Opportunities are now in progress for research developers. These people interview workers, conduct surveys, and build tools that provide a more quantitative perspective on what is happening on various Internet platforms. There is great optimism pertaining to AI future impact on health care. Further, this impact extends to possible applications of AI in diagnosing and treating patients or helping senior citizens live fuller and healthier lives. In addition, AI maybe a factor in broad public-health programs constructed around enormous amounts of data that may be attained in the coming years approaching everything from personal genomes to nutrition. AI impact extends also to long-expected transformations in formal and informal education systems.

Quite a few projects involve labeling data, such as image data (*i.e.*, facial recognition). This data can be supplied into supervised or unsupervised machine learning models. Further, other projects involve transcribing audio. For example, when you talk to Goggle Assistant or Amazon Alexa, they can be capable of answering questions, as well as executing the smart home commands. These voice recognition algorithms learn to understand speech better. Moreover, organization workers can label websites that might be filled with hate speech or pedophilia. This process will eliminate the possibility of the user being exposed to such websites.

AI has made fantastic strides to date, but it often needs huge amounts of data and computer power to arrive at a decision. Researchers are using powerful AI algorithms onto simple, low-power computer chip that can run for months on a battery. These new developments could facilitate in developing more advanced AI capabilities, like image and voice recognition, to home appliances and wearable devices, along with medical gadgets and government, commercial, and industrial sensors. This technology could also assist in keeping data private and secure by diminishing the prerequisite to send anything to the cloud.

Microcontrollers are moderately simple, low-cost, low-power computer chips located inside billions of products, comprising automobile engines, power tools, TV remotes, and medical implants. These tools include deep learning algorithms and neural network programs that liberally mimic the manner in which neurons connect and fire in the human brain. Deep learning algorithms normally run on dedicated computer chips that apportion the parallel computations required to train and operate the network more effectively.

For example, chatbots have recently emerged as a new communications conduit for consumer brands and customers. Apprehending language is one factor of perfecting chatbots. Another factor is employing empathy (see www.wired.com/wiredinsider/2018/04/ai-future-work/). A new upsurge of startups is inserting the emotional intelligence into chatbot-based communication. This is an AI component of natural language processing (NLP), which is the ability of a computer program to understand human language as it is spoken.

Another type of AI technology is computer vision, which works on enabling computers to see, recognize and process images in a similar way that human vision does, and then provide appropriate output [1].

Computer vision is an interdisciplinary field that deals with how computers can be made to achieve high-level comprehending from digital images or videos. From the perspective of engineering, it seeks to automate tasks that the human visual system can do. Therefore, as NLP is to speech, computer vision is to sight. Further, it is a representation of imparting human intelligence and instincts to a computer. Nonetheless, it is an arduous task to empower computers to recognize images of different objects.

Although early computer vision attempts date back to 1950, the convergence of hardware and software improvements, along with an inflow of new visual data from mobile devices and other cameras, are positioning a computer vision resurgence. Moreover, as AI proficiencies have developed, it can empower machines to assess items that individuals cannot. As a result, computer vision can learn to view and interpret the visual world in much the same way humans process through their vision.

Computer vision's objective is not only to see, but also to process and deliver useful results based on the observation. For example, a computer could generate a 3D image from a 2D image, such as those in automobiles, and furnish critical data to the automobile and/or driver.

Automobiles tailored with computer vision could be able to identify and discriminate objects on and around the road such as traffic lights, pedestrians, traffic signs and so on, and act appropriately to the situation. This AI device could offer inputs to the driver or even make the automobile stop if there is an unexpected obstacle on the road. Finally, computer vision capabilities can process, categorize, and understand images and video at a scale and speed that would otherwise be unattainable for humans.

By utilizing NLP as well, computer vision technology may be able to not only encapsulate, index, store, and extract information from visual data, but also to curate, normalize, and understand content from images or documents [15]. Computer vision technology assists healthcare providers ameliorate the arrangement of conditions as well as fuels automated driving solutions like Google's Waymo and Tesla's Autopilot. Amazon Web Services invented a programmable deep learning-enabled camera and kits that organizations can implement to develop their own computer vision applications.

Other future commercial applications could include smart glasses, augmented reality devices that continuously operate target detection. Another application will be sensors that are designed to predict problems with industrial machinery. Currently, sensors need to be wirelessly networked so that computation can be done remotely, on a more powerful system. Finally, another important application could be in medical devices that use machine learning to continuously monitor blood pressure.

Nonetheless, there are limits to the capabilities of today's AI. Although AI is prodigious at optimizing for an exceedingly narrow objective, it is incapable to select its own goals or to think creatively. And while AI is phenomenal in the ruthless world of numbers and data, it is deficient in social skills or empathy. The capability to make another individual feel understood and cared for is presently lacking from AI apparatuses. Correspondingly, in the domain of robotics, AI is capable to operate many rudimentary tasks like stocking goods or driving automobiles; however, it lacks the tactful adroitness required to attend to elderly people or toddlers.

## Financial Robots

There has been intensifying interest in robotics and automation, both in accounting and the financial markets in the use of big data. Robotics can deliver other benefits, such as improved compliance, faster turnaround times and higher quality.

Financial robots are based on robot process automation technology. Robot process automation mainly imitates a user's manual operation, such as automatic generation of accounting data, simulation generation of accounting decision-making risk, *etc.* The goal of robot process automation is to substitute workers with automation. Moreover, robot process automation refers to the process automation of robots. Furthermore, robot process automation is a technical means to automate and process human labor by executing repetitive instructions based on data programming and rules [15 - 20].

According to the definition of robot process automation the Institute for Robotic Process Automation and Artificial Intelligence [15] designates a technology application that enables organizational employees to conFig. computer software or 'robots,' collect and construe prevailing applications to process transactions, manipulate data and trigger responses, and communicate with other digital systems [16]. The financial robot is the application of robotic process automation in accounting and finance that relies on big data, Internet, and AI.

In May 2017, Deloitte Touché Tohmatsu took the lead in launching financial robot products, which had an immediately impact in the financial circle [21]. KPMG, PricewaterhouseCoopers and Ernst & Young, which belong to the four largest international accounting firms, have also successively launched their own financial robots and financial robot solutions [22 - 26].

Robotic process automation indicates that more and more retail financial consumers interact with financial service providers through a financial robot driven by algorithms or other mathematical models [24]. The financial robot is based on the robotic process automation technology that is based on computer coding and rule-based software. In addition, it can automate manual activities by performing repeated rule-based tasks [25]. Robot process automation mainly simulates the manual operation of users, such as automatic generation of accounting data, simulation of generation of accounting decision risks, *etc.* The goal of robotic process automation is to replace people with automation [16].

The financial robot performs the same tasks as a human by issuing program commands from a computer. For example, some of the tasks it performs include but are not limited to data entry, analysis, report generation and other work in accordance with the computer command in an orderly manner. Further, the accounting robot can work with other software on an existing desktop. The accounting robot can trigger the record button to generate a script robot when the user wants to perform an automated task. With some programs, the script robot can browse e-mails, open files, identify useful information, and enter data into the system. Also, the financial robot can monitor the progress of the program in real time, send emails to managers and report abnormal data.

Financial robots require precise programming commands to perform tasks. Imprecise program commands can skew data collection [17]. exclaimed that the task instructions performed by the financial robot are targeted, which is to automate the commonly known work. If the task being performed is the first time, the financial robot is not suitable for the task. It must include the premise of the manager's prejudgment that there can be no uncertain results.

The traditional accounting work is to deal with the post event records of business activities, including the accounting of economic results, the entry of vouchers, the statistics of data, and the accounting process of financial statements. These basic accounting tasks require accountants to summarize and report. Moreover, the basic accounting work is simple and has a high repetition rate, which requires a lot of time and energy to complete. To a certain extent, it extracts very valuable human resources of an organization. Nonetheless, with the implementation of financial robots can liberate accountants from the above simple and repeated work and enable accountants to have the energy to complete higher-end financial management and pre-decision-making work.

As for the industry, accounting firms are vigorously developing financial robots to aid their work. From the vantage viewpoint of auditing, coordination, internal control testing and other human intensive audit tasks can be completed through financial robots. Hence the role of auditors is changing from yesteryear of data collectors, processors, and analysts to the evaluation components of audit procedures. Auditors are gradually assigning the part of the audit process that can be automated to the financial robot for work implementation. For the financial bots' program commands to run as expected, they require particularized instructions for performing specific tasks. For example, executing the check unread message command, through, which an individual will need many pre-embedded conditions to perform the same task. In this case, the financial robot will require to open an Internet browser, enter the relevant password to log in to the organization's mailbox, and check the unread mail [17].

The Public Company Accounting Oversight Board [18, 19] emphasizes that revenue is an area with high audit risk, which indicates that there is a chance for additional audit work. Research has indicated that financial robots can improve audit quality by testing the overall situation of income transactions. In addition, financial robots can allow auditors to more accurately assess and deal with the risk of significant misstatement of income [17]. The promotion of financial robots does not imply that there is no need for accountants. That is, financial robots are good at data integration and report generation, but it cannot evaluate the economic environment and make scientific and reasonable decisions. This requires traditional accounting practitioners to make management decisions through professional knowledge [20].

There are also risks in the use of financial robots. Because the financial robot needs to manage data information, data information is generally stored in the cloud, so there will be privacy and security issues. In the information age, it is not uncommon for the network security to be invaded by hackers [21]. As one of the famous accounting firms, Deloitte Touché Tohmatsu suffered an abnormal network security attack in 2017. Hackers broke into the cloud of Deloitte email system and illegally obtained customer records [27].

Financial robots work with big data. Barocas and Selbst [28] suggested five mechanisms by which Big Data and the algorithms that process it may unfairly affect different groups:

1. *Target variables*. A proxy is selected when the goal of "quality" is not accessible. For instance, how to identify a prospective employee? If performance reviews are designated as a measure, then any bias in an organization will be transmitted by the hiring algorithm. More so, longevity with an employer and other amalgamation of measures each have its own uncertainties.

2. *Training data*. Similar to target variables inheriting ingrained bias, so may data implemented to train the model. Using social media data builds in other sources of bias. There is no easy escape.

3. *Feature selection*. Features are the variables or attributes that an organization may assemble into a model. Should the algorithm include the reputation of the applicant's university in the score for a job applicant? Or should the algorithm include the zip code of their home address? Both may show a relationship with

categories such as race, class, or social economic status.

4. *Proxies*. Criteria that are authentically pertinent in making rational and well-informed decision choices may also occur to operate as dependable proxies for membership in a particular group. Employers may find that subject members of certain groups to constantly receive disadvantageous treatment since the criteria that establish the desirability of employees happen to be held at systematically lower rates by members of these groups.

5. *Masking*. All the above apparatuses can occur unintentionally; nonetheless, they can also transpire with intent if the employer has erroneous preconceived notions, and the algorithm may then serve to mask their bias.

Furthermore, robots require detailed process accuracy and require to be taught at the keystroke level. Nonetheless, organizations are discovering that processes are not always well understood, even where strong process documentation exists. Operations that are viewed as standard in the process documentation, often diverge substantially in reality across nations and/or business units. Implementation teams need to work meticulously together with the organization to fully comprehend the particularized processes and proactively address any issues [29, 30].

**Where are we headed?**

In simple terms, algorithmic designs began with symbolic AI, which involved the explicit embedding of human knowledge and behavior rules into computer programs [31, 32]. Symbols are items that are implemented to represent other items. Symbols perform an important role in the human thought and reasoning process. For example, symbols are used to define things (dog, truck, airplane, *etc.*) and people (professor, fireperson, carpenter). Symbols can characterize abstract concepts (bank transaction) or items that do not physically exist (web page, blog post, *etc.*). They can also depict actions (*e.g.*, walking) or states (*e.g.*, sleeping). Symbols can be categorized into hierarchies (an automobile is constructed of doors, tires, windows, chassis, seats, *etc.*). They can also be utilized to designate other symbols (*e.g.*, a rabbit with fluffy ears, a blue wall, *etc.*).

Communicating in symbols is one of the center pieces that make humans intelligent. Consequently, symbols have also portrayed a imperative role in the creation of AI. Moreover, the practice of symbolic AI exhibited a lot of promise in the early decades of AI research. Nonetheless, in recent years, as neural networks, also known as connectionist AI, gained traction, symbolic AI has fallen over the curb.

Neural networks are almost as old as symbolic AI. Nevertheless, they were principally discharged since they were inefficient and warranted computing resources that were not accessible at the time. Thanks to the enormous availability of data and processing power, recently deep learning has achieved status and has advanced past symbolic AI systems.

The advantage of neural networks is that they can deal with disorganized and unstructured data. For example, instead of manually laboring through the rules of detecting dog pixels, a person can train a deep learning algorithm on many pictures of dogs. The neural network then develops a statistical model for dog images. When you provide it with a new image, it will return the probability that it contains a dog.

Deep learning and neural networks do extremely well at precisely the chores that symbolic AI tussles with in completing a design. They have fashioned a revolution in computer vision tools such as facial recognition and cancer detection. Deep learning has also propelled improvements in language-related tasks.

Deep neural networks are also very suitable for reinforcement learning. Reinforcement learning is a subset of machine learning that utilizes programmers' classical approaches to manually code every rule that defined the behavior of the AI software. Hence, machine learning apparatuses are AI models that develop their behavior through frequent trial and error methods. This is the type of AI that masters complicated games such as Go, StarCraft, and Dota.

Contrast to other types of machine learning, reinforcement learning does not entail a great deal of training examples. As an alternative, reinforcement learning models are provided an environment, a set of actions they can perform, and a goal or a reward they must pursue.

The AI agent is required to try to construct moves that maximize its reward or bring it closer to the objective. At the outset, the AI system knows nothing about the environment and makes random actions, measuring the rewards and conveying the quality of each action in something called a Q-table. Chiefly, a Q-table is a function to which you give the current state of the environment and an action, and it returns the reward that action will generate. The more training a deep learning model goes through, the more data it collects from its environment and the more precise its Q-table becomes.

Nevertheless, according to Ben Dickson, software engineer, Deep learning has several deep challenges (see: https://bdtechtalks.com/2019/05/28/what-i--reinforcement-learning/) the benefits of deep learning and neural networks are not without tradeoffs. Deep learning has a few challenges and disadvantages in contrast to symbolic AI. Particularly, deep learning algorithms are impervious, and attempting to determine how they operate mystifies even their inventors Hence, it is very difficult to communicate and troubleshoot their internal mechanisms.

Furthermore, neural networks require mountains of data. And unlike symbolic AI, neural networks have no concept of symbols and hierarchical representation of knowledge. This limitation makes it extremely difficult to employ neural networks to tasks that entail logic and reasoning, such as science and math.

Therefore, the Throughput Model can assist in designing and implementing an algorithmic process, since humans require assistance in generalizing their skills. Deep neural networks is great at ingesting large amounts of data and exploiting huge computing resources to solve very narrow problems, such as detecting specific kinds of objects or playing complex video games in certain situations. Nonetheless, the designing and implementation of key features are missing from current deep learning systems.

## CONCLUSION

AI is a precipitously developing scientific technology that is commonly utilized in many fields. A variety of different industries has historically been based on 'human work' and, therefore, these fields are bound to be by the growth of AI. Moreover, this technology changes the original way of working in different industries, reduces fraud, and speeds up the processing of information, making the efficiency of work much higher. Nonetheless, it also can contribute to unemployment rate increasing in certain industries. Therefore, across the board in a variety of different industries, individuals must improve their personal self-learning ability, make themselves more aware of aspects of AI knowledge and change their traditional mindset in order to better adapt to the new work environment permeated by AI.

The significance of AI has taken over society at large. AI can have an impact on everyday life on the workforce, society, the financial industry, and healthcare. People that are against technology growth will have negative feedback about AI and people that support technology growth will have positive feedback about AI. Some of the benefits that AI can provide is to lessen loss regarding time efficiency and redundant material information. Now more than ever AI is highly valued especially due to the covid-19 pandemic that has caused pandemonium around the world. Now more than ever hospitals, schools, parents, businesses, and the working class must rely on the advancement of AI to make their lives more comfortable.

The term AI portrays computing systems that demonstrate some form of human intelligence. It covers several intertwined technologies, comprising of data mining, machine learning, deep learning, neural networks, natural language processing, speech recognition, and sentiment analysis. AI is a quickly evolving area of technology that promises to be a game-changer for numerous industries and applied in areas like driverless cars, home energy systems, and investment portfolio management.

Furthermore, AI technologies goes as far as a reformation of the human brain, which is capable of learning, analyzing, and interpreting information. AI assists in the development, innovation, success, and daily improved efficiency of people and organizations.

AI can be viewed as a broad umbrella of cognitive and computational science that facilitates intelligent decision-making. Main branches under AI include machine learning, deep learning, neural networks, and natural language processing fields, which are all systems that work to make prescriptions, predictions and descriptions based up to date.

The Throughput Model is composed by four major concepts:

1. *Perception*: Basically, it is the first process on the throughput model, means the categorization and classification of the environment [1].

2. *Information*: It is important to keep in mind the relevant and reliable information that may affect the process. For example, economic situations that are related to the environment.

3. *Judgment*: Evaluates the situation by applying information and perceptual framing of the problem to be analyzed by the individual.

4. *Decision choice*: Finally, based on the results obtained, the decision maker must be ready to act or not.

Through these four concepts, there are six dominant algorithmic pathways that can influence decision choices. The Throughput Model shows us different pathways that lead to a certain decision choice. Fig. (**1.2**) illustrates six algorithmic pathways in the process of decision making:

(1) **P→D,** (2) **P→J→D,** (3) **I→J→D,** (4) **I→P→D,** (5) **P→I→J→D,** and (6) **I→P→J→D.**

When AI is implemented into this model, the decisions become more accurate and reliable. Individuals typically frame a problem by using their perception and judgment. Nonetheless, this process can become time consuming and can lead to misconceptions about information. AI can use pattern recognition and analyze an entire population of information faster and more accurately than a person can process and analyze. However, the more we use AI to make decisions, the more we must focus on the risk.

The emergence of financial robot has a certain impact on the accounting field. As technology enhances, robots will be able to do more complex tasks faster and more efficiently than people. Definitions that are now becoming a part of the business and AI lexicon include the following:

1. *Cognitive automation*, which is the utilization of cognitive or AI tools such as machine learning, deep learning, and natural language processing to enable more complex automation that is generally based on the laws of probabilities.

2. *Digital workforce*, which is utilized to depict the automated solutions that are delivering processes within an organization. These solutions include AI generated robots, chatbots, and algorithms. Typically, the digital workforce will be either working in the background on virtual machines or accessed by consumers and co-workers through a command-based interface. Presently, robots dominate most digital workforces, which supports robotic process automation.

3. *Robotic process automation* (RPA) represents the automation of rules-based processes with software that utilizes the user interface, which can perform on any software, including web-based applications, ERP systems, and mainframe systems.

4. *Natural language processing* (NLP) is a very wide-ranging area and can comprise of many different skills. At its straightforward form, NLP can assist computers perform commands given to them through text commands. Smart speakers and smartphone AI assistants utilize NLP to process users' commands. Fundamentally, what this implies is that the user does not have to remain true to a stringent arrangement of words to activate a command and can utilize diverse alternatives of the same sentence.

In sum, AI can be a tremendous tool to assist individuals and organizations to carry out their duties. The development and application of AI has not only changed our lifestyle but also improves our work efficiency. AI is a programmed computer system that can act or think like a human being, such as decision-making, communication with human language, and learning from knowledge. AI algorithms, machine learning, biometric, deep learning, and natural language processing utilize programs to recognize and employ patterns from data collected on the computer to provide faster and more accurate analysis for individuals and organizations. AI technology increases people's work efficiency and enables them to spend more time concentrating on high-level decision-making.

AI is a growing industry that has many ways to be used. Virtual reality, programing, automated pages, or simply by having a computer system taking care of all day-to-day tasks and be able to provide the company way to improve.

Similarly, to an automobile replacing a carriage, the advent of the automobile assuredly compelled the carriage driver into an outdated position. On the same grounds, the surfacing of AI will eradicate now popular areas in business and non-business workers. Nevertheless, this does not imply that these people will not find a new position or occupation. The emergence of automobiles necessitated that people learn how to drive automobiles. While the materialization of AI compels those individuals learn how to design, deploy, and manage AI.

Although it has its pros, it also has cons. A lot of employees are being afraid to be replaced by an AI. This should not be the case, instead of being afraid, they should be excited to be receiving help from this program. They have been created to be implemented and use as an advantage.

## REFERENCES

[1]   W. Rodgers, *Artificial Intelligence in a Throughput Model: Some Major Algorithms?* Science Publications (CRC Press, Taylor and Francis Group): Florida, 2020.

[2]   C.S. von Bartheld, J. Bahney, and S. Herculano-Houzel, "The search for true numbers of neurons and glial cells in the human brain: A review of 150 years of cell counting", *J. Comp. Neurol.,* vol. 524, no. 18, pp. 3865-3895, 2016.
[http://dx.doi.org/10.1002/cne.24040] [PMID: 27187682]

[3]   S. Herculano-Houzel, "The human brain in numbers: a linearly scaled-up primate brain", *Front. Hum. Neurosci.,* vol. 3, no. 31, p. 31, 2009.
[http://dx.doi.org/10.3389/neuro.09.031.2009] [PMID: 19915731]

[4]   N.T. Lee, P. Resnick, and G. Barton, "Algorithmic bias detection and mitigation: Best practices and policies to reduce consumer harms", *Brookings Institute,* 2019. Available at: https://www.brookings .edu/research/algorithmic-bias-detection-and-mitigation-best-practices-and-policies-to-reduce-consumer-harms/#footnote-1

[5]   W. Rodgers, F. Yeung, C. Odindo, and W. Degbey, "Artificial Intelligence-Driven Music Biometrics Influencing Customers' Retail Buying Behavior", *J. Bus. Res.,* vol. 126, pp. 401-414, 2021.
[http://dx.doi.org/10.1016/j.jbusres.2020.12.039]

[6]   C.C. Aggarwal, *Data Mining: The Textbook.* Springer: Switzerland, 2015.

[7]   G. Shmueli, N.R. Patel, and P.C. Bruce, *Data Mining for Business Intelligence: Concepts, Techniques, and Applications in Microsoft Office Excel with XLMiner.* Wiley: New York, 2010.

[8]   W. Rodgers, "Ethical Beginnings: Preferences, rules, and principles influencing decision making", *iUniverse,* 2009.

[9]   EPRS--European Parliamentary Research Service, *Understanding algorithmic decision-making: Opportunities and challenges,* 2019.

[10]    W. Rodgers, Usefulness of decision makers' cognitive processes in a covariance structural model using financial statement information, (Doctoral Dissertation, University of Southern California), 1984.

[11]    W. Rodgers, *Process Thinking: Six pathways to successful decision making.* iUniverse, Inc: NY, 2006.

[12]    W. Rodgers, *Throughput Modeling: Financial Information Used by Decision Makers.* JAI Press: Greenwich, CT, 1997.

[13]    W. Rodgers, "How do loan officers make their decisions about credit risks? A study of Parallel Distributed Processing (PDP)", *J. Econ. Psychol.,* vol. 12, no. 2, pp. 243-265, 1991. [http://dx.doi.org/10.1016/0167-4870(91)90015-L]

[14]    W. Rodgers, E. Alhendi, and F. Xie, "The impact of foreignness on the compliance with cybersecurity controls", *J. World Bus.,* vol. 54, no. 6, p. 101012, 2019. [http://dx.doi.org/10.1016/j.jwb.2019.101012]

[15]    IRPA AI, "Institute For Robotic Process Automation & AI", https://irpaai.com

[16]    M. Bichler, and A. Heinzl, "Robotic Process Automation, Decision", *Bus. Inf. Syst. Eng.,* vol. 60, no. 4, pp. 269-272, 2018. [http://dx.doi.org/10.1007/s12599-018-0542-4]

[17]    K.C. Moffitt, A.M. Rozario, and M.A. Vasarhelyi, "Robotic process automation for auditing", *J. Emerg. Technol. Account.,* vol. 15, no. 1, pp. 1-10, 2018. [http://dx.doi.org/10.2308/jeta-10589]

[18]    Public Company Accounting Oversight Board. (PCAOB), *Technology and the Audit of Today and Tomorrow.,* 2017a. Available at: https://pcaobus.org/News/Speech/Pages/Harris-statement-PCA-B-AAA-4- 20-17.aspx

[19]    Public Company Accounting Oversight Board (PCAOB), *Staff Inspection Brief,* 2017b. Available at: https://pcaobus.org/Inspections/Documents/inspection-brief-2017-3-issuer-scope.pdf?utm_source= PCAOB+Public+Affairs&utm_campaign=d5eec61254-Press_Release_2017-issuer-scope-b-ief-outlook&utm_medium=email&utm_term=0_7e8f08cfb3-d5eec61254-125366813

[20]    H.J. Holzer, "The robots are coming", In: *Let's help the middle class get ready.* Brookings Institute, 2018. Available at: https://www.brookings.edu/blog/up-front/2018/12/13/the-robots-are-coming-lets-help-the-middle-class-get-ready/

[21]    Deloitte, *First financial robot put into use,* 2020.*First financial robot put into use,* 2020. Available at: https://www2.deloitte.com/cn/zh/pages/innovation/articles/deloitte-robot-cbn-interview.html

[22]    KPMG, *How Cognitive Tech Is Revolutionizing the Audit.,* 2016. Available at: https://assets. kpmg.com/content/dam/kpmg/us/pdf/2016/11/us-audit-reprint_v5_web-FINAL.pdf

[23]    PwC, *PricewaterhouseCoopers: The adoption of robotic process automation (RPA) continues to spread across industries.,* 2021. Available at: https://www.pwc.com/gx/en/news-room/analyst-citations/2021/idc-white-paper-pwc-a-robot-for-every-worker.html

[24]    S. Degeling, and J. Hudson, "Financial Robots as Instruments of Fiduciary. Loyalty", *Decision in the Sydney Law Review,* vol. 40, no. 1, p. 63, 2018.

[25]    S. Zheng, "Financial Management Innovation of Electric Power Enterprises Based on Robotic Process Automation", In: *3rd International Seminar on Education Innovation and Economic Management (SEIEM 2018).* Atlantis Press, 2019. [http://dx.doi.org/10.2991/seiem-18.2019.53]

[26]    Ernst & Young, *Robotic process automation Automation's next frontier.,* 2016. Available at: https://assets.ey.com/content/dam/ey-sites/ey-com/en_gl/topics/digital/ey-robotic-pro-ess-automation.pdf

[27]    Deloitte, *Deloitte Statement on Cyber-Incident.,* 2017. Available at: https://www2.deloitte.com/global/

en/pages/about-deloitte/articles/deloitte-statement-cyber-incident.html

[28]  S. Barocas, and A.D. Selbst, "Big Data's Disparate Impact. 104 California Law Review 671", *SSRN*, 2016.https://ssrn.com/abstract=2477899
[http://dx.doi.org/10.2139/ssrn.2477899]

[29]  G. Cui, M.L. Wong, and H-K. Lui, "Machine Learning for Direct Marketing Response Models: Bayesian Networks with Evolutionary Programming", *Manage. Sci.,* vol. 52, no. 4, pp. 597-612, 2006.
[http://dx.doi.org/10.1287/mnsc.1060.0514]

[30]  A. Dafoe, *AI Governance: A Research Agenda Allan Dafoe Centre for the Governance of AI Future of Humanity Institute, University of Oxford,* 2018. Available at: https://www.fhi.ox.ac.uk/wp-content/uploads/GovAI-Agenda.pdf

[31]  W. Rodgers, "The influences of conflicting information on novices' and loan officers' actions", *J. Econ. Psychol.,* vol. 20, no. 2, pp. 123-145, 1999.
[http://dx.doi.org/10.1016/S0167-4870(99)00002-1]

[32]  W. Rodgers, "Three primary trust pathways underlying ethical considerations", *J. Bus. Ethics,* vol. 91, no. 1, pp. 83-93, 2010.
[http://dx.doi.org/10.1007/s10551-009-0069-1]

**CHAPTER 2**

# Understanding Throughput Decision-making Modeling

"You don't have to be a genius or a visionary or even a college graduate to be successful. You just need a framework and a dream".

---Michael Dell, founder of Dell Computers

Data is every company's secret weapon, the new oil, the gasoline that powers algorithms. Use whatever metaphor you like, but as a company manager, if data, machine learning and artificial intelligence are not at the top of your agenda, then you should be removed of your position. We still don't know who the data will belong to, we don't know if artificial intelligence will be proprietary or open, but we do know that now is the time to stop being afraid of artificial intelligence and to get working on understanding its impact.

---Enrique Dans

The field of Artificial Intelligence is set to conquer most of the human disciplines; from art and literature to commerce and sociology; from computational biology and decision analysis to games and puzzles.

---Anand Krish

**Abstract**

Individuals and organizations need to make decisions daily. Given limited time in formulating issues and addressing problems, individuals and organizations must enjoy a certain degree of discretion in planning, revising, and implementing strategies. The Throughput Model facilitates individuals and organizations to simplify process models by modeling perception, information, judgment, and decision choice in a parallel modeling and neural network system. In addition, the Throughput Model allows for a fundamental and wide-ranging approach to understanding first through fifth dimensions dealing with problem solving as well as advancing our knowledge towards quantum computing.

**Keywords:** Analytical Algorithmic Pathway, Expedient Algorithmic Pathway, Fifth dimension, First dimension, Fourth dimension, Global perspective algorithmic pathway, IoT, Limited memory, Parallel computing, Quantum computing, Qubit, Reactive machines, Revisionist algorithmic pathway, Ruling guide algorithmic pathway, Second dimension, Self-awareness, Theory of mind, Third dimension, Throughput model, Value-driven algorithmic pathway.

## INTRODUCTION

The planet as we know today has transformed considerably, in 1995 cell phones were huge bricklike objects. Jump forward to 2021 and the advancements made are astounding to say the least. With the World Wide Web having taken off and establishing itself as a huge power, organizations have learned and adapted to these changes. Thereby, this has contributed to automation and computer systems being more important and central for day-to-day business. Just a few years ago people thought that introducing AI like machine learning and deep learning software's and predictive algorithms would mean a replacement of workforce. Not only in the industrial and labor work but also influencing many types of office jobs. Making all types of professions nervous and uncertain for the future.

The Fourth Industrial Revolution (which is also known as "Industry 4.0") has a positive impact on everyday lives of humans based on the convergence of new technologies [1 - 3]. The most dynamic change of human history takes place currently when individuals face the Fourth Industrial Revolution, which combined various digital and physical technologies (which can be termed digital transformation) [4] such as AI, machine learning, cloud computing, augmented reality (AR) and virtual reality (VR). During this process, AI is a key driver of the Fourth Industrial Revolution. Thus, there is no doubt that a significant and active role for AI in this revolution.

Over the past several years, more and more algorithmic accountability has become an important concern for social scientists, computer scientists, journalists, and lawyers. That is, the potential of the Fourth Industrial Revolution advances a captivating vision of AI algorithms installed in manufacturing systems that can sense, analyze, and react to physical conditions. Enlivened by improving digital technologies, similar scenarios have projected the future of intelligent buildings, hospital systems, farms, and cities.

Computation for AI algorithms is inexpensive, powerful, and small. Sensors are ubiquitous. Networks are becoming speedier and more specialized. Further, AI algorithms have transition beyond hype into broad application, powered by specialized semiconductors. For example, algorithms are all the time more substituting human decision-making on whether a loan is issued or whether an employment candidate gets through to the next round, removing the "human element out of the loop". Nevertheless, the justification behind this decision-making is "black-boxed" to those in the organization, such as executives or managers, much less those directly affected by the decision.

The Throughput Model enables an increased understanding regarding the structure and background of algorithms used in organizational contexts. The Throughput Model is "instrumental" in the process of adopting a strategy for decision-making. That is, the Throughput Model describes the process of decision-making that enables individuals and organizations to recognize risks and opportunities in order that they can make appropriate decisions to react to different circumstances.

Algorithmic decision making can be depicted as automated decision-making based on predefined rules and/or goals. Algorithmic decision making comes with a set of assumptions. In order to better understand what algorithmic decision-making is and how it may affect individuals and organizations, the Throughput Model highlights six decision-making algorithmic pathways regarding to particular context.

The deep the impact of AI based algorithmic decision-making is already dominating across numerous spheres of social, political, and economic life [5]. For example, AI grounded algorithms are utilized to achieve what is determined to be the appropriate medical diagnosis in a much speedier and more efficient way [6], as well as the best possible way to process financial transactions and associated revenues [7].

AI can influence people, processes, and technology. Nowadays, the traditional business operation model is facing the challenge of new IT technology. The application of new technology has brought a huge impact to traditional enterprise managers and employees, which ranges from positive and negative influences. For example, in China, by way of facial recognition, traffic offenders are issued fines for jaywalking in real time, which they receive as text messages on their phones. The role of algorithms in warfare (cyber or "traditional") is increasingly apparent.

Big data technology, AI, robotic process automation (RPA), *etc.*, have widely served various industry. AI is becoming the best solution to promote many standardized and repetitive tasks with clear rules in various offices and consulting agencies. AI greatly reduces labor costs, improves work efficiency and work quality, thereby increasing productivity and work performance. The Throughput Model is a tool which can assist individuals and organizations to determinate the steps and strategies before they decide. In this way, the organizations can reduce issues of biases that may creep into the decision-making process.

In recent years, the Throughput Model has been found applicable in a variety of areas. For example, managers and accountants can use the algorithmic pathways of the Throughput Model when operating or analyzing the business. The Throughput Model assists decision makers to better scrutinize steps taken to resolve issues. Further, the distinct pathways suggest that decision-making logic can lead to very different results. Further, the Throughput Model can also be applied to AI oriented algorithms as operationalize by machine learning or deep learning to achieve a more reasonable, improved, accurate process and results.

The role of the Throughput Model is to determine the links and strategies that decision makers emphasize before deciding. The six algorithmic pathways of the Throughput Model can help organizations to build AI based systems. With the development of the times, the improvement of technology has greatly increased the growth of big data and reduced the difficulty and cost of data storage. The most critical thing is the improvement of computing power. The computing power has reached a level where analysis can be performed without specific programming. On this basis, the algorithms in the Throughput Model as a brand-new tool and technology can effectively help organizations.

## APPLICATION OF THROUGHPUT MODELS-CREATING A TRUSTED ENVIRONMENT USING ALGORITHM PATHS

The shared, and habitual, outlook of the cutting-edge innovations in AI research is that sentient and intelligent machines are just on the horizon. Machines understand verbal commands, distinguish pictures, drive automobiles, and play games better than humans do.

Existing software algorithms are proficient of performing chores that necessitate human intelligence and are driving the enlargement of technologies such as visual perception, speech recognition, decision-making, language translation, robotics, and driverless vehicles. Although AI has become a familiar term in many sectors, there is an across-the-board discernment of the concept in the corporate and general community, whereby the focus is on machine and deep learning. Mainly, wealthier information sources can be gotten from bigger, more precise data sets, using standard predictive analysis models for the express aims of self-learning, general development, planning and the eventual improvement of organizational intelligence.

Neural networks are generally organized in layers (see Fig. **2.1**). Layers are made up of several interconnected 'nodes' that comprise of an 'activation function.'

Patterns are presented to the network by way of the 'input layer,' which communicates to one or more 'hidden layers' whereby the actual processing is performed by a system of weighted 'connections.' The hidden layers then are associated to an 'output layer.'

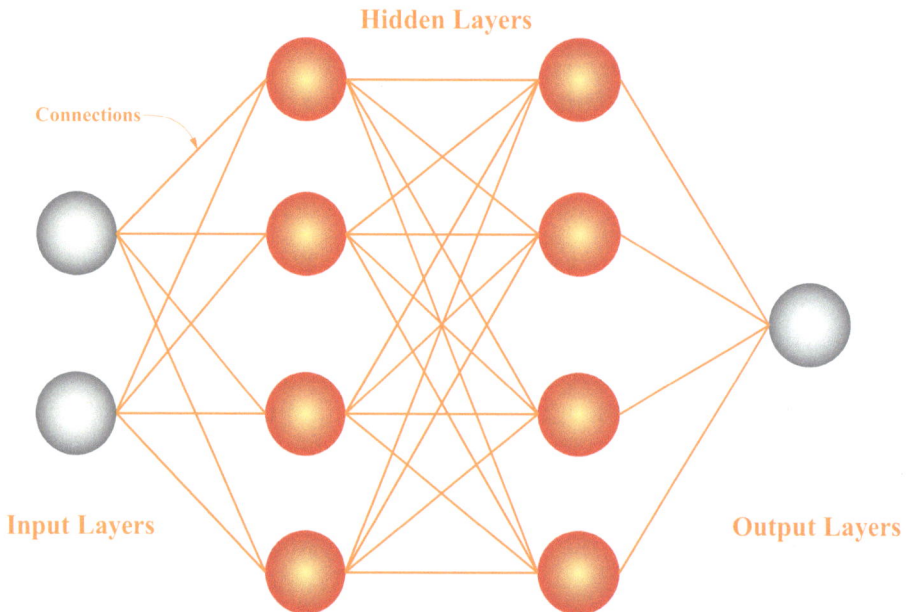

**Hidden Layers**

Connections

**Input Layers**

**Output Layers**

**Fig. (2.1).** Neural networks. Adopted from Rodgers [9].

In addition, most ANNs comprise of some arrangement of 'learning rule' that transform the weights of the connections corresponding to the input designs that it is presented to the model. Hence, ANNs learn by example as do their biological counterparts; a child learns to recognize cats from examples of cats.

There are many kinds of learning rules used by neural networks. An ANNs' learning rule or learning process is a method, mathematical logic or algorithm that enhances the network's performance and/or training time [8]. A lot of the learning methods in machine learning work like each other and are based on each other which makes it difficult to classify them in clear categories. Nonetheless, they can be broadly comprehended in four classifications of learning methods. In addition, these classifications do not have clear boundaries and they tend to belong to multiple categories of learning methods such as Hebbian theory, Gradient descent, Competitive learning, and Stochastic learning.

*Hebbian theory* is a neuroscientific theory asserting that a surge in synaptic efficacy comes about from a presynaptic cell's recurring and persistent stimulation of a postsynaptic cell [10]. Hebbian Learning is stimulated by the biological neural weight adjustment mechanism. It describes the method to convert a neuron an inability to learn and enables it to develop cognition with response to external stimuli.

The essential notion pertaining to Hebbian learning is that if two neurons are apt to trigger on similar inputs, the weight connecting them is increased. There is no notion of guidance here, and hence, gradient descent *via* backpropagation is utilized in supervised setting. That is, where the target may come from explicit labels, or from self-supervision like in auto-encoders. Further, Hebbian learning can be used in the unsupervised setting where there is no target that you are directly trying to match.

Backpropagation is a method implemented to adjust the connection weights to counterbalance for each error found during learning. The error amount is effectively divided among the connections. In principle, backprop calculates the gradient (*i.e.*, the derivative) of the cost function linked with a given state with respect to the weights. The cost function is a function that maps an event or values of one or more variables onto a real number intuitively symbolizing some "cost" allied with the event. The desired weight updates can be done *via* stochastic gradient descent or other methods

*Gradient Descent* is a helper algorithm that aims to achieve the required optimal solution through trial-and-error method. In terms of defining the problem and discovering a solution, a linear regression model can be depicted that involves a supervised machine learning model. In this model, a specific dataset is provided, for example the rate at which a particular house sells as a function of its size. Therefore, the selling price is equal to the function (size).

A plot of the given dataset is made in a graph and as for this model, the best possible straight line is drawn through this graph such that it covers most of the values given. In this manner, it can be found that a relatively accurate selling price for a house whose size is not there in our dataset. Therefore, the problem lies in finding the appropriate coefficients for the line to be drawn. That is, finding 'm' and 'c' in the straight-line equation, $y = mx + c$.

Consequently, a function can be found, which is called the cost function that assists to determine these coefficient values. It links a cost value with a specific pair of coefficients and performs this for a wide range of combinations. Among these cost outputs, a selection is achieved for the least since only the least cost value confirms the minimum deviation of the line from the dataset.

The gradient descent algorithm can assist in the discovery of a route to the lowest cost value given all the cost values.

The process can unfold as follow (*i.e.*, tantamount to climbing down a hill):

1. It starts with a specific pair of coefficients and sees their cost value.

2. It then observes for a cost value lesser than what it is now.

3. For that reason, it moves to the lower value and updates the coefficients.

4. Following a certain time, it arrives at a local minimum beyond which it cannot proceed any further.

5. Hence, it has located the correct pair of coefficients needed at that point where it cannot proceed further.

*Competitive learning* is a form of unsupervised learning whereby nodes challenge for the privilege to respond to a subset of the input data [11 - 12]. A variant of Hebbian learning. That is, Hebbian learning and competitive learning works by increasing the specialization of each node in the network. It is well suited to finding clusters within data.

## Stochastic Learning

Stochastic gradient descent (also known as SGD) is an iterative method for optimizing an objective function with appropriate smoothness features (*e.g.*, differentiable, or non-differentiable). Further, it can be viewed as a stochastic approximation of gradient descent optimization since it replaces the actual gradient. This is calculated from the entire data set by an estimate of a randomly selected subset of the data.

Although the mathematics involved with neural networking is not a trivial matter, a user can rather easily gain at least an operational understanding of their structure and function. People cannot interactively participate in the world; in the same manner they can imagine AI systems one day may be able to perform. As an alternative, these machines will behave the same manner whenever they come across the same circumstance. This process can be appropriate for the very reason for ensuring an AI system trustworthiness [13].

## FOUR FORMS OF AI

In current theory and practice, AI consists of four forms; the first is 'reactive machines.' This form of intelligence necessitates a computer to perceive the world and respond accordingly to what it sees without reliance on inherent internal concepts of the extant world. The second form is 'limited memory;' this encompasses machines which can track the past, remembering details and processes which they have previously encountered. The third form is 'theory of mind'; this form of AI is becoming more sophisticated, developing an overall understanding of the world along with specific knowledge of individuals and their activities. The fourth form is 'self- awareness,', is the final stage of AI development. The concept of a self-conscious machine remains distant, and the focus for the development of this is on the ability of machines to interpret memory, actively learn, and make choices based on experience. Currently, the situation is that AI is well past the first type and actively perfecting the second. Now, the third and fourth types exist only in theory. Therefore, the following four major areas are now discussed: (1) reactive machines, (2) limited memory (3) theory of the mind, and (4) self-awareness.

## Reactive Machines

The most fundamental types of AI systems are simply reactive and have the capability neither to form memories nor to utilize previous experiences to notify recent decisions. For example, of AI successes is IBM's Deep Blue chess playing supercomputer, which defeated global grandmaster Garry Kasparov in the late 1990s [14]. Deep Blue can recognize the pieces on a chess board and know how each move. It can make predictions regarding what moves may be next for it and its opponent. Further, it can select the most optimal moves from among the possibilities. Nonetheless, it neither has any concept of the past, nor does it have any memory of what has happened before. Apart from a seldom utilize chess-specific rule against repeating the same move three times, Deep Blue pay no attention to everything beforehand. That is, it only examines the pieces on the chess board as it presently stands and select from possible next moves.

These methods do improve the ability of AI systems to play specific games better, but they cannot be easily changed or applied to other situations. These computerized imaginations have no concept of the wider world. That is, they cannot function beyond the specific tasks they are assigned and are without difficulty hoodwinked on other chores.

Moreover, this kind of AI tool involves the computer to directly perceive the world and performing on what it grasps. It does not depend on an interior notion of the world. Further, AI development provides a better "representation" of the world since individuals are not very accomplished at programming precise simulated worlds for computers to use. Nonetheless, the current AI reactive machines neither have no concept of the world, nor do they have a unlimited reservoir for other duties.

Likewise, Google's AlphaGo, which has defeated the best human Go experts, cannot appraise all potential future moves. Its analysis technique is more sophisticated than Deep Blue's, using a neural network to evaluate game developments. Neural networks or 'artificial' neural network (ANNs) are processing devices (algorithms or actual hardware) that are freely modeled after the neuronal structure of the human cerebral cortex; however, on a much smaller scale. A sizable ANN might have hundreds or thousands of processor units, whereas a human brain has billions of neurons with a paralleling increase in intensification of their general interaction and evolving behavior.

## Limited Memory

This AI class (*i.e.*, limited memory) consists of machines that can view the past. Self-driving automobiles can perform these tasks. For example, they monitor other automobiles' speed and direction. That cannot be performed in a just one moment, but rather necessitates distinguishing objects and observing them over time.

These observations are inserted to the self-driving automobiles' preprogrammed portrayal of the world, which also consist of lane markings, traffic lights and other important components, such as curves in the road. They are incorporated when the automobile decides when to change lanes, to circumvent blocking another driver or being hit by an adjacent vehicle.

Nevertheless, these straightforward fragments of information regarding the past are only momentary. They are not set aside as part of the automobile's library of experience it can learn from in the future. However, human drivers do compile experience over years behind the wheel.

## Theory of Mind

This important divide represents the difference between the machines that are in existence today and the machines that will be constructed in the future. Machines in the next, more advanced, class not only arrange the portrayals regarding the world, but also descriptions about other people, places, or things in the world.

A machine has a theory of mind if it can assign mental states to itself and others [15] (Gernsbacher, and Yergeau, 2019). A system of inferences of this kind is properly viewed as a "theory of mind" since such states are not directly observable, and the system can be used to make predictions about the behavior of others.

Moreover, the understanding that people, creatures, and objects in the world can have thoughts and emotions that affect their own behavior is essential for the theory of mind. This is critical to how people formed societies since they allowed us to have social interactions. Without understanding each other's motives and intentions, and without considering what somebody else knows either about me or the environment, working together is at best difficult, at worst impossible. Therefore, possessing a functional theory of mind is considered important for success in everyday human social interactions and is utilized when analyzing, judging, and inferring other people behavior.

If AI systems or machines can operate among us, undoubtedly, they will have to be able to understand that each of us, as well as having thoughts and feelings and expectations for how humans will be regarded. In addition, the machines will also need to adjust their behavior accordingly to the circumstances.

## Self-awareness

The final stage of AI development is to construct systems that can form representations about themselves [9] (Rodgers, 2020). In due course, AI machines will communicate as though they have and understand consciousness.

This step is an extension of the "theory of mind" stage of AI. Consciousness is also referred to as "self-awareness". Consciousness, in its most simplistic form is sentience or awareness of internal and external existence. For instance, "I want that item" is a very distinct statement from "I know I want that item". Conscious entities are aware of themselves, know about their internal states, and can predict feelings of others. We assume someone honking behind us in traffic is angry or impatient, because that's how we feel when we honk at others. Without a theory of mind, we could not make those sorts of inferences.

The growing popularity of the Internet and intelligent neural networks have meant that AI technologies such as machine learning and deep learning are being increasingly used in different areas. AI technology is likely to increase the efficiency of companies. AI technology will ensure that the batch processing of large quantities of data can be carried out, improving the accuracy and timeliness of accounting processes. Despite this, AI technology will potentially have negative impacts. That is, if the security and stability of the systems involved are insufficient, information leakage and other serious consequences will result. AI itself does not have the capacity to form independent judgments. Further, AI is currently used in the business sector to perform calculations according to the requirements of individual accountants; nonetheless, it is unable to independently think on its own with a conscious. This, paradoxically, places higher demands on the professional knowledge and skills on designers of systems as well as the monitors. Organizations have increased the quantity and quality of their staff and have accelerated their information flows and network constructions, also increasing their investment in research and development (R & D) in AI. It is particularly important to observe and evaluate the ways in which companies use AI to support their business development.

The emergence of AI tools has provided organizations with new resources which have an important role to play in providing increased and more accurate information. For example, the implementation of AI to mechanize work processes saves time while also reducing the risk of erroneously calculated data. In addition, AI apparatuses can perform in-depth quality checks based on user-defined conditions. Rodgers [9, 16] suggests the establishment of a company culture should be characterized by ethical considerations. Algorithms which are capable of ethical decision-making using Throughput Model (discussed in the next section) can create an authentic, ethical, and trusting environment which enables mutual support among company staff, producing optimum results for their organization [13, 17].

## INTRODUCTION OF THE THROUGHPUT MODEL

In recent years, the Throughput Model [1, 9, 16, 18, 19] have been found applicable in accounting, cyber security, engineering finance, marketing, management, and organization behavior. Companies can use the algorithmic pathway of the Throughput Model when operating or analyzing their operations. The Throughput Model helps decision makers to have more augmented steps and decision choices when making key decisions. Different decision pathways can lead to very different results. Hence, the Throughput Model can also be applied to AI apparatuses, to achieve a more reasonable, optimized, accurate calculation process and results from specific algorithmic pathways.

With the recent development of technology, the improvement of AI applications has greatly increased the use of big data and reduced the difficulty and cost of data storage. The most critical item is the enhancement of computing power. The computing power has reached a level where analysis can be performed without specific programming. On this basis, the algorithmic pathways in the Throughput Model as a pristine tool can effectively assist AI, and work of individuals and organizations.

This aim of this section is to discuss the Throughput Model influences on AI apparatuses. Nowadays, the traditional business operation model is facing the challenge of new AI technology. The application of new AI technology has brought a huge impact to traditional organizational managers and employees regarding positive and negative impacts.

Big data technology, AI, robotic process automation (RPA), *etc.*, have widely served various industry. For example, it can assist individuals to battle against the coronavirus and may has a contribution on the deterrence of money laundering. It is well known that Deloitte is one of the organizations who introduce AI into the business. Moreover, AI can assist to simplify employees' daily work processes and operations as well as achieving automation and heighten productivity.

There are at least two forms to achieve automation. First, AI may reduce the manpower directly by performing repetitive work. Furthermore, AI is becoming the best solution to promote the standardization of repetitive tasks with clear rules in various offices and consulting agencies.

Second, it may enhance employees' capabilities to perform the task better and faster, which may improve the efficiency during the working process. Thus, AI can greatly reduce labor costs, improves work efficiency and work quality thereby improving the overall productivity and profitability of a company.

Since AI may be viewed as a new digital innovation that requires more explanation regarding its usefulness. First, AI systems are dependent on the amount and the quality of the data. Therefore, how to obtain enough large amounts of high-quality data is a question. Second, some AI algorithms have many hidden layers of decision-making routines during the training process, which will increase the difficulty of auditability and traceability. To this end, the Throughput Model is a tool, which can assist a manager to determinate the steps and strategies before they make decision choice [20]. In this way, organizations may reduce kinds of opacity issues that occurs when applying certain AI algorithms for problem solving.

To address the opacity issue pertaining to the use of algorithms, the Throughput Model proposes four major concepts, which are, *perception, information, judgment,* and *decision choice.* Each algorithmic pathway that adopts different concepts can present unique decision-making positions.

This section reviews the key literature with the implementation of AI and organization design as well as the Throughput Model. AI is becoming more and more applied in the market and have already impacted on several areas, such as automotive technology, healthcare, service industry and other manufacturing entities. In essence, AI has provided a lot of opportunities to individuals and organizations. In the area of business, the introduction of AI has provided a more advanced platform for areas such as accounting and auditing. In the interim, the Throughput Model may assist organizations to make decisions, which are an essential component for productivity and profitability. Numerous scholars have conducted extensive research regarding the advantages and disadvantages in AI (*e.g.,* [20]). The Throughput Model advances research and practice by focusing on a theoretical perspective and empirical analysis of the challenges in the implementation in practice. Thus, this review critically contrasts and evaluates available literature in a bid to address how the Throughput Model can assist organizations.

First, some studies support the notion that AI has its weaknesses and limitations for organizations [21]. That is, AI supported machine learning and deep learning has weaknesses pertaining to transparency and accountability when it assists an organization in decision-making. Therefore, ethical problems may become a challenge.

In the business environment [22], concluded that the risk of using AI in corporate accounting may be that the majority employees are professional in one or more areas on accounting. Nonetheless, they do not have enough education and experience in the AI arena. Further, AI does not have enough imagination, creative work, and emotional communication to "think out of box" compared with humans. Nowadays, the value of accountants and auditors are more and more reflected in performing creative work, such as communicating with others, and providing attention to the changing market environment. In addition, there is an increasing threat on the newest AI tools, which implies that during the training, the employee will be trained in AI, but not in the concepts, rules, and details of the underlying accounting standards. Therefore, Guyader's [23] work on AI in the corporate realm is complemented by Baldwin, Brown and Trinkle's [22] study, in that it is essential for the chief financial officer to make sure their team has the necessary ability to implement AI technology. Meanwhile, as AI is a kind of new generation of machine learning and deep learning systems, it may bring sociological side effect which is the increasing rate of unemployment [9] and the professionals need to be prepared for the challenges of AI revolution [24]. Goh *et al.* [25] argued that due to overfitting, the data cannot be generalized even if the AI techniques are powerful. At the same time, there is a limitation on modelling of statistical and mathematics, which is the foundation of AI modelling. The primary reason is that some of the business issues cannot be solved simply by mathematical computations.

In contrast, other studies have argued there are some positive impacts of AI in organizational areas such as corporate accounting. For example, Rodgers [18, 19] stated that biometrics identification is a way that assess one or more different biological features. Through the authenticate of the AI based biological features, the application, service, or device can be used effectively in organizations. This view is supported by Kairinos [26] who argues that there are many ways that AI is implemented to protect consumers and businesses. AI based biometrics are especially useful in the arena of diminishing the occurrence of the fraudulent use of payment cards. Further, in corporate accounting, AI may improve the quality of accounting information and ensure the true and fair nature of accounting information. In addition, AI based systems can strengthen the prevention of financial risk and enhance corporate competitiveness (Rodgers, 2012). In the perspective of the society, AI plays an important role in combating money laundering and crime, which is becoming a trend in the global community. The application of AI in biometrics is not only limited on online fraud, but also it can be time and cost saving. There are many ways that AI based solutions can protect consumers and businesses [26].

Second, AI is an essential part of the accounting profession future [22, 27]. That is, there is a tremendous potential for automation in financial accounting and reporting. In the early 1980s and 1990s, some management systems were introduced which were used to evaluate the cash flow, analysis the business combinations and financial reports. This view is supported by Le Guyader [23] who stated that the introduction of AI may have an ascription from an uncomplicated excel based valuation and accounting matchups to the variety of decisions that complex accounting rules leave to management. Under this situation, AI may have an influence on the process of management practices. AI may assist to manage and analyze the cost, planning and control, forecasting, capital budgeting, resource allocation, variance analysis and cash flow evaluation, which may decrease the cost of labor and time. Moreover, it may assist a manager to make decisions acting on targets set. Therefore, this process may increase the accuracy of meeting a goal.

Third, AI systems may reduce an organization overall cost as well as improving and the accuracy and efficiency of computing the accounting information. Vasarhelyi and Kogan [28] argued that AI high accuracy and efficiency in calculations is way ahead of what humans are capable of accomplishing. As the providers of information and the assessors of the risk, accountants require novel tools to enhance their overall efficiency and effectiveness within the corporate accounting contexts [22].

Fourth, there is an argument that suggests that there is an increasing risk that the professional accountant may be replaced by AI. This is primarily due to the repetitive tasks and duties that accountants perform [25]. Nonetheless, it may not be such a terrible idea to replace some of the accountants' tasks with AI. That is, some of the accountant' time can be free up to be utilized on higher level duties, which may produce more efficiencies in the organization. At the same time, accountants may create other duties, which may add and deliver more value to the company [25].

It is well known that AI can largely imitate a human's cognitive ability to learn and recognize patterns even though it cannot replicate human intelligence completely. Therefore, this is an opportunity for workers to develop their skills to create more benefit for their company. For example, workers' communication skills and critical thinking will become more important in the AI age [29]. Jazaie [30] maintained that there are at least seven significant skills for workers. They are:

1. skill of presentation (storytelling),
2. credibility,
3. confidence,
4. friendliness,
5. eye contract,
6. understanding other's point of view, and
7. give or receive the feedback.

Moreover, the critical thinking skills is also important for employees, which cannot replace by the AI. The skill of critical thinking has been "broadly acknowledged as a instrumental requirement for success in most practical and professional spheres [31]. Furthermore, critical thinking skills have become one of the main aims in for individuals in organizations [24]. Furthermore, the skill of leadership is playing a significant role in corporate accounting since an increasing professional accountant participate in the management of their organization's strategic plan, Thus, Stancheva-Todorova [24] stated that some major types of leadership will become increasingly indispensable in the AI age. Overall, the development of AI may become a major opportunity that exists for people throughout an organization combining interdisciplinary work with AI applications. This sort of collaboration could catapult the development of AI in many areas [22]. Overall, AI systems can reliably handle and process voluminous data while also ensuring that there is continuous monitoring to learn from new data and errors and create more value for an organization.

In sum, AI is influencing the business and non-business. Further, AI will continue to influence the traditional accounting process, which implies that it can be more efficient and accurate. Meanwhile, the AI system may help individuals and organizations dealing with the decision-making process which is the bedrock of performance. The Throughput Model may influence the organizational decision-making, which can serve as the theoretical underpinnings of the algorithms used in full force in AI applications such as machine learning and deep learning. To this end, the next section will be grounded in the details and operations of the Throughput Model.

Many of the exciting technological advances can be illustrated by the Throughput Model in capturing the first, second, third, fourth and fifth dimensions (see Fig. **2.2**). That is, research suggests that the dimensions are states of consciousness, and the elevated dimensions are neighboring to the source energy [9] (Rodgers, 2020). AI neural networks endeavors to imitate the human brain to provide faster, more efficient, and more effective problem solving in reaching better decision choices (see Fig. **2.2**).

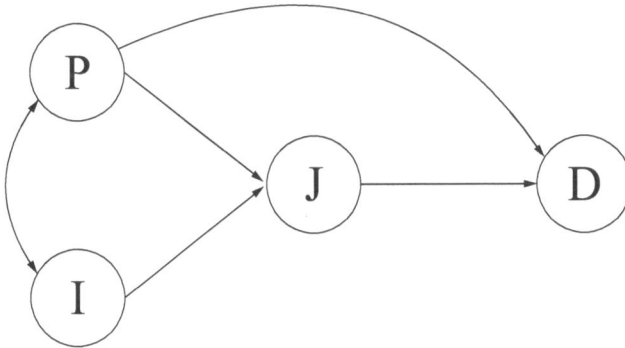

*Where P = perception, I = information, J = judgment, and D = decision choice*

**Fig. (2.2).** Throughput modelling diagram.

The first dimension is a single point. For example, the constructs of perception, information, judgment, or decision choice. For example, one dimensional single point "perception" system includes the number line (Fig. **2.3**).

**Fig. (2.3).** First dimension showing perception as a single point. Partially adopted from Rodgers [32].

The second dimension contains two axis, x & y. For example, the two axes in the Throughput Model can be symbolized as follows:

1. P→J

2. P→D

3. I→J

4. J→D

Further, the second dimensional consciousness is awareness as point and line from perception and judgment starting points (Fig. **2.4**).

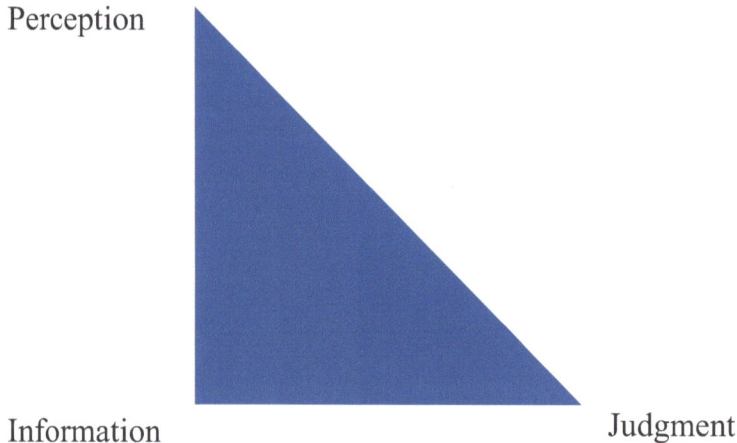

**Perception**

**Information**                    **Judgment**

**Fig. (2.4).** Second dimension showing perception, information, and judgment (length and width). Partially adopted from Rodgers [32].

In the third dimension we perceive duality, polarities *etc.* Further, in the third dimension, we experience the information sources as distinct from ourselves so that we can perceive information objectively. And by observing information, we establish that energy into the physical realm. Whereas, the second dimension has height and width, the third dimension represents height, width, and depth. Therefore, the height, width, and depth imply density and volume. The relationship of P←→I depict the third-dimension properties of density and volume. Prior research has long-established that the relative volume of visible space can designate the proportional perceived density and volume [34]. In other words, research has advised that three-dimensional (3D) structure-from-motion (SFM) perception in people comprises numerous motion-sensitive occipital and parietal brain areas. Furthermore, research on people's density has revealed that how individuals perceive a high-density situation pungently influences their behavior, and that density itself seldom has a direct unmediated consequence on individual's behavior [35].

Some of the density of perception include:

- Vision
- Touch
- Sound
- Taste
- Smell

There are also other senses that permit us to perceive things such as balance, time, body position, acceleration, and the perception of internal states. Many of these are multimodal and encompass more than one sensory modality. Social perception (*i.e.*, "P") or the capability to recognize and employ social cues about people and relationships, is another vital mode of perception (Fig. **2.5**).

**Fig. (2.5).** Third dimension showing the density of perception. Partially adopted from Rodgers [32].

First, second and third dimensions are the usual length, width, and height of a person, place, or thing we perceive around us. Special theory of relativity of Einstein displayed that time also should be treated like these [36]. The reason is that if you perceive an event from dissimilar reference frames, for example, one observer is on the platform and the other one is in a moving train, what each one calls space and time get muddled that is x(train) is contingent both on x(platform) and t (platform). Recent developments in theoretical physics (such as string theory or M-theory) are advocating that there could be more spatial dimensions (as many as 7 more), which we do not perceive in our daily lives. For example, viewing a hose from a distance, it looks like a thin string of one dimension, length only. Nonetheless, if closer, it has a circular cross section (another dimension which was not visible before). The theory is that it is conceivable that the higher dimensions will be perceptible in experiments at very high energy. Today, people have not been able to verify this idea. Higher dimensions are challenging to portrait with our brain since we are three dimensional beings. Nevertheless, mathematically there is not a problem to capture. At this moment, as there are two-dimensional (plane) and three-dimensional (solid) geometries, there can exist (*i.e.*, for now mathematically) n-dimensional geometries as well.

The fourth dimension involves "time," and what that suggests is uncertainty. Our viewpoint of time is relative, and that "time" is most prone to be nonlinear. The investigation of time perception is a subject within psychology, cognitive linguistics and neuroscience that symbolizes the subjective experience, or sense, of time, which is gauged by an individual's perception ("P") of the period of the unlimited and developing of events (captured by "I"). Hence, the following

Throughput Model sequence of relationship represent the 4$^{th}$ dimension encapsulating "time":

1. P→D,
2. P→J→D,
3. I→J→D,
4. I→P→D,
5. P→I→J→D, and
6. I→P→J→D.

Further, in the P←→I relationship, individuals do not only perceive events ("I") only, but also their temporal relations. For example, just as it is natural to depict that people perceive spatial distances and other relations between objects (*e.g.*, I see the butterfly as floating above the surface of the water), it appears natural to discuss perceiving one event following another (*e.g.*, the thunderclap as following the flash of lightning) (Fig. **2.6**).

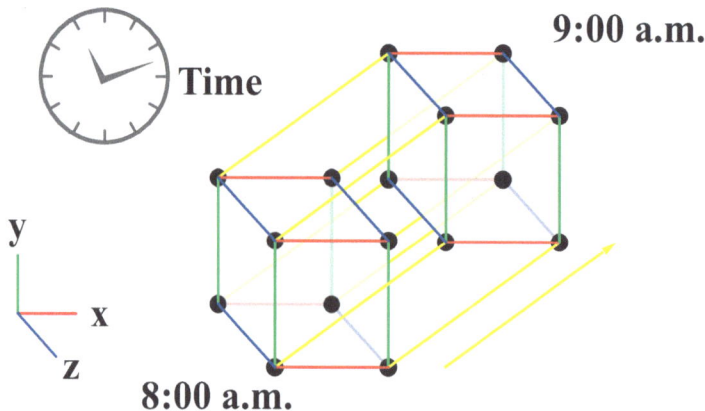

**Fig. (2.6).** Fourth dimension representing time. Adopted from various web sources.

Finally, the *fifth dimension* is a reality whereby the vastness and complexity of "time" could be perceived as the second dimension is perceived in the third dimension. A five-dimensional space can be viewed as a sequence of numbers that can represent a location in an N-dimensional space (Einstein and Bergmann, 1938). If interpreted in the Throughput Model, it is one or more algorithmic pathways influencing a decision choice. Therefore, P→D and J→D represents two algorithmic pathways that are parallel and influencing decision choice.

In the fifth dimension we experience different information sources from a perspective of unity that assist us in problem solving. Therefore, the Throughput Model parallel processing is the use of multiple processing elements simultaneously for solving any problem. Further, the Throughput Model emphasizes the fifth dimension by analyzing different parallel pathways navigated in combination with AI that traverses through to come to a decision. We can also see the types of classifications and how they can be perceived as human decision making. Giving us a clear view and understanding of how AI can replicate human's decisional outcome. This analysis also requires us to have a clear understanding of AI systems. What they are and the type of categories they fall under to able to assess its process in decision-making. Moreover, the Throughput Model enables more focusing on machine learning or deep learning software's as well as predictive analytics, and their connection to the type of AI needed in organizational effectiveness and efficiencies.

The Throughput Model design permits an understanding of the fifth dimension as employed by quantum computing. That is, parallel processing allows quantum computers to take a distinctive method to information processing. As an alternative of solving a problem one outcome at a time, a quantum computer computes every possible outcome *simultaneously* (Fig. **2.7**).

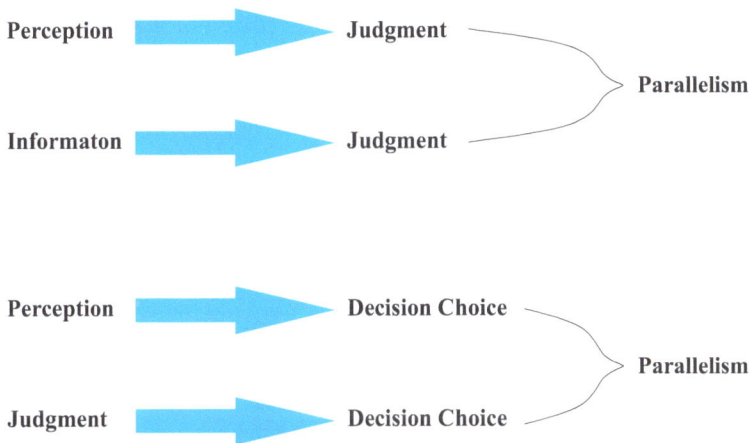

**Fig. (2.7).**  Fifth dimension showing parallelism in the throughput model.

For example, as explained by Rasmusson [37]: "Imagine you want to find the deepest place on Earth and a single point on the planet can be uniquely identified by a group of bits, like GPS coordinates. To move the point toward low ground, the processor modifies the group of bits so they represent a neighboring point that's further downhill. This is repeated until the point reaches a minimum. But is this the lowest minimum? To truly know if that minimum is the deepest place, the computer must search the whole planet. It must start at every point, go downhill, and then find the lowest minimum among all the discovered minimums. That's a lot of starting points! If each point were enlarged to a square mile, the computer would need to try 196.9 million points!" Hence, a quantum computer may be able to solve the aforementioned problem, 196.9 million times faster.

Recently, Chinese Developers claimed that the Zuchongzhi device can do in just over an hour a task that supercomputers would take years to accomplish. These results surpass those produced by Google's Sycamore processor in an experiment two years ago (see: https://www.scmp.com/news/china/science/article/3140968/chinese-quantum-computer-sets-record-processing-test#amp_tf=From%20%251%24s&aoh=16267349570845&csi=0&referrer=https%3A%2F%2Fwww.google.com).

One of the advantages of the Throughput Model is that it depicts parallelism, which assist in solving a problem. Similarly, quantum computer solves for each point in parallel (meaning at the same time) as every other point. Accordingly, through a process called "superposition," qubits permit a quantum computer solve this problem in parallel instead of one point at a time.

Superposition is analogous to a rotating coin. While a coin is rotating, is it heads (0) or tails (1)? Well, we know that "measuring" the coin will give heads (0) 50% of the time and tails (1) the other 50%. Because the rotating coin can deliver a head (0) and tails (1) result, the rotating coin is, theoretically speaking, both heads and tails at the same time. Similarly, a qubit in superposition is both 0 and 1, but when evaluated, the qubit will read either 0 or 1. Parenthetically, rigorous experimentation has shown qubit superposition is in both states.

Why parallel computing?

a. In everyday life runs in dynamic nature, that is various things occur at a certain time; however, at dissimilar places concomitantly. This data is lengthily vast to manage.
b. Real-world data necessities more vibrant simulation and modeling, and for accomplishing the same, parallel computing is essential.
c. Parallel computing delivers concurrency and saves time and money.
d. Multifaceted, sizable datasets, and their management can be structured only and only using parallel computing's method.
e. Warrants the applicable use of the resources. The hardware is assured to be managed effectively whereas in serial computation only some part of the hardware was employed, and the remaining rendered groundless.
f. Also, it is impractical to implement real-time systems using serial computing.

Applications of Parallel Computing:

a. Databases and Data mining.
b. Real-time simulation of systems.
c. Science and Engineering.
d. Advanced graphics, augmented reality, and virtual reality.

Limitations of Parallel Computing:

a. It addresses such as communication and synchronization between multiple sub-tasks and processes, which is complicated to accomplish.
b. The algorithms must be administered in such a manner that they can be conducted in a parallel mechanism.
c. The algorithms or programs must have low coupling and high cohesion. Nonetheless, it is challenging to generate such programs.
d. More technically skilled and expert programmers can code a parallelism-based program well.

The hope of what quantum computers can do. Though many of these goals are far away, scientists are cautiously optimistic that a quantum computer of the future will accomplish them (see Fig. **2.8**).

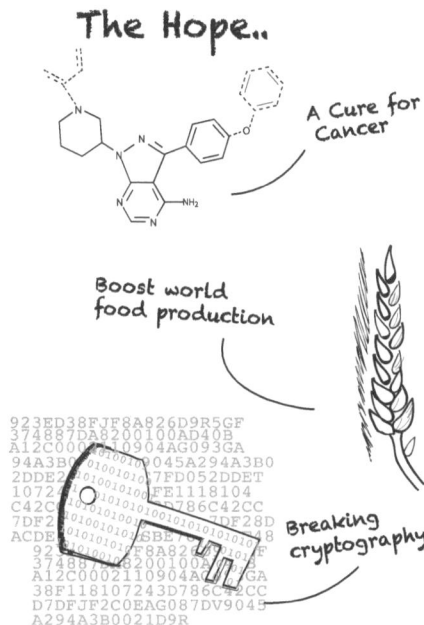

**The Hope..**

A Cure for Cancer

Boost world food production

Breaking cryptography

**Fig. (2.8).** Quantum computing helping society. This figure came from the EPiQC zine on quantum computing.

The Throughput Model imitates human cognitive processes, which occurs in the mind of individuals prior to a decision choice [32]. The decision-making perspective suggests that a choice can be motivated by one of six dominant algorithmic pathways by the context in which it is made. This perspective is focused on learning the factors (*i.e.*, perception and/or information) that bring value to the selections (*i.e.*, judgment) before a decision choice is made (see Fig. **2.2**).

The Throughput Model can also be described as a conceptual quantitative model that links the phases of individuals' cognitive processes in terms of "perception" (P), "information" (I), "judgment" (J), and "decision choice" (D), where "P" or "I" (or iterations between both) lead to "J," which then leads to "D" (and/or "P" directly leads to "D"). Hence, understanding of the different algorithmic pathways that lead to "D" can help to suitably design a system to uncover consumer decision models. Moreover, the algorithmic pathway that customers link to an option can vary depending on the number of alternatives, the decision maker's mood, her/his former experience with that kind of decision, and so on.

The six typical decision algorithmic pathways [33] in Fig. (**2.2**), which can be clarified as:

1. **The Expedient Algorithmic Pathway P→D**
2. **The Ruling Algorithmic Guide Pathway P→J→D**
3. **The Analytical Algorithmic Pathway I→J→D**
4. **The Revisionist Algorithmic Pathway I→P→D**
5. **The Value Driven Algorithmic Pathway P→I→J→D**
6. **The Global Perspective Algorithmic Pathway I→P→J→D**

The *Expedient Algorithmic Pathway* is mostly utilized when individuals are confronted with greater time pressure to decide. Nevertheless, when it comes to making quick decisions, time pressure is a big issue for human decision-makers. Therefore, this is where AI machines may be more beneficial given the particularity of the situation.

The *Ruling Guide Algorithmic Pathway* takes consideration of judgment (*i.e.*, analysis). Individuals make decisions using their internal or external rules. This algorithmic pathway sometimes may be effective and efficient in a stable environment. Nonetheless, today the environment is changing rapidly. Changes in regulations and rules escalate the chance of fraudulent activities. Ignoring relevant and relative information can lead individuals and organizations to make horrible decisions.

The *Analytical Algorithmic Pathway* is established on the availability of information to conduct a detailed analysis before reaching a decision. It is useful to minimize risk in certain areas. Further, individuals and organizations can gather all relevant and reliable information on past performance of an entity; however, due to changing environments, previous information made not be sufficient for actions. This algorithmic pathway assumes that all the information is accurate, and the environment is stable and controllable.

The *Revisionist Algorithmic Pathway* combines information and perception. Relevant and relative information will update or modify investors' perception before reaching a decision. However, missing judgment component in this pathway will provide individuals or organizations little time to analyze all the information. Consequently, if all the information considered is relevant, relative, and correct, it will be useful for people to decide when time pressure is great. Yet, if the information is biased and incomplete, it will lead people to unsatisfactory decisions.

The *Value-Driven Algorithmic Pathway* represents perceptual framing modifying the information source and, thereby a decision. The determining factor using this algorithmic pathway is the individual's subjective preference, which can result in a decision that is not the most rewarding but one that is the most satisfying to the individual since the decision is based first and foremost on his or her individual perception.

The *Global Perspective Algorithmic Pathway* is the most ideal algorithmic pathway among all the six decision making pathways. It takes into consideration all types of information that updates or revises people's perception, and then is followed by judgment before the final decision is made. If individuals and organizations are open-minded allows for broader ethical considerations. Detailed analysis will also follow the reframed perception before final decisions are made. Individuals will not only exam various information sources, but also closely observe an organization's activities and changes in the regulations. In this way, their perception can be reframed timely, and a more favorable decision can be made especially in a rapidly changing technologically oriented world. Nevertheless, the Global Perspective pathway and the Value-driven pathway are both very time consuming. If time pressure is too great, incomplete, or mis-interpreted information will weaken these two decision-making perspectives. Therefore, this is where AI technology can be quite beneficial to individuals and organizations.

The Throughput Model advances individuals and organizations decision-making process on what is required to be accomplished. The advantage of this method is that it can assist decision makers to understand why certain individuals selectively present information to support their own positions. This approach also helps to illustrate the particular "way of thinking" in which individuals base their positions on essential issues. Since information is usually subjectively processed by decision makers, it correlates with perception in conceptual models. The influence of incoming information is related to a decision maker's previous experiences or beliefs about this information and the degree of covariance between these factors; these two sources of information together determine covariant perception held that, due to the duplication of cues (*i.e.*, prior expectations and information provided by information), the implementation of individual decision-making options may become ambiguous and difficult; cues are both interrelated and linked to perception [32]. This fact implies that the interdependence of perception and information should be considered in the model. Finally, perception and judgment influence the decision-making process. Rodgers [38] concluded that most decisions made involved automatic, perceptual heuristics and thoughtful information processing strategies (judgments). One of the main contributions of the Throughput Model is that individuals can decide to weight certain approaches based on their own decision-making perspectives. Decision makers can benefit from the knowledge that alternative approaches can improve or modify their decision choices. Finally, this novel approach enables organizations to supplement multiple decision-making strategies with unique algorithmic pathways to make decisions. The Throughput Model begins with consideration of how individuals think about perceived way of problem solving. In the global environment, decision-making issues can affect stakeholders who are internal or external to an organization. Further, the level of influence of deciding is determined by their importance of the algorithmic pathway the decision maker implements in problem solving.

These six algorithmic pathways are viewed as the most dominant and influential for decision-making, especially when aided by AI apparatuses. Further, one of the primary assertions regarding the Throughput Model algorithmic pathways is that they provide more flexibility in decision-making when compared with the traditional model.

The traditional model is based on two major assumptions [39, 40]. The first assumption suggests that choices are understood to follow the principle of utility maximization. Utility can be thought of as levels of satisfaction, happiness, or personal benefit. Individuals act to maximize personal subjective benefits by assessing each option aligned with the weighted criteria and choosing the option with the highest total score. The second assumption of the rational model is that individuals' preferences are well-defined and constant over time [40, 41].

In addition, the Throughput Model represents a parallel distributed processing (PDP) two-stage model, which depicts individuals and organizations' knowledge representation of information that may influence their judgments (*i.e.*, analysis), which in turn may have an impression on their decision choices [11]. That is, the perceptual and judgmental processes have different parallel pathways leading to an action (see Fig. **2.2**).

## PARALLEL PROCESSING DIMENSIONS OF THE THROUGHPUT MODEL

Computer software was written conventionally for serial computing. This meant that to solve a problem, an algorithm divides the problem into smaller instructions. These discrete instructions are then executed on the Central Processing Unit of a computer one by one. Only after one instruction is finished, next one starts.

For example, let's assume people standing in a queue waiting to purchase a movie ticket and there is only one cashier. The cashier is handling tickets one by one to the people inline. The complexity of this situation increases when there are two queues and only one cashier.

Therefore, serial computing represent:

a. A problem statement is broken into discrete instructions.
b. Next the instructions are implemented one by one.
c. Finally, only one instruction is executed at any given moment in time.

Step number three above presents a tremendous problem in the cognitive decision-making process as only one instruction was obtaining execution at any moment of time. In addition, from a computing viewpoint, this is a tremendous waste of hardware resources as only one part of the hardware will be running for instruction and of time. Therefore, utilizing parallel processing in the example, the complexity will decrease when there are two queues and two cashiers providing tickets to two individuals simultaneously. This is an example of parallel processing.

The Throughput Model assumes that parallel processing takes place through the interactions of many simple processing elements called units, each sending activations to other units [11, 12]. At times, the units represent potential hypotheses regarding such facets such as loan officers' perceived notions regarding a possible loan to a client, or their prognostic judgments about a client's capability to payback a loan. In these cases, the activations stand roughly for the strengths connected with distinct possible hypotheses.

McClelland *et al.* ([42] p. 11) advocated that PDP models offer the hope of computationally sufficient and psychologically accurate mechanistic accounts of the phenomena of decision makers' cognition which have eluded successful explication in conventional computational formalisms; and they have radically altered the way we think about the time-course of processing, the nature of representation, and the mechanisms of learning. The Throughput Model takes the serial processing model one step further by portraying decision makers' perceptual and judgmental parallel processing before they arrive at a decision choice [11].

This leads us to parallel computing, which is the use of multiple processing elements simultaneously for solving any problem. Problems are broken down into instructions and are solved concurrently as each resource that has been applied to work is working at the same time.

The advantages of parallel computing (or parallel processing) over Serial Computing (or input-output models) are as follows:

1. It can save time and money as many resources working together will reduce the time and eliminate potential costs.

2. It may be impractical to solve larger problems on serial computing (*i.e.*, input-output models).

3. It can take advantage of non-local resources when the local resources are finite (*e.g.*, IoT, cloud computing).

4. Serial Computing 'dissipates' the potential computing power, therefore parallel computing (or parallel processing) makes better work of the hardware (or software).

**Types of Parallelism:**

**a. Bit-level or Qubit Parallelism –**

It is the form of parallel computing which is based on the increasing processor's size. It reduces the number of instructions that the system must execute to perform a task on large-sized data.

*Example:* Consider a scenario where an 8-bit processor must compute the sum of two 16-bit integers. It must first sum up the 8 lower-order bits, then add the 8 higher-order bits, thus requiring two instructions to perform the operation. A 16-bit processor can perform the operation with just one instruction. Quantum computing, a qubit or quantum bit (sometimes qbit) is the basic unit of quantum information. That is, the quantum version of the classic binary bit physically realized with a two-state device. A qubit is a two-state (or two-level) quantum-mechanical system, one of the simplest quantum systems displaying the idiosyncrasy of quantum mechanics.

## b. Instruction-level Parallelism –

A processor can only tackle less than one instruction for each clock cycle phase. These instructions can be re-ordered and grouped which are later implemented concomitantly without influencing the result of the program. This is called instruction-level parallelism.

## c. Task Parallelism –

Task parallelism engages the breakdown of a task into subtasks and then apportioning each of the subtasks for implementation. The processors accomplish the execution of sub-tasks concurrently.

## 5. Data-level Parallelism (DLP) –

Instructions from a single stream operate concurrently on several data – Regulated by non-regular data manipulation patterns and by memory bandwidth

The Throughput Model differs from the traditional economic theory (*i.e.*, rational model or input-output model), since it is (1) a process model (*i.e.*, opens up the black box), and (2) similar to a human neural network provides parallel routes in two stages (*i.e.*, I→J and P→J in the first stage and P→D and J→D in the second stage) (see Fig. **2.2**), (3) include a symbolic neural network function (*i.e.*, P←→I) that imitate a Bayesian model (see Fig. **2.2**), and (4) provides different stages before a decision is made.

For example, based on the simple evaluation of alternatives, the six AI algorithms can be fortified through an artificial single layer neural network as shown in Fig. (**2.9**).

Also, when a data set applied to individuals and organizations becomes more complex, an artificial deep-layer neural network can be set for the algorithmic pathways (see Fig. **2.10**).

As an introduction, the Throughput Model can benefit technologies such as the Internet of Things (IoT), which is depicted by instruments such as mobile devices, tablets, and smart appliances. On the most basic level, the IoT refers to objects which can connect and communicate *via* the Internet. The IoT technology influences individuals' behavior on online users' daily lives. In this manner, when online users decide to purchase goods, their mobile applications can automatically save and record this data for autonomously monitoring the consumption of goods and beverages and re-ordering of goods through a reminder application or announcement by means of retail applications.

The utilization of the IoT in unification with cloud technologies has become an impetus for parallel distributed processing models, such as the Throughput Model. The IoT and cloud computing are now related to each other. These are dedicated technologies of the future that will bring many benefits.

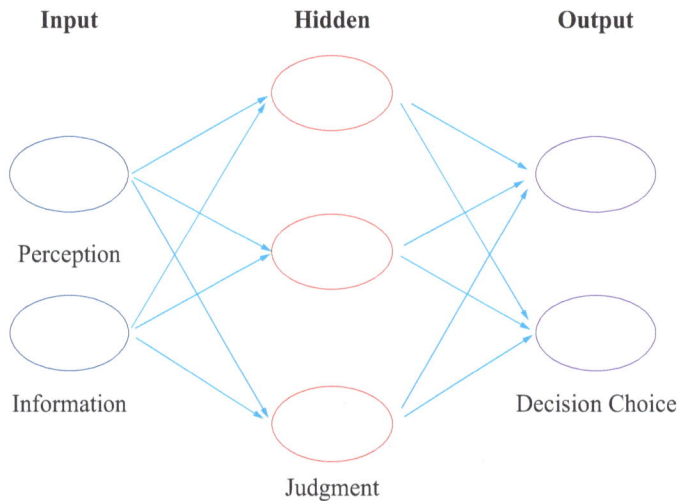

**Fig. (2.9).** Artificial single layer neural network for evaluation of alternatives of the purchase decision algorithm.
Source: Author generated

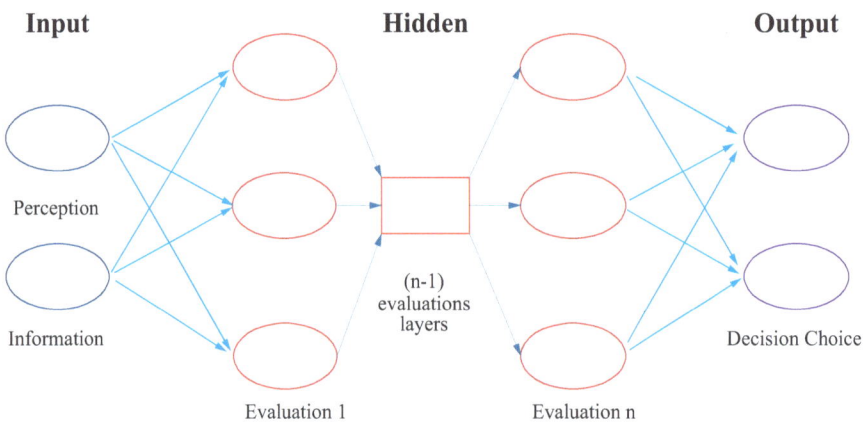

**Fig. (2.10).** Artificial deep layer neural network for evaluation of alternatives to purchase decision algorithms.
Source: Author generated

## IoT and Cloud Computing

Cloud Computing is a tremendous factor that improves the success of the IoT [43]. Cloud computing facilitates individuals to perform computing tasks providing services over the Internet. That is, due to the tremendous growth of AI technology, the problem of storing, processing, and retrieving considerable volumes of data has ascended to new heights. Numerous innovations relate to the mutual use of the IoT and cloud technologies. In combination, it will be conceivable to utilize influential processing of sensory data streams and novel monitoring services. For instance, sensor data can be stacked and banked implementing cloud computing for later use. Further, this later use can be for intelligent monitoring as well as for activation of other devices. The objective is to transform data into insights and thereby pushing for cost-effective and productive action. Moreover, the three main components of the cloud listed below can transform the use of IoT:

1. Computing power

2. Reliability

3. Connectivity

In addition, the benefits of cloud are as follow:

1. IoT assisted by cloud computing offers many connectivity alternatives, entailing large network access. Individuals utilize a variety of devices to acquire access to cloud computing resources such as mobile devices, tablets, laptops. This is accessible for users; however, generates the problem to acquire for network access points.

2. Developers can utilize IoT cloud computing on-demand. Namely, it is a web service retrieved without special permission or assistance. The only condition is Internet access.

3. Based on the request, people can use the service according to their requisites. Prompt and accommodating implying you can magnify storage space, edit software settings, and work with the quantify of users. Attributable to this feature, it is conceivable to deliver deep computing power and storage.

4. Cloud Computing infers the amalgamating of resources. It inspires amplified associations and erects close connections between users.

5. As the number of IoT devices and automation in use propagates, security concerns emerge. Cloud solutions offer organizations with reliable authentication

and encryption protocols.

6. IoT cloud computing is fitting since costs vary depending on use. The provider measures the usage statistics. A mounting network of objects with IP addresses is needed to connect to the Internet and exchange data between the components of the network.

## Comparison of Internet of Things and Cloud Computing

The Cloud is a centralized system facilitating the transfer and delivering of data and files to data centers over the Internet. An assortment of data and programs are simple to access from a centralized cloud system. The Internet of Things (IoT) denotes those devices are connected to the Internet. In the IoT, data is stored in real-time, as well as historical data. The IoT can analyze and instruct devices to make effective decisions, as well as track how certain actions function.

Cloud computing encompasses the delivery of data-to-data centers over the Internet. IBM divides cloud computing into six different categories (https://www.ibm.com/cloud/learn/cloud-computing-gbl):

**1. Platform as a Service (PaaS)** –The cloud contains everything you need to construct and distribute cloud applications so there is no need to maintain and buy equipment, software, *etc.*

**2. Software as a Service (SaaS)** –In this case, applications run in the cloud and other organizations operate devices that connect to users' computers through a web browser.

**3. Infrastructure as a Service (IaaS)** – IaaS is an option providing organizations with storage, servers, networks and hubs processing data for each procedure.

**4. Public Cloud** – Organizations administer spaces and provide users with quick access through the public network.

**5. Private Cloud** – The same as a public cloud, but only one individual has access here, which can be an individual or organization.

**6. Hybrid Cloud** – Established on a private cloud; however, offers access to a public cloud.

Commonplace devices such as automobiles and household appliances may have an Internet connection, and with the development of the IoT, more and more devices will join this list.

## Pairing with Edge Computing

Data processing at the network edge or edge computing is handled with IoT solutions and permits quicker processing and response times. For example, consider a large factory with many applied IoT sensors. In this circumstance, before sending data to the cloud for processing, it will be aggregated it close to the border to prevent cloud overload by reducing direct connections.

Edge computing is a distributed, open IT architecture that includes decentralized processing power, empowering mobile computing and IoT technologies. In edge computing, data is managed by the device itself or by a local computer or server, rather than being transmitted to a data center.

Data centers with this methodology craft data processing much faster. Nevertheless, a methodology that is only grounded on the edge will not deliver a complete view of a company operations. If there is no cloud solution, then the factory only controls each unit individually. Likewise, it has no way of imagining how these units work in relation to each other. This is why only the combination of edge computing and the cloud will facilitate organizations to advance from IoT developments.

## Leading to Quantum Computing

Quantum computers rely on complex physical laws that are completely distinct from the relatively simple logic of classical computers (Table **2.1**). Dominated by the unpredictable behavior of subatomic particles like photons and electrons, quantum computing includes novel ideas such as how matter can exist in two states at once [44 - 46].

**Table 2.1. Difference between Bits and Quantum Bits.**

| Bits | Quantum Bits or Qubit |
|---|---|
| It is a single unit of information that has a value of either 0 or 1 (off or on, false or true, low, or high). | In quantum computing, a qubit or quantum bit is the basic unit of quantum information—the quantum version of the classical binary bit physically realized with a two-state device. A qubit is a two-state quantum-mechanical system, one of the simplest quantum systems displaying the peculiarity of quantum mechanics. |
| The device computes by manipulating those bits with the help of logical gates (and, or not). | The device computes by manipulating those bits with the help of quantum logic gates. |
| A classical computer has a memory made up of bits where each bit grasps either a one or zero. | A qubit (quantum bits) can grasp a one, a zero or essentially a superposition of these. |

*(Table 2.1) cont.....*

| Bits | Quantum Bits or Qubit |
|---|---|
| Bits are employed in classical computers. | Qubits (Quantum bits) are employed in quantum computers |
| Information is collected in bits, which take the discrete values 0 and 1. | Information is collected in quantum bits, or qubits. A qubit can be in states marked \|0} and \|1}; however, it can also be in a superposition of these states, a {0} + b{1}, where a and b are complex numbers. If we consider the state of a qubit as a vector, then superposition of states is merely vector addition. |
| For instance, if accumulating one number takes 64 bits, then storing N numbers takes N times 64 bits. | For instance, for every extra qubit, then twice as many numbers can be stored. For example, with 3 qubits, coefficients can be {000}, {001}, {010}, {011}, {100}, {101}, {110} and {111}. |
| Bits are slow. | Qubits are faster. |
| Its circuit behavior grounded on classical physics. | Its circuit behavior grounded on quantum mechanics. |

In this age of supercomputers, quantum computing is deemed as the next big device to enhance our capabilities. In addition, quantum computing may leapfrog over the supercomputers. To put this into proper perspective, supercomputers have accomplished an apex of performance of around 200 petaflops or 200,000 trillion calculations per second. Quantum computers may be able to attain a billion times more performance power (https://www.nature.com/articles/s41586-019-1666-5).

Quantum computers perform quite differently than classical computers. This is primarily due to quantum effects known as *superposition* and *entanglement*, and *quantum bits* (called qubits), which can take on non-binary states embodied by complex numbers. This enables computational solutions to mathematical problems that cannot be solved by classical computers since they demand sequentially computing an astronomical number of combinations or permutations.

Unlike a bit that must be a 0 or a 1 (or its probabilistic combination), a qubit can be in a complex-value-weighted grouping of states called a *superposition*. Multiple qubits could be decisively *entangled* into linear combinations of (complex-valued-weighted) states across the qubits, which "correlates" them so their quantum state cannot be depicted independently, *i.e.*, entangled states (Table **2.1**).

A quantum computer will be able to perform any chore that a classical computer is able to achieve (Dietz, Henke, Moon, Backes, Pautasso, and Sadeque, 2020). Nonetheless, if classical algorithms on a quantum computer are use, then it will simply perform the calculation in a comparable way to a classical computer. A quantum computer can be employed to its full potential if quantum algorithms are formulated. The Throughput Model provide guidance for parallel processing, which could assist in the design of quantum parallel algorithms. Despite this, these algorithms are not easy to produce, which necessitates a great deal of research and development.

## CONCLUSION

AI can be considered as an umbrella term that houses various fields of study. These include cognitive psychology, computer science, linguistics, among others. AI tools and their applications are continually growing and evolving. With the explosion of data in recent years, new technologies for analyzing this data have materialized on the scene. AI coupled with Big Data analytics are among the top in such technologies. Furthermore, AI technology has triggered the human imagination. AI tools are now being implemented across almost every industry and sector, including transportation, healthcare, defense, finance, and manufacturing. Organizations of all types across the globe all the time more consider the development of AI capabilities as essential to remaining competitive. AI future can be depicted as helping to spur enormous productivity gains over the next decade, making it essential to the competitiveness of national economies.

AI based machine learning and deep learning (along with NLP and computer vision) have come to appear like the new path forward. Algorithms, freed from human programmers, are training themselves on massive data sets and producing results. Many industries will be recalibrated as individuals and organizations prepare for the ensuing conversion to an AI-driven economy. That is, the efficiencies and other economic advantages of code-based machine intelligence may contribute to the disruption of all aspects of human work. While some industries will welcome new job creation, others worry about massive job losses, widening economic divides and social upheavals, including populist uprisings.

Similarly, as software did a few years ago, AI can amplify humans' creative thinking with a computer's relentless capability to stir through a multitude of data, hypothesize alternatives or optimize outcomes. Nonetheless, scholars, stakeholders, and policymakers question the adequacy of existing apparatuses overseeing algorithmic decision-making and wrestle with new challenges staged by the rise of algorithmic power in terms of transparency, fairness, and equal treatment.

Automated decision-making algorithms are implemented throughout industry and government, buttressing many processes from dynamic pricing to employment practices to criminal sentencing. Given that such algorithmically cognizant decision choices have the potential for momentous societal impact, one of the goals of this book is to help developers and product managers design and implement algorithmic systems in publicly accountable ways. In addition, individuals and organizations' appetite for AI-driven transformation is at an all-time high. That is, the private and public sectors are progressively focusing on AI algorithms to program simple and complex decision-making processes. Technology has never moved at such a rapid pace, which indicates that the decision makers' tasks are harder than ever to stay current and up to date with AI tools. In addition, understanding the vast array of AI capabilities is a stretch for most individuals and organizations globally.

Basically, we desire for an autonomous vehicle to be a reliable driver. Nonetheless, until appropriate ethical and trust systems are in place, it may not be such a good thing for machines to truly engage with, and respond to, the world. The simplest AI systems will not ever be bored, or interested, or sad.

The cloud computing in combination with the IoT will make fundamental changes to the life of individuals and organizations. How information is managed to support daily activities especially with AI apparatuses. To date, the cloud is the only technology that can analyze, store, and access the IoT depending on the utilization of a model. For example, some of the Throughput Model concepts can be harnessed through the employment of cloud computing with the IoT. That is, efficiencies are enhanced due to the nature of on-demand information whereby cloud computing with an Internet connection is available on any device at any time. As hybrid cloud adoption grows, many organizations are comprehending its benefits and the necessity to implement this technology. Cloud computing will continue to open novel prospects for the IoT and Throughput Modeling for the future.

A classical computer would take, in some situations, more than the age of the universe to produce a result. Breakthroughs are required not just in technology, but also in algorithm and require other supporting technology such as leverage of machine learning, deep learning, AI, Big Data, cloud computing to accelerate quantum computing development.

In sum, AI is a powerful general-purpose technology. Future progress could be speedy, and some experts expect that extraordinary capabilities in strategic areas will be attained in the coming years. The Throughput Model has the capability to augment human intelligence and enable smarter decision-making. AI applications applied to the Throughput Model can assist in detecting wrong decisions and thus speeds up the entire process of decision making.

The enlighten use of the Throughput Model may provide digital cooperation to serve humanity's best interests is the top priority. The Throughput Model six dominant AI algorithms are offered as a means for people around the world to come to common understandings and agreements. This modeling process facilitates the innovation of widely accepted approaches aimed at tackling wicked problems and maintaining control over complex human-digital networks.

## Is there a Need for Throughput Modeling to Represent Symbolic AI and Neural Networks?

Connectionists maintain that approaches based on pure neural network structures will eventually lead to robust or general AI (https://iep.utm.edu/connect/). After all, the human brain is made of physical neurons, not physical variables and class placeholders and symbols.

The technology world has undergone a great transition from serial computing to parallel computing. Technological giants such as Intel has already taken a step towards parallel computing by employing multicore processors. Parallel computation will revolutionize the way computers work in the future, for the better good of the world. With all the world connecting (*e.g.*, IoT) to each other even more than before, parallel computing does a better role in aiding us stay that way. With faster networks, distributed systems, and multi-processor computers, it becomes even more necessary.

To this end, the Throughput Model can further this field since it represents symbol manipulation in six algorithmic pathways that seems to be essential for *human* cognition, such as when a child learns an abstract linguistic pattern, or the meaning of a term like *cousin* that can be applied in an infinite number of families, or when an adult extends a familiar linguistic pattern in a unique manner that extends beyond training distributions.

The Throughput Model provides the first steps towards building architectures that combine the strengths of the symbolic approaches that can be adapted for machine learning, to develop better techniques for extracting and generalizing abstract knowledge from large, often noisy data sets.

Moreover, symbolic systems such as the Throughput Model exist in our everyday lives. For example, our web browsers, operating systems, applications, games, *etc.* are grounded on rule-based platforms. These same tools are implemented in the specification and execution of practically all the planet's neural networks. Decades of computer science and cognitive science have proven that being able to store and manipulate abstract concepts is an essential component of any intelligent system. And that is why the Throughput Model's symbol system can be a vital component of any robust AI system.

What is more, the Throughput Model may assist with hybrid architectures that combine symbol manipulation with other techniques such as deep learning. The benefit of hybrid AI systems is that they can combine the strengths of neural networks and symbolic AI. Neural nets can find patterns in the messy information we collect from the real world, such as visual and audio data, large corpora of unstructured text, emails, chat logs, *etc*. And on their part, rule-based AI systems can perform symbol-manipulation operations on the extracted information.

The apparatus of symbol-manipulation is the Neuro-Symbolic Concept Learner (NSCL) AI system developed by researchers at MIT and IBM (http://nscl.csail.mit.edu/). The NSCL learns visual concepts, words, and semantic parsing of sentences without explicit supervision on any of them. Instead, this model learns by simply looking at images and reading paired questions and answers.

The NSCL combines neural networks to solve visual question answering (VQA) problems, a class of tasks that is especially difficult to tackle with pure neural network–based approaches. The researchers demonstrated that NCSL was able to solve the VQA dataset CLEVR with remarkable accuracy (http://nscl.csail.mit.edu/). CLEVR is a diagnostic dataset that tests a range of visual reasoning abilities (https://cs.stanford.edu/people/jcjohns/clevr/). It comprises minimal biases and has detailed annotations depicting the type of reasoning each question requires.

Google's search engine is a massive hybrid AI that combines state-of-the-art deep learning techniques such as symbol-manipulation systems such as knowledge-graph navigation tools. AlphaGo, is yet another example of combining symbolic AI and deep learning.

As AI is tapped more and more for applications where decisions necessitate explanation, the Throughput Model provides the capability to look under the hood of the AI and understand how those decisions are reached by organizations. This is fundamental for employing ethical and trustworthiness systems. Hence, Throughput Modelling ought to be considered from the start as it will inform the design of an AI system.

## REFERENCES

[1]     B.E. Penprase, "The Fourth Industrial Revolution and Higher Education", In: *Higher Education in the Era of the Fourth Industrial Revolution.,* N.W. Gleason, Ed., Springer Singapore: Singapore, 2018. [http://dx.doi.org/10.1007/978-981-13-0194-0_9]

[2]     A. Kaplan, and M. Haenlein, "Siri, Siri in my Hand, who is the Fairest in the Land? On the Interpretations, Illustrations and Implications of Artificial Intelligence", *Bus. Horiz.,* vol. 62, no. 1, pp. 15-25, 2019. [http://dx.doi.org/10.1016/j.bushor.2018.08.004]

[3]     M. Xu, J.M. David, and K.S. Hi, "The Fourth Industrial Revolution: Opportunities and Challenges", *International Journal of Financial Research,* vol. 9, no. 2, p. 90, 2018.
[http://dx.doi.org/10.5430/ijfr.v9n2p90]

[4]     H. Lee, and C-H. Cho, "Digital advertising: present and future prospects", *Int. J. Advert.,* pp. 1-10, 2019.

[5]     D. Lindebaum, and F. den Hond, "Insights From "The Machine Stops " to Better Understand Rational Assumptions in Algorithmic Decision Making and Its Implications for Organizations", *Acad. Manage. Rev.,* vol. 45, no. 1, pp. 247-263, 2020.
[http://dx.doi.org/10.5465/amr.2018.0181]

[6]     A.M. Froomkin, "Introduction", In: *Robot law: x–xxiii.,* R. Calo, I. Kerr, Eds., Edward Elgar: Cheltenham, UK, 2016.
[http://dx.doi.org/10.4337/9781783476732.00005]

[7]     T. Hendershott, C.M. Jones, and A.J. Menkveld, "Does algorithmic trading improve liquidity?", *J. Finance,* vol. 66, no. 1, pp. 1-33, 2011.
[http://dx.doi.org/10.1111/j.1540-6261.2010.01624.x]

[8]     S. Haykin, *Neural Networks: A Comprehensive Foundation.* 2nd ed. Prentice Hall: New York, 1998.

[9]     W. Rodgers, *Artificial Intelligence in a Throughput Model: Some Major Algorithms.* Taylor and Francis publication.: Florida, 2020.

[10]    D.O. Hebb, "Distinctive features of learning in the higher animal", In: *Brain Mechanisms and Learning.,* J.F. Delafresnaye, Ed., Oxford University Press: London, 1961.

[11]    W. Rodgers, "How do loan officers make their decisions about credit risks? A study of Parallel Distributed Processing (PDP)", *J. Econ. Psychol.,* vol. 12, no. 2, pp. 243-265, 1991.
[http://dx.doi.org/10.1016/0167-4870(91)90015-L]

[12]    D.E. Rumelhart, and A. Ortony, "The representation of knowledge in memory", In: *Schooling and the acquistion of knowledge* Erlbaum: NJ, 1977.

[13]    W. Rodgers, *Trust Throughput Modeling Pathways.* Nova Publication: Hauppauge, NY, 2019.

[14]    K. Warwick, "A Brief History of Deep Blue, IBM's Chess Computer", *Mental Floss,* 2017.https://www.mentalfloss.com/article/503178/brief-history-deep-blue-ibms-chess-computer

[15]    M.A. Gernsbacher, and M. Yergeau, "Empirical Failures of the Claim That Autistic People Lack a Theory of Mind", *Arch. Sci. Psychol.,* vol. 7, no. 1, pp. 102-118, 2019.
[http://dx.doi.org/10.1037/arc0000067] [PMID: 31938672]

[16]    W. Rodgers, *Ethical Beginnings: Preferences, rules, and principles influencing decision making.* iUniverse, Inc: NY, 2009.

[17]    W. Rodgers, and S. Gago, "Cultural and ethical effects on managerial decisions: Examined in a throughput model", *J. Bus. Ethics,* vol. 31, no. 4, pp. 355-367, 2001.
[http://dx.doi.org/10.1023/A:1010777917540]

[18]    W. Rodgers, *E-commerce and biometric issues addressed in a Throughput Model.* Nova Publication: Hauppauge, NY, 2010.

[19]    W. Rodgers, *Biometric and auditing issues addressed in a Throughput Model.* Information Age Publishing Inc.: Charlotte, NC, 2012.

[20]    W. Rodgers, S. Al Fayi, H. Al-Refiay, and J. Murray, "Artificial Intelligence Algorithms Implemented for Ethical Issues in Management Accounting", *China Management Accounting Review,* vol. 11, no. 1, pp. 116-131, 2020.

[21]    C. Kavanagh, "New Tech, New Threats, and New Governance Challenges: An Opportunity to Craft Smarter Responses", *Carnegie Endowment for International Peace,* 2019. https://www.jstor.org/stable/resrep20978.5

[22] A.A. Baldwin, C.E. Brown, and B.S. Trinkle, "Opportunities for artificial intelligence development in the accounting domain: the case for auditing. Intelligent Systems in Accounting, Finance & Management", *Int. J.,* vol. 14, no. 3, pp. 77-86, 2006.

[23] L.P. Le Guyader, "Artificial intelligence in accounting: GAAP's "FAS 133", *J. Corp. Account. Finance,* vol. 31, no. 3, pp. 185-189, 2009.
[http://dx.doi.org/10.1002/jcaf.22407]

[24] E. Stancheva-Todorova, "How artificial intelligence is challenging accounting profession. Journal of International Scientific Publications", *Economy & Business,* vol. 12, pp. 126-141, 2018.

[25] C. Goh, G. Pan, P.S. Seow, B. H.Z. Lee, and M. Yong, *Charting the future of accountancy with AI.,* 2019.

[26] N. Kairinos, "The integration of biometrics and AI", *Biometric Technology Today,* vol. 5, no. 5, pp. 8-10, 2019.
[http://dx.doi.org/10.1016/S0969-4765(19)30069-4]

[27] R.K. Elliott, "The third wave breaks on the shores of accounting", *Account. Horiz.,* no. June, pp. 61-85, 1992.

[28] M.A. Vasarhelyi, and A. Kogan, *Artificial Intelligence in Accounting and Auditing.* vol. 4. Towards New Paradigms, 1998.

[29] ICAEW, "Institute of Chartered Accountants in England and Wales", *Artificial intelligence and the future of accountancy,* 2017.https://www.icaew.com/- /media/corporate/files/technical/information-technology/technology/artificial-intelligence-

[30] R. Jazaie, *Communication Skills for Accountants: Lessons from GGU's Director of Accounting Programs,* 2017.business.com/2017/10/12/communication-skills-for-accounting- presentations/

[31] S. Sin, A. Jones, and Z. Wang, "Critical Thinking in Professional Accounting Practice: Conceptions of Employers and Practitioners", In: *The Palgrave Handbook of Critical Thinking in Higher Education.,* M. Davies, R. Barnett, Eds., Palgrave MacMillan: London, 2015, pp. 431-456.
[http://dx.doi.org/10.1057/9781137378057_26]

[32] W. Rodgers, *Throughput Modeling: Financial Information Used by Decision Makers.* JAI Press: Greenwich, CT, 1997.

[33] W. Rodgers, *Process Thinking: Six pathways to successful decision making.* iUniverse, Inc: NY, 2006.

[34] A.L. Beer, T. Watanabe, R. Ni, Y. Sasaki, and G.J. Andersen, "3D surface perception from motion involves a temporal-parietal network", *Eur. J. Neurosci.,* vol. 30, no. 4, pp. 703-713, 2009.
[http://dx.doi.org/10.1111/j.1460-9568.2009.06857.x] [PMID: 19674088]

[35] P.C. Cozby, "Effects of density, activity and personality on environmental preferences", *J. Res. Pers.,* vol. 7, no. 1, pp. 45-60, 1973.
[http://dx.doi.org/10.1016/0092-6566(73)90031-7]

[36] A. Einstein, and P. Bergmann, *On A Generalization of Kaluza's Theory of Electricity.* vol. 39. Annals of Mathematics, 1938, no. 3, pp. 683-701.
[http://dx.doi.org/10.2307/1968642]

[37] A.J. Rasmusson, "The power of quantum computing: Parallelism", *SciU Conversations in Science at Indiana University,* 2019.https://blogs.iu.edu/sciu/2019/07/13/quantum-computing-parallelism/

[38] W. Rodgers, *"Usefulness of decision makers' cognitive processes in a covariance structural model using financial statement information",* Dissertation, University of Southern California, 1984.

[39] A. Tversky, and D. Kahneman, "Extensional vs. intuitive reasoning: The conjunction fallacy in probability judgment", *Psychological Review,* vol. 90, pp. 293-315, 1983.

[40] D. Kahneman, P. Slovic, and A. Tversky, *Judgment under uncertainty: Heuristics and biases.*

Cambridge University Press: New York, 1992.

[41]   A. Tversky, and D. Kahneman, "Availability: A heuristic for judging frequency and probability", *Cognit. Psychol.,* vol. 5, no. 2, pp. 207-232, 1973.
[http://dx.doi.org/10.1016/0010-0285(73)90033-9]

[42]   J.L. McClelland, D.E. Rumelhart, and G.E. Hinton, "The appeal of parallel distributed processing", In: *Parallel distributed processing.,* D.E. Rumelhart, J.L. McClelland, Eds., vol. 1. , 1986, pp. 3-40.

[43]   L. Francis, S. Woerner, and E. Yndurain, *Getting your financial institution ready for the quantum computing revolution.,* 2019.https://www.ibm.com/downloads/cas/MBZYGRKY

[44]   D. Deutsch, "Quantum theory, the Church–Turing principle and the universal quantum computer", *Mathematical and Physical Sciences,* vol. 400, 1985no. 1818, pp. 97-117

[45]   M. Dietz, N. Henke, J. Moon, J. Backes, L. Pautasso, and Z. Sadeque, *McKinsey & Company*, 2020.

[46]   M.G. Levy, "New Quantum Algorithms Finally Crack Nonlinear Equations", *Quanta Magazine,* 2021.https://www.quantamagazine.org/new-quantum-algorithms-finally-crack-nonlinear- equations-20210105/

**CHAPTER 3**

# Six Dominant Decision-making Algorithms

*Success in creating AI would be the biggest event in human history. Unfortunately, it might also be the last, unless we learn how to avoid the risks.* ---Stephen Hawking

The insight at the root of artificial intelligence was that these "bits" (manipulated by computers) could just as well stand as symbols for concepts that the machine would combine by the strict rules of logic or the looser associations of psychology.

---Daniel Crevier

Even the smartest AI will relentlessly follow its code once set in motion -- and this means that, if we are meaningfully to debate the adaptation of a human world into a machine-mediated one, this must take place at the design stage.

---Tom Chatfield

**Abstract**

Algorithms have been implemented to benefit decision-making for hundreds of years and pre-date computers. While algorithms are hardly a contemporary invention, they are nonetheless progressively intricate in systems implemented to support decision-making. Algorithmic decision-making is the processing of input data or perceptual processing to influence a judgment or decision choice. Further, algorithms are utilized to support decisions such as prioritization, classification, association, and filtering. This chapter illustrates a broad introduction to six fundamental algorithms for decision making. These algorithms in total make up the Throughput Model. Each algorithm is clearly presented and can comprehensively assist individuals and organizations in considering a wide range of issues.

**Keywords:** Algorithms, Analytical algorithmic pathway, Artificial intelligence, Chatbot, Computer vision, *Deep learning*, *Decision choice*, *Human-computer interaction (HCI)*, Expedient algorithmic pathway, Global perspective algorithmic pathway, Heuristics and biases, Information, Judgment, Machine learning, Neural networks, Perception, Throughput model, Revisionist algorithmic pathway, Ruling guide algorithmic pathway, Value-driven algorithmic pathway.

# INTRODUCTION

Social science is the science branch dedicated to the study of societies and the relationships among people within those societies. This term incorporates an all-embracing range of academic disciplines, which include accounting, anthropology, archaeology, economics, history, human geography, linguistics, management science, media studies, political science, psychology, and sociology.

AI taps into these fields to provide a enhance representation of how individuals make decisions.

Computer vision, neural networks, predictive analytics, speech recognition, natural-language understanding, machine-learning and deep learning systems are some of the necessary tools that provide researchers and practitioners to capture the human thought process. Research is progressing apace, media attention is at an all-time high, and organizations are progressively implementing AI-based algorithms in quest of automation-driven efficiencies. AI-based algorithms for decision making purposes are being utilized more and more in everyday life. To name a few, this comprises the delivery of government services, justice and policing, entertainment, employment, and banking.

One of the foremost open questions in both neuroscience and machine learning is: How precisely do human brains operate, and how can we estimate that with our own algorithms? To this end, researchers and practitioners have employed machine learning, deep learning, and natural language processing to depict how we as humans make decisions. These apparatuses incorporate algorithms that mimic the human thought process enhancing decision-making in a variety of tasks.

Machine learning and deep learning are types of AI that employs algorithms, which supplies computers with the ability to automatically draw inferences when exposed to new data, without being explicitly programmed. Natural language processing enables computers to assess and understand human language to process and analyze huge quantities of natural language data. This is data that may be unstructured and that does not fit conveniently into the conventional row and column systems of relational databases.

Algorithmic decision choices may be based on handcrafted systems that exercise modest scoring mechanisms, or the identification of keywords, or natural language extraction. Rules may be expressed directly by programmers or be dynamic and flexible based on machine learning of contextual data. As discussed in chapter 1, opportunities, and implications of the usefulness of machine learning algorithms in decision-making are growing. As more data is produced, a surge in the utilization of machine learning algorithms will provide organizations to contemplate a much all-encompassing range of datasets or inputs than was heretofore possible. This allows an opportunity for better decision-making. That is, combining human and machine intelligence in an intelligent way.

Algorithms viewed from a very detail mathematics and computer science level represent a finite sequence of well defined, computer-implementable instructions, generally to solve a class of specific problems or to perform a computation. Well-defined incorporates an unambiguous way an expression has a unique interpretation or value.

Therefore, algorithms are always unambiguous and are utilized as stipulations for performing calculations, data processing, automated reasoning, and other tasks. In contrast, a heuristic is a technique used in problem solving that uses practical methods and/or various estimates to produce solutions that may not be optimal but are sufficient given the circumstances.

Algorithms in the Throughput model is basically a means of representing step-b--step solutions to a problem. These algorithms can be used to represent automated reasoning that involves knowledge representation and reasoning as well as metalogic dedicated to understanding distinct views of reasoning. This process of reasoning symbolizes the capacity of applying logic to seek truth and draw conclusions from new or existing information.

Information can be thought of as the resolution of uncertainty [1]. Whereby, it addresses the question of "What an entity is" and therefore denotes both its essence and the nature of its features. More so, the concept of *information* has different meanings in different contexts. Therefore, the concept becomes synonymous to notions of constraint, communication, control, data, and form.

Uncertainty refers to epistemic (*i.e.*, concerned with knowledge) situations concerning imperfect or unknown information. It applies to predictions of future events, to physical measurements that are already constructed, or to the unknown. Uncertainty occurs in partially observable (*i.e.*, system is not fully visible to an external sensor) or stochastic (*i.e.*, random probability distributions) environments, as well as due to ignorance, indolence, or both [2].

This chapter centers on six dominant decision-making AI algorithmic pathways described as follows: *The Expedient Pathway, The Ruling Guide Pathway, The Analytical Pathway, The Revisionist Pathway, The Value Driven Pathway, and The Global Perspective Pathway* [2, 3].

1. **The Expedient Algorithmic Pathway P→D**
2. **The Ruling Guide Algorithmic Pathway P→J→D**
3. **The Analytical Algorithmic Pathway I→J→D**
4. **The Revisionist Algorithmic Pathway I→P→D**
5. **The Value Driven Algorithmic Pathway P→I→J→D**
6. **The Global Perspective Algorithmic Pathway I→P→J→D**

The *first algorithmic pathway* is the **P→D**, the expedient pathway, which usually happens in circumstances whereby a decision choice ought to be made rapidly. The *second algorithmic pathway* is the **P→J→D**, the ruling guide pathway, where time pressures may be essential; however, are not as immediate as the **P→D** pathway. For the **P→J→D** *algorithmic* pathway, a person frames the problem, analyzes it, and then makes a decision choice. The *third algorithmic pathway* is the **I→J→D**, designated as the analytical pathway whereby relevant and reliable information is the reassurance of beneficial decision choices. When exploiting this pathway, information will directly guide the judgment stage before a decision choice is made. If possible, the information is pre-determined and is weighted by other sources, without biases.

The *fourth algorithmic pathway* is **I→P→D**, the revisionist pathway where information can stimulate the manner in that a person perceptually frames the problem or circumstance before coming to a final decision. The information affects the perceptual frame significantly while one is seeking for a decision choice. Moreover, information is deemed a crucial piece of this decision-making process. The *fifth algorithmic pathway* is **P→I→J→D**, or the value driven pathway illuminates perceptual framing affect on information sources that bear on judgment before a decision is made. The perceptual frame can modify the information sources utilized to be analyzed in the judgment stage. Further, a person's experience, education, training, economic, and social perspective has a key influence on how a circumstance is conducted. The *sixth algorithmic pathway* is **I→P→J→D**, or the global perspective pathway illuminates how information buttresses people to adjust their perceptions before the judgment (analysis) stage begins. In addition, this pathway offers that an open-minded decision choice is more likely to be made due to new information that has been received by an investor [2 - 4].

These six dominant decision-making AI algorithmic pathways can be instrumental for the design and use of more detailed algorithms such as:

1. Regressions (*e.g.*, least square regression, logistic regression, *etc.*),

2. Decision Trees,

3. Forest Trees (which are multiple decision trees),

4. Naive Bayes Classification (represents a classification technique based on Bayes' Theorem with an assumption of independence among predictors).

5. Support Vector Machines (*i.e.*, supervised learning models with associated learning algorithms that analyze data for classification and regression analysis),

6. Clustering of data (*e.g.*, multidimensional scaling, exploratory and confirmatory factor analysis, K-means, *etc.*).

AI systems have become both more powerful and increasingly promising for integration in a variety of application areas. Nonetheless, an awareness towards the social challenges has also been called to these AI systems, particularly in how they may fail or even actively disadvantage marginalized social groups, or how their opacity, which may make them a challenge to oversee and manage. The expanding application of algorithms to decision-making in a variety of economic, political, and social contexts has encouraged demands for algorithmic accountability. For example, A growing number of organizations are considering "algorithms" will be the way to reinvent talent acquisition and create a more inclusive workforce. In some situations, this may imply eliminating the traditional dimensions of the hiring process [5].

Responsible decision-makers must supply their decision-subjects with good reason for their automated system's algorithmic outputs. On the other hand, discrimination and bias could be the unintentional result of AI algorithms to automate decision choices. Such algorithmic systems are influencing important outcomes such as who views online housing ads, which patients will benefit from additional medical care, which applicants will be selected for interviews, risk assessment in criminal sentencing, and teaching evaluations. Furthermore, policymakers and researchers are questioning how to fully assess the short and long-term implications of these AI algorithmic systems. Whose interest do they serve? Are the systems sophisticated enough to deal with complex social contexts? In addition, risks come not only from the algorithmic technology by itself, and not just from the people who embed their values into the algorithms during its construction and training, but from how individuals implementing the algorithm are trained and constrained, or not constrained, in their use of it.

Finally, a practical approach that can be applied to most machine learning and deep learning problems can be depicted as follow:

1. *Categorize the problem.* This is a two-step process.

   a. *Categorize by input.* If it is labelled data, then a *supervised learning* problem emerges. If it is unlabeled data and a structure is required, then it is an *unsupervised learning* problem. In order to optimize an objective function by interacting with an environment, requires a *reinforcement learning* problem.

   b. *Categorize by output.* If the output of a model is a number, it is a *regression* problem. Moreover, if the output of a model is a class, then it is a *classification* problem. Finally, if the output of a model is a set of input groups, then it is a *clustering* problem.

2. *Locate the available algorithms.* After categorizing the problem, then identify the algorithms that are applicable and practical to implement utilizing the tools at your disposal.

3. *Employ all of them.* Set up a machine learning or deep learning apparatus that compares the performance of each algorithm on the dataset utilizing a set of judiciously chosen evaluation criteria. The topmost one is automatically selected. This can be performed once or select a process that does this in intervals when new data is added.

4. *Optimize hyperparameters (optional).* Using cross-validation, tune each algorithm to optimize performance, if time permits it. If not, manually selected hyperparameters will work well enough for the most part.

## HUMAN-COMPUTER INTERACTION (HCI) AND DECISION-MAKING

The omnipresent adoption and prevalence of AI in real-world contexts have raised concerns among both researchers and practitioners for issues of bias, accountability, fairness, and discrimination. To address these problems, AI researchers and practitioners have engaged on offering mathematical insights to remedy issues such as bias, discrimination, and transparency of algorithm choice. Further, researchers have focused on tweaking the algorithms themselves to correct for bias and to enhance interpretability [6].

Human-computer interaction (also called HCI) bridges the gap between ethics and practice with specific recommendations for making successful tools that augment, amplify, empower, and enhance individuals. At the outset, human-computer interaction is a field of research and practice that developed in the early 1980s, which initially was a specialty area in computer science comprising cognitive science and human factors engineering. Presently, human-computer interaction is a multidisciplinary field of study focusing on the design of computer technology and the interaction between humans (the users) and computers in many avenues. The flow of information between the human and computer is expressed as the loop of interaction. The loop of interaction has several aspects to it, including:

a. **Visual centered:** Undoubtedly, it may be the most prevalent area in human computer interaction (HCI) research.
b. **Audio centered:** This is an essential area of HCI systems. This area deals with information developed by distinct audio signals.
c. **Task environment:** The conditions and goals set upon the decision maker.
d. **Machine environment:** The environment that the computer is associated to a laptop in a working environment.
e. **Areas of the interface:** Non intersecting areas comprise of processes of the human and computer not relevant to their interaction.
f. **Input flow**: The flow of information that commences in the task environment, when the decision maker has some choices that necessitates utilizing their computer.
g. **Output:** The flow of information that begins in the machine environment.
h. **Feedback:** Loops through the interface that assess, moderate, and verify processes as they pass from the individual through the interface back and forth to the computer.
i. **Fit:** This is the complement between the computer design, the decision maker, and the chore to improve the human resources required to complete the chore.

Moreover, pertaining to the machine side, relevant techniques are appropriate in computer graphics, operating systems, programming languages, and development environments. A programming language is a formal language consisting of a set of strings that create various types of machine code outputs (*i.e.*, machine language instructions). Programming languages are one kind of computer language and are utilized in computer programming to implement algorithms.

Whereas, on the individual side, the relevant factors include communication theory, graphic and industrial design disciplines, linguistics, social sciences, cognitive psychology, social psychology, and human factors such as computer user satisfaction are relevant. Due to the multidisciplinary nature of HCI, people with different backgrounds contribute to its success. HCI is also sometimes termed human–machine interaction (HMI), man-machine interaction (MMI) or computer-human interaction (CHI).

## Future of Human Computer Interaction (HCI)

The potential of HCI is emerging impressively in every walk of our life. For example, the HCI may include in the future the intelligent refrigerator that orders groceries in an automatic manner. Moreover, the design innovations that are most useful and least troublesome to individuals will survive. The HCI will develop in a revolutionary fashion with developments in the technology of making connections with human sensory experience at the neural level. The definitive "virtual reality" experience is one that centers into the human brain on the same nerves that bring it sense experiences. Connection to visual and auditory nerves will be undoubtedly the next generation of HCI. Several interests drive development of his technology. The other non-mental interaction, service mode of HCI can be found in current medical devices, automobile computers homes, which are progressively more operated by computers. People typically interface with these apparatuses by "programming buttons" or by voice command. For example, automobiles GPS includes voice commands. Finally, the typewriter keyboard (written language) will remain intact even if transformed for mobile telephones and handheld computers until there is a satisfactory language recognition technology that dramatically changes the cumbersome keyboard entry.

## Applications and Services Pertaining to HCI Includes:

1. Healthcare

2. Games and Gamification

3. Learning and Education

4. In-Vehicle Interaction

5. Voice Search apps such as Alexa, Siri, Cortana

6. Hypertext

## ONWARDS TO THE USE OF ALGORITHMS

An Algorithm is typically depicted as a mathematical logic underscoring any kind of system that executes tasks or makes decision choices. For example, how Facebook arranges what posts a user view in their Facebook feed are an "algorithm". The logic implemented in a software program to designate criminal defendants a public safety risk score can be construed as an "algorithm". Moreover, "algorithms" do not necessarily have to be grounded in software on computers. Nevertheless, in the occurrence of various types of risk assessments utilized in courts or human services agencies, the "algorithm" can be exemplified by a piece of paper that provide a framework in which the steps a person should take to assess a specific case.

Algorithms are broadly used in society to make decisions that influence most features of people lives. For example, which school a child can attend, whether an individual will be tendered credit from a bank, what products are advertised to consumers, and whether a person will be offered an interview for a job. Governments and municipalities are more and more implementing algorithms to perform government services. Algorithmic systems are utilized to make decisions regarding government resource allocation (*e.g.*, where police are dispatched or where fire stations are constructed), pick up speed on government procedures (*e.g.*, public benefits eligibility and compliance), and aid government officials in making essential decisions such as whether a person will receive bail, or a family will receive a follow up visit from a child welfare agency.

Organizations are now moving to adopting AI algorithmic methods to frame decision choices. Its training approach, data, and its purpose must be placed in reliable examiners as well as understood by management. Traditionally, AI algorithms benefited immensely by using variables that closely imitated human biases and preferences. That is, the bias of a loan approval officer towards certain stereotypes usually constitutes the "historical labelled data" of whether an applicant will receive a loan approval or not.

Chatbots used for loan analysis may reduce biases. That is, "personalized" information such as demographics, chatter (*i.e.*, from chatbots) of a loan applicant has useful predictive power. AI chatbots can understand language outside of a set of pre-programmed commands and continue learning based on the inputs it receives. They can also make changes based on patterns and become smarter over time as they experience new situations. This type of chatbot can be applied to a range of uses – from sentiment analysis to making predictions about what a visitor is looking for on your website.

Chatbots is an AI tool that attempts to closely mimic the human mind. In other words, computer software scrutinizes problems at multiple layers in an endeavor to simulate how the human brain evaluates problems. Visual images, natural language, or other inputs may be construed into numerous factors to extract meaning and construct context, refining the probability of the computer software arriving at an appropriate conclusion. Deep learning techniques utilizes "neural networks" that learn from processing the labeled data provided for the period of training and utilizes this answer key to learn what features of the input are required to assemble the accurate output. Once enough examples have been processed, the neural network can commence to handle new, unseen inputs and efficaciously return correct results.

## Other Algorithmic Patterns

Comparatively, machine learning is the broader field, and this is apparent in the algorithms that can be harnessed to other fields. Machine learning is exercised in computer vision in the interpreting device and interpretation stage. Computer vision pertains to pattern recognition. Moreover, computer vision signifies the capability of a computer to see and perceive the surrounding area [7]. The computer vision algorithms are mathematical and graphical models that endeavor to assist a computer to interpret an image. Humans interpret images in countless multifaceted ways, where the actual capability of computers to interpret images is very limited, even with the up-to-date technology. The challenge of engineers and computer scientists implementing computer vision algorithms is that vision relies on a series of deductions related to unknown elements of the image. Computer vision algorithms also assist to make improvements in the manner that computers can get types of data from an image.

Computer vision applications envelops areas such as: object detection and recognition, self-driving cars, facial recognition, ball tracking, photo tagging, and many more. Computer vision pertains to pattern recognition. Therefore, to train a computer how to recognize visual data is to provide it with an enormous number of images. These images can range from thousands to millions that have been labeled, and then subject those to an assortment of software techniques, or algorithms, that provide the computer to search for patterns in all the components that relate to those labels.

For example, feeding a computer software package a million images of dogs will subject it to algorithms that allow it to analyze the colors in the photo, the shapes, the distances between the shapes, where objects border each other, *etc*. Therefore, it will identify a profile of what "dog" means. When the program has completed its analysis, then it will be able to use its experience if provided other unlabeled images to find the ones that are liken to a dog.

A broad spectrum of computer vision algorithms labor in assorted ways. Some of them work to categorize certain parts of a photograph or image. This type of technology is known to uncover new facial recognition features on cameras or in security equipment.

In addition, there is also a whole distinct class of computer vision algorithms associated to the automotive industry. Some of these are offering techniques for what automobile experts refer to as "augmented reality". In the state-of-the-art vehicle technologies, computers can assist people to understand the onward thoroughfare and prevent road dangers or even looming collisions. Also, these tools repeatedly depend on computer vision algorithms that construe the visual data around the vehicle, providing the deduced results to the individual driver.

Studying algorithms for computer vision can often lead to enhanced learning from some of the different algorithm types implemented for distinct image tasks. One of these types can be described as "morphing". This morphing effect allows one image turns into another. Another algorithm type is described as multi-view reconstruction. That is, image processing program tools are used to capture specific data and handle it in precise ways, or even for physical reproduction through 3D printing applications.

## Broader Design Algorithms and Decision-Making Processes

A more nuanced outlook for AI-based algorithms is essential. It is profusely clear that, left unconstrained, AI algorithms entrenched in digital and social technologies can encode societal biases, accelerate the spread of rumors and disinformation, amplify echo chambers of public opinion, commandeer people attention, and even weaken their mental welfare. To arrest the aforementioned items, EU's General Data Protection Regulation (GDPR) requires that organizations be able to enlighten their algorithmic decisions [8].

The GDPR "Article 22" makes legal or significant decisions pertaining to individuals based solely on automated processing, unless:

a. The decision is necessary for entering into or performing a contract,
b. The individual affected by the decision has consented, or
c. A legal authorization exists.

The GDPR also provides individuals a right to receive an explanation of the logic behind automated decisions and to have such decisions reviewed by a human. The other GDPR principles, such as transparency and compliance with individuals' rights, apply equally to the processing of personal data using AI as to other types of processing.

Algorithms can be depicted as fallible human creations; therefore, they can be embedded with errors and biases from human processes. When algorithmic tools are adopted by organizations without adequate transparency, accountability, and oversight, their use can harm customers, threaten civil liberties, and exacerbate existing issues within organizations (*e.g.*, bias, inefficiencies, opacity regarding decision-making). Although organizations are increasingly implementing algorithmic systems in their daily practices, it is quite uncertain in how widespread and integrated such algorithmic systems are used at any organizational level.

Consequently, what might an AI algorithm synopsis look like? First, it should embrace a holistic perspective. Computer science and machine learning techniques will be necessary; however, these techniques are unlikely satisfactory underpinnings for an algorithm branch of learning and study. Strategic thinking, contextually apprised professional judgment, communication, and the scientific method are also necessitated for individuals and organizations understanding.

What is more, what kinds of broader principles should we expect such algorithmic justifications to appeal to? To answer this question, this chapter presents from the Throughput Model's six dominant algorithmic pathways.

## THROUGHPUT MODELLING SIX DOMINANT ALGORITHMS

The Throughput Model identify, analyze, explain, and predict decision choices related to transactions. Previous research has developed an input-output relation between information and the action or development of decisions. This model also emphasizes the same information and decision processes of perception and judgments not occurring at the same time. The information is reanalyzed, resorted, and reconfigured in further informational stage [2, 9]. The Throughput Model consists of four concepts that can deliver different decision models, these concepts explained below are perception, information, judgment, and decision (Fig. **3.1**).

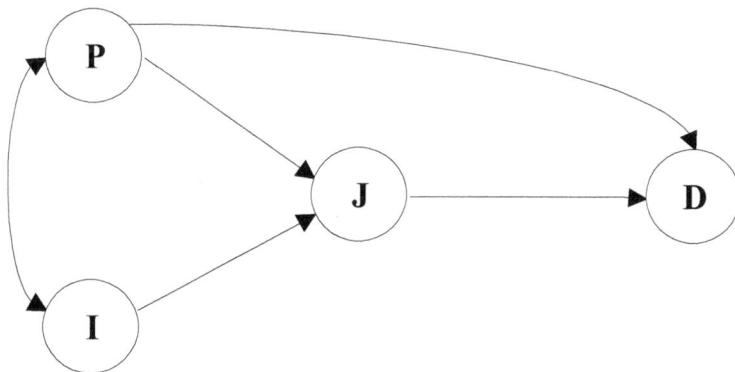

*Where P= perception, I= information, J= judgment, and D= decision choice.*
Source: Rodgers

**Fig. (3.1).** Throughput modelling diagram.

(a) *"Perception"* involves the process individual use to frame their problem-solving set or view of the world". This concept can be related to the personal experience perceived through the individual's life.

## The Process of Perception

1. *Reception*: In this process, an individual obtains the information through stimuli.

2. *Selection*: This is administered by two kinds of elements:

a. External elements: These are density represented by size, intensity, proximity, motion, and novelty.
b. Internal elements: These are attitude, motives, experiences, interests, and expectations.

3. *Organization*: It is the procedure whereby a person arranges stimuli into a profound pattern. It comprises the following:

a. Grouping: Congregating of stimuli on the grounds of similarity.
b. Proximity: This is the nearness of stimuli to one another that affects perception.
c. Closure: It is the capability to combine stimuli so that jointly to form a whole pattern.

4. *Interpretation*: It is the structure of an idea regarding the information that is sensed, selected, and organized. It includes but limited to the following heuristics: primacy effect, selective perception, stereotyping, halo effect, projection, and expectancy effect. They are the kinds of perceptual heuristics that are prone to errors.

a. *Primacy/ Recency Effect*: The first impression is given the most salience that is known as the primacy effect. Recency effect, on the other hand, is that individuals remember newest events more than the less recent ones.
b. *Stereotyping*: It is the effect instigated by establishing a certain belief about a class of stimuli and simplifying that view to encounters with each member of that class. There is a difference between the perceived idea of each class and the definite traits of the members.
c. *Halo effect*: It is the process of generalizing from an all-inclusive analysis to a single feature or trait. A negative halo effect is known as the reverse halo effect. For example, it can affect the performance appraisal of employees in an organization.

d. *Projection*: It is a psychological protection device that makes individuals evaluate their negative traits with other people and conclude that they are better off than others. Perceptual checking minimizes the negative effects of projection.

e. *Selective Perception*: This implies that individuals see, feel, or hear what they desire or want to and omit other information which are inconsistent to their viewpoint.

f. *Expectancy effect*: It is the tendency of people to construe any person or object based on how they expect the person, place, or object to be in the first place. It is also called as Pygmalion effect.

b. "*Information*" includes the set of available information to a decision-maker for problem-solving purposes. Generally, we hope that information is both reliable and relevant.

Information utilized in decision-making is to diminish or eliminate uncertainty. Nonetheless, excessive information may affect problem processing and tasking, which indirectly affect decision choice. Moreover, information is any kind of pattern that shapes the formation or transformation of other patterns. In this sense, there is no requirement for a conscious mind to perceive, much less appreciate, the pattern. Consider, for example, DNA. The sequence of nucleotides is a pattern that induces the formation and development of an organism without any need for a conscious mind.

c. "*Judgment*" represents the process that individuals implement to analyze incoming formation as well as the influences from the perception function. From these sources, rules are implemented to weigh, sort, and classify knowledge and information for problem-solving or decision-making purposes.

Further, judgment is a capability to make weighed analysis using either compensatory or non-compensatory schemes [2]. That is, in the process of formulating a judgment, two methods of analysis of perception and information are implemented for evaluation: compensatory and non-compensatory. In the compensatory method of analysis, when choosing between two choices, it is to ascertain what the critical criteria are to make a comparison. Next, a summation of the weights is performed on each of the items that are compared to determine which one has the highest value. The non-compensatory approach for analysis for a modification of the basic compensatory strategy of adding and summing the criteria values. That is, a selection of only one criteria value of the product may only be necessary. Further, Rodgers [2] acclaimed that "In a non-compensatory strategy, a good value on the attribute cannot make up for a poor value on another. We can view compensatory *versus* non-compensatory as a bipolar dimension to identify decision-making strategies".

d. *Decision choice* represents an action taken or not taken [9]. Decision choice encompasses selection of the best alternative solution or course of action. During this stage, individuals should apply their capabilities to warrant that the decision is carried out corresponding to guidance. There are three types of decisions: choices, evaluations, and constructions [2]. In a *choice* circumstance, people are challenged with a well-defined set of alternatives, and the customary task is to choose one of them. *Evaluations*, on the other hand, represent indications of worth for people's alternatives. Finally, *constructions* are decisions whereby individuals attempt to accumulate the most satisfactory alternative, possible. Typically, these constructions are driven by perceptual framing of the problem, which results are based on biases, strategies, or framing of past events related to the problem at hand.

Moreover, in Fig. (**3.2**) the directional arrows (*i.e.*, "→") are used as a guide of the next step in the decision-making process. Further, the double arrow between "P" and "I" (*i.e.*, P←→I) explain that incoming information can change the current perception. And perception can influence the type of information to be "attended to" as well as to be utilized in further processing in the judgment stage ("J").

The Throughput Model's six dominant algorithmic pathways are interdisciplinary with social science methodology and concepts from such fields as psychology, behavioral economics, human-centered design, and ethics (Rodgers [2, 9 - 11]. This modeling process provides different stages as well as pathways that depict the patterns in data use.

1. **The Expedient Pathway P→D**
2. **The Ruling Guide Pathway P→J→D**
3. **The Analytical Pathway I→J→D**
4. **The Revisionist Pathway I→P→D**
5. **The Value Driven Pathway P→I→J→D**
6. **The Global Perspective Pathway I→P→J→D**

This format allows the algorithms suitability in transparency for end-users. This transparency assists whether a particular set of algorithms are likely to be used in a socially acceptable manner. For example, will it produce undesirable psychological effects or inadvertently exploit natural human frailties? Is the algorithm being implemented for a deceptive purpose? Is there evidence of internal bias or ineptitude in its design? Is it effectively reporting how it arrives at its recommendations and representing its level of confidence?

The risk of constructing AI that fortifies societal biases has prompted calls for enhance transparency about algorithmic processes. Moreover, societal call is for ways to understand and audit how an AI agent arrives at its decision choices. While the utilization of AI systems grows, being able to explain how a given model or system will be imperative, especially for those used by industry, governments, or public sector agencies.

The Throughput Model six algorithmic pathways widen the lens from algorithms as a technology in isolation, to algorithms as systems embedded in human systems (see Fig. **3.1**) for both those that design the algorithmic technology, and those that use it. The six dominant algorithmic pathways can partially address the issue surrounding transparency and explainability. There is a growing awareness that addressing problems of unfairness or bias in algorithms in the abstract will be inadequate for mitigating problems when an algorithm is implemented in practice. Hence, the Throughput Model six dominant algorithms provide a more concrete basis for ongoing assessment and performance evaluation.

Further, since the outputs produced by machine learning and deep learning models are in part a reflection of the training datasets they are exposed to, the six algorithmic pathways may serve as a guide in gathering data. Moreover, training data are samples of expected categories that are consumed by a neural network. These samples echo the data exposed to the neural network when employed in a real-life scenario.

Training data can instigate algorithm bias within AI systems from *"personal bias"* held by data gatherers as well as "environmental bias imposed directly or indirectly within the data gathering process [2]". Knowingly or unknowingly, individuals have internal biases that can be projected in the data collection process involved when building machine learning models. Whereas environment bias may occur as a function of locally sourcing training data for an AI system that is purposed to be used on a global scale. The AI system may not have been trained with enough data that is representative of the actual condition it is expected to perform in the circumstances.

## Six Dominant Decision-Making Algorithms

The Throughput Model AI-driven algorithms can be used to process large amounts of data to provide meaningful individual or organizational based insights. While humans face decision fatigue, The Throughput Model AI-algorithms do not have such limitations, and this makes the entire decision-making process more accurate and consistent in its application. The Throughput Model algorithms can assist in analyzing customer data related to their browsing history or data collected *via* questionnaire to gain meaningful insights [12]. Based on these insights, organizations can make effective marketing decisions. These may include running marketing campaigns to target prospects, sending product recommendations and personalized mails to offer customers with what they want exactly when they want it.

Neural networks include image recognition, speech recognition, natural language understanding and machine translation. The Throughput Model six dominant algorithms are useful especially since neural networks are a key component of many AI applications. A primary reason for this is that neural networks are something of a 'black box' when it comes to elucidating exactly how their results are generated.

Neural networks are so-called since they mimic, to a degree, the way the human brain is designed. That is, neural networks are constructed from layers of interconnected, neuron-like, nodes. Further, they embrace an input layer, an output layer, and a variable number of intermediate 'hidden' layers. In addition, 'deep' neural nets merely have more than one hidden layer. The nodes themselves perform moderately simple mathematical operations. Nonetheless, between them, after training, they can process prior unseen data and produce correct results established on what was learned from the training data.

For example, based on the simple evaluation of alternatives, the dominant six algorithmic pathways can be fortified through an artificial single layer neural network as shown in Fig. (**3.2**).

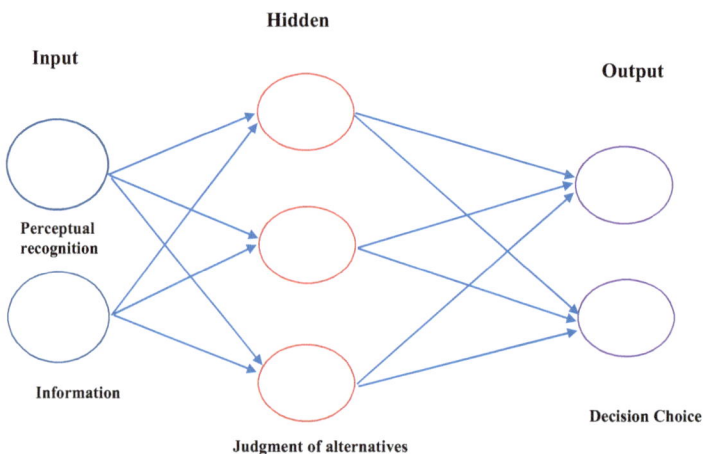

**Fig. (3.2).** Artificial single layer neural network for decision choice algorithm. Adopted from Rodgers [5].

With the Throughput Model AI-based algorithms, data can be revealed to tools that analyze and draw insights from the analysis. Nevertheless, it is also vital to understand the algorithmic stages and patterns that arise during the analysis and utilize it to further enhance the results. The Throughput Model six dominant algorithms can recognize patterns and share insights for better decision-making. For instance, retailers can map the buying or selection patterns of customers and identify an algorithmic pattern, which may assist in refining the look and feel of the website or designate the need for more product details or something else of importance in an organization. This experience not only helps in decision-making but also empowers organizations to optimize processes and add value to the services offered.

Even though the Throughput Model algorithms cannot completely replace managers, it can provide much valuable support and guidance when it comes to management. That is, one of the possible aims of AI refers to cognitive processes and specifically to reasoning. Before making any decision, people also reason, it is therefore natural to explore the six dominant decision-making algorithms connected with AI.

Many organizations have data that may sit idle since it is beyond the comprehension of the human mind. Nevertheless, with AI and Throughput Modeling applied, new vistas can open. In other words, AI-based algorithms can assist in the leveraging of the power and the limitations of tacit knowledge. What many organizations maybe overlooking is that they are sitting on mountains of administrative data from the past that can be harnessed in a predictive sense to help make better decision choices. AI based mechanisms can assist in the following problem areas.

1. *AI spots outliers*: AI can swiftly identify and seize outlying factors. These AI mechanisms fall in the descriptive analytics pillar, a branch of machine learning, which produces organization value by exploring and recognizing noteworthy patterns in hyper-dimensional data, something at which individuals are not as efficient to handle. Dimensionality in statistics refers to how many attributes a dataset must be analyzed by a person or machine. For high-dimensional data, datasets are inclined to be unstructured, which may present additional challenges to exploit. Moreover, noise and uncertainties frequently exist in big datasets. Such noisy data can become more challenging to process and to employ any suitable data mining techniques.

2. *AI promotes counter-factual thinking*: Data by itself can be maneuvered to validate pre-existing notions, or missing variables may affect the outcomes. This may lead to sub-optimal decision-making and inadequate resource allocation. Causal analytics emboldens counter-factual thinking. By not addressing questions in a causal manner may provide a pathway to an individual or organization making the wrong decision choice.

3. *AI enables "combinatorial" thinking*: The boldest decision choices are moderated by constraints to the point where new projects may not be able to deliver. Most decision-making functions in the setting of elevating some object. These objectives could be maximizing revenues or minimizing costs in the existence of a range of constraints. budgets, or service quality levels that must be maintained. In these settings, combinatorial optimizations algorithms, based on prescriptive analytics, can predict favorable outcomes that deliver more value for individuals or organizational resources.

Throughput Modeling can assist individuals and organizations in achieving better decision-making through various stages and six algorithmic pathways. The modeling process provides:

1. Faster decisions – Individuals and organizations implementing algorithmic pathways can better ably understand the decision paths used for decision-making. Algorithmic pathways can heighten decision-making using critical statistics from structural equation modeling software packages such as partial lease squares, LISREL [13, 14].

2. Multiple inputs handling –Gathering insights from different sources and handling various factors altogether, AI algorithmic modeling are more efficient than a human. It is because human is unable to process huge amount of information at once to reach complex decisions. For AI-enabled algorithms, it is possible to process the same data and predict the best decision for an organization.

3. Fixation of certain points – Functional fixedness is a type of cognitive bias that involves a tendency to see objects as only working in a particular way. It is human psychology when an individual is obliged to make quite a few decisions at short notice, the quality gets compromised. AI generated algorithms can assist organizations in making better decisions without making the management team fatigue. It gathers the insights and shares the information with the management to come to a decision choice.

4. Original inputs – AI algorithms helps in identifying patterns that are not possible to fathom with just the human mind. The inimitable insights advanced to organizational executives can avoid pitfalls damaging to companies.

Furthermore, while AI-based algorithms are supporting decision-makers, it is also imperative to leverage individual's judgment to accomplish the best possible result. AI-based algorithms could strategically address data and analyze it to obtain insights. Moreover, individual's judgment can manage the inferences to attain enriched decision-making. AI-based algorithms may also have bias and the inability to see beyond the data and analytics. Thus, one of the different six dominant algorithmic pathways may bring in value to the results sprung from a specific algorithmic pathway. In addition, this may deal with grey areas that other algorithms are unable to realize, enabling strategic and more meaningful decision-making.

In sum, the effects of AI on organizational decisions are as good as the data that is employed in the algorithms. Therefore, it is essential to be mindful of the data utilized for analyzing and deriving insights. Separately from checks on the source of the data and its credibility, it is also critical to be knowingly aware of the problem attempted to be deciphered or the decision choice to reach. This can lead to improved use of the information that is required to achieve individual or organizational goals.

## ADVANTAGES AND DISADVANTAGES OF THE USE OF AI ALGORITHMS

AI is considered as part of the 4th industrial revolution technologies that attempts to mimic human reasoning in machines. John McCarthy first coined the term AI in 1956 when he invited a group of researchers from various disciplines, which included language simulation, neuron nets, complexity theory and more to a summer workshop called the Dartmouth Summer Research Project on Artificial Intelligence to discuss what would eventually become the field of AI [15].

Emanating from this conference emerge the platform that all facets of learning or any other attribute of intelligence can in principle be specifically expressed that a machine can be made to mimic it. Further, from this platform lay the foundation that attempts will be made to find how to make machines can utilize language, form abstractions, and concepts, solve kinds of problems now reserved for humans, and improve themselves.

AI is the ability of a computer program to learn and think. Everything can be considered Artificial intelligence if it involves a program doing something that we would normally think would rely on the intelligence of a human. The *advantages* of AI applications are colossal and can transform any organizational sector. Next, the brief sections covering (1) reduction in human error, (2) take more risks, (3) operating 24/7, (4) assisting in repetitive tasks, (5) assisting digitally, (6) prompt decisions, (7) regular applications, and (8) novel inventions illustrate AI usefulness.

1. Reduction in Human Error:

Individuals' heuristics and biases can occur from time pressures and memory lapses (skill-based errors), and mistakes [2]. Nonetheless, computers do not make these mistakes if they are programmed correctly. With AI, the decision choices are taken from the previously gathered information employing a certain arrangement of algorithms. Hence, errors are decreased and the chance of attaining accuracy with a higher degree of precision is a possibility.

**Example:** Weather Forecasters implementing AI have diminished the preponderance of human errors.

## 2. Takes More Risks:

Many risky restrictions of individuals can be incapacitated by exploiting an AI Robot that can accomplish more risky functions. AI can be instrumental in travelling to another planet, defusing a bomb, exploring the deepest segments of the oceans, mining for minerals, as well as handling natural or man-made disasters.

**Example:** The Chernobyl nuclear power plant explosion in Ukraine had severe consequences to individuals living in the area. Moreover, in the beginning, there were no AI-powered robots that could assist to minimize the radiation effects partly produced by fires. People close to the core were killed suddenly. Rescue workers in due course poured sand and boron from helicopters from a distance. As such, AI Robots can be appreciated in such situations where human involvement can be very hazardous.

## 3.Available 24/7:

Generally, people can work for 4–6 hours a day not including the breaks and rest periods. Moreover, people are composed in such a manner to revitalize themselves as well as preparing for the next day of work. Nevertheless, implementing AI can designate machines to work 24x7 without any breaks and unlike people, they will not get bored.

**Example:** Educational Institutes and Helpline centers are receiving many queries and issues that can be managed successfully making the most of AI technology.

## 4. Assisting in Repetitive Jobs:

Performing many repetitive efforts every day such as editing email messages, scheduling meetings, *etc.* are essential in the global economy. Hence, implementing AI can enhance productivity by automating routine tasks as well as creating more time for other matters.

**Example:** In financial institutions, numerous verifications of documents to obtain a loan are a very arduous task. Nonetheless, implementing AI software can augment the process of verifying the documents whereby both the customers and financial institutions will be benefited.

## 5. Assisting Digitally:

Some of the exceedingly progressive organizations exercise digital assistants to interact with users, which benefit the reduction for human resources. Digital assistants are also utilized in many websites to deliver services that users deem important for their work. Digital assistants such as modern chatbots are designed in a manner that it has become difficult to determine that we are chatting with a chatbot or a human being.

**Example:** Organizations' customer support team can reduce the doubts and queries of the customers. Exploiting AI, the organizations can set up a voice bot or chatbot that can assist customers with all their queries. Today many organizations are benefit from these digital assistants on their websites and mobile applications.

## 6. Prompt Decisions:

Implementing AI together with other technologies can produce machines to make faster decisions faster than a human and carry out actions people. While taking a decision human will analyze many factors both emotionally and practically; however, AI-powered machine labors on what it is programmed and delivers the results in a quicker and more successful manner.

**Example:** When individuals play chess games on the computer, it is almost impossible to defeat the central processing unit (CPU) in the hard mode because of the AI software that supports the game. It will take the best possible steps in a very short time according to the algorithms implemented in the AI software.

## 7. Regular Applications:

Day-to-day applications such as Apple's Siri, Window's Cortana, Google's OK Google are repeatedly utilized in our daily routine whether it is for exploring a location, taking a selfie, making a phone call, replying to an email and many more.

**Example:** In the past when we are planning to go somewhere we would use printed material such as a map or ask someone for the directions. But now all we have to do is say "OK Google where is Alaska". It will illustrate Alaska's location on google map and the best route between your location and Alaska.

## 8. Novel Inventions:

AI is fueling many inventions in practically every domain which will help people resolve the mainstream of multifaceted problems.

**Example:** Recently medical doctors can predict colon cancer in people at earlier stages utilizing updated AI-based technologies.

Disadvantages of AI tools can spell problems for individuals and organizations if they are not aware of its imperfections. Algorithms may become group-aware when they are not intended to operate in a bias manner. AI pulls out correlations in the data that function as substitutes for group membership. For example, in a geographically segregated society, ZIP codes and other location data can be a standard proxy for race, religion, or nationality. Ride-sharing companies found the problem when a particular study [16] revealed that their location-based pricing algorithms charge customers more for rides to or from neighborhoods predominantly dominated by people of color. Moreover, programming an AI system to discount people's gender or race or leaving this information out of the data set is not sufficient to ensure an algorithm is group blind. In other words, although there may be an absence of identity being explicitly considered in how an algorithm's results are ascertained, the structural and historical nature of prejudice and the way it informs geography, opportunity and life chances mean that prejudicial disparities can still appear.

Other Disadvantages of AI are as follow:

## 1. Could be Expensive:

AI is continuing updating software to meet the latest requirements. Moreover, the costs of repairing and maintaining machines may be very expensive to organizations.

## 2. Making People Lethargic:

AI may cause sluggishness with people due to its applications automating the majority of the work. People tend to get addicted to these inventions which can cause a problem to future generations.

## 3. Unemployment:

AI is substituting the preponderance of the repetitive tasks and other works with robots, people interference is becoming less which will trigger a foremost problem in the employment standards. Presently, most organizations are surveying options to replace the minimum qualified individuals with AI robots that can do comparable work with more efficiency.

## 4. No Emotions:

Typically, machines are much better when it comes to working efficiently; however, they cannot replace the human connection that makes the team. Machines cannot develop a bond with people, which is an indispensable attribute when comes to management.

## 5. Lacking Out of Box Thinking:

Machines can perform only those tasks which they are designed or programmed to executive.

In sum, these are some advantages and disadvantages of AI. For the most part, very new invention or breakthrough will have both. Nevertheless, people ought to compare the differences between the positive and negative sides of the invention to lead to better future outcomes.

Machine learning, deep learning, and natural language processing models are progressively utilized to apprise decisions of great consequences about people. Discrimination in machine learning, deep learning, and natural language processing becomes objectionable when it places privileged groups at the systematic advantage and certain unprivileged groups at the systematic disadvantage. Dr. Kalinda Ukanwa at the University of Southern California argued that organizations can make algorithms treat people more fairly by inducing three key steps (https://www.bostonglobe.com/2021/05/23/opinion/algorithmic-bias-isnt-just-unfair-its-bad-business/). They are:

1. Instead of eradicating group identifiers, organizations should include demographic features in their data so they can recurrently audit their algorithms to establish whether they accidentally discriminate against certain groups. For example, IBM's AI Fairness 360 is an open-source tool kit that assists in detecting bias in machine learning models. In addition, Microsoft's FATE research group generates reports and tools that are targeted at diminishing bias and enhancing AI transparency and accountability. AI Fairness 360 (AIF360), a wide-ranging Python package (https://github.com/ibm/aif360) that comprises nine different algorithms, developed by the broader algorithmic fairness research community, to lessen that unwanted bias. These software packages assist the facilitation of computational techniques that are both innovative and responsible, while prioritizing issues of fairness, accountability, transparency, and ethics as they relate to machine learning, deep learning, and natural language processing by extracting from the fields with a sociotechnical orientation, such as HCI, information science, sociology, anthropology, science and technology studies, media studies, political science, and law.

2. Organizations can model how their routine decisions will affect demand over a period of time among consumers who learn that some groups are handled differently.

3. Algorithms should be constructed to make decisions utilizing context-specific data about people. For example, as opposed to inferring information from various information sources pertaining to where they live or their education level, factors that should be examined relate to a person's credit card payment frequency in credit rating decisions, or a patient's blood pressure levels in health care, or a student's grades in education. The data implemented to train the algorithm is essential as it relates to biases. That is, increasing the variation among and representation of different kinds of consumers permits algorithms to better appraise people on their own merits.

In general, algorithms can lead to fairer outcomes, but only if they are constructed and administered to in a proper manner. As computers gradually make influential decisions about our lives, from the health care and financial services we receive to our educational and career prospects, we must stay vigilant to the possibility for bias. There are persuasive ethical and trust motives to do so, as well as societal and business reasons.

## CONCLUSION

The Throughput Model's six algorithmic pathways are a very structured way to make decisions, especially when it is a very subjective matter. For example, auditors typically go through some or all these pathways when performing an audit. AI algorithms help facilitate the process in an audit and help client's implement efficient internal controls to reduce the risk of material misstatements. In this chapter, perception, information, and judgment are the major concepts utilized as steps to arrive to a decision choice. These algorithmic pathways can assist, for example, making the audit process more efficient by relieving the auditor from time consuming test work that is substituted by a reduction in risk of material misstatement and an improvement in internal controls.

The use of AI to make important decisions is on the rise and is attractive to industry and government organizations. Algorithms can help streamline decision-making and, due to the vast amount of data they can process, can lead to better-informed decision choices. The Throughput Model six dominant algorithms allow for beneficial decisions that are an assembly of various factors such as data and its analysis, human expertise and experience, consultation, contextual awareness, application of data in a particular situation, *etc*. AI algorithms have become indispensable to individual and organizational decision-making, bettering drive insights and leading to solutions faster, more accurately and in a scalable manner.

AI-based algorithms are being applied in a range of sectors, from medicine to retail, automobile, human resources, and education. It presents a wide band of benefits to industry and government.

Furthermore, AI-based algorithmic decision-making possess immense potential and are likely to obtain impressive economic, social, and political achievements. The use of algorithms, data, and AI is typically beneficial in various processes across different industries and governments as it provides more accuracy and efficiency. An algorithm is a self-contained step-by-step set of operations that computers and other 'smart' devices accomplish to perform calculation, data processing, and automated reasoning tasks. Progressively, algorithms use institutional decision-making based on analytics, which involves the discovery, interpretation, and communication of meaningful patterns in data. Particularly beneficial in areas resonant with recorded information, analytics relies on the concurrent application of statistics, computer programming, and operations research to quantify performance.

While the extent of the future use of algorithms in decision-making will be different by industries and governments, the underlying risk is which of the six dominant algorithms (or combinations thereof) will govern decision-making processes. As AI-based algorithms transfers from research environments to practical decision-making environments, it goes from being a computer science challenge to becoming an economic, political, and societal challenge as well.

## REFERENCES

[1]    L. Floridi, *Information - A Very Short Introduction.* Oxford University Press, 2010.
       [http://dx.doi.org/10.1093/actrade/9780199551378.001.0001]

[2]    W. Rodgers, *Process Thinking: Six pathways to successful decision making* iUniverse, Inc: NY, 2006.

[3]    W. Rodgers, and T. McFarlin, *Decision Making for Personal Investments: Real Estate Financing, Foreclosures and Other Issues.* Palgrave Macmillan: London, 2017.
       [http://dx.doi.org/10.1007/978-3-319-47849-4]

[4]    W. Rodgers, and T. Housel, "The effects of information and cognitive processes on decision-making", *Account. Bus. Res.,* vol. 69, no. 69, pp. 67-74, 1987.
       [http://dx.doi.org/10.1080/00014788.1987.9729349]

[5]    W. Rodgers, *Artificial Intelligence in a Throughput Model: Some Major Algorithms?* Science Publications (CRC Press: Taylor and Francis Group): Florida, 2020.

[6]    G. Montavon, S. Lapuschkin, A. Binder, W. Samek, and K-R. Müller, "Explaining nonlinear classification decisions with deep Taylor decomposition", *Pattern Recognit.,* vol. 65, pp. 211-222, 2017.
       [http://dx.doi.org/10.1016/j.patcog.2016.11.008]

[7]　R. Szeliski, *Computer Vision: Algorithms and Applications.* 2nd ed. Springer, 2020.

[8]　GDPR (General Data Protection Regulation), *Insoft Consulting.,* 2020.https://gdpr-info.eu/

[9]　W. Rodgers, *Throughput Modeling: Financial Information Used by Decision Makers.* JAI Press: Greenwich, CT, 1997.

[10]　W. Rodgers, *Ethical Beginnings: Preferences, rules, and principles influencing decision making* iUniverse: NY, 2009.

[11]　W. Rodgers, *Trust Throughput Modeling Pathways.* Nova Publication: Hauppauge, NY, 2019.

[12]　W. Rodgers, F. Yeung, C. Odindo, and W. Degbey, "Artificial Intelligence-Driven Music Biometrics Influencing Customers' Retail Buying Behavior", *J. Bus. Res.,* vol. 126, pp. 401-414, 2021. [http://dx.doi.org/10.1016/j.jbusres.2020.12.039]

[13]　W. Rodgers, "Evaluating accounting information using causal models: Classification of methods and implications for accounting research", *J. Account. Lit.,* vol. 10, pp. 151-180, 1991.

[14]　W. Rodgers, and A. Guiral, "Potential Model Misspecification Bias: Formative Indicators Enhancing Theory for Accounting Researchers", *Int. J. Account.,* vol. 46, no. 1, pp. 25-50, 2011. [http://dx.doi.org/10.1016/j.intacc.2010.12.002]

[15]　J. McCarthy, M.L. Minsky, N. Rochester, and C.E. Shannon, "A Proposal for the Dartmouth Summer Research Project on Artificial Intelligence", *AI Mag.,* vol. 27, no. 4, 2006.

[16]　D. Lu, "Uber and Lyft pricing algorithms charge more in non-white areas", *NewScientist,* 2020.https://www.newscientist.com/article/2246202-uber-and-lyft-pricing-algorithms--harge-more-in-non-white-areas/#ixzz6xAxyZZy7

# CHAPTER 4

# The Expedient Algorithmic Pathway

**Abstract: Abstract.**

*By their very nature, heuristic shortcuts will produce biases, and that is true for both humans and artificial intelligence, but the heuristics of AI are not necessarily the human ones.* ---Daniel Kahneman.

*What all of us have to do is to make sure we are using AI in a way that is for the benefit of humanity, not to the detriment of humanity.* ---Tim Cook.

Computers will overtake humans with AI at some [point] within the next 100 years. When that happens, we need to make sure the computers have goals aligned with ours.

---Stephen Hawking.

**Abstract**.

The Expedient Algorithmic Pathway (P→D) represents an individual or organization with a certain level of expertise providing a decision without the assistance of information since the information may be too noisy, incomplete, inadequately understood, or the alternatives cannot be differentiated. In addition, time pressures may circumvent an individual or organization from analyzing the available information. This algorithm is very useful in AI applications ranging from data gathering to problem solving.

**Keywords:** Algorithms, Behavioral biometrics, Big data, Biometrics, Blockchains, Body Odor Recognition, DNA, Dynamic signature, Ear Recognition, Expedient Algorithmic Pathway, Face Recognition, Face Thermography, Fingerprint, Gait, Hand Geometry, Iris Scan , Keystroke Dynamics, Palm Print, Physiological biometrics , Retina Scan, Vein Patterns, Voice (Speech) Recognition.

## INTRODUCTION

AI is a branch of computer science that shows the capacity of intelligence a computer system or robots must be able to mimic what a human can do. In AI the computer system can do almost everything a human can do, they can think,

.

process information, and then make action on the information they have. One of the purposes of AI is to create robots or machines that are intelligent enough to perform the task of a human, without always needing the human by its side.

AI may become one of the most disruptive technological developments in the last two hundred years. AI algorithms can create new opportunities and risks in every aspect of business, government, and human life. For example, AI represents opportunities for the audit profession to provide leadership in audit services by educating industry and government leaders on the ethical use and implementation of AI algorithmic systems.

The Decision Makers' Processes Diagram, also known as the Throughput Model, explains how a decision is made and which factors are involved. In this diagram the "P" stands for perception, the "I" for information, the "J" for judgment, and the "D" for decision choice. This diagram does not have one exact way for showing how a decision is made because there are several different ways to come to a decision and everyone will interpret the information in a different way. Someone's perception can be influenced by their previous experiences, their background including their education. Information will always be the same information provided to every individual but based on their perception they can process the information differently. Some people might have the ability to make further assumptions based on the knowledge they already have. Therefore, all these factors will lead to everyone's judgement being distinct from one another. Based on their judgement, everyone's decision will be different, it does not necessarily mean it is right or wrong, but they have different reasons for their decisions (Fig. **1**).

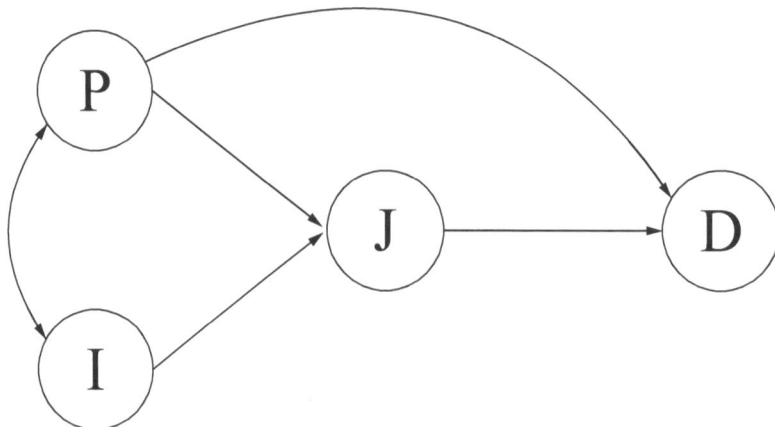

**Fig. (4.1).** Decision makers' processes diagram. Source: Rodgers [1].

There are three basic ways everyone comes to a decision which are represented through algorithms. An algorithm is a process used in calculations and problem-solving operations. The three basic algorithms can then be further expanded making a total of six algorithms for the way a decision can be made. The other three algorithms are very similar to the first three algorithms just with an additional concept of "*perception*" or "*information*" added to the algorithm. These algorithms are:

1. **The Expedient Pathway P→D.**
2. **The Ruling Guide Pathway P→J→D.**
3. **The Analytical Pathway I→J→D.**
4. **The Revisionist Pathway I→P→D.**
5. **The Value Driven Pathway P→I→J→D.**
6. **The Global Perspective Pathway s I→P→J→D.**

The main concepts do not change for the algorithms, they are just placed in different order, which causes the outcome to be different. The Expedient Pathway (P→D) is the center of discussion in this chapter.

The Expedient Pathway (P→D) is an AI algorithm based only on an individual's perception [1]. This is the most efficient of the pathways because it is the one that takes the least time to perform. Perception is how we frame the environment based on our past experiences. Perception is influenced by several factors, such as emotions and personal biases. The Expedient Pathway ignores information perhaps because it is unclear or unreliable. This pathway is most effective when the available information is unreliable and there is a limited time period, or the environmental conditions are shifting to make a decision choice. The main advantage of this algorithmic pathway is that it takes very little time, and the main disadvantage is that it ignores the available information sources, so if the person deciding does not have the appropriate experience, the decision may be wrong.

The Expedient Pathway only has one step to reach a decision and it serves well when an individual or organization have limited time to make a decision choice. Often, decision makers must make quick and simple decisions all the time. AI can help standardize this process by implementing regressions, decision trees, forest trees, and/or graphics. For example, there is software that automatically calculates depreciation and amortization expense, and you only have to input the variables, such as initial cost, depreciation method, salvage value, and useful life. This software eliminates the risk the risk of material misstatement in the calculation for depreciation expense.

The Expedient Algorithmic Pathway also comes into play when we have a limited time to make a decision choice. Time limitation can result in not choosing the correct decision for what is best for a particular project. In addition, not understanding clearly the task can also lead individuals to not selecting the correct course of action, and this could get worst due to increasing time limitations. This algorithmic pathway represents and provides the most efficient way to a decision. It also represents the shortest distance.

The **"P"** or perception represents the categorization or classification of information. That is, perception represents how we "think," "frame," or set up a problem our environment based on our experiences, training, and education. In other words, our decision choices are augmented by the education we have received, training provided by others, and our experiences in our economic, political, and social manner of living.

Sometimes, in our lives we may face situations where we have just a few seconds of time to decide. Furthermore, many events in our lives are unplanned and unexpected. Moreover, environmental circumstances can change thereby making it difficult to plan.

It is also important to understand an aspect of our lives in how we may frame a particular situation is due to our emotions and biases that can influence in decision choices. These patterns allow us to make quick decisions due to the heuristics that are employed in our decision-making apparatus. Moreover, perceptions assist in the categorizing and classifying events in our memories to decide. Fig. (**4.2**) is an illustration of the **PD algorithmic pathway**, which depicts how we frame our world.

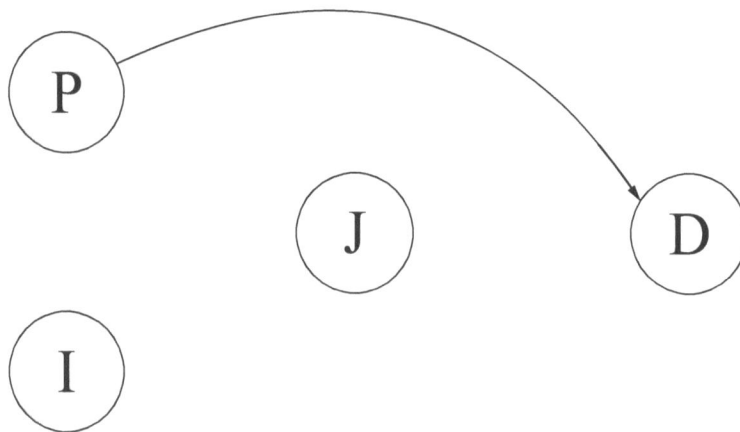

**Fig. (4.2).** P→D The algorithmic pathway consists of perception to decision choice. Source: Rodgers [1].

AI is the simulation of human intelligence that is programmed into machines to think and mimic how humans perform a task. This can refer to any machine that can carry out a task such as problem solving. AI has evolved to the point where we are able to deposit checks from the comfort of our homes, using an application, without having to make a trip to the bank. Alexa is one example of the P→D algorithmic pathway. Alexa is an intelligent tool designed to listen, frame a problem, and carry out human like commands. Users of the Alexa program usually install it in their homes for simple demands such turning lights on or off, turning music on, lowering volumes, changing songs, *etc*. AI influence our daily lives.

AI also applies to many accounting systems. In accounting the systems are designed to recognize patterns and derive algorithms based on feedbacks. It is machine intelligence built from machine learning. This helps with accounting because the computers identify similar relationships to associate them to contracts and/or documents. Computers can be trained to complete tedious tasks by processing large amounts of data and calculate different types of information all at once. As data grows in a company or across industries the demand for AI has increased. Machine intelligence provides for computer capability to harness understanding of data, relationships, and rules as well as comprehend through implication of a set information to provide analysis. Accounting firms need to be able to assess and process customer data to be able to present and ensure up to date financial recording. The benefits of AI include but are not limited to faster and efficient audit completion, increased business insights, and the workload is more tolerable. Even though AI Is very efficient it also has its disadvantages, such as getting laid off your job to be replaced by a machine, there is a great risk with errors, distrust, and cybersecurity *etc*. The main technical problem has been if AI can really be trusted for an audit or not and what the impact would be.

The pathway from **PD** provides as the most efficient pathway when a person has impending time constraints to make a decision choice. This can occur when an unforeseeable emergency occupies our thoughts leaving no space in our mind to think about anything else. This can also occur when we have a certain expectation or standard in which we were raised culturally or due to societal norms. In addition, facts and other informational sources not presented in a timely manner due to miscommunication, procrastination, or insufficient context portrayal encourages the utilization of this pathway. This pathway provides the quickest way to make a decision. In which, it represents the least time consuming, compared to the other 5 pathways to a decision choice. An emphasis is placed on the **"P"** or perception.

The foundation of perception is based on how we structure our surrounding based on crucial events in our life. These events in our life are influenced by demographics, gender, technology, politics, religion, culture, *etc.* Perception is also formed by our tactical strategies, and how our mind stores information we memorize and understand and place in storage blocks.

In addition, stereotypical and societal pressure can determine how we choose to interpret a situation based on our rationalization of the chain of events that have occurred due to our personal feelings. The tactics learned through our experiences give us a guide in how we approach every situation we encounter; we have an enormous number of manuals filled with instructions for situations varying from how to tie your shoe to how to drive a car. Perception assists us in compartmentalizing and rating events in our memories to take us down one of six pathways to make a decision. The **P→D** pathway, emphasizes how we depict the world. Further, due to our personal experiences, training, and education there may be times whereby information (I) is insufficient or ignored as indicated in Fig. (**4.1**).

A decision tree is useful in illustrating applying the Expedient Algorithmic Pathway to the auditing process would reflect in the relationship between an organization and an auditor (see Fig. **4.3**). There are times where a choice between ethical or a non-ethical response may occur in the blink of an eye, but the decision choice made can result in the loss of reputation of a company and credibility. The error of this decision may be influenced by external factors such as bias, bribes, and ineffective auditing.

*P→D (stable environment)*

In this scenario a trendy business has started to receive an influx of customers. They are making revenue at record times, and there has been no complaints or negative reviews on any platforms. With all the positive attention this organization is receiving the owner comes to the realization hiring an auditor would add even more credibility to his business and attract investors to take a chance on his company. After meeting with several external auditors, the owner comes to discovers that a colleague from his alma mater has applied for the auditing position. He catches up with his old friend, now candidate, and decides she is the best fit for the evaluation of financial statements, and record keeping.

After notifying the applicant she has received the job, the owner questions his decision of hiring an acquaintance. He is worried the relationship may affect the effectiveness of the auditor and may appear as unethical. However, he reassures himself that she has the best credentials in comparison to the other auditors and the relationship between them was always professional. The business owner makes the *decision choice* to hire the old colleague and places trust that the auditor will follow due professional care and enforce the Principles of Professional Conduct. As expected, the auditor effectively conducts her report, and ensures no material misstatements are occurring within the company by properly conducting tests on the internal controls of the organization.

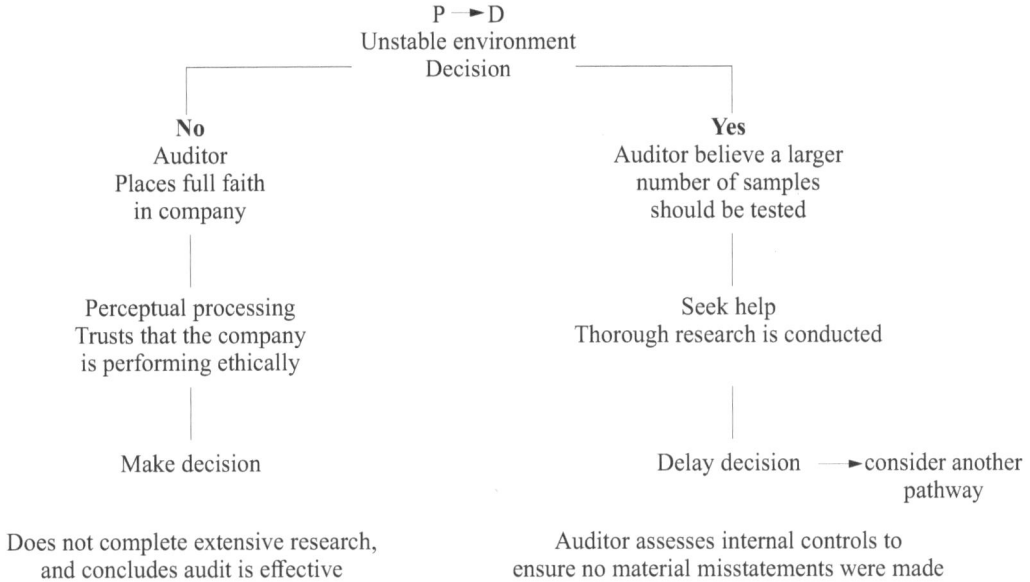

P → D
Unstable environment
Decision

**No**
Auditor
Places full faith
in company

**Yes**
Auditor believe a larger
number of samples
should be tested

Perceptual processing
Trusts that the company
is performing ethically

Seek help
Thorough research is conducted

Make decision

Delay decision ──► consider another
pathway

Does not complete extensive research,
and concludes audit is effective

Auditor assesses internal controls to
ensure no material misstatements were made

**Fig. (4.3).** The expedient algorithmic pathway decision tree process. (Adapted from Rodgers [1]).

## *P→D (unstable environment)*

Although it's great to believe individuals will always conduct themselves in an ethical manner and meet the set expectations this is not always the case. For example, if you're a hiring manager you interview several candidates, review applications, and assess which would be the best fit for the position. However, if you give a candidate the job due to having a previous relationship you cannot be 100% sure they are going to perform with an unbiased opinion or if favoritism can occur. After hiring the applicant, you may also come to the realization that the employee does not have the required tools and skills to excel in this position (*unstable environment*). The hiring manager performs to the best of their abilities in evaluating each of the employees equally while attempting to assess each candidate equally and fairly.

Suppose a manager responsible for hiring staff must decide whether to hire the candidate that also happens to be their acquaintance, but she wants to consult with the human resources department before she makes her decision. This process illustrates how the hiring manager uses her perceptual frame (based on her *expertise*) to decide if the candidate is the most qualified, and how his desire to delay the hiring process can negatively affect the auditing process *(decision choice)* and may influence him to use another *pathway*.

## BIOMETRICS INFUSED WITH AI TECHNOLOGY

Biometrics is the measurement of both physical and behavioral human characteristics and is most often used to verify the identity of a person. Physical characteristics include fingerprint, iris, facial and vein recognition, whereas behavioral characteristics include geographic location, travel patterns, and purchase habits. Biometrics is becoming increasingly advanced, expanding into the way a person holds their phone or even tap a screen. Artificial intelligence algorithms will reject access to a system or stop a transaction if a set of biometric information does not match a pattern previously identified though machine learning. Although the combined use of biometrics and artificial intelligence is cutting edge to prevent fraud, it is essential that algorithms within the neural network are continuously enhanced, and antifraud practices are utilized to combat acts to circumvent security measures. Fraudsters have attempted to bypass biometric identification measures by using silicone finger molds for fingerprint recognition, contact lenses with another person's iris printed on lens for iris recognition, and plastic surgery to circumvent facial recognition. Furthermore, artificial intelligence must be utilized to protect biometric information collected in general, as this information in the wrong hands could be detrimental to the fraud victim.

Biometrics is the measurement of human physical and behavioral characteristics and is most often used to identify and verify individuals. As the cost of technologies continue to decrease, many organizations are gradually switching from manual paper identification to automated biometric identification. Manual paper identification can be difficult to store, is easily stolen and forged, and is subject to human forgetfulness and biases. Fraud techniques have also become more sophisticated creating a tug-of-war between organizations and fraudsters in keeping ahead of each other. These shortcomings allow for identity theft occurrences that often plague our current society, such as credit card fraud, costing organizations millions of dollars each year. The transition to biometric identification eliminates human biases, improves accuracy, and promotes efficiency. Furthermore, the variety of biometric data available for identity purposes provides organizations with flexibility in developing their systems (see Table **4.1**).

Table 4.1. Biometrics Behavioral and Physiological Tools.

| Biometric Types | |
|---|---|
| *Behavioral* | *Physiological* |
| Voice (Speech) Recognition | Fingerprint |
| Gait | Retina Scan |
| Dynamic Signature | Face Recognition |
| Keystroke Dynamics | DNA |
| - | Face Thermography |
| - | Hand Geometry |
| - | Iris Scan |
| - | Palm Print |
| - | Ear Recognition |
| - | Vein Patterns |
| - | Body Odor Recognition |

Source: from Rodgers [4].

Biometric identification utilizes computer systems to create templates composed of binary code for each person's unique characteristics. When a computer system receives biometric data, it will compare the data to its neural network to match the data with previously stored patterns. This matching process is part of deep learning. If the data comes from a new person whose biometric information was not previously archived, the system will assign mathematical algorithms to the data and convert it into binary code. This information will be stored in the form of templates within the neural network for future identification purposes.

When a request is received by the computer system to confirm the identity of an individual, it must have a representation of someone's identity, such as an email address, and a piece of biometric data, such as retina patterns. In this example, unique retina patterns of the individual would be used to create a template, and the email address would be used to obtain the template within the computer system. Then the computer system would perform one of two functions to confirm or authenticate the individual's identity. These independent functions are called verification and identification. Verification is a much easier process for the system to perform because the authentication request includes information about who the individual claims to be. The verification process is simply confirming that the individual is in fact the person they are claiming and is matching the information provided with the template. This process is overt, meaning that the individual is aware of the authentication process or knows that data is being collected about them. When an individual drives outside of a fifty-mile radius from El Paso, the federal government collects data from vehicles and their occupants while passing through the U.S. Customs and Border Protection interior checkpoints. This data collection process is overt because individuals are aware of all the cameras collecting biometric data when speeding through the checkpoint. The identification process is more complex than verification because the authentication request does not include information about the identity of the individual. Instead, the computer system must use a database containing biometric data to Fig. out the identity of the person. Data collection could be overt or covert in the identification process. Covert means that the individual is not aware of the authentication process or does not know their data is being collected. A criminal investigator collecting fingerprints from a garbage can is an example of covert data collection.

When a computer system confirms an individual's identity it can use three different forms of authentication. The first form is "something you are," which is biometric data like face recognition or DNA. Biometric data is unique to everyone and is not replicated within another individual. The second form of authentication is called "something you have," such as an access badge or a social security card. This type of authentication is familiar in current society; however, its pitfalls include the possibility that the identification forms can be lost, stolen, or forged for another's use. Biometric data on the other hand cannot be used by another person to confirm their identity. The third type of authentication is called "something you know," such as a pin number or password. This form of proof of identity is also common; however, it is not fool proof. To circumvent fraudsters that may Fig. out passwords and pins, requirements for those items have become more stringent and complicated. Furthermore, organizations often require that passwords and pin numbers be changed on interval cycles often leading to users forgetting these items. In comparison, biometric data cannot be guessed or forgotten.

Biometrics and AI can work together to develop effective and reliable security systems. In the high-tech digital age, security is one of the foremost concerns of any organization. Every organization has appreciated that data is a major resource. Therefore, organizations deploy sophisticated security apparatuses to safeguard important information. Nevertheless, many commercial titans such as Google, Facebook, Cathay Pacific, Exactis, and many more have experience major data breaches in the recent few years. These data breaches have uncovered essential data of millions of customers. Therefore, organizations are constantly looking for enhance options to traditional security models.

AI driven biometrics such as fingerprint and iris scans are being utilized for authenticating employees at the workplace and identifying smartphone owners. Such biometrics can be implemented in organizations to authorize data access for confidential data. Biometrics can be utilized along with traditional passwords or PIN numbers for multi-factor authentication. Moreover, the integration of AI with biometrics can assist in the development of data-driven security protocols. Hence, combining AI and biometrics together will lead to the creation of dynamic security models.

There are two different kinds of AI, one is software based and the other is physical agents, such as robots. Robots' mimic what a human does, therefore doing the work of a human only requiring supervision of the robots. Physical Agents were created to be able to do the daily functions that a human can do, therefore making it easier for the tasks a human must perform. The software-based AI should be able to do things that humans cannot do, like sorting through big amounts of data within seconds and making a conclusion based on their findings. AI has been around for a long period of time but has become more popular recently due to the increase of technological advances and the increased amounts of data. AI has many subsets including machine learning, deep learning, big data, blockchain, and natural language processing [3].

Machine learning is the technique that uses certain methods to make machines carry out certain tasks. Machine learning can be put in two categories, supervised or unsupervised [2, 3]. Supervised machine learning makes the machine make predictions based on functions to get from known inputs to known outputs. Unsupervised machine learning works only with inputs, no outputs. It finds patterns in the data it has without an expected output. Unsupervised machine learning is like thinking quick on your feet, you take the information available and make a prediction based on that. Machine learning is just the opposite it has a set of steps that it will follow to get to the outcome or prediction of the input. An algorithm is described as the process or the rules that problem solving operations follow. Engineers use algorithms when designing a learning machine, the algorithm is what will make the machine process the data. Machine learning is the way to teach machines to adapt to changes within the technology or to adapt additional information to a current problem and make a rational decision. Machines have the advantage of speed, accuracy, and the amount of volume they can hold and still conclude, something that the human mind lacks.

Deep learning is a set of techniques that will study what the human brains does for a computer to then recreate [3]. Deep learning models are trained by using large sets of data that learn features directly from the data without the need for manual feature extraction. None needs to teach the computer how to perceive the information or where to apply it, the computer knows what to do with the information. Deep learning goes a further level than machine learning being able to interpret new or unknown information and going deeper into more layers of information. Some great examples of deep learning in the everyday life can be something as small as cellular devices to something as big as self-driving cars. As technology evolves the deep learning in machines gets better, in your mobile phone while on a search-engine many advertisements will pop-up and those advertisements will be something you will most likely look into. A mobile phone can remember what you previously searched and store that information for later and when you open the search engine again it will try to take you back to what you were previously looking to buy. Self-driving cars also became very popular when Tesla, a car manufacturer, was the first the company to create a car that did not require a driver. The self-driving car was able to take you to and from places safely just as a regular car would. The technology in this type of car recognized all the traffic signals, such as stop signs and traffic lights just as any human would. The concept of self-driving cars is not perfect yet but as more information becomes available, and technology advances it will be mastered.

Big data is exactly what is sounds like, a big amount of data. It represents data sets that are very big and complex that human minds and the technology in earlier years could not process or understand. The information could be misunderstood or not adequately processed because it was too much to comprehend. Now that technology has evolved and became something much bigger, researchers are trying to find a process to make information from big data useful and valuable. There are several ways that this can be done but they have not found the most practical way of doing this. The more technology advances the more information can be taken out of big data, the more information more relationships can be made.

Big Data has become a popular topic amongst business professionals eager to harness its power to advance its operations. It is defined as a massive amount of data generated and saved from both traditional and non-traditional means that can be either structured or unstructured. This data is used as an input to the "I" component of the Throughput Model. Processed information along with artificial intelligence is utilized in a myriad of ways, including to: predict behavior, identify cost, and time efficiencies, optimize decisions, and detect fraudulent activity. "Big data" generally consists of three "V's": (1) volume, (2) velocity, and (3) variety. *Volume* describes the amount of data coming from multiple sources, including traditional sources such as consumer transactional data or non-traditional sources such as twitter feed information. *Velocity* entails the ability to process information that is generated at hypersonic speed in a timely fashion. Humans would not be able to utilize the continuous information generated from big data sources in a timely fashion without artificial intelligence analyzing the real-time data. *Variety* encompasses the culmination of numeric to alphabetic text information from thousands of sources. A challenge with the "I" component, thus big data, is determining the integrity of the information. Decision makers through artificial intelligence must ensure that the information has not been intentionally modified without permission and that the source of the information is reliable. Without AI, it would be difficult for a human to verify the integrity of the information obtained because of the nature of the three "V's." Big data information can be used by utilities to refine its resource planning, by law enforcement to predict crime, and by healthcare professionals to develop treatment plans.

The convergence of blockchain and AI can augment machine learning and enable AI to generate many financial and non-financial products. Blockchain facilitates secure storage and sharing of data or anything of value. AI apparatuses can evaluate and generate insights from data to produce value. Hence, AI models can be used to analyze, classify, and make predictions from data. Data is key to AI effectiveness, and along with blockchain enabling capacity to collaborate and secure data sharing. From a fraud prevention and security system platform, blockchain can ensure the trustworthiness of data and can enable more data to be securely shared before AI extracts insights from it.

Blockchain is fundamentally a centralized and transparent data network system. For example, this technology may change the way travel managers and travel management companies utilize and exchange a traveler's identity. Further, this technology stores information in unalterable encrypted blocks. This information can only be accessed through codes shared by authenticated users, who can view the data, but not alter it, and thereby generate incorruptible records of their transactions. Suppliers, travel managers and travel management companies can track the identity of travelers at different points on their journey without compromising data security.

Moreover, an authentication system such as blockchain enhances protection against fraud and decreases the risk of identity theft. Additionally, invoicing, settlement, payments, contract negotiation and identity verification are activities executed by travel industry companies through manual processes with multiple controls and verification systems. Distributed records protected by blockchain will ensure that all parties agree on a single version of the truth in real time by eliminating such time-consuming processes. For example, a traveler's can be verified from anywhere, thus eliminating an awkward and burdensome exchange with passport control when it does not look like the traveler's photo. Furthermore, according to CWT (see https://www.mycwt.com/de/de/TPFtechnology-en/#02) an application is being tested that clearly assigns luggage to passengers to minimize risk of lost baggage. Finally, in relation to loyalty programs, points, and bonuses, blockchain tools can assist in the collection across different vendors, which can be made immediately and utilized similarly to currency. This potential combination is increased with the availability of biometrics technology.

Biometrics can be depicted as the authentication of an individual, it is what makes them who they are, it is the measure of someone's biological characteristics. Biometrics includes how the individual looks like, their facial features, their fingerprints or palm print. As technology is evolving biometrics is used as an identification factor for many places where confidential or personal information is included. Fraud is defined as the criminal intent to take personal or confidential information for someone's own personal gain. To prevent fraud biometrics are being used in the simplest things such as cellular devices to more complex things such as accessing a bank account or a safe. Personal devices use protection such a password, or a personal identification number (PIN), or even fingerprint recognition. Bank Accounts use more complex protection such as facial or voice recognition to help prevent fraud with more complex and personal information. Using these protective authorizations with biometrics it is much harder for anyone to steal personal information and use it to their advantage. The decision-making model starts with information, without it no decision can be drawn therefore nothing will be accomplished. As technology advances the use of biometrics also advances. The biometric technologies can be separated into two categories, behavioral and physiological (see Table **4.1**).

Various types of behavioral biometrics include, voice recognition, gait recognition, dynamic signature, and keystroke dynamics. Whereas, physiological biometrics include, fingerprint, retina scan, face recognition, DNA, face thermography, hand geometry, iris scan, palm print, ear recognition, vein patterns, and body odor recognition [4].

Some examples of the physiological characteristics in biometrics include the use of fingerprint, palm print, hand geometry, retina scan, face recognition, DNA, and many more (also [4, 5]). These biometrics are used in everyday life with gadgets at home such as cellular devices to some not so common gadgets like accessing vaults or safes. The use of the fingerprint is the most common one and it can be used for identification and verification. It can be used to help identify who you are without any other sort of identification, or it can also be used to verify who you are while comparing another form of identification.

The fingerprint can be used by two different approaches, the minutiae-based approach, and the pattern-based approach. The minutiae approach implements the ridge ending and bifurcation on the finger to plot points known as minutiae (Fig. 4.4). This approach makes it easy to compare two distinct fingerprints in an electronic system. The second approach is the pattern-based approach, and it is performed in two blocks called image enhancement and distortion removal. In both approaches the fingerprint is being scanned and can be used to make a reasonable conclusion on your verification or identity. Another common use biometric is the palm print and it works very similarly to the fingerprint recognition. Every palm print is distinct; therefore, it is also fairly easy to compare to other and make a decision to an individuals' identity. The palm is also scanned and the ridge patterns, endings, and paths of the raised portion of the palm are all measured. There is also another type of biometric called hand geometry. The hand geometry can be taken as an image of your entire hand or as a two-finger reader only, and just like it sounds, an image of just two fingers will be taken. The devices to take a hand geometry are very accessible and small that it can be taken pretty much anywhere. As technology advances the goal is to be able to store all these palm prints and fingerprints into one big database that is accessible to many people to try to determine the identity of someone's fingerprint or palm print.

**Fig. (4.4). Fingerprint.** Source: from Rodgers [4].

The retina scan is not as common, but it is being used with very safe and confidential information. The way the retina scan works is that the individual is forced to look at a specific point and focus on that point, then the scanner can scan the individual's retina (see Fig. **4.5**). The retina scan is not very user friendly but is it very accurate and can distinct one person from another. The iris scan is also very similar, this method will high resolution images to compare the patterns in someone's iris. This type of technology is used with a camera and will reduce the amount of light to therefore reduce the amount of reflection from the convex cornea to be able to produce a very detailed picture. This process will then use the picture to make a conclusion as to the identification of that person.

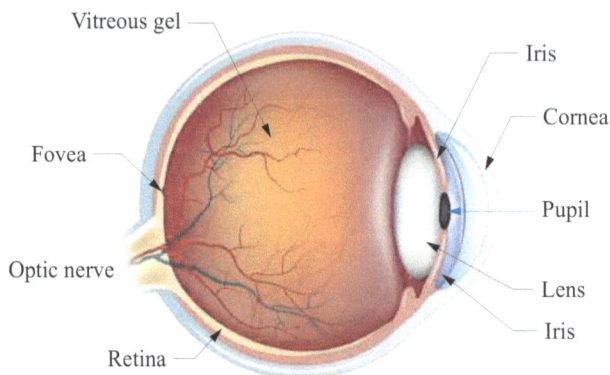

Vitreous gel

Iris

Cornea

Fovea

Pupil

Optic nerve

Lens

Iris

Retina

**Fig. (4.5). Retina.** Source: from Rodgers [4].

A very popular biometric that is being used a lot more frequently now is the face recognition. Face recognition was not very popular because technology wasn't as advanced as it is now (Fig. **4.6**). Artificial intelligence is also a lot more advanced, and it allows for use of some of these techniques a lot more user friendly. The way facial recognition works is that it will use a camera or a picture of an individual to recognize whether it is a positive identification or not. An individual does not have to cooperate or agree to use this type of biometric is it simply taken, making this type of biometric a passive biometric. This tool has advanced greatly because now an individual does not have to be right in front of the camera or close to the camera for that matter. An individual might be scanned within a distance, and they will not even know it. It has also advanced greatly from simply matching the someone's pattern to now matching distinctive features and complex points in someone's face. This was mainly used by officials before in missing case or as security measures in places like a bank. Now this type of technology is used almost every day, facial recognition is used in cellular devices, tablets and even computers, this comes to show how much technology has advanced in a short period of time.

Face thermography is also another form of biometric that is being used more frequently. This works by detecting heat patterns in someone's face by the shape of their blood vessels. There is no physical contact as a camera will import a picture and will be collected quickly. This type of biometric is very similar to the facial recognition.

The biometric software applies machine learning or deep learning algorithms to match a live portrayed image to the stored face print to verify one's identity. Image processing and machine learning are the mainstays of this technology. Facial recognition has gathered substantial attention from researchers due to human activities found in various applications of security like an airport, criminal detection, face tracking, forensic, *etc*. Contrasted to other biometric traits like palm print, iris, fingerprint, *etc*., facial biometrics can be non-intrusive.

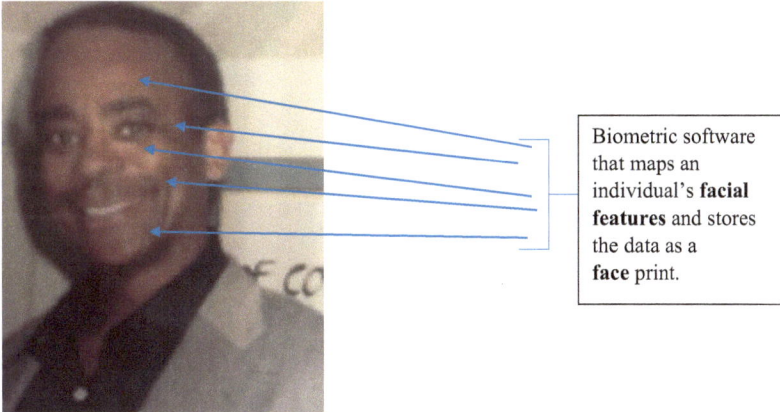

Biometric software that maps an individual's **facial features** and stores the data as a **face** print.

**Fig. (4.6).** Facial recognition. Source by author. Features identified by machine intelligence.

DNA is a very well-known physiological biometric, it is the double helix structure presented in the human cells. DNA can be used to produce a DNA fingerprint or a DNA profile (Fig. **4.7**). DNA can be taken from many different sources, blood, hair, saliva, fingernails, and anything else that was once attached to the body at one point. The one downfall to DNA biometrics is that it is very slow, it cannot recognize someone within a matter of seconds or even minutes. Therefore, results will take weeks and months to be received and that can be very frustrating. Another downfall to DNA is that it is very costly therefore it will not be used as frequently as other biometrics will be used. There are many other types of physiological characteristics in biometrics, but these mentioned are the most common ones used today. Maybe as artificial intelligence advances some more, the other types of biometrics will soon become more common and will be a part of someone's life on the daily.

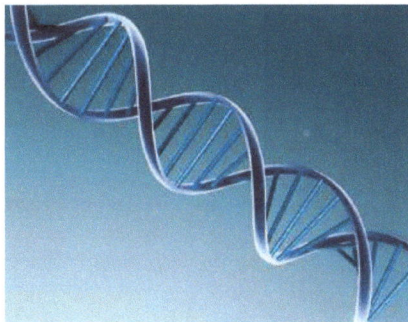

**Fig. (4.7).** DNA. Source: from Rodgers [4].

DNA technology can implement an AI neural network to identify the lab of origin of an engineered DNA sequence. The design choices made when building a new DNA tool are commonly prescribed by laboratory history and culture, which leads to sequence similarities in DNA surfacing from any given laboratory.

Users of GenePlaza, for example, can upload their 23andMe data and pay $4 extra to access an "Intelligence App," which rates their DNA using data from their big 2017 study on IQ genes. It shows users where their genes place them on a bell curve from lower to higher IQ. A similar calculation is available from DNA Land. (https://www.dnaweekly.com/blog/geneplaza-interview/).

More and more companies are providing an app development platform designed for scientists to create and sell genetic mobile applications. Their growing collection of Genetic Applications enables end-users with valuable insights on various aspects including cognitive abilities, health traits, and potential for addictions.

Voice (Speech) Recognition was first introduced by IBM in 1962 when it unveiled the first machine capable of converting human voice to text. Today, powered by the latest tools such as machine learning and deep learning, speech recognition is reaching new milestones.

Voice recognition biometrics is the ability to recognize an individual's voice, just like it sounds (Fig. **4.8**). Speaker or voice recognition relies on the structure of a person's vocal tract and their personality. Speaker and speech recognition are not the same thing, speech recognition is the recognition of certain words not someone's voice. One big downfall to speaker recognition is that it will not recognizes an individual on a recording, it must be in person. The other downfall is that it depends on scripted text.

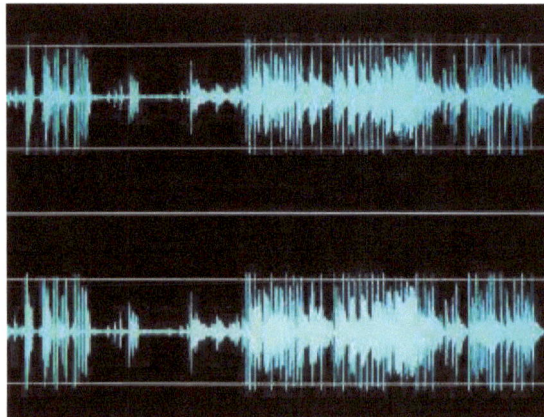

**Fig. (4.8).** Voice (speaker) recognition. Source: from Rodgers [4].

Further, this human disposition presents a challenge for machine learning in speech recognition. Listening to and understanding what an individual verbalizes is so much more than hearing the words the person speaks. Machines are learning to "listen" to accents, emotions, and inflections; however, there is still much needed research in this area.

Recently, Nuance is best known for its *deep learning voice* transcription service, which is very prevalent in the healthcare sector was sold. In April 2021, Microsoft's announced a $19.7 billion acquisition of Nuance, a company that provides speech recognition and conversational AI services (https://blog. probyto.com/microsofts-aquistition-of-nuance/#:~:text=Nuance%20is%20 best%20known%20for%20its%20deep%20learning,that%20provides%20speech %20recognition%20and%20conversational%20AI%20services.).

Gait recognition is also becoming more popular it is the ability to recognize the unique way someone walks (Fig. **4.9**). It analyzes a lot of factors like the space between every stroke, how fast someone is walking, the length of their legs and many others. Some researchers maintain that each human has approximately 24 different factors and movements when walking, resulting in every individual person having a unique, singular walking pattern (see: https://www.airport-technology.com/features/ai-at-airports-security/).

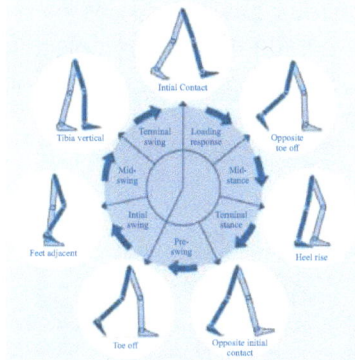

**Fig. (4.9).** Gait recognition.

Scrutinizing the distinctive gait signature from a person by stressing, which variables at what time windows of the gait cycle are employed by the model to identify an individual. The portrayed approach examines the appropriateness of understanding and interpreting the classification of gait patterns using state-o--the-art machine learning methods. Non-linear machine learning methods such as artificial neural networks use graspable prediction strategies and can learn meaningful gait characteristics.

This is also an example of a passive biometric, the individual does not have to do anything in specific or agree to taken into consideration with the simple task of walking, this biometric is used. Someone can fake their gait by purposely walking different, taking shorter steps or longer steps, walking slower or faster. There are many ways to beat the system but if that individual does not know about gait recognition, it will not try to beat the system.

In the everyday environment around the globe, security is very essential. A fundamental component of security is authentication, which is based on an individual's identity that is authorized to certain privileges.

Signature recognition and verification involves two distinct; however, soundly related tasks: The first one is the identification of the signature owner. The second one is the decision choice regarding whether the signature is genuine or forged. Moreover, depending on the requirement, signature recognition and verification problem is placed into two major categories: (a) online signature recognition and verification systems and (b) offline [8].

There are many means for authentication, and signature is one among them. Dynamic signature is the ability to recognize if someone signed or even wrote a word using a pen or pencil and paper (Fig. **4.10**). The way every individual write, is distinct therefore the way everyone signs is even more distinct. The dynamic signature will analyze the various characteristics in someone's signing style to determine if it really was that person or someone else. The angle of the signature, the amount of pressure of certain letters, the formation of the letters and many other can distinguish a person's signature.

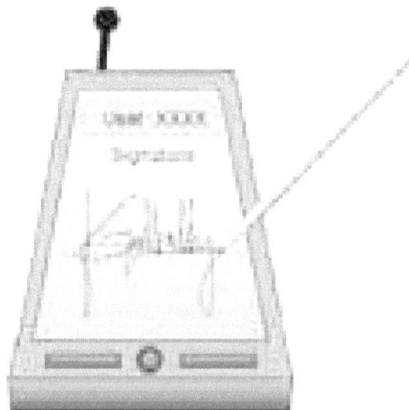

**Fig. (4.10).** Dynamic signature. Source: from Rodgers [4].

AI enabled signature forgery detection software can significantly upgrade efficiency in sectors that deal with a large volume of paper works that require signatures. It saves time and effort and can eradicate fraudulent practices to a large degree. The insurance sector is a chief beneficiary of AI enabled signature verification systems because it relies principally on documents submitted during policy enrollment to confirm claims accordingly. Any signature mismatch or fraud can lead to the advantages being given away to illegitimate claimants and can instigate harsh implications.

Developed algorithms are more and more based on the dynamic analysis of electronically handwritten signatures employing neural networks. These handwritten signature's dynamic parameters include the process of generating the signature, which facilitates its fuller and more stable representation. The group of dynamic parameters comprises the length of forming a signature, the pen pressure on the surface, the tilt of the pen, and others.

These parameters are varying during the signature creation; thereby. making it possible to extract the individual features. Based upon the continuous recording of the signature's parameters, it is much less likely to impersonate another individual than utilizing the static (graphical) signature representation. The dynamic signature can operate as a biometric modality that utilizes the writer for recognition purposes given their individual anatomical and behavioral characteristics. In addition, dynamic signature apparatuses should not be mistaken with electronic signature portrayal systems utilized to capture the signature's graphic image, which is frequent in locations where merchants are capturing signatures for transaction authorizations (see Fig. **4.11**).

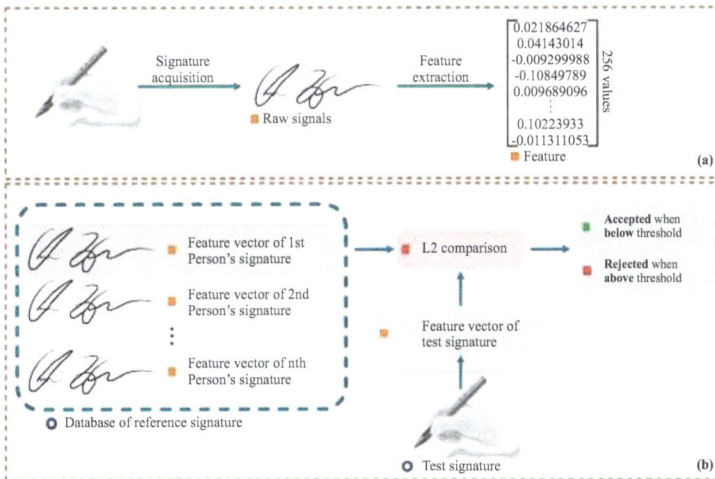

**Fig. (4.11).** Processing of signature. Adopted from Kurowski, Sroczyński, Bogdanis, and Czyżewsk [6].

Keystroke dynamic biometrics is the way people type (Fig. **4.12**). This biometric measure the different types of speeds and the timing between every key pressed on the keyboard. Everyone takes more time typing out certain words or if it is something they are used to typing like a username or a password they might type faster, it just depends. Therefore, the timing between keys or words is distinct and can be used to make a conclusion about the identity of the individual. There are not as many behavioral biometrics currently being used as there are in physiological biometrics; nonetheless, implemented properly, they are a useful way of making a positive identification. As technology and AI advance the use of these biometrics will also advance.

**Fig. (4.12).**  Keystroke dynamics. Source: from Rodgers [4].

AI and biometrics can be combined to make keystroke dynamics more precise and a dependable typing pattern recognition technology. AI systems can track information regarding how people type and the time interval between two keys for the most exercised keys to identify individuals.

As these types of biometrics are used for privacy and information protection purposes the level of fraud begins to increase. People will find ways to beat the system and pretending to be someone they are not to be able to get into certain databases. There are three different categories that tie into authentication factors, something you know, something you have, and lastly something you are. Something you "know" can be as simply as knowing someone's passwords, or username to something more complex like personal information. Security questions are now being used more frequently and if someone knows some personal information, they might be able to guess the answer to the security question. Something you "have" can be like a credit card or a debit card to be able to access the funds within that account. Something you "are," which is tied into biometrics with using certain features that only that individual has. These can be things like their fingerprint, voice recognition and many more. These feature types can be more protective but will not assure that information will not be stolen, therefore a combination of the three types should be used to help keep information safe.

Biometrics can be applied in any type of environment and are used for the benefit of the public. A great example where using biometrics will benefit both a customer and a vendor would be in a warehouse. A warehouse is used to store valuable goods that can widely range in prices. The use of biometrics in a warehouse can help with security, protecting the valuable goods. Any type of warehouse has some type of security such as a security guard that patrols the property where the warehouse is located. Some other type of security examples are cameras to monitor the activity outside and inside the warehouse and some type of fence to help protect the valuables. Some other common types of security a warehouse might have is an alarm system. This alarm system can be a pin pad where a code is entered or a card key that will be paired up with a card key reader to activate or deactivate the alarm system. The primary goal of the vendors that hold their merchandise in a warehouse is to keep unauthorized personnel out of the warehouse. Unauthorized personnel will be there for one common reason and that is to take merchandise that does not belong to them. For vendors to not lose out on their goods they have to implement good security features.

More to the point, Mastercard has 2 billion cards in use in more than 210 countries and territories. Further, Mastercard processes 165 million transactions per hour, implementing machine-learning algorithms and employing 1.9 million rules to investigate each transaction. AI technology allows this to occur very rapid in a matter of nanoseconds [7].

Moreover, the transactions are ingested by the algorithms inspect items such as the cardholder's buying habits, geographic location and travel patterns, along with real-time data on card usage. Algorithms are used to address the following questions. What are they trying to buy? Where are they are trying to buy it? What else have they bought in the same day? In addition, each transaction is scrutinized in terms of the rules that is associated to what a valid transaction would appear like and what appearances reflect fraudulent transaction.

Mastercard is progressively exhausting AI in conjunction with biometrics. Biometrics such as fingerprint, iris and facial recognition are as tools to authenticate the identity of card users. For example, the Mastercard Identity Check service permits online shoppers to authenticate a purchase by touching the screen of a smartphone or by merely presenting their faces to the device and blinking (*i.e.*, a concept sometimes referred to as "selfie pay").

Furthermore, Mastercard is using technology that identifies and verifies users based on their online interactions' behavior, which cannot be replicated by a third party [7]. For example, the technology considers how individual users hold a device, the way they swipe it and tap it, and the pressure they put on the screen.

Machine learning is used to build that profile, and it continuously builds that profile over time. Machine learning apparatuses can acknowledge it is you from your signature. In cases in which a user's biometrics do not match the profile established by machine learning, AI steps in and stops the transaction.

## EXAMPLE 1: EXPEDIENT ALGORITHMIC PATHWAY APPLIED TO STABLE AND UNSTABLE ENVIRONMENTS

Fraud risk is an internal control system that protects the mechanisms of the audit. These fraud risk assessment models are a resource to help for the internal fraud specially in audit. Ethics and fraud have a really close relationship with audit helping understand the connection with audit. First if to gather all of the information and in this case in the inventory management department then identify the risks that can be found looking at the inappropriate journal entries or reports and if they are any unusual things in the expenses. Determine if they are a huge risk based on the frequency of the reports and identify also the ineffective cases. Lastly respond with the fraud investigators and auditors to handle fraudulent situations.

The use of biometrics combined with fraud security systems already in place can assist to decrease the number of individuals that access the warehouse without permission. Some common types of biometrics that can be used for security measures include fingerprint recognition, iris scan, gait recognition, face recognition and even voice recognition. Depending on the amount of value of the goods stored in the warehouse will influence the type of biometric tool that can be utilized for security. If the value of the goods stored at the warehouse is high, then it is apropos to spend a high amount on the security. On the other hand, if the value of the goods stored at the warehouse is inexpensive, then it is not likely an organization will spend a great deal of money to purchase biometric tools. For example, assume that a warehouse is holding the inventory of a grocery store or a retailer where the amount per piece is very low then it might not be worth spending a lot of money on biometrics to increase the security. On the contrary, If the warehouse is storing inventory that is very expensive such as luxury automobiles, special parts for machinery or something as valuable as confidential information then it is worth spending money on biometrics to increase the security. The most affordable biometric that exists currently is fingerprint recognition, fingerprint recognition, which can be used to identify and verify someone's identity. Fingerprint recognition is very affordable since it is a small portable machine that can be easily moved around and does not require a big system. The process requires everyone's fingerprints to be stored into a database, once a comprehensive database is constructed, then when a person finger is scanned, it will either match it or not match it to a fingerprint already in the database. This biometric does not require deep learning, such as determining to find more algorithms or performing more research beyond the database employed in the system. Nonetheless, the biometric tool can provide deep learning methodology within the information it has stored in the database. One of the weakness in this system is that this biometric can be easily fooled by taking someone's fingerprint and pretending to be someone else.

Next, other biometrics tools become more complicated, which can result in a hike in price. A very effective biometric is the iris scan, this biometric will have the person glance into a camera that will then scan the iris and compare it to the previous iris scans in the database. This type of biometric is not that easily fooled and, therefore becomes more effective when it comes to positively identifying a person.

Fingerprint and iris scans biometrics can be operationalized in an Expedient Algorithmic Pathway system since there is only pattern recognition from the person's iris being matched with an iris scan located in the database. That is, the fingerprint or iris image is already recorded in the system; therefore, it will either match or not match the fingerprint or iris scan. Once a person scans his/her fingerprint or iris, the database system will suggest approval based on the records or not approve it if there is no match. Hence, it will be a complete match or be denied entirely.

The use of biometrics for the security in a warehouse could lean towards a type one error rather than a type two error. It does not matter how much time or money is spent into various types of biometrics since there will always be a possibility for these two types of errors. There should be planning to recognize the two types of errors to determine how much will be tolerated for each type of error. In the case of a type one error would be considered rejecting the entrance of an authorized personnel. A type two error would be accepting the entrance to un-authorized personnel. The purpose of integrating biometrics into an AI warehouse security system would be to not allow unauthorize people from entering the warehouse. Therefore, it would not make sense to lean towards a type two error since that would allow someone in the warehouse who does not belong in there. For example, if the margin of error is ninety-five percent based on a type one error and five percent based on a type two error. The unwanted error should be limited as much as possible considering the budget for the biometric, but a ninety-five and five percent based in a good allocation for a low and high budget biometric.

The decision-tree for the biometrics used in warehouse security does not replace existing security but can work as a two-factor authentication. Therefore, regular security will stay in place to help correctly identify authorized personnel and the biometric can be utilized to verify the identification of the personnel. The decision tree will start with a simple task to see if the person attempting to enter the warehouse premise is authorized or un-authorized, this will branch out into two simple answers, other yes or no (see Fig. **4.11**). If this person is identified as un-authorized personnel, then the door or gate to enter the warehouse will not open. The other option is yes, if this person was identified as authorized there needs to be further investigation, how was this person identified. If the identification occured through regular security measures, it requires to verification with a biometric, if it is not verified with a biometric the gate or door will not open once again. If it is verified with a biometric and the result is a match, the door or gate will open, permitting access to the personnel. If the biometric does not match any fingerprint or iris scan in the system, the personnel will be labeled as un-authorized personnel even though the security proved otherwise. Therefore, the door will not open again. The result is that it will always need to be a match with the biometric tool system for the person to gain access into the warehouse. The utilization of a biometrics tool as a second verification of identity will provide the best result to keep un-authorized personnel outside of the warehouse. The application of the biometric tool will start-off in a straightforward manner for any type of warehouse with for example, fingerprint and/or iris recognition. Different types of warehouses will be able to afford this biometric and as time passes by, they will decide whether there is a need to upgrade the biometric AI system into something more elaborate.

As technology advances, the use of biometrics tools will also advance. Biometrics tools integrated into an AI system is flexible and cost effective to be applied at anywhere. Although, some biometrics tools may be more complicated than others; however, they can help reduce the amount of fraud that happens in a workplace. These biometrics can take different forms by applying information available and coming to a decision weighting many factors. Fig. **(4.13)** is an illustration of a general biometric tool integrated in an AI system based upon the Expedient Algorithmic Pathway.

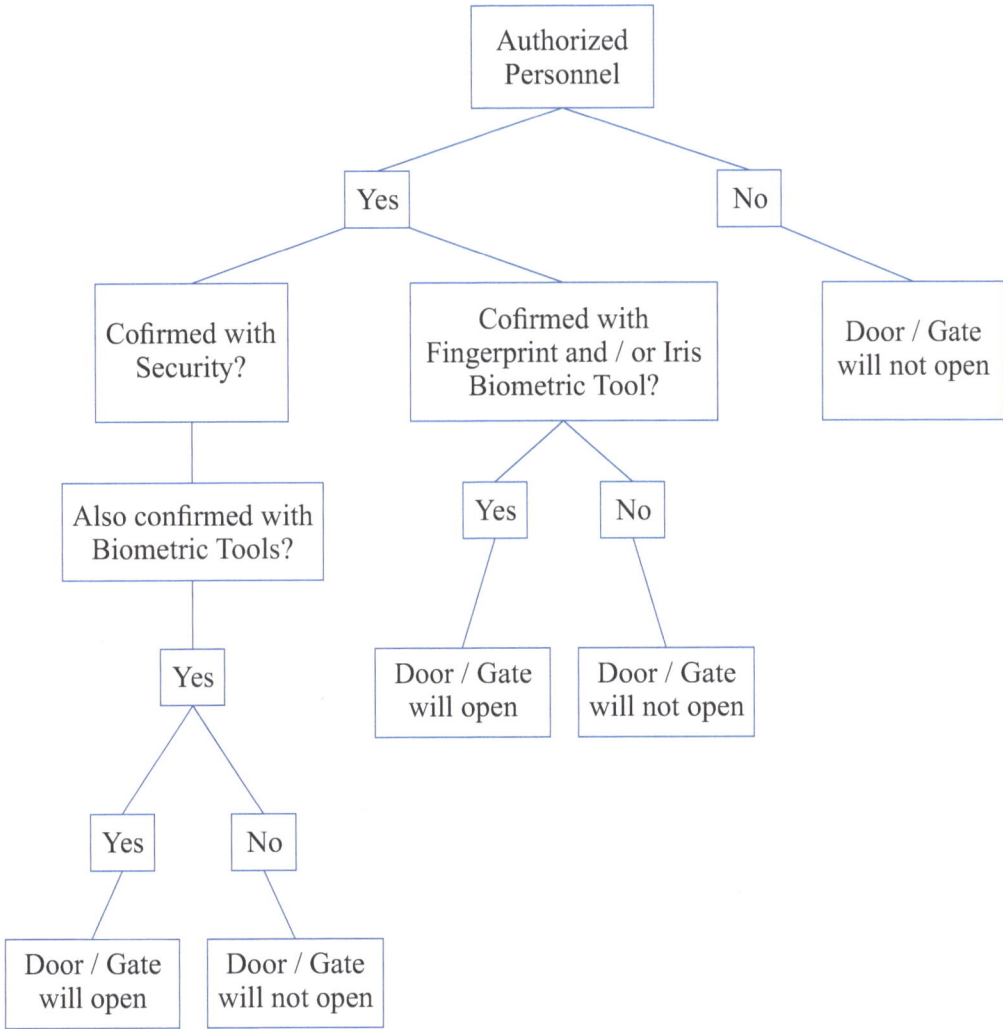

**Fig. (4.13).**  Personnel authorizing biometric. Source: Adopted by students and author.

## Example 2: Expedient Algorithmic Pathway applied Vault Doors

Fraud entails intentional deception by a fraudster for their personal benefit and to the detriment of a victim. The victim can either be another individual or it can also be an organization. To commit a fraudulent act, three components must exist: (1) opportunity, (2) pressure, and (3) rationalization. These components are often depicted in the form of a "Fraud Triangle", which is shown below (Fig. **4.14**). Proper analysis of the Fraud Triangle and the Throughput Model, along with the utilization of biometric data can deter fraud, reduce costs, promote efficiency, and enhance accuracy.

## The Fraud Triangle

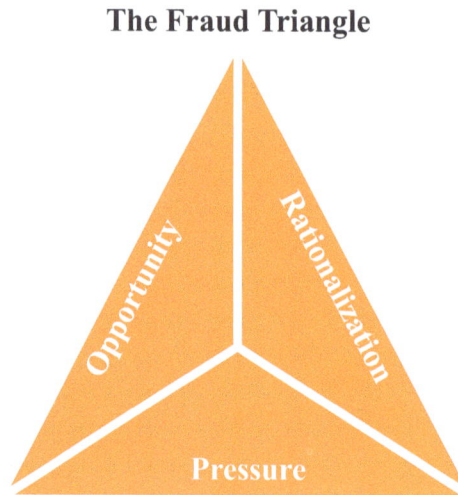

**Fig. (4.14).**  Source: Rodgers [5].

To commit fraud, individuals must have the *opportunity* to commit a crime along with the perception that they will not be caught. Often the opportunity for fraud exists due to weak internal controls or lack of adequate supervision. The opportunity leg of the Fraud Triangle aligns with the "information" component of the Throughput Model. Auditors are particularly interested in analyzing whether there are opportunities for fraud during their audit and search for information indicating whether there is a potential for fraud to prevent losses to an organization. Biometrics is a form of information that can be utilized to strengthen internal controls. An organization's management team must ensure that adequate processes, procedures, and controls are enforced to deter fraud.

The second leg of the Fraud Triangle is *"pressure,"* which alludes to that something occurring in a fraudster's life must push them to commit the fraud. Pressure may come in the form of the inability to meet debt obligations, the inability to meet basic needs, or the desire to obtain a certain level of social status. Pressure aligns closely with both the Perception and Information components of the Throughput Model. To combat the Pressure to commit fraud, an organization should promote a culture that makes employees feel like they are part of the entity. The organization may consider offering free lunches, provide on-site gym access, or guarantee pay raises at the end of the year. Auditors may collect information about employees concerning previous errors made on the job or gather information about criminal activity. Auditors may also recommend that employees in jobs with the potential for high losses resulting from fraud be bonded as a condition of employment.

The final leg of the Fraud Triangle is *"rationalization,"* which indicates that fraudsters justify their criminal behavior to make themselves feel better about committing the crime. An individual may justify a crime by believing that it is their only way out of a bad situation, fraudsters may plan to return what they have stolen, or the fraudster may believe that they are entitled to the stolen property due to the lack of a promotion or raise. Rationalization most closely aligns with the "judgment" component of the Throughput Model. With proper internal controls, fraud should not occur within an organization, and biometrics are essential component in modern day security.

To illustrate how an organization can use the Throughput Model, Fraud Triangle, and biometrics to combat fraud, will be analyzed using the Expedient Algorithm Pathway as an example. The Expedient Algorithm Pathway (P→D) represents the following: If an organization utilizes this algorithm, it believes that a person's values will affect decision choice in a decision-making process. To combat the pressure to commit fraud, an organization may offer tuition assistance, continuing education courses, and subsidized daycare to incentivize employees to not commit fraud. If these incentives do not deter all employees from committing fraud, information measures may assist in stopping the fraud. To protect cash located in a safe, an organization may implement iris recognition biometrics to access the safe room and palm print recognition to open the safe. Furthermore, the organization may require that access to cash within the safe always be performed under dual control. Further, it is important that the organization implements tight internal controls, promote an organizational culture of integrity, and ensure that the tone at the top discourages fraudulent behavior. Organizations utilizing the Expedient Algorithm Pathway believe that it is likely that a correct decision choice will be made by following the order of the algorithm (Fig. **4.15**).

What happens if the biometric authentication system makes an error in properly identifying a person? There are two main types of performance metrics: type 1 errors (false accept rate or false match rate) and type 2 errors (false reject rate or false non-match rate). Type 1 errors occur when a biometric system incorrectly authenticates the identity of an individual and grants them access to what the system is protecting. Type 2 errors are opposite in that the biometric system rejects the identity of an individual that has authority to access what is being protected. In our decision tree example above, the cash inventory held within the safe is very valuable. It would be preferable to have a type 2 error where an authorized person is denied access to the cash. A type 1 error could be detrimental to the financial stability and reputation of the credit union in a situation where an unauthorized individual accesses the safe and takes all the money. Type 1 errors may be preferable in situations where high value items are not at stake and occasional unauthorized access is preferable to inefficient processing. An example of this would be access to a movie theater. A movie ticket is not an expensive item, and the movie theater will not go out of business if an unauthorized individual sneaks into a movie without paying. However, the movie theater may not be able to sustain business if it implements complicated security systems for customers to access the theater rooms and it becomes inconvenient for customers to watch their movies.

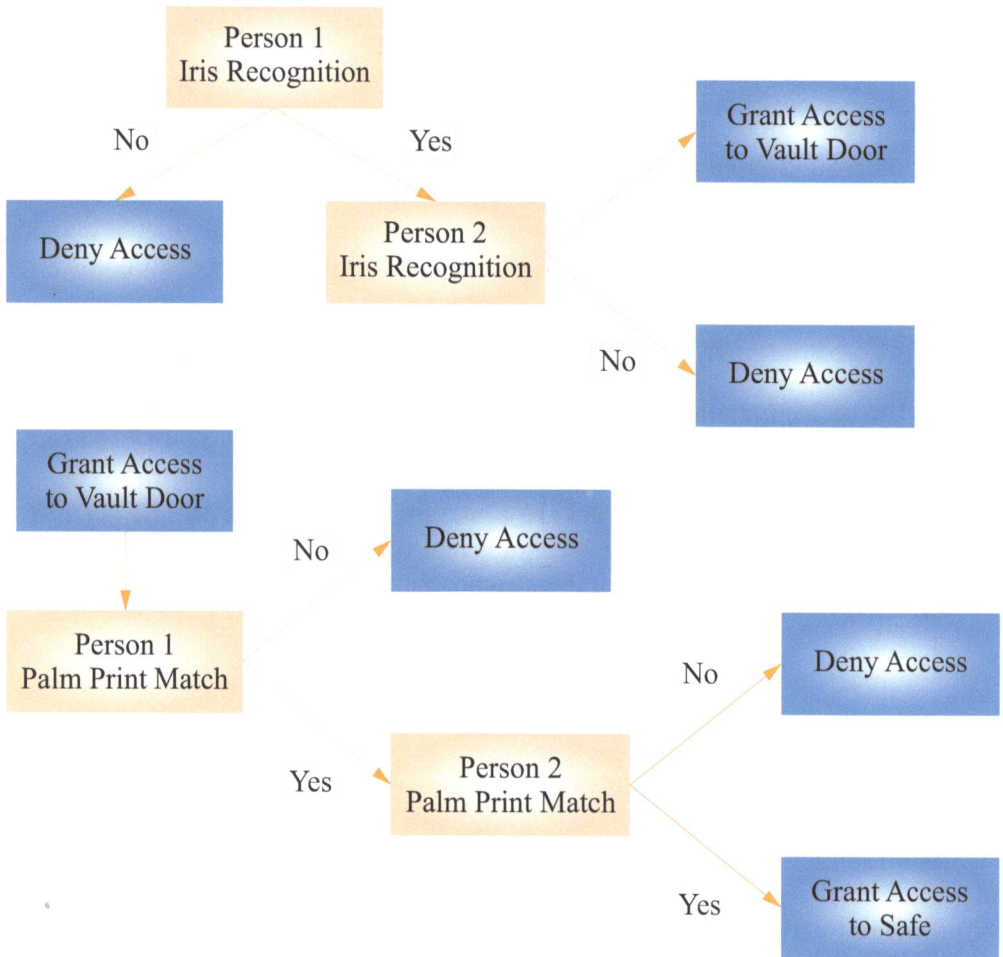

**Fig. (4.15).** Source: From students.

AI generated biometrics using algorithms, machine learning, deep learning and biometrics has become integral to assess large amounts of data created by society. This data is generated from both traditional and non-traditional sources and can be presented in a structured or unstructured manner. Society uses artificial intelligence for planning, decision-making, problem-solving, reasoning, and learning, and humans are unable to perform these functions as efficiently as artificial intelligence due to big data's qualities of volume, velocity, and variety. To better assess the information provided to AI systems and to make better decisions, algorithms should be developed using the Throughput Model and the appropriate algorithms. This will help increase accuracy and eliminate potential human bias. Artificial intelligence will continue to evolve to assist us in all aspects of society, including governance, healthcare, education, and scientific advancement.

## CONCLUSION

AI is a subset of the computer science field in which machines are created to function with human-like traits through use of complex algorithms. These machines learn and adapt from experiences created by utilizing large amounts of data without human intervention. AI human-like traits includes planning, decision-making, problem-solving, reasoning, and learning, and machines can perform these functions more efficiently and timely compared to a human's ability. The Expedient Algorithmic Pathway (P→D) examples explored the implementation of AI benefiting from machine learning, deep learning, and big data. Further, this conversation continued along the lines of how AI and biometrics are being utilized along with the Throughput Model to combat fraud.

An algorithm is a set of specific instructions given to a computer to solve a set of problems. It is often described as being much like a recipe in that the instructions are given in a step-by-step format. Simple algorithms can be linked together to perform more complex tasks, forming artificial neural networks within artificial intelligence models. Algorithms are most often used in mathematical operations, such as performing calculations and data processing. For example, instead of a human taking several days reading a five-hundred-page paper in search of the word "regulatory," a word processing system utilizes algorithms to find the word every time it is used in the paper within seconds. It is important to maintain the integrity of algorithm inputs because computers follow instructions very well. If the inputs are incorrect, the computer will follow the algorithm exactly, leading to an incorrect output.

Throughput Modeling is a decision-making structure that is used by businesses to assist with better decision choices, as well as in artificial intelligence modeling.

Decisions are made using the model to comprehend and predict the best path forward. The model consists of four (4) components: 1) perception ("P"), 2) information ("I"), 3) judgement ("J"), and 4) decision choice ("D"), and these components are combined into six (6) different decision-making algorithms.

Perception involves viewing the problem to be solved through the lens of one's own viewpoint or through the culmination of a person's unique education, training, and other experiences. Usually this involves assessing the problem for patterns that mimic experiences recalled from memory. The information component consists of new external data and information that is gathered to assist a decision maker with determining a solution to a problem. It is important for the decision maker to assess the quality of the information by determining its reliability and relevancy to the problem at hand. The decision maker then uses judgement to process both their perceptions and the new information together to formulate a decision choice or solution to the problem. Often the decision choice is also impacted by the cost and risk to the organization and its assets.

In this chapter, the **PD Expedient Algorithmic Pathway** is discussed as the most efficient decision-making pathway since it is the quickest route from perception to decide. Perception is how we analyze or frame the environment based on our own experiences. That is why, our emotions and personal biases play an important role in this pathway and our lives. This pathway is characterized by a limited period to influence a decision. Most of the decision using this pathway are based on personal experiences that allows us to reinforce a strategy.

Furthermore, the Expedient Pathway, the **PD** pathway, may be the only pathway available if an individual is planning to make decisions quickly, without the benefit of information. **Perception** is how we view every encounter and interaction based on previous experiences. In this pathway our personal biases can quickly influence our decision-making process. This pathway is characterized by a limited time period to influence a decision and the disregarding of available informational sources. Many of our decisions using this pathway are based on knowledge we already have stored in our mind, and educational expertise we have already learned.

Machine Learning is a branch of the AI field in which systems produce outputs based upon learned information rather than solving for a predetermined result. It learns by gathering enormous amounts of data in a quest for establishing patterns. Those patterns are used to establish a model and new information is compared to the patterns within the model. As more information is gathered, the model is validated with consistent decisions and results. These models are built either through Supervised Learning or Unsupervised Learning. With Supervised

Learning, computers are given training data detailing correlations between patterns and expected outputs. For example, training data could be offered to decrypt between an octopus and a spider. If the animal has eight legs, swims, and is found in water, the expected result is an octopus. However, if the animal has eight legs, crawls, and is not living in water, the expected result is a spider. Nevertheless, unsupervised Learning, does not provide information regarding which patterns result in what outputs. Instead, the inputs are presented, and the computer deduces patterns and outputs on its own. In the previous example, pictures of octopuses and spiders would be furnished. On the other hand, the computer would separate out the spiders from the octopuses on its own grounded upon identified similarities and differences in the photos.

Deep Learning is a more advanced form of machine learning in that it utilizes artificial neural networks (ANNs) to learn from large amounts of data and was developed to mimic the neocortex of the human brain. ANNs are comprised of layers of differing combinations of the six Throughput Model Algorithms, much like the layers of neurons within our brains. Deep learning, like machine learning, identifies complex patterns from swaths of data to provide solutions efficiently to problems. Nonetheless, deep learning utilizes its neural networks to solve problems from data repetitiously and can change its "neurons" slightly based upon changes it receives within the data. These changes are made by the data and not by the algorithms themselves. It does this through acquiring new information, which is then processed through perception in the mind, and ultimately converted to knowledge (*i.e.*, P←→I). Knowledge becomes part of the unique education, experiences, and training of perception. Stored perception and information can be analyzed and restructured an infinite number of times within the ANNs when new data is processed. Thus, deep learning allows for model modifications within its deep neural network layers, if data is gathered that contradicts previously established patterns, hence the notion that the computer is learning. Deep learning also has the ability to analyze diverse and unrelated data to solve problems that machines learning would not be able to perform on its own. Given the amount of data that is generated every day by society, the advancement of deep learning has become progressively essential in efficiently processing information accurately and timely. Common examples of deep learning include virtual assistant like Siri or Alexa that use complex neural network systems to recognize the nuances of language. Deep learning is also used for autonomous cars that must recall previous experiences within its vast neural network to navigate unfamiliar roadways and traffic situations.

# REFERENCES

[1]     W. Rodgers, *Process Thinking: Six pathways to successful decision making.* iUniverse, Inc.: NY, 2006.

[2]     C. McClelland, "The Difference Between Artificial Intelligence, Machine Learning, and Deep Learning", Retrieved from: https://medium.com/iotforall/the-difference-between-artificial-intellig-nce-machine-learning-and-deep-learning-3aa67bff5991

[3]     W. Rodgers, *Artificial Intelligence in a Throughput Model: Some Major Algorithms?* Science Publications (CRC Press, Taylor and Francis Group): Florida, 2020.

[4]     W. Rodgers, *E-commerce and biometric issues addressed in a Throughput Model.* Nova Publication: Hauppauge, NY, 2010.

[5]     W. Rodgers, *Biometric and Auditing Issues Addressed in a Throughput Model.* Information Age Publishing, Inc.: Charlotte, NC, 2012.

[6]     M. Kurowski, A. Sroczyński, G. Bogdanis, and A. Czyżewsk, "An Automated Method for Biometric Handwritten Signature Authentication Employing Neural Networks", *Electronics (Basel),* vol. 10, no. 4, p. 456, 2021.
[http://dx.doi.org/10.3390/electronics10040456]

[7]     J. Morss, *Outsmarting Fraudsters with AI and Biometrics.,* 2018. Retrieve from https://www.cio.com/article/3326549/outsmarting-fraudsters-with-ai-and-biometrics.html

[8]     A.A. Dongare, and R.D. Ghongade, "Artificial Intelligence Based Bank Cheque Signature Verification System", *International Research Journal of Engineering and Technology,* vol. 3, no. 1, pp. 167-171, 2016. [IRJET].

# CHAPTER 5

# The Ruling Guide Algorithmic Pathway

Artificial intelligence is no match for natural stupidity.

---Anonymous

Computers bootstrap their own offspring, grow so wise and incomprehensible that their communiques assume the hallmarks of dementia: unfocused and irrelevant to the barely-intelligent creatures left behind. And when your surpassing creations find the answers you asked for, you can't understand their analysis and you can't verify their answers. You have to take their word on faith.

---Peter Watts

Our ultimate objective is to make programs that learn from their experience as effectively as humans do. We shall ... say that a program has common sense if it automatically deduces for itself a sufficient wide class of immediate consequences of anything it is told and what it already knows.

---John Mccarthy

**Abstract**

The Ruling Guide Algorithmic Pathway (P→J→D) elucidates a decision-making process from perception through judgment to decision choice. This algorithmic pathway is portrayed as a perceptual framing of the decision in which a person or organization may have biases and strategies, time pressures, a rejection of new informational sources, and a certain degree of expertise. This algorithmic pathway is correspondingly helpful in handling situations from both stable and unstable environments.

**Keywords:** Artificial Intelligence, Behavioral Biometrics, Blockchain, Contracts and Liability, Data Privacy, Decision choice, Decision tree, Deep learning, Fingerprint recognition, Fraud, Human Rights, Identification, Intellectual Property, Judgment, Machine learning, Perception, Physiological Biometrics, Ruling Guide Algorithmic Pathway, Verification, Voice recognition, XBRL.

## INTRODUCTION

The purpose of this chapter is to analyze the ruling guide algorithmic pathway that can be utilized by AI tools. Technology employing AI can mimic some of the tasks that people can perform. Such tasks included: decision-making, recognition, and perception. Artificial intelligence technologies can be from computer systems to robotics. The purpose of these technologies is to get it to think and rational, in order to solve problems similar to a human as closely as possible. The Ruling Guide Pathway is based on perception, judgment, and decision choice. Perception includes personal biases and experiences, time pressures, rejection of information sources, and the individual making the decision, usually has some experience. In the ruling pathway, the framing of the problem, the perception, drives all of the analysis, the judgment. This pathway is typically used by individuals who are not experts. Like the Expedient Algorithmic Pathway, the Ruling Pathway also eliminates available information sources.

The **P→J→D** pathway implies our framing of the problem **(P)** drives how and what is analyzed, **(J)** before deciding. Much of what we believe contributes to influence the items we deem important for our analysis. Search patterns can also affect our analysis. It is important to note that this pathway plays down or eliminates available information sources. We must understand time pressures, problematic information, unstable environmental conditions may affect the available information use in handling a particular problem situation (see Fig. **5.1** below).

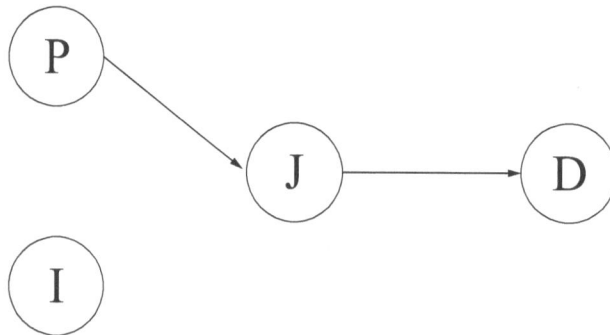

**Fig. (5.1).** P→J→D algorithmic pathway is from perception to judgment to decision choice. Source: Rodgers [2].

At the core of AI is a tool based on learning and adapting to new data based on software. The ruling guide algorithmic pathway is a response to this uncertainty, many legitimate questions need to be addressed to assess and control the risks related to an AI solution. Issues pertaining to the ruling guide algorithmic pathway include:

## Human Rights

If the dataset is biased at the outset, what happens with the output coming from the algorithm? Will certain groups/populations be disadvantaged? What will the consequences be for an organization and the individuals?

## Contracts and Liability

Most organizations cannot possibly assume all risks related to their product (particularly the unpredictable ones). Therefore, the ruling guide algorithmic pathway is a guide to draft a fair contract between entities.

## Data Privacy

The ruling guide algorithmic pathway provides a guiding light for confidential or sensitive information. This algorithm also provides a gateway to making sure that information is useful for the product, but also protects the owners of said information.

## Intellectual Property

Organizations are becoming difficult to value reliably and accurately due to the economy becoming increasingly intangible. Many of the criticisms of traditional methods result from its inability to value these intellectual property or knowledge assets [1]. AI technology is influencing the complexity in production processes and products. Stock market valuations are frequently several times higher than book values. This gap is viewed as evidence that the effects of AI technology and knowledge are very imperative to corporate and individual's wealth.

Since AI algorithms are highly collaborative, built upon the prior research and development, the ruling guide algorithmic pathway helps to strike a balance on how we balance the competing concerns of the public good and market advantages. It sheds light on how to increase collaboration between academia and industry. Finally, this algorithm is a start on how organizations can address the private legal concerns of creating intellectual property as well as the valuation [1].

The Ruling Guide Pathway is based on the specific rules, guidelines or procedures used by the people making the decisions. For example, in the case of auditors use the International Auditing Standards (IAS) or the Generally Accepted Auditing Standards (GAAS) as the guidelines to conduct an audit on a company's financial statements. In this pathway, it is assumed that the rule governs the process even though the provided information may paint a different story. In other words, rules are over substance (*i.e.*, information). The lack of relevant or reliable information forces the auditor to rely on rules to make decisions. GAAS do not provide hard rules, they provide subjective guidelines which allow auditors to tailor the audit procedures based on every specific client. This is where the auditor's perception of a rule, combined with his/her judgement of the situation results in a decision.

A straightforward example of this algorithmic pathway is the analysis of the quality of an internal control system by an auditor. Internal controls are complicated to implement especially for small business which do not have sufficient resources. The information an auditor is able to get from a client depends on their systems, if the system on hand is too basic and does not provide enough detail, and the information it provides is contradictory or unreliable, the auditor chooses to ignore that information. Inherent risk factors may come into play, like some financial transactions may require complex calculations that make it more likely for there to be material misstatements. Without having reliable information, the auditor can only use his perception and judgment to come to a decision. AI additions that could prevent issues of internal control, especially for small businesses, are using simple software that standardizes the processes. Some clients give the auditors access to their software, so they can evaluate if the procedures were performed correctly. The Ruling Guide Pathway relies on the auditor's experience and analysis of the client, to give an accurate opinion on the financial statements and internal controls.

Employing this algorithmic pathway, relies on perception, as rules, guidelines, and procedures are part of the framing in this mode. In other words, **P→J→D** depicted as the "ruling guide pathway," implies that we first frame the situation that will determine how we analyze the problem before making a decision choice. Nonetheless, biases may also play an incalculable role in this pathway, such as personal, social, and political heuristics can change what we believe the utilized procedures (especially internally generated) should be framed in this pathway.

## EXAMPLE 1 –RULING GUIDE ALGORITHMIC PATHWAY

For the past 5 to 10 years, AI has evolved rapidly and is affecting many industries. Currently, AI technology has helped many businesses detect fraud and discrepancies. AI technology has assisted auditing firms to better uncover fraud.

In the following sections, this section will discuss the general functions of the algorithms, big data, machine learning, and deep learning, and how everything is related to the Ruling Guide Pathway. This section will also discuss how these functions may assist audit firms detect fraud. Additionally, this section examines the difference between machine learning and deep learning technology. The analysis of AI is an important issue to understand since this technology will continue to evolve in the future and will change how organizations conduct their operations. A critical concept of AI is algorithms.

## Machine Learning

The Ruling Guide Algorithmic Pathway, P→J→D, can be used in a machine learning technology. Machine learning is an AI technology constructed with algorithms, that have rules set to learn and adapt for data. Machine learning technology has two categories: supervised and unsupervised. These two categories can help detect fraud within the business, by learning patterns of the accounts and behaviors of people. Supervised learning is a train technology that uses its input data to checks new data in order to determine new patterns. Unsupervised learning is when it learns by itself different patterns, just using its input data.

When the machine learning technology learns a new pattern, it can change its algorithm. The change can happen when it finds further information related to its input data. Machine learning can be programmed to modify and adapt to new data since new data may be continuously changing. Big data is very complicated whereby researchers have attempted to find ways to collect and analyze data. Currently, AI can manage and analyze data faster than humans can. It is essential for humans to be able to interpret this data. In another note, one more artificial intelligence technology is deep learning.

## Deep Learning

Unlike machine learning, deep learning uses neural networks techniques. Neural networks AI technology works similar to a human brain. Deep learning does not follow an algorithm like machine learning, because it works side by side with perception (P) and information (I). It works together going back and forward trying to learn to make human-like decisions.

One more difference between machine learning and deep learning is that deep learning can create more actions with the input data than machine learning. Deep learning creates a lot of small calculations that allows it to recognize images. Machine learning would not be able to identify a picture because it would be too complex for the algorithm. Deep learning data can be used to learn about image recognition, called biometrics. Biometrics is the technology used to check the individual identification and verification, by using the physical measurements and the characteristics of an individual. The physical measurement could be the measurement of the gap in inches of a step an individual takes as it is walking. The characteristics of an individual could be fingerprint recognition, even body odor recognition. Deep learning technology can be used for businesses to verify work-personal faster and identify those that do not work there.

Deep learning, biometrics, can also be used to identify fingerprints, DNA, keystroke dynamics, along with other classifications. These classifications are more secure than having an identification card. The fingerprints can work for both identification and verification process. First, multiple fingerprint samples are taken from the individual to get process; then it gets stored in a database. When the individual wants to access the system, a fingerprint is required. Then it is process and match with a reference from the database. This process decreases fraud within the workplace because it only allows the individual that have their fingerprints in the system to access it.

## Biometric Technology

Biometrics technology is part of AI along with its subsets of machine learning and deep learning apparatuses. Biometrics is the study of the measurement of the body and the characteristics of a human. Biometrics are used for security purpose to identify individuals. There are three different types of security systems that organizations can install. The first type to identify a person is with something they know. The second type is with something they have. The final way to identify a person is with something they are [3].

Biometric technology relates to two forms of recognition: identification and verification. In identification, the procedure of this system is searching for the individuals' information in a database to find who this person is. For verification, the procedure seeks to confirm who the individual says they are. Biometrics technology uses algorithms and deep learning, and it separates the technologies measurements between physiological and behavioral.

The relationship between biometric and fraud will be discussed in relationship with the Throughout Model. It will explain, how an organization can come up with a decision of what is the best biometric technology to implement. The organization will be able to analyze and understand what changes are needed to decrease fraud in the workplace.

As stated previously, biometric is the study of the measurement of the body and the characteristics of a human. Biometric technology mainly used for security purposes; it is used in to identify individuals. There are three different types of security system that can be used to identify individuals.

The first type of security system is the identification of an individual with an intangible pass, something they know, that the individual can remember, such as passwords or PIN. This security system works if the individual does not forget the password or PIN. Individuals can make up the password and PIN, based on personal information; example, the password or PIN can be their date of birth.

The issue is if the PIN is this simple and if there is anybody that knows this person date of birth, they will be able to access the system. Now, what if the individual uses a more complicated password. The issue here is that the individual may forget her/his password, and then would require security personnel to assist with identifying her/him.

The second type of security system is a tangible object, such as an identification card or smart card. These cards can be scanned to enter a secure facility such as building, office, bank, *etc.* The issue with these tangible objects is that they can be lost, borrowed, or stolen. Another problem is that security technology has been improving over the years making identify fraud difficult; nonetheless, these cards are still open to falsification.

The third type of security system is using biometric technology; this technology uses the characteristics of an individual such as face and speaker recognition; which are just two of many biometric technologies used. The example in this section using a Ruling Guide Algorithmic Pathway will get more into detail later regarding the different types of biometric technology. That is, the example will employ a rule-type system by integrating AI biometric tools. Further, biometric technology is the best and most suitable form of security out of the three security systems. Biometrics cannot be forgotten or lost since every individual is unique. For organizations to improve safety, a combination of two of the three security systems can be done.

## Recognition: Identification *vs.* Verification

Biometric technology uses two kinds of recognition: identification and verification [3, 4]. A technology that uses identification it is recognizing "Who is this person?" The system has to search the database looking through a list to find the individual. While verification, recognizes "Is this the person who they claim to be?" The system will search to find if this individual is who they say they are. If the data does not match, it will reject the individual.

A biometric technology that uses both identification and verification is fingerprint technology. In the fingerprint identification process, samples are taken, processes and then kept in the database. To identify an individual, a sample is taken, process, and searches through all the samples in the database until it comes up with a match. To verify an individual, is the same process but it does not have to search through all the samples, it just matches it. The fingerprint is telling the system who they are, and the system must match the fingerprint to verify it is the truth. It is a 1:1 matching, while identification is 1: N matching, (N = number of samples).

## THROUGHPUT MODELING ALGORITHMS AND FRAUD PREVENTION

Biometric technologies are made of algorithms from the Throughput Model. There are six different algorithms in the model. The algorithms are designed to solve all sort of problems. The Throughput Model consists of four concepts: perception (P), information (I), judgment (J), and decision choice (D), as shown in Fig. (**5.2**).

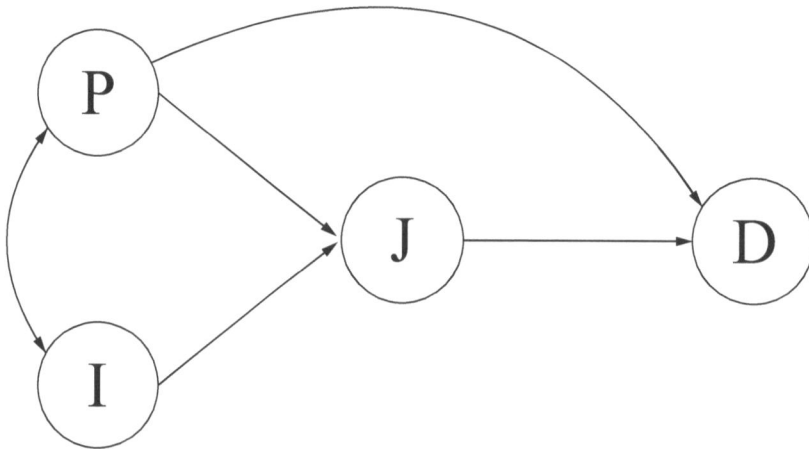

**Fig. (5.2).** Throughput model. Source: Biometric and Auditing Issues Addressed in a Throughput Model [4].

For AI technology to solve a problem, it must be given a process or procedures to follow, called algorithms. Algorithms are fundamental to AI technology. The previous chapters highlighted that there are six different sets of algorithms in artificial intelligence that consist of four concepts: perception (P), information (I), judgment (J), and decision choice (D). Below are the six different algorithms, represented as the Throughput Model.

1. **The Expedient Pathway P→D**
2. **The Ruling Guide Pathway P→J→D**
3. **The Analytical Pathway I→J→D**
4. **The Revisionist Pathway I→P→D**
5. **The Value Driven Pathway P→I→J→D**
6. **The Global Perspective Pathway I→P→J→D**

Each algorithm provides a different order of coming up with a decision choice. The concept of perception is based on data it knows by memory. The concept of information is based on the data that was put in, such as facts. Information is also based on big data, which hold a great volume of all sorts of data. In the concept of judgment, the data from perception and information is analyzed and used to come up with a decision choice. In the Throughput Model, in algorithms (1), the decision choice is only going to be based on the data from perception. In algorithm (5), the algorithm is going first to use the perception data and use it to relate it to the information (facts). Data gathered from perception and information; the concept judgment will exam it and make a decision. In algorithm (6), in this case, the algorithm is going to use the data from information first and then make a perception utilizing this data. A decision will be made, based on the judgment of the perception of the information. Depending on the customers' needs and the data entered, each of the six algorithms will choose the best choice. An AI technology that uses algorithms is machine learning.

Perception is based on memory and experience, while information on big data and facts. For judgment, the data collected from perception and information will be evaluated to concluded with a decision. The algorithms learn from incoming data, also known as deep learning. Deep learning is a big part of biometric technology because deep learning learns to adapt to new data. Before any organization decides which biometric technology to use, they should consider the above components.

## Biometric Technologies: Physiological *vs.* Behavioral

Biometric technologies are divided into two categories, physiological and behavioral. Physiological technology uses human body parts to identify the individual. Examples are fingerprint, iris scan, facial recognition, thermography, *etc.* Contrast, behavioral technology uses human movements and voice, such as voice recognition, gait, and keystroke dynamics. For these technologies, the individual will have to touch the machine or stand in front of a camera.

## Fraud and Biometrics

Fraud exists everywhere, and organizations have tried to eliminate this factor from their businesses. Fraud is when a person steals from the company to get some sort of gain, while the company takes a loss. Examples of fraud are false reports, awareness of false statements, theft of funds or assets, or the selling of information that can affect the organization.

In order for an individual to commit a fraudulent act, three components have to happen, called the Fraud Triangle (Rodgers,. The components are pressure/ incentives, opportunities, and attitudes/rationalization. Organizations must be aware of these components in orders to reduce fraud. Every organization is different and utilize different types of biometric technology to decrease fraud within the business. The Fraud Triangle and the Throughput Model can help determine what biometric technology to use to prevent fraud from the internal and external organization.

Pressure and incentives are when an individual is motivated to commit fraud caused by financial problems, addiction, even just for greed, *etc.* Pressure and incentives fall under perception (P) in the Throughput Model. Opportunity to commit fraud happens when there is weak or no internal control within the business. If there is no separation of duties or security system, an individual can easily commit fraud. Opportunity falls under information (I) in the Throughput Model. Fraud happens with attitudes and rationalization when individuals believe they deserve the money. Other justified they need it, or they are just borrowing it. These individuals make themselves believe they have the right to steals. Attitudes and rationalization fall under judgment (J) in the Throughput Model.

With the algorithms from the Throughput Model, an organization can decide what biometric technology to choose. An example: the Ruling Guide Algorithmic Pathway, P→J→D, can be depicted as the perception of pressure/incentives/opportunity→rationalization/attitudes (*i.e.,* embedded in judgment)→decision choice. First, you recognize that an employee has financial problems, perception (P), and perceive the company as having a weak internal control system. Next, you are going to come to a rationalization, (*i.e.,* judgment), that this individual may commit fraud. Therefore, you decide, (decision choice), to implement a biometric technology as operationalize by an AI algorithmic P→J→D system. For example, the company can implement facial recognition, fingerprint, and iris scan. These security systems can be placed to enter offices, inventory warehouse, or logins into the software.

In sum, the primary purpose of biometric technology is to identify individuals. Biometric technology uses two forms of recognition: identification and verification. The technology also separates the measurements into physiological and behavioral, as discussed above. Many organizations are now moving to biometric technology because it is more secure. As technology improves and gets better, the cost of these technologies will decrease making it more affordable.

In addition, an AI biometric technology system can assist in decreasing fraud within the workplace by implementing the technology in internal controls. The Throughput Model assists in representing the algorithmic pathway suitable for implementation of the technological software. Nonetheless, although biometric technology can strengthen and safeguard an organization's assets, ethical issues should be addressed regarding individuals' privacy rights.

## Decision Tree and Biometrics

The decision tree is a tool that helps show the possibilities and outcomes of an event or situation. The decision tree can be used for many things, but this report, it will be used to show how biometric security technology works.

Furthermore, a decision tree is a very distinctive kind of probability tree that empowers an individual or organization to make a decision choice regarding a particular type of process. For example, an organization may desire to select between producing item A or item B, or financing in selection 1, selection 2, or selection 3. The Throughput Model can be used to help the organization view the implementation of AI apparatuses.

For example, let's assume that a medical office desires to secure valuable information into a software system. The information is highly sensitive and if in wrong hands it can cause a significant embarrassment and create legal trouble. The medical office firm would have to design and develop a high-level security system that is inexpensive. The firm would like to establish an inexpensive security system by using two different biometric technologies. Furthermore, based on the Throughput Model the firm would use the Ruling Guide Algorithmic Pathway. This algorithmic pathway implies a procedure that authorizes access into the system, *e.g.*, medical doctors, nurses, and managers. This decision tree provides an example of a high-level security system using two different biometric technology, fingerprint recognition, and voice recognition based upon the P→J→D algorithmic pathway (see Fig. **5.3**).

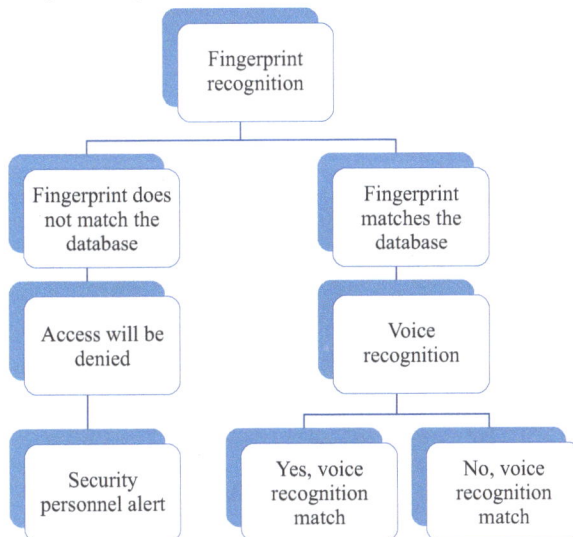

**Fig. (5.3).** Decision tree with two biometric tools. Source: student generated.

Fig. (**5.3**) illustrates the medical office firm decision on how using two different biometric technology works. The decision tree shows fingerprint recognition as its first biometric tool. If individuals want to access the software system based upon their authorization (P), they will have to provide their fingerprint by placing their right index finger on the device (see Fig. **5.4**). This event will create two judgment scenarios (J), matching or not matching. If the fingerprint does not match the database, access will be denied, and it will alert security personnel. Security personnel will go check to see who is trying to access the system and or do a verification check to see if "they are who they say they are." Once verified, the security personnel will allow the individual to continue to the next step.

**Fig. (5.4).**  Fingerprint biometric. From Rodgers [3].

If the fingerprint matches the system database, it will let the individual continue with the next step, voice recognition. With voice recognition, the individual will say a word or phases that will match the voice recognition database (see Fig. **5.5**). If the phases or voice do not match the database, security personnel will be alerted to check and verify. If it matches, the individual will have access to the software system (D).

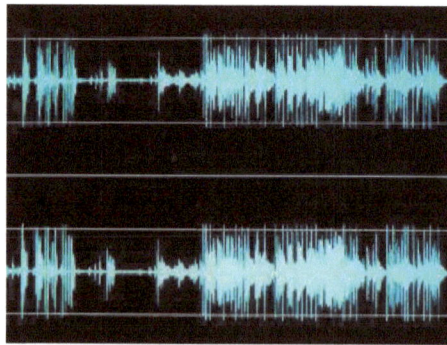

**Fig. (5.5).**  Voice (speaker) biometric. From Rodgers [3].

The fingerprint and voice recognition security systems are easy and inexpensive compared to other biometric technology. Unfortunately, this technology can get fooled; for example, the fingerprint recognition can get fooled by a mold of an individual's fingerprint and the voice recognition with a recording of the individual's voice. That is why having two biometric security systems, the fingerprint and voice recognition will keep important information safe.

## Type 1 and 2 Errors

This decision tree could have two types of errors, Type One, and Type Two. Type One error is when the authorized individuals get denied into the system. In this case, the partners, supervisors, and managers could get denied access even though they are authorized. Type Two is when the systems fail to deny unauthorized individuals, which means that it allows unauthorized individual access. For this reason, two biometric security technology is better than one. Going back to the example, if fingerprint recognition gets an error and allows an unauthorized individual access to the next step. The voice recognition could most likely stop the individual.

The Throughput Model conceptualization can be essential to select a biometric technology since it helps understand individuals' views in each situation. The decision tree model is made based on the Ruling Guide Algorithmic Pathway the biometric system. Having a strong internal control system provides patients, managers, and employees with a secure system. Organizations aspire for a secure internal control system to protect their asset and valuable documents from internal and external individuals or competitors that want to gain something from it. The biometric technology security systems help, but the organization must also implement and follow its policies and procedures (*e.g.*, separation of duties) to help prevent fraudulent activities in the workplace.

## EXAMPLE 2 –RULING GUIDE ALGORITHMIC PATHWAY

Managers and accountants perform an important role in business; from managing transactions to sorting out and processing financial reports in a form that supports decision making. Besides managing the large volumes of financial data in organizations, they need to ensure all the results are accurate, consistent, and timely delivered. This is where AI is very beneficial to an organization.

Combining AI with financial operations can enhance output quality by reducing human errors. Business applications have been built to using artificial to produce predictive models that get better with time. These applications also lead to an increase in sales from data regarding consumer behavior on a product. Chatbots are gradually replacing the human workforce in the financial sector. AI models can support adherence and related audits by analyzing reports alongside laws and flagging issues. This can be achieved using machine learning tools that read reports and perform trend analysis and identify outliers. Although AI has clear benefits, the realization of the technology in accounting functions can be quite challenging. A key risk is a resistance to change from people within an organization. They argue that the value of data generated by AI cannot be trusted compared to data from traditional financial systems. Other fears cited concerning converting non-financial data into reports are maintaining data security, data privacy, and the inability to have robust data management systems.

Machine learning requires the use of huge volumes of data to work effectively. The technology can analyze and learn from a variety of data and generate valuable information. Moreover, this data needs to be extracted, transformed, and stored appropriately and securely. In instances of improper data management or cybersecurity systems, the organizations may be at the risk of inaccurate insights, data breaches, and internet attacks. Smaller institutions may also be confronted with the problem of insufficient data to build models. Acclimating a system to be compatible with existing data can be very expensive and time-consuming. While these challenges pose a problem to accounting functions, there are ways to manage the risks that come with AI. Data quality and management are key to maintain the trust of the data from the beginning and believe that the insights generated thereafter are beneficial to the decision-makers.

Legal risks and liabilities can be managed by extensive and rigorous testing before the deployment of the systems to provide enhance performance. Where errors are considered high, management may come in to validate the results and manage the risk. A culture transformation can also be accomplished by appointing ambassadors who drive technological initiatives to the other parts of the organization. Working with AI in accounting tasks can improve the overall results leading to better decision-making. This enables management and accountants to focus on other sensitive tasks requiring their expertise. Nonetheless, organizations should formulate ways to manage these risks and develop workable strategies that benefit from AI.

Research indicates that many accounting firms are adopting the AI technologies in their operations [5]. The use of AI in the global economy and municipalities is essential as it helps in simplifying and automating the management of accounting information and records. In addition, a variety of industries have adopted AI in their management and accounting procedures since it supports large-scale information as well as supporting intelligent decision-making by the firm's management.

Furthermore, the development and adoption of different accounting software and the introduction of AI have transformed accounting information management. The use of AI has positively influenced the performance of a firm's accounting operations. Research also indicated that the adoption of AI has helped increase the accuracy of reported accounting information, increased the speed of analyzing, and reduced paperwork during the internal and external reporting of accounting information [6]. The utilization of AI has increased the flexibility and efficiency of the database systems used by firms. The development of AI has led to the introduction of accounting software tools such as robots.

Traditional accounting tasks are often burdensome and repetitive. AI utilization can assist organizations to overcome the repetitive challenges of documentation and filling data. It is very burdensome for accountants to manage the large volumes of documents and data, which must administer and manage.

Data management involves performing complex tasks accurately and timely. Further, data organization and management by accountants is people intensive requiring specific instructions. Therefore, the adoption of AI helps to overcome some of these challenges. AI software can perform as the automated workhorses that support businesses in conducting their accounting activities, streamlining a wide range of core business activities, and supporting customer relations. Accounting firms have shifted from using on premise software solutions that required high investment in hardware and lengthy systems implementation to use AI and cloud-based applications. Firms have shifted from traditional business intelligence that is often utilized in house data and storage houses to use AI. Data management and accounting is significant in any organization, and that traditional intelligent software are obsolete when matched with the current need for accounting information. The current accounting departments deal with significant data. Businesses currently must deal with millions of customers and different operations that involve transactions of money that must be accounted for by the firm. Thus, the traditional software model does not have the appropriate software architecture and capabilities to conduct the requisite computations in the accounting department. That is, organizations utilizing traditional models find it difficult to solve their accounting challenges [6]. There are challenges in utilizing custom-made software as the firms had to constantly renew and upgrade their custom-made software whenever a function is required. Grounded on this argument, most firms have transitioned from the traditional on the premise accounting software to using AI analytics and cloud-based software packages.

Accounting is an integral part of the business that entails measuring the financial activities and communicating reliable and relevant information to the stakeholders to such as creditors, investors, and other interested third parties. The use of manual and traditional accounting systems is labor-intensive; thus, the adoption of AI in accounting has supported the introduction of significant changes in the field of accounting. Research by the British Broadcasting Corporation (BBC) indicated that the accounting profession was ranked at position 21 among 366 professions that may be obliterated due to the adoption of AI [13]. According to Zhang *et al.* [14], a survey conducted indicated that more than 120 internal auditors between 2016-2017 in KPMG IT internal auditors indicated that more than half of the firms indicated the use of AI. Research also indicated that there is increasingly widespread use of AI in accounting firms. For example, the big four accounting firms globally have adopted financial robots that utilize AI. The developed AI robots can automatically recognize data, entering their invoices, and generating financial reports. Accounting is an intensive human task and requires the information to be accurate to help in decision making. The adoption of AI-guided robots in the accounting sector has replaced several people in the accounting sector of a firm [14]. The financial robots have led to the replacement of accounting clerks, rendering organizations to have zero accounting knowledge. Nonetheless, AI supports organizations' decision-making in most financial matters. Further results suggest the accounting sector is likely to change when firms fully adopt the use of AI in all financial matters of a particular business.

According to Zhang *et al.* [14], the utilization of AI in the accounting sector is significant and has gained popularity since it supports unveiling financial fraud, supporting stock market forecasting, and auditing. Accounting fraud is one of the major significant issues that affect firms globally. The use of human beings in the development of financial statements and the overall accounting of a firm's information is vulnerable to manipulation and alteration of financial information to suit their malicious ambitions. Accounting fraud is a significant issue that an organization or person may decide to perform. According to Pamungkas *et al.* [11] accounting fraud denotes the misstatement or the deliberate commission or commission of amount to lure the fusers of financial statement. It also involves misstatement resulting from inappropriate handling of assets and liabilities. Accounting information specifies the performance of a given firm, and thus, a firm may manipulate financial information to develop the impression that it is functioning in the correct manner. Thus, firms laden with fraud may manipulate the financial statements [11]. Based on prior research, several conditions must be present when accounting fraud impacts on an organization record. These conditions involve the factors and abilities that make a person or the firm cheat. The traditional way of accounting provides different opportunities for people to conduct accounting fraud.

From previous research conducted, AI and machine learning have facilitated the accounting profession to overcome fraud challenges [12]. The use of AI is noteworthy in detecting anomalies and fraud cases within the accounting arena. Firms have suffered from erroneous payment and loss of accounting records such that they require the services of an external auditor to evaluate all the firm's accounting information. Deployment of an auditor to the firm to evaluate the accounting information of a firm is time-consuming, tiresome, and expensive to conduct an audit. Therefore, the adoption of AI in the accounting department is significant in reducing or eliminating accounting errors in a firm. According to research by Cangemi and Taylor [6], when a firm deploys the use of an accounting AI software package, the firms can unveil some of the erroneous payments encountered through its system. Adopting an AI oversight system helped a particular company receive $1.5 million of cash that would have been lost due to sloppy billings. It also helped the firm to receive approximately $300,000 to $500,000 of cash that would have been lost due to other inefficiencies. These examples demonstrate that AI is essential in accounting process improvement, and organizations could operate more efficiently with the adoption of AI in their accounting departments. The use of AI-powered accounting analytics assisted firms to gain better analysis and oversight of their financial position. The adoption of AI analytics in accounting assists organizations to overcome the challenges of evaluating the multiple documents they have during the accounting process.

Moreover, the use of humans in the processing of accounting information may not be accurate since people are prone to make mistakes due to fatigue, biases, and inappropriate skill sets. People can also easily fail to comply with new guidelines that control how accounting is performed in the organization. According to Cangemi and Taylor [6], the use of AI-packaged accounting analytics supports the development of enhanced AI software. The adoption of AI software packages can aid firms in developing accounting analyses with a higher degree of accuracy based on audit techniques. Thus, AI support assists firms to boost stakeholders' overall confidence in management's decision-making capabilities. Firms currently can develop their own AI processes and operations compliant with the rules and regulations the firms adhere to within the accounting principles framework. The result of adopting AI is promising as the firms currently have better control of the accounting environment [6]. The use of AI benefits firms to evaluate accounting information and without doubt detect fraud and errors in recording information. Therefore, the adoption of AI accounting systems is significant in reducing accounting errors, unproblematic retrieval of analyzed data, and reporting the information more efficiently and effectively.

Furthermore, according to research by Raji *et al.* [7], the audit results of a firm are approached with skepticism since they are dependent on vulnerable human judgment. Organizations and individuals need to develop and establish the integrity of the process and assure all the users of the accounting information that the results are valued and independently conducted. In addition, decision makers should be assured that the audit process is conducted according to the guidelines developed for auditing. Users of the information must affirm the auditor in charge is not compromised to provide information that may cause a company to appear more attractive by concealing the critical financial information of the firm. According to Raji *et al.* [7], there is a significant need to develop a process to support compliance and provide a robust framework to conduct an independent audit. The audit should focus on the adopted model to ensure the accounting process is performed with integrity and follow the right code of conduct. Thus, the adoption of AI in the accounting of financial data is a significant issue in promoting the integrity, code of conduct, and assurance they the whole process was conducted in the appropriate manner. The use of AI system provides a level of assurance that the information communicated is accurate and free from manipulation.

According to Faccia, Al Naqbi, and Lootah [8], the current firms engage with a vast amount of financial data that is difficult to deal with when using human labor to analyze the information. Their results suggested that the adoption of AI in accounting assists firms overcome the challenges of managing bid data generated in their firms. Technological development has supported different firms to adopt big data management aided by financial management. It is undeniable that the availability of a significant amount of data is incredibly challenging to analyze; however, big data analytics has helped to overcome the challenge. Currently, in accounting, AI has aided firms with the bookkeeping and storage of data. The Adoption of AI in the accounting sector has made it possible for firms to classify accounting transactions automatically. It also supports firms in developing financial statements and tax returns more accurately and reliably. Furthermore, the use of AI is significant as it benefits the different firms control their considerable amounts of data. Firms have embraced AI technology that helps in collecting, analyzing, and processing the accounting data safely and securely.

AI in accounting is supplemented by adopting machine language, deep learning, and natural language processing to increase efficiencies in productive activities. The adoption of AI in financial accounting requires developing the appropriate software and machine language/deep learning processing to report accounting documents implemented in the analysis. One of the noteworthy languages embedded with AI in financial accounting is eXtensible Business Reporting Language (XBRL). According to Faccia, Al Naqbi, and Lootah [8] XBRL is a major machine language that assists different accounting firms to manage their financial data. It is a language utilized in the electronic communication of a firm's financial data that has supported business reporting globally. The adopted language enables firms to produce the required data for reporting purposes. It is an essential tool that assists in comparability and consequent evaluation of business accounting information. Adopting the language facilitates the avoidance of replicating accounting data, thereby reducing the level of data loss. Millions of firms worldwide are currently utilizing XBRL, especially after the language was certified by the American Institute of Public Accountants (AICPA). The language has evolved with the addition of new functionalities that support the analysis of financial data that is very safe and without cases of errors in financial reporting.

According to Rodgers [5], the neural network is a significant aspect of AI that assist to model the human brain. The learning and teaching methods supporting the neural networks are grounded on the experience of the electronic models and the developed natural neural networks. The advancement in AI development and other technologies has supported the use of neural networks in accounting as they have complex computational models that are adopted by the computer system. The neural network implements that ability to learn into computer programs. The adoption of neural networks in management supports a firm to conduct predictions using complex algorithms in the neural networks. As the neural networks perform their task as humans, they have the capacity to predict the financial position of a firm based on the data collected over the years. Firms have adopted to use AI embedded neural networks such as deep learning to overcome the challenges associated with the manual computation of management and financial information [5]. Further, this methodology also helps to develop accurate reporting of financial and management information. In addition, the use of neural networks reduces the level of skepticism of accounting information compared to when humans conduct auditing procedures.

## Can Blockchain Augment XBRL

A blockchain is a growing list of records, called *blocks*, that are linked together utilizing cryptography [9]. Cryptography is a tool of safeguarding information and communications through the implementation of codes, whereby that only those for whom the information is intended can read and process it. Further, blockchains are public and consequently all transactions on the chain can be observed. Nonetheless, since the buyers and sellers are characterized through digital signatures, their identity is camouflaged.

Moreover, a blockchain is typically designated as a distributed, decentralized, public ledger. The "blocks" in blockchain encompass records of information in the following manner:

1. transactions (for example, the date, time, and amount of a purchase),
2. the digital signature of the buyer and seller of the transaction, and
3. a distinctive identifier called a "hash" that permits to describe apart from every other block. The "chain" in blockchain is the links between all the blocks. Each time a new transaction ensues, it is adjoined as a permanent block to the chain.

Blockchain supported by AI are valuable new technologies that will need data standards to work effectively. Blockchain has completely different uses and purpose from the XBRL standard; hence may not be used in place of data standards. Moreover, blockchain is a particular type of database. It varies from a typical database in how it stores information. Blockchains stockpile data in blocks that are then chained together. As new data comes in it is entered into a fresh block.

XBRL and blockchains are both used to communicate. Nonetheless, blockchain requires data standards blockchain thereby implements data standards to record and exchange information. Universal, machine-readable standards are particularly essential when automating processes, for example in smart contracts. Further, blockchain technology can be implemented to generate a permanent, public, transparent ledger system for assembling data on sales, tracking digital use and payments to content developers, such as wireless users or musicians. In addition, blockchain comes with the concept of maintaining and decentralizing the data or transactions. Data once sent to a blockchain network cannot be deleted or detached from all the systems.

AI based machine learning requires a large amount of machine-readable data. To facilitate the development of AI an open data ecosystem and consistent standards for structuring and labeling the data are essential. In other words, better quality data equals more beneficial AI tools. The XBRL standard is a facilitation of machine-readable, consistent, unambiguous data is crucial for smooth AI and blockchain applications.

In sum,

The objective of the blockchain is to establish:

a. trust, which indicates that a transaction has occurred,
b. the amount has been paid when an untrust relationship between parties occurs, especially when the identity of the parties to a transaction are unknown.

In the absence of blockchain, trusted third parties like banks, brokers, large retail distributors, such as Amazon facilitate transactions between two parties who are unfamiliar with one another. The middleman serves an essential role since it can verify identities, confirm that the transaction in fact transpired, and that it was accomplished for the amount that both parties agreed upon. The blockchain eradicates the requirement for such centralized authorities since it embraces all the data regarding the transaction and is observable by all parties. Nevertheless, it disguises the identity of the parties. And the blockchain offers an audit trail that never goes disappear.

## AI Generated Solutions for Fitness Training

AI generated algorithms have been quite useful in the analysis of accounting information. Recent research has indicated that there is a huge development of deep learning algorithms involved in the accounting sector. The adoption of deep learning algorithms supports the development of the implementation of various functionalities and the development of machine learning. According to AL-Aroud [10], accounting has benefited from the use of deep learning algorithms. The developed powerful algorithms are essential in applying to financial modeling and in the analytical facets in accounting. Due to the increased volume of data required in the accounting process, AI and the adoption of deep learning algorithms have helped ease the challenges of engaging in complex procedures and processes using traditional accounting methods. According to Pamungkas *et al.* [11], the application of AI has helped various firms forecast bankruptcy among firms. The use of AI and deep learning algorithms support intelligent accounting models that assist forecast whether a business will suffer from bankruptcy. The AI-powered techniques include discriminant analysis and support vector machines that help analyze and predict a firm's financial position in each period. The models use market-based and accounting-based variables that are developed using numeric data that are well structured in the same format [11]. The data collected helps in quantitative analysis and plays a significant role in predicting the right information that helps various stakeholders to make the right decision. It also helps firm managers make the right accounting adjustment and corrections to avert the impending danger of insolvency.

Nevertheless, when utilizing biometric technology to prevent or detect fraud companies or individuals must be able to draw a line between an individual's privacy and the biometric technology being used. The privacy act of 1974 protects individuals and establish the line that companies should consider [4]. The act regulates the collection, maintenance, and use of personal information from US citizens. Although the act itself does not mention biometrics there are several amendments that also protect individuals from the private information.

The US Constitution has 27 amendments that protect the rights of individuals. Further, the United States Constitution is often denoted to as a "living document" that matures and varies as society moves forward. And no matter an individual's perspective pertaining to constitutional interpretation, there is no doubt that amendments to the Constitution have transformed the course of the American legal system. The first ten amendments became known as the Bill of Rights that embraces several of the freedoms we conjoin very meticulously with the United States, such as freedom of religion, freedom of speech, and freedom of the press. These constitutional rights guard the people lives from intrusion by the government. This is especially true in the case of AI based infusion into biometrics systems.

Overall, the amendments have been for the better, and some of them very much better. In addition, the amendments have advanced rights, liberties and momentously enhancing the democratic content of the system. For example, the Fourth Amendment which protects people from unreasonable searches and seizures establish a line so that cops or the government cannot randomly show up to an individual's house and search the house, there must be a reason and the authority must have a warrant specifying the reason of the search. The fifth amendment covers integrity and values of society, which can be incorporated in the Ruling Guide Algorithm Pathway (P→J→D). The 9th Amendment overall notes that all rights not stated in the constitution and not forbidden by the Constitution belong to the citizens. Finally, the Fourteen Amendment, states that no state should deprive any person of life, liberty, or property, without due process of the law, which can be depicted by the Ruling Guide Algorithm Pathway (P→J→D). Overall, the amendments and the privacy act of 1974 must be considered to a high degree when establishing biometrics. It is also important to know how to use biometrics for security purposes and consider whether the biometric is best for society as a public interest that would maximize the good of society *versus* individual privacy interest.

Moreover, biometrics can assist in strengthening an organizations internal control by providing an internal control system that protects users from scam emails, identity theft, and potential fraudulent transactions. A very popular form of identity theft is called phishing and it is when a user receives spam email that recommends the receipt to click on the link attached to the email and update their personal data. The link will then more than likely take the victim to a fictitious website that would than ask for financial information.

A particular security problem is "website defacement," which is the sabotage of internal control biometrics systems-based web pages by hackers placing in or altering information. The altered web pages may deceive unknowing users and represent negative publicity that could affect an organization's image, brand name and credibility. Despite the technological advances with the implementation of biometrics, a Type 1 and Type 2 error may arise. A Type I error is the rejection of a true hypothesis while a type to would be the failure to reject a false null hypothesis.

As discussed previously, AI is a branch of computer science involved with imitating human intelligence in machines. For fitness training, employing AI requires asking the following question. How does a computer system might perform things that individuals can do, such as fitness training decisions? When applied to fitness decision tree operationalize by an AI machine learning software development, this might mean whether an app can "decide" on the workload, number of steps, offer a suitable set of exercises, *etc.*

In addition, machine learning software provides the context in the form of data, while AI responds to that context within a set of parameters. Machine learning depend upon automating the analysis of statistics to make sense of very large sets of data, using complex algorithms to find specific patterns.

Fig. (**5.6**) presents a decision tree that is useful in illustrating the implementation AI-based biometrics. Decision trees are a great tool to use when a dilemma is present, and a decision must be made. A decision tree is a model that can be utilized for both the classification and regression. The tree ultimately answers sequential questions until a final answer is reached. The decision tree is a flowchart that provides a handful of alternatives and outcomes that are based on the decision to be made. Applying AI-based biometrics and the Throughput Model provides a good example of the Ruling Guide Algorithmic Pathway.

The decision tree consists of a wearable device that will ultimately track an individual's heart rate, sleeping patterns, calorie intakes, and steps. The wearable device will be a ring that its purpose is to motive individuals to be fit. The ring will be referred to as the fitness ring. The objective of the ring can be described in the Ruling Guide Algorithmic Pathway.

Based upon the Ruling Guide Algorithmic Pathway perspective a series of rules is placed in a system. The morality is based on the actions itself not because the result of the action would be good. Additionally, this perspective also considers acts to be obligatory regardless of the consequences and follows the rule structure of the system. Therefore, the purpose of the fitness ring under a Ruling Guide Algorithmic Pathway perspective, would be for fitness training. That is, an athlete must be fit to be competitive, which is implied that the athlete must exercise, eat healthy, and get enough sleep. Fig. (**5.6**) presents a representation of a decision tree incorporating the Ruling Guide Algorithmic Pathway.

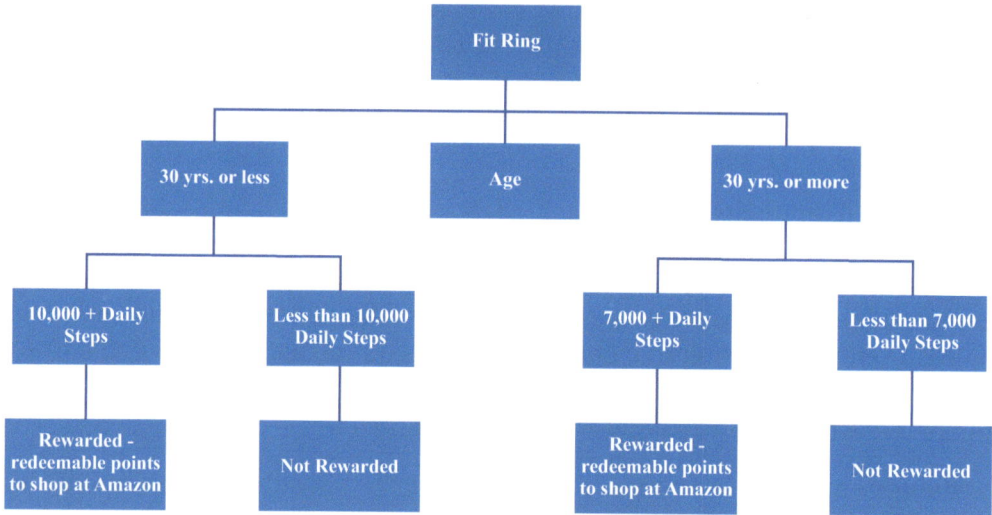

**Fig. (5.6).** Ruling guide algorithm for fitness. Source: Student generated.

Based on the decision tree above, the fit ring will be divided into two categories by age, under 30 and over 30. If the individual is under 30 years of age, she/he would be required to complete 10,000 steps to be rewarded, if less than 10,000 steps individual will not be rewarded. The incentive provided for completing the required daily steps will be based on points that the individual will be able to accumulate and redeem on Amazon to purchase items. Now, if the individual is over 30 the same rules would apply, however, the individual would only be required to complete 7,000 daily steps. Besides promoting fitness, the fitness ring will additionally track biometrics by measuring the individuals heart rate, BMI, sleeping pattern, calories, and of course steps. The ring will be able to track trends of the individual through a ratio analysis and establish weekly goals to improve the individual's fitness as the 10,000 and 7,000 steps would simply serve as a benchmark. Now, the ring would also be influenced by a Type 1 or Type 2 error. A Type 1 error would happen when the ring tracks the 10,000 or 7,000 steps but the individual did not complete the steps as the ring may have measured some distance when the individual was driving, or the individual may have cheated and placed the ring on a dog. On the other side a Type 2 error would be present when the individual completes the required steps, however, the ring incorrectly measures the steps, and the individual is not rewarded.

In relating the fitness ring to the Throughput Model, the ring would have a database of the individuals stats that are being track and use that information to establish future goals for the individual to improve its health trends through ratio analysis and compare the biometrics with previous statistical measures completed by the individual. The algorithm being implemented depicts the P→J→D algorithm. The rules govern the steps involving storing information in a database and then the ring would determine if the steps were completed based on the age of the individual. Finally, a decision choice would be made by either rewarding the individual or not rewarding the individual. The ring would additionally use AI supported machine learning software by detecting the individual's health patterns and make corrective recommendation if appropriate or recommendations that would improve the individual's health and performance based on the sampled information. The ring would provide the feedback automatically to the induvial through an App on a weekly basis. On the other hand, the ring would implement deep learning by using the trend analysis or health pattern and improve the individual's health each time.

In sum, the application of biometrics can help improve society whether through fitness or through the safeguarding of assets. Biometrics can help the prevention and detection of fraudulent activity. As mentioned, the use of biometrics can assist an organization by providing an internal control system that will help and improve its overall objectives.

## CONCLUSION

This chapter presented a discussion of the Ruling Guide Algorithmic Pathway (P→J→D) that included examples of AI technology and its subsets of machine learning and deep learning. Machine learning and deep learning, both technologies are made to learn from output data, using its input data. However, deep learning is more complex because it uses neural networks techniques, which indicates that works like a human brain. It works side by side with the concept of perception and information. Deep learning is biometric technology and is used for recognition of identification and verification.

One of the primary purposes of AI is to make technology to think and perform like humans — technology based on computers system and robotics. As the year has gone by, technology has gotten better. Currently, many businesses depend on artificial intelligence to conduct business. As stated earlier in the essay, audit firms depend deeply on AI to help them find discrepancies; from here it is on the firm to investigate. Having these systems, auditors can learn from these mistakes and can provide future clients with better information.

Artificial intelligence consists of six different algorithms, which are compost of four concepts: perception, information, judgment, and decision choice, the Throughput Model. The six algorithms arise with a decision choice, based on the order of these concepts.

The adoption of AI impacts upon a variety of different systems utilized by organizations. That is, the use of AI programs is mimicking humans pertaining to the decision-making process. AI systems are easily adapted in the manufacturing centers, healthcare, and current accounting arenas. Further, AI systems encompass software that can perform in a similar manner of an expert in a particular field. AI systems are developed to solve various challenges in combining different fields. The AI systems powered by deep learning neural networks learn from the data they are fed, whereby supporting the need of users.

AI is about producing technology that permits machines and computers to operate in an intelligent way. Machines with AI can mimic cognitive functions, like learning and problem solving. Examples of AI are self-driving cars, and drones. AI can be implemented to detect fraud in the banking and insurance industries, or to assist in pinpointing the proper healthcare treatments, by scrutinizing large volumes of data.

The XBRL data standard renders information into machine-readable format, abolishing the necessity for manual data entry. AI is oftentimes depicted as a tool that could render text or numeric facts into machine-readable information. Blockchains can be summarized as supportive of AI technology as follow:

(1) Blockchain is a particular kind of database.

(2) It varies from a typical database in the manner it stores information; blockchains store data in blocks that are then chained together.

(3) As new data comes in it is recorded into a fresh block. Once the block is complete with data it is chained onto the previous block, which makes the data chained together in chronological order.

(4) Distinct kinds of information can be stored on a blockchain; however, the most general use thus far has been as a ledger for transactions.

(5) In Bitcoin's case, blockchain is utilized in a decentralized manner whereby that no individual or group has control. Instead, every user collectively retain control.

(6) Decentralized blockchains are immutable, which implies that the data entered is unalterable. For Bitcoin, this implies that transactions are everlastingly recorded and observable to anyone.

In summary, the Ruling Guide Pathway, **P→J→D**, illustrates a decision-making process from **perception** through **judgment** to **decision choice.** This pathway is also useful in handling situations from stable and unstable environment. People's experiences, training, and education can also provide them with tools to handle situations that they recognize. However, the other side is that if the individual is not an expert or does not have the experiences may lead to detrimental decisions. The **P→J→D** pathway can be divided into two parts of a stable or unstable environment.

AI will continue evolving, and it will impact the world in the coming years. As AI technologic develops, the human will have to grow with it too. Human will have to learn to adapt to technology and learn to evaluate the data that the AI technology provided because just like humans, technology can also fail.

## REFERENCES

[1] W. Rodgers, *Knowledge Creation: Going Beyond Published Financial Information.* Nova Publication: Hauppauge, NY, 2016.

[2] W. Rodgers, *Process Thinking: Six pathways to successful decision making.* iUniverse, Inc.: NY, 2006.

[3] W. Rodgers, *Biometric and Auditing Issues Addressed in a Throughput Model.* Information Age Publishing, Inc.: Charlotte, NC, 2012.

[4] W. Rodgers, *E-commerce and biometric issues addressed in a Throughput Model.* Nova Publication: Hauppauge, NY, 2010.

[5] W. Rodgers, *Artificial Intelligence in a Throughput Model: Some Major Algorithms?* Science Publications (CRC Press, Taylor and Francis Group): Florida, 2020.

[6] M.P. Cangemi, and P. Taylor, "Harnessing artificial intelligence to deliver real-time intelligence and business process improvements", *EDPACS,* vol. 57, no. 4, pp. 1-6, 2018.
[http://dx.doi.org/10.1080/07366981.2018.1444007]

[7] I.D. Raji, A. Smart, R.N. White, M. Mitchell, T. Gebru, B. Hutchinson, and P. Barnes, "Closing the AI accountability gap: defining an end-to-end framework for internal algorithmic auditing", *Proceedings of the 2020 Conference on Fairness, Accountability, and Transparency,* pp. 33-44, 2020.
[http://dx.doi.org/10.1145/3351095.3372873]

[8] A. Faccia, M.Y.K. Al Naqbi, and S.A. Lootah, "Integrated Cloud Financial Accounting Cycle: How Artificial Intelligence, Blockchain, and XBRL will Change the Accounting, Fiscal and Auditing Practices", In: *Proceedings of the 2019 3rd International Conference on Cloud and Big Data Computing,* 2019, pp. 31-37.
[http://dx.doi.org/10.1145/3358505.3358507]

[9] M. Iansiti, and K.R. Lakhani, "The Truth about Blockchain", *Harvard Business Review,* 2017.https://hbr.org/2017/01/the-truth-about-blockchain

[10] AL-Aroud, "The Impact of Artificial Intelligence Technologies on Audit Evidence", *Academy of Accounting and Financial Studies Journal,* vol. 24, pp. 1-11, 2020.

[11] I.D. Pamungkas, I. Ghozali, T. Achmad, M. Khaddafi, and R. Hidayah, "Corporate governance mechanisms in preventing accounting fraud: A study of fraud pentagon model", *J. Appl. Econom. Sci.,* vol. 13, no. 2, pp. 549-560, 2018.

[12] W. Rodgers, A. Söderbom, and A. Guiral, "Corporate Social Responsibility Enhanced Control Systems Reducing the Likelihood of Fraud", *J. Bus. Ethics,* vol. 91, suppl. Suppl. 1, pp. 151-166, 2014.

[13]   E.P. Stancheva-Todorova, "How artificial intelligence is challenging accounting profession", *Economy Business Journal,* vol. 12, no. 1, pp. 126-141, 2018.

[14]   Y. Zhang, F. Xiong, Y. Xie, X. Fan, and H. Gu, "The Impact of Artificial Intelligence and Blockchain on the Accounting Profession", *IEEE Access,* vol. 8, pp. 110461-110477, 2020. [http://dx.doi.org/10.1109/ACCESS.2020.3000505]

**CHAPTER 6**

# The Analytical Algorithmic Pathway

*Artificial intelligence (AI) is manna from heaven for sci-fi writers. We've seen a sentient computer called HAL wreak quiet havoc in* 2001: A Space Odyssey. *We've watched a robot girl's will to survive in 2015's* Ex Machina. *Most recently we've seen an AI-meets-the-wild-west scenario in TV series* Westworld. *Writers do a great job of making AI entertaining, but does it work the other way around? Can AI itself create, develop and write storylines, scripts and other art forms? AI is spreading into every corner of human existence. So it should come as no surprise that it's helping authors, journalists and writers to create in ever more inventive ways.*

---Jamie Carter

The human brain has about 100 billion neurons. With an estimated average of one thousand connections between each neuron and its neighbors, we have about 100 trillion connections, each capable of a simultaneous calculation ... (but) only 200 calculations per second.... With 100 trillion connections, each computing at 200 calculations per second, we get 20 million billion calculations per second. This is a conservatively high estimate.... In 1997, $2,000 of neural computer chips using only modest parallel processing could perform around 2 billion calculations per second.... This capacity will double every twelve months. Thus by the year 2020, it will have doubled about twenty-three times, resulting in a speed of about 20 million billion neural connection calculations per second, which is equal to the human brain.

---Ray Kurzweil

As a global futurist and futurephile, one of the things that excites me about artificial intelligence is the death of procrastination -- anything 'left brained' that we avoided and delayed doing, like taxes, filing, travel expense coding, receipt management, and updating our calendars will be procrastinated on no longer. That in and of itself should sell you on the virtue of AI -- unless you of course derive a lot of pleasure from these activities, in which case I urge you to upgrade and diversify your thinking.

---Anders Sorman-Nilsson

**Abstract**

The Analytical Algorithmic Pathway, I→J→D, involves of attaining the most usefulness from an individual or organization decision given reliable and relevant information. On the other hand, information that is incomplete, noisy, and/or difficult to interpret deteriorates the interpretation of this algorithmic pathway. This algorithmic pathway shoulders that all information is known, the environment is controllable, and the information is precise, in that it can be related to other events, or that it can be rated or ranked. Characteristically, the environment is stable, and the information and events are precise.

**Keywords:** Analytical Algorithmic Pathway, Artificial intelligence, Biases, Biometrics, Decision tree, Dynamic Signature Verification, Facial Recognition, Fingerprint Biometrics, Fraud, Fraud triangle, Hand geometry reader, Hand geometry recognition, Iris reader, Misstatements risks, Opportunity, Palm print reader, Pressure, Rationalization, Retina Scanner, Vein Patterns.

## INTRODUCTION

The Analytical Pathway is based on information, judgment, and decision choice. This algorithmic pathway suggests that information has a direct impact on our analysis of the situation. In this pathway, perception is ignored or played down; therefore, biases, strategies, and emotions has very little import in influencing the decision choice. In the information step, information sources that are typically reliable and complete are determined and in the judgment step, those information sources are weighted on how they impact the analysis. This pathway is usually useful when the environment is stable and when information sources are reliable and relevant [1].

The Analytical Pathway is implemented by decision makers when information influences the analysis and therefore the final decision (See Fig. **6.1**). For example, in an audit, the information received by the client determines the types of procedures that will be performed in order to give a professional opinion on the financial statements and internal controls. For instance, think of a not-for-profit organization that provides medical attention to women that have income under a certain threshold. The auditor must perform procedures to ensure that adequate documentation was requested from patients to make sure they comply with the eligibility requirements. This specific information regarding the client is utilized by the auditor to select the appropriate procedures to determine if the company did a good job in only accepting patients that were eligible. AI may assist in this process if the company has access to the patient's tax records. Hence, the auditors can confirm the annual income of possible patients. This is similar to what universities' student aide administration does to evaluate the financial need of students when they apply for grants and loans. Having the AI system to access records facilitates this process. Without access to records, the company must request documentation, such as paystubs, which makes the procedure more time consuming for the auditors.

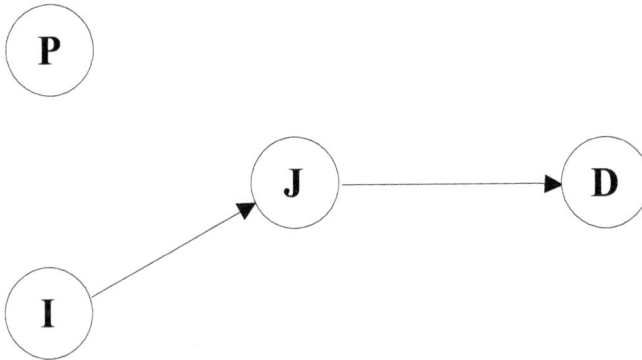

**Fig. (6.1).** I→J→D. The decision path consists of information to judgment to decision choice. Source: Rodgers [1].

The Analytical Algorithmic Pathway (I→J→D) does not focus on perception at all, it relies primarily on the information that is available. Nonetheless, when this pathway relies only in information, we have the risk that problems may appear and this is because sometimes information may be incomplete, or difficult to interpret. It works most admirably when information is reliable and relevant, this pathway can also be divided in two parts: stable and unstable environment [1] (see Fig. **6.2**).

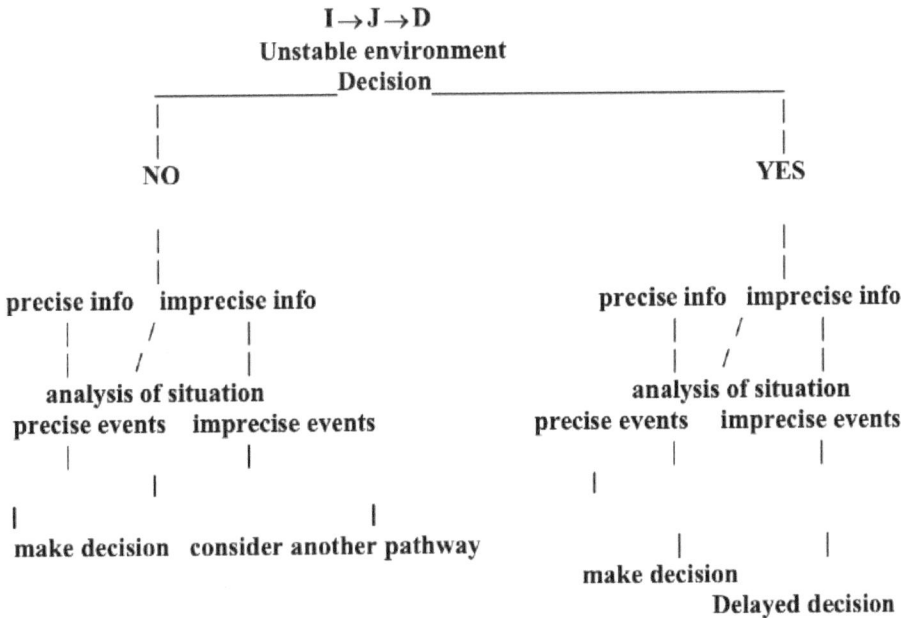

**Fig. (6.2).** Analytic pathway decision tree (I→J→D). Adopted from (Waymond Rodgers, Process Thinking, [1]).

That is, the **I→J→D** pathway aims of achieving the most usefulness from our decision given the reliable information. Information that is incomplete, or difficult to interpret will affect the pathway. As we continue in this pathway, it assumes all the information is known, also that we can "control" our environment. Typically, the environment and the information are stable and precise.

## EXAMPLE 6.1 -- ANALYTICAL PATHWAY (I→J→D)

Fraud interviews, internal control testing, and general interviews with employees, managers, supervisors, *etc.* are analyzed to obtain a major understanding of the company's internal controls and profile. Moreover, biometrics are depicted by a company to protect its major assets and the procedures as well as its procedures, such as payroll, cash, ethics, *etc.* The company described as the Native American Incorporated (NAI) operates under tribal government. It has no formal constitution and by-laws; however, it is governed under a compact signed in 1895. The NAI is a federally recognized Indian tribe governed by an elected governor and tribal council. The accounts of NAI are organized on the basis of funds and account groups, each of which is considered a separate accounting entity. The operations of each fund are accounted for with a separate set of self-balancing accounts that are comprised of assets, liabilities, net assets, revenues and expenses, as appropriate.

NAI's activities are accounted for on the flow of financial recourses measurement focus and use the accrual basis of accounting and, accordingly, reflect all significant receivables, payables, and other liabilities. Management is responsible for the preparation and fair presentation of these financial statements in accordance with accounting principles generally accepted in the United States of America; this includes the design, implementation, and maintenance of internal control relevant to the preparation and fair presentation of financial statements that are free from material misstatement, whether due to fraud or error.

### Company Profile

NAI operates in the entertainment (gaming), food/beverage, free music concerts, among other social activities. The American Institute of Certified Public Accounting (AICPA) guidelines and Industry Audit Risk Alerts, industry publications, *etc.*, which provide information on these industries is the Audits of Nonpublic Companies, Audits of Governmental Entities. Furthermore, NAI is treated as an enterprise fund on the financial statements of the Pueblo. The accounts of the Pueblo are organized on the basis of funds and account groups, each of which is considered a separate accounting entity. The operations of each fund are accounted for with a separate set of self-balancing accounts that are comprised of assets, liabilities, net assets, revenues and expenditure of expenses, as appropriate. NAI's activities are accounted for on the flow of financial recourses measurement focus and use the accrual basis of accounting and, accordingly, reflect all significant receivables, payables, and other liabilities. Moreover, NAI's Entertainment Center is located and transacts all of its business on the Reservation. As mentioned before, the Company is an enterprise fund of the Pueblo and as such, is not subject to federal or state income tax on the income earned in the conduct of commercial business.

## Internal Controls System

The company has different internal controls. Ethical behavior is communicated to employees *via* the employee handbook and by the managers. Management demonstrates a concern for control by performing important internal control procedures, such as approvals and the regular preparation and review of summary cash audit sheets. Cash from the major profit areas (machine, poker, restaurant, bar) flow through the entertainment center cage and is reconciled in three shifts daily. In addition, the accounting department consists of accountants, payroll clerks, and MIS specialists, all of whom seem sufficiently knowledgeable and experienced to perform their job duties. ADP is an outside specialist who handles the payroll. A formal organizational structure is in place as well as formal job descriptions throughout the organization. In addition, human resources conduct background investigations and drug screening on all prospective employees. Management establishes human resource policies and procedures that demonstrate its commitment to integrity, ethical behavior, and competence. NAI has a security department and a surveillance department. Surveillance focuses on the entertainment center floor as well as the cashiers to ensure they handle cash properly. A supervisor is notified of suspicious activity. All employees have color coded badges. For example, only employees with red badges are allowed into the main bank and Employees tend to have the competence and training necessary for their assigned level of responsibility. Employees are periodically evaluated and reviewed. There are currently three shifts at NAI. All reporting for the three major profit centers is done through the cash vault. The three profit centers include the entertainment center floor, a restaurant and a bar. There are three primary source documents generated by NAI's financial reporting system: Cash disbursements from vendors; Payroll-ADP *via* journal entry and the summary cash audit sheets which includes all profit centers.

The cash balance and controls over cash is one of the most significant items on the balance sheet. Clients pay cash to play the machines and are paid back in cash at the cashier windows. Cash operation procedures and internal controls are proper. A physical count of the 2nd shift in NAI's bank. It is noted that only cashiers, security, and main bankers are permitted in the Main Bank. Also, Cash is counted using a bill counting machine and coin counting machine. Amounts are recorded on a reconciliation sheet. Additionally, Cash from NAI's three major revenue sources flow through the bank. As mentioned earlier, these are the restaurant, the Bar, and the machines. Then, a count is performed at the end of each shift and the beginning of the next shift (3 shifts daily); the beginning balance must match the ending balance from the prior shift and a cash audit worksheet is created at the end and beginning of every shift. The bank is monitored by surveillance at all times. Clearance to enter bank is approved by security and a special badge is provided; no one can enter the bank without this badge and all cash is kept in a high-quality safe. Moreover, if a bank employee cannot reconcile to the prior shift's balance; main banker will assist the employee. The error is usually simple in nature and resolved quickly. In the event that a count does not reconcile, a Variance sheet is created by a banker: if -/+ \$20 1$^{st}$ occurrence verbal warning, 2nd written and further to be handled by manager. If the variance is -/+ \$60 it is then investigated by security through surveillance. Furthermore, The GM has requested that \$500,000 be maintained in the bank at all times but, there is sometimes more or less cash on hand. Finally, deposits are picked up on daily basis.

Processing Cash receipts is a main operation in the company. First, customers cash out at the cashier windows with tickets printed from the machines. Revenue is moved to the mini-vault. All employees in the bank and mini vault are properly screened and constantly monitored while conducting the physical count. They have strict procedures they must follow such as "washing" their hands, *etc.* Then, the main banker and employees verify the revenue and sign a reconciliation sheet. Next, from the mini-vault, revenues move to the main bank where they are again counted, verified and signed off. Only \$5000 is maintained at each cashier and \$50,000 Monday thru Thursday and \$40,000 Friday thru Saturday in total at the cashiers' cage. After these, all cash on hand is counted (and signed off) at the end of each of the 3 shifts and at the beginning of the next shift for accuracy. The cash receipts and disbursements are identified and captured on each shift's daily cash audit sheet prepared by the main bank.

As mentioned above, using the cash audit sheets, a monthly summary journal entry is posted to the general ledger by a staff accountant and reviewed and approved by the CFO. Finally, daily flash reports, as well as month end financial statements are generated from daily cash audit sheets; the information is captured *via* journal entry by staff accountant for inclusion into the monthly financial statements upon CFO approval.

## Fraud and Misstatements Risks

Some potential financial statement fraud risks related to the nature of the entity are Management override of controls. Machine revenues at NAI increased dramatically in 2020 due to aggressive marketing and promotions and free concerts to generate additional traffic. In addition, NAI pays commission for the use of the sweepstakes. This creates a major expense for the company and takes a large portion of the machine revenues. In 2008, NAI was hard hit by the economy and its clients had less disposable income. The publicity from NAI's case vs the State regarding the 8-liners was also likely to blame. In 2010, NAI began hosting free concerts to generate traffic at the center. The result was a doubling of revenues to approximately 117 million. A high volume of cash transactions occur on a daily basis and the company has 235 employees. Furthermore, the client continues to maintain a very large workforce. As of June 2020, 500 employees were reported.

Other risks are that the client has contracts with several different vendors and the commission rates vary per each contract. There is an interest by management or the owner/manager in maintaining or increasing the entity's earnings trend, the entity maintains or processes large amounts of cash, the entity's inventory is easily susceptible to misappropriation, the entity has fixed assets that are easily susceptible to misappropriation due to small size, portability, marketability and the entity's lack of an updated fixed assets inventory. Moreover, there is a concentration of risk because the Company maintains cash balances at one bank. Cash accounts are insured by the Federal Deposit Insurance Corporation (FDIC) for up to $250,000. The Company also maintains large cash balances in the entertainment center vault on its premises.

Other accounts that required high internal controls due to its amount and importance in the financial statements are:

- Cash and Cash Equivalents – For purposes of the statement of cash flows, the Company considers all short-term debt securities purchased with an original maturity of three months or less to be cash equivalents.
- Allowance for Doubtful Accounts – Receivables are presented in the statement of financial position net of estimated uncollectible amounts. The Company records an allowance for estimated uncollectible accounts in an amount approximating anticipated losses. Individual uncollectible accounts are written off against the allowance when collection of the individual accounts appear doubtful.
- Investments – The Company classifies its securities that are held for short-term resale as trading account securities which are recorded at their fair values.

Realized and unrealized gains and losses on trading account securities are included in other income.

- Inventories – Inventories are stated at lower of cost or market using the first-in, first-out method and consist of food, beverages, and cigarettes.

- Property, Plant and Equipment– Property, plant and equipment are carried at cost. The cost of property, plant and equipment is depreciated over the estimated useful lives of the related assets. The costs of leasehold improvements are amortized over the lesser of the length of the related lease or the estimated useful lives of the assets. Depreciation and amortization are computed primarily on the straight-line method over the estimated useful lives of the assets for financial reporting purposes. Expenditures for major renewals and betterments that extend the useful lives of property and equipment are capitalized. Expenditures for maintenance and repairs are charged to expense as incurred. When property, plant and equipment are sold or otherwise disposed of, the asset and related accumulated depreciation are relieved, and any gain or loss is included in operations.

- Impairments – The carrying amounts of assets are reviewed at each balance sheet date to determine whether there is any indication of impairment. If any such indication exists, the asset's recoverable amount is estimated to determine the amount of the impairment loss.

- Paid Time Off – The Company's regular employees are granted paid time off for vacation and sick leave in varying amounts based on length of service. Employees who work 40-hour work weeks earn the equivalent of 80 paid time off hours for each full year worked for the first two years of service. Employees start accruing the equivalent of 120 paid time off hours for each full year worked after completion of 2 years. Employees who work less than full work week calendar year earn paid time off on a pro-rated basis.

- Accounting Estimates – The preparation of financial statements in conformity with generally accepted accounting principles requires management to make estimates and assumptions that affect the reported amounts and disclosures. Accordingly, actual results could differ from those estimates.

- Income Tax – The Company is located and transacts all of its business on the Reservation. The Company is an enterprise fund of the Pueblo and as such, is not subject to federal or state income tax on the income earned in the conduct of commercial business.

- Advertising Costs – The Company expenses advertising costs as incurred.

- Reclassifications – Certain accounts in the prior-year financial statements have been reclassified for comparative purposes to conform with the presentation in the current-year financial statements.

There is a moderate risk in the area of Property, Plant and Equipment. The Department manager obtains a quote for equipment or improvement. General manager must approve all fixed asset purchases. Then, the check request forms are completed for each vendor invoice to be vouchered in the accounts payable system. Depending on the nature of expense, it will be expensed or capitalized. Each form notes the account to be charged and is signed off by the manager, CFO or General Manager. The review of the certain fixed asset records reveals that there may be assets that have not been correctly recorded in the Organization's records and/or there may be assets recorded on the Organization's records that are no longer in use. We believe that this indicates the need for a complete physical inventory of fixed assets, which will be the best and most efficient method for developing an accurate listing of all fixed assets. Additionally, this will allow the Organization to develop procedures whereby the fixed asset listing is reconciled to the general ledger, which will ensure an accurate accounting for assets. Currently, there are no physical counts of assets, under the value of $750 such as chairs on the floor, chairs are broken or thrown out daily. The CFO makes decision on how to adjust fixed assets for retirements and deletions.

## Biometrics

AI biometric technologies provide new kinds of digital identity data, new ways to collect it, and new opportunities for its use [2]. Although the client has excellent controls, the use of AI supported biometrics in this type of industry is highly recommended and necessary. Considering the size and complexity of the entity, general computer controls are properly designed and implemented to meet the significant control objectives. For instance, a few of the current biometrics in use include: the palm print reader (see Fig. **6.3**) and hand geometry reader for computer access and for payroll purposes (see Fig. **6.4**).

**Fig. (6.3).** Palm print reader. Adopted from Rodgers [2].

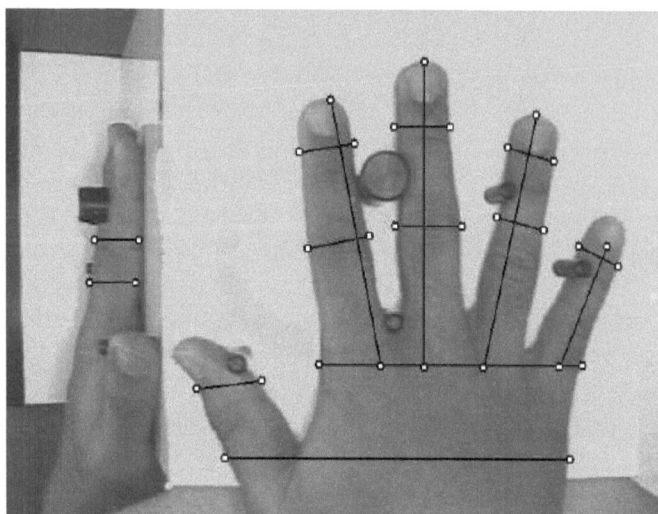

**Fig. (6.4).** Hand geometry reader. Adopted from Rodgers [2].

The palm print reader is used for physical security and access to programs and data are appropriately controlled to prevent unauthorized use, disclosure, modification, damage, or loss of data. Furthermore, security on the premise is high. Access to the accounting department and the main bank are restricted by the flash drive thumb reader. Moreover, ADP is used for payroll processing. Employees punch in and out daily on a handprint device located in the access control, biometric handprint device is used to monitor employee time. Daily punch information for each employee is entered *via* handprint device into ADP system for review and approval. Once payroll hours are approved by the respective manager, biweekly payroll reports are generated for review and acceptance. Month end payroll entry is summarized and entered into the general ledger *via* journal entry. Monthly summary journal entry is posted to the general ledger by staff accountant after it is reviewed by Chief Financial Officer (CFO).

An individual's hand is more distinctive than the human eyes can perceive. This uniqueness can be measured with computer-based imaging and measurement procedures and identity of a person can relate to the uniqueness of his/her hand. Hand geometry is a biometrics tool that recognizes users from the shape of their hands. Hand geometry readers determine a user's hand along many dimensions including height, width, deviation, and angle and compare those measurements to measurements stored in a file. Hand geometry or hand shape technology is the oldest employed biometric technology, even more ancient than the implementation of fingerprint biometric technology [2].

Similar to all other biometric systems, hand geometry recognition has its own set of advantages and disadvantages as listed illustrated below:

Advantages of hand geometry recognition biometrics

- Fast, simple, precise and easy to use.
- Less insensitive than many other biometric modalities like fingerprints and retina recognition.
- Functioning of the recognition systems does not fluctuate with the condition of the skin surface (*e.g.*, skin color, wet/dry skin, smudged or dirty skin, scars, grim, diseases that only affects skin surface, *etc.*).
- Can be implemented in some of the severest environmental situations such as extreme heat and cold, where many other biometrics will fail.
- Difficult to circumvent. It would require entire 3D replica of a subject's hand to sidestep the system.
- Can be incorporated with other systems like proximity and smart card readers.
- It can be utilized in warehouses, storage facilities, and factories, where the population sizes are very large.
- More consistent audit trails than traditional card or paper-based systems.
- Elevated level of public acceptance than many other biometric technologies.
- Eradicates the necessity to generate, administer or carry cards, hence reduces overall cost, time and efforts over traditional attendance systems.

Disadvantages of hand geometry recognition biometrics

- Not very distinctive biometric characteristics: therefore, it cannot be leveraged for high security applications. Nevertheless, when combined with other forms of identity verification (biometric or non-biometric), it can be implemented with moderate to high security applications as well.
- Certain medical conditions such as swelling or injury in hand that changes the shape of the hand can affect the performance of the system. Shape of hand can also change with change in weight and aging.
- Hand geometry readers can be pricier than many other biometric recognition options, for example fingerprint attendance system can start as low as $50 while price of an entry level hand geometry reader may start with $1000.
- Hygiene may be an issue as subjects have to place their hand on the scanning platen. Nonetheless, manufacturers use silver nanotechnology on the base plate surface to resolve this issue. Silver nanotechnology has anti-microbial properties, causing the system suitable for hygiene sensitive applications like hospitals, healthcare outfits, schools, *etc.*

Due to the high risks in this type of industry, an iris reader for security access to the bank and accounting department (see Fig. **6.5**). Or a retina scanner can be implemented as a biometrics security device that is designed to capture retina samples (see Fig. **6.6**) [2].

**Fig. (6.5).** Iris reader. Adopted from Rodgers [3].

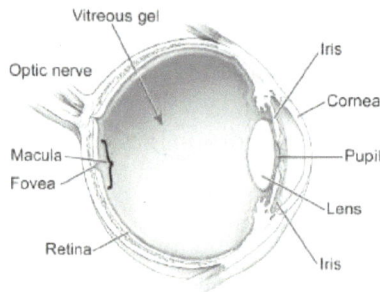

**Fig. (6.6).** Retina scanner. Adopted from Rodgers [3].

The samples captured help with various processes, including identification, authentication, and verification. One reason that a retina scanner is a top choice is because it happens to be more accurate than biometric type scanners that scan fingerprints [3]. Retina patterns cannot be duplicated, the patterns of the retina are very unique, and the false acceptance and rejection rates are much lower with these scanners than with others, such as fingerprint scanners. Furthermore, biometric iris scanners carefully examine the iris of a person's eye and uses pattern recognition techniques to identify and authenticate that person's identity. High resolution images are taken with the biometric iris scanners and passed through a biometrics system with high tech software to match up the iris to the person. While retina scanners use similar scanning camera technology, iris and retina biometrics are different. The iris is the colored portion of the eye and special camera techniques create images of the iris, then turning them into mathematical representations so that an individual can easily be identified. Most scanners are of high quality and will not be affected by the use of contacts or glasses. It is also recommended to improve the security and automatic lock of doors.

A biometric scanner is an essential part of the biometrics world. In order for biological data to be measured and analyzed, some type of scanner must be present to scan in the human body characteristic, whether it is a fingerprint, the iris, the retina, or even facial characteristics (Which Biometrics)[6]. Today public security systems, corporate offices, and consumer electronics often boast these scanners to provide better security and convenience. Many different scanners are available today whereby different types of biometrics can be employed by organizations. The type of assets that NAI handles, and the amount of revenue earned by the company, requires the use of high security which is reached using strict biometrics, such as handprint reader, eye readers, USB thumb reader and flash drive thumb reader, among other tools. In addition, QuickBooks functionality is used to close the year and print financial statements. The staff performs a QuickBooks balance sheet and profit/loss review. Backup schedules and supporting detail are examined for all balance sheet accounts. The accounts payable aging schedule is agreed to the general ledger as well as all outstanding payroll tax, garnishments, *etc*.

Finally, the review of the certain property, plant and equipment records reveals that there may be assets that have not been correctly recorded in the Organization's records and/or there may be assets recorded on the Organization's records that are no longer in use. This indicates the need for a complete physical inventory of fixed assets, which will be the best and most efficient method for developing an accurate listing of all fixed assets. Moreover, this will allow the Organization to develop procedures whereby the fixed asset listing is reconciled to the general ledger, which will ensure an accurate accounting for assets. Specifically, the listing should include the following data:

• Description of the asset
• Cost, voucher number, and vendor name
• Date placed in service
• Estimated useful life
• Depreciation method
• Depreciation expense and accumulated depreciation for the year
• Date asset was retired and selling price, if applicable

Complete information such as the above on all property, plant and equipment assets would provide excellent control for the safeguarding of these assets, which are a significant cost. A better assessment and evaluation could also be made regarding the reliability of certain fixed assets, and the need for replacements, and so on (see Fig. **6.7**).

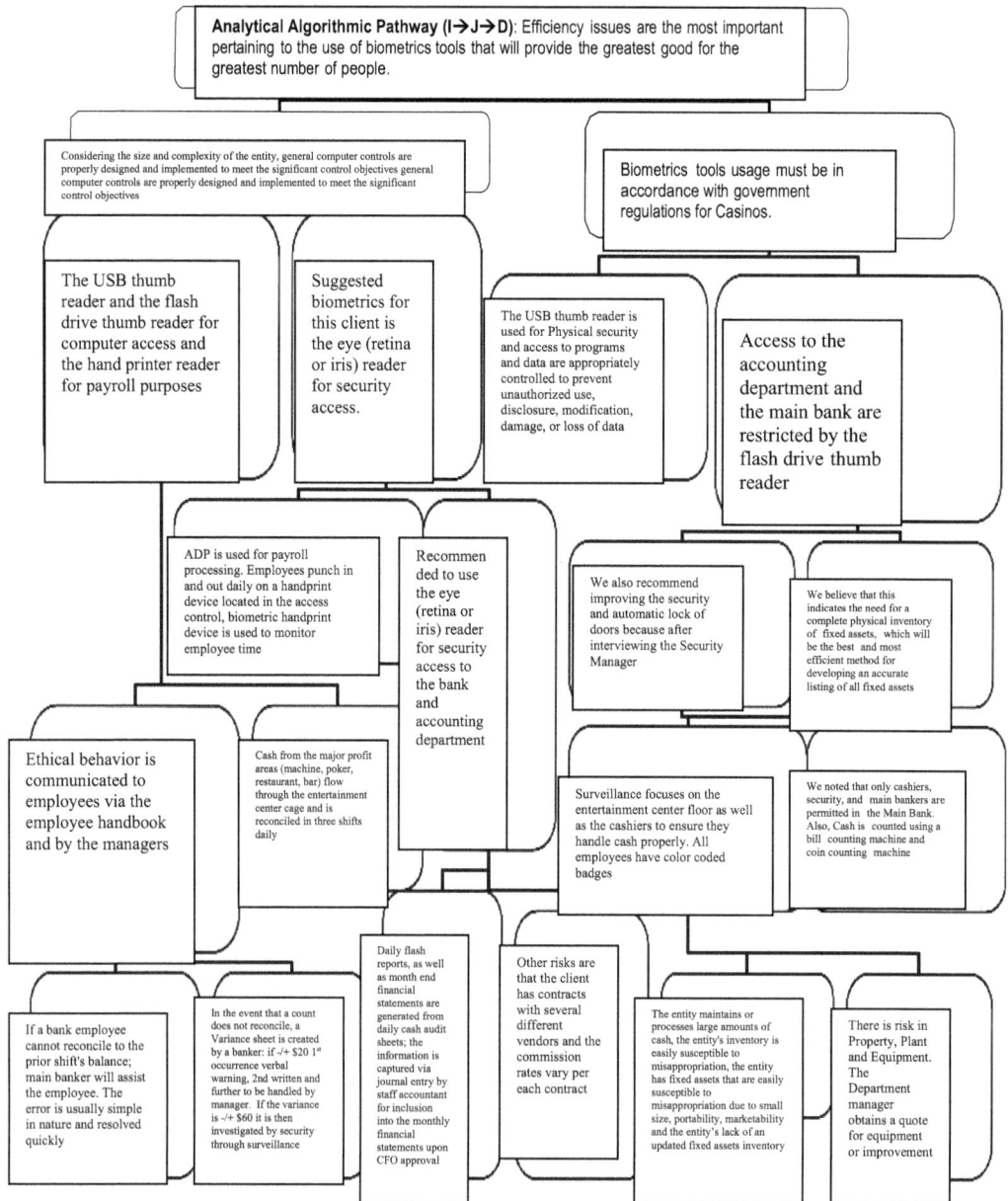

*(Fig. 6.7) cont.....*

The type of assets that NAI handles, and the amount of revenue earned by the company, requires the use of high security which is reached using strict biometrics, such as hand print reader, eye readers, hand print reader and hand geometry reader, among other tools.

The Company is treated as an enterprise fund on the financial statements of the Pueblo. The accounts of the Pueblo are organized on the basis of funds and account groups, each of which is considered a separate accounting entity. The operations of each fund are accounted for with a separate set of self-balancing accounts that are comprised of assets, liabilities, net assets, revenues and expenses, as appropriate

Although the client has excellent controls, the use of biometrics in this type of industry is highly recommended and necessary. Considering the size and complexity of the entity, general computer controls are properly designed and implemented to meet the significant control objectives

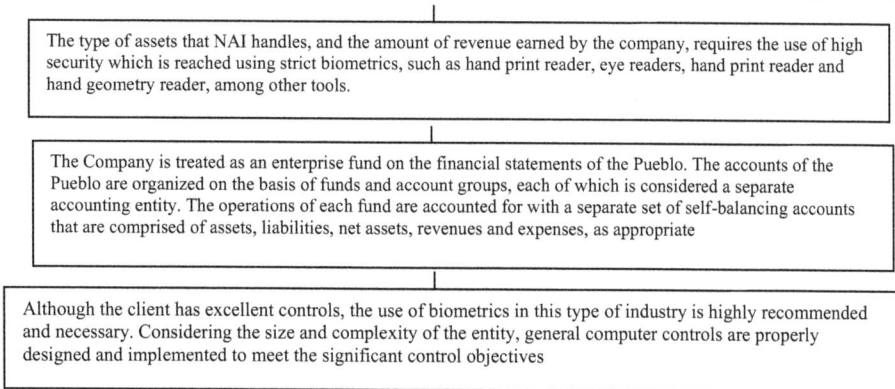

**Fig. (6.7).** Biometrics and internal controls in NAI. Source: Partially produced by students and author.

## EXAMPLE 6.2 -- ANALYTICAL PATHWAY (I→J→D) EMPLOYED IN ELANDA COMPANY

AI systems employing biometrics represent novel technology used to safeguard important assets, and its application provides a distinctive operational advantage for Elanda Inc. This organization is in a very competitive industry in which safeguarding its assets is an essential part of the company. This protection needs to be achieved in the most efficient and safe manner and the current internal controls reflect a lack of stability and protection. The company is in risk of being a victim of fraud, creating massive costs related to theft, legal issues, and unsafe products. The recommended biometric system consists of the implementation of seven systems that working together can reduce the risks that the company faces. This system will allow Elanda Inc. to obtain the protection that the organization requires not only to be safe but also successful. Further, consultants have recommended a system to safeguard assets, whereby the recommendation will create a sense of trust between employees, creating a trustful environment in which individuals will be able to support one another and obtain the best results for the organization. The six recommended biometrics are voice, keystroke dynamic, dynamic signature, vein, face, and retina scanners. These biometrics are focused on two cycles which are the purchasing/inventory cycle and the conversion of material cycle. Reducing risks and increasing productivity are the main focus on implementing these two cycles The recommended biometric system focuses on the analysis of different concerns and risks that exist in the aforementioned cycles. The first risk factor relates to the possible manipulation of inventory, which implies the misrepresentation of balances, theft, high costs and breaking the laws related to the protection of a control substance. Voice Recognition is recommended to access the databases and create updates in order to minimize this risk. The second risk factor can be depicted as the falsification of documents, which can create an issue of overpaying for inventory, misrepresentation of assets, and opportunity of theft between others. The recommended biometric is the implementation of Keystroke Dynamics to allow the productions of purchase orders and requests. The third risk factor relates to vendor selection, which is related to collusion between vendor and employee; increasing inventory costs and decreasing profitability opportunities. The internal control recommended is supervision and approval by using dynamic signature. The fourth risk factor pertains to vendor employee collusion thereby focused on the receiving department as well as the count and analysis of inventory received. This risk may create deficiencies related to incorrect quantity and quality reporting and the misuse of drugs in production, creating high costs of production, loss by theft, and legal issues. The biometric tool recommended for this risk is the use of Dynamic Signature. The fifth risk factor relates to the inventory in warehouse and laboratories theft. This risk relates to cost of stolen inventory, and the recommended biometric is the use of vein recognition to access inventory. The sixth risk factor is the Intangible access by unauthorized person, this issue is related to the main assets of the company that are formulas and research and development. To protect the intangible assets, we recommend the usage of a two biometrics tools, which are facial recognition to access the assets and dynamic signature to create copies or updates. Finally, the seventh and last risk factor pertains to pharmaceutical wrongdoing legal suits, in which the costs or possible liabilities can be unimaginable. Since there could be a tremendous monetary impact of this type of risk, a recommendation of three sets of approval process based on management hierarchy and strong biometrics, which are the dynamic signature, finger vein scanner and a retina scanner.

The implementation of the recommended system will generate a vast opportunity for growth for the organization in the pharmaceutical industry. The reasons for the growth are protection, whereby a business is able to protect their most significant assets by implementing good internal controls resulting in higher efficient, effective, and successful operations. The key to these results is the avoidance of unnecessary costs and losses that can arise from a fault in the security system (*i.e.*, common in using only passwords). The recommended biometric system has the advantage that it can be applicable to other needs in the different business cycles not only the ones specified previously.

**Background and Organization for Elanda Inc., Pharmaceutical Business**

Elanda Inc. is an organization that develops, creates, and sells different medicines. The constant changes and new developments in the industry creates a need for Elanda Inc. to have a large research and development system, which basically creates different formulas for new drugs and searches new ways of implementing chemical substances to improve and innovate the formulas of their products. The enterprise has the mission to create the best drugs possible creating huge profits for its competitive advantages related to the R&D.

## Biometric Internal Control Needs

The organization has different cycles including the revenue, expenditure, conversion, financing, and the fixed assets cycle. The cycles which have a higher business risks, regarding the need of implementation of biometrics to safeguard of assets are the inventory/purchasing (part of the expenditure cycle) and the conversion cycles mentioned before. Both of these cycles deal with important parts of the organization which are development of new drugs, safeguarding inventory or chemical substances, safeguarding formulas, patents and trademarks. The implementation of a biometric internal control is an essential part of the business since there is the need to protect the assets. As part of the internal controls, they implement several different technologies that are around the facilities to be able to protect their laboratories and warehouses from intruders and any unauthorized access. The control varies from passwords to access cards. Elanda Inc. has faced several issues related to the protection of its inventories especially because of the importance of the substances that it manages. To protect itself from employees with problems, the company has a policy to run background checks on every hire to prevent the company from ethical dilemmas.

## Fraud Analysis

Elanda Inc. has two cycles that are essential to its business, which are the inventory/ purchasing cycle and the conversion cycle. These two cycles are very essential since they deal with Elanda Inc.'s development procedures directly, which are the products (medicine), the process of conversion and the usage of different controlled substances. To design the fraud analysis which would be best suited for the organization, this section promotes the fraud triangle to guide the process, complementing it with the understanding of the tone of top management, and application of biometrics as a control towards the protection against fraud.

The fraud triangle is a model, which is used to analyze the potential risks of fraud. This model identifies three elements that allow a fraud to occur, or which can lead to it. These three elements are opportunity, pressure and rationalization; by themselves they can create a risk regarding fraud but combined they can be a huge threat for any business survival. The first element is *"opportunity,"* which relates to an organization internal control to diminish fraud or errors. Opportunity represents the giant loopholes within organizations that are prone to the riskiness of fraud. In other words, opportunity is the chance the employees of any organization can exploit internal control weaknesses by pilferage, manipulation, or misstatement of the organization's assets. The second element, *pressure* can be referred to as incentives or motives. Moreover, this motivation or incentive provide an employee or person a reason to commit a fraud, which can vary from financial problems, addictions, gambling, *etc*. The third element, *rationalization* is the justification of actions of the person committing the fraud. In addition, people who commit frauds commonly are first offenders who are trying to survive a difficult time or a complicated financial problem. These three elements are essential to create a successful plan to reduce fraud. Nonetheless, the only element that can be manipulated, controlled, and protected by the any company is "opportunity." Therefore, for this reason, the focus will be on this issue along with a supporting influence from pressure and rationalization.

## THE FRAUD TRIANGLE

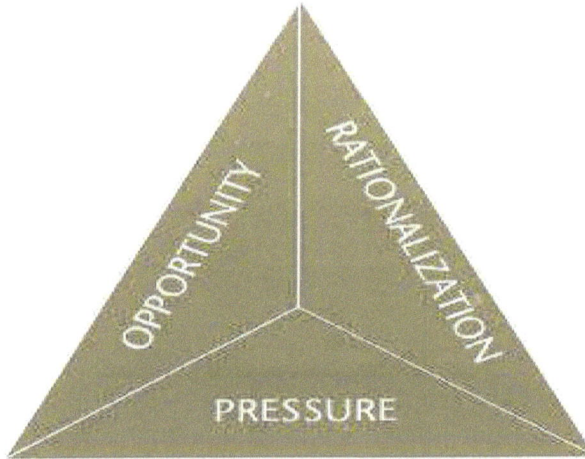

**Fig. (6.8).** Source: Rodgers, Söderbom, and Guiral [4].

The tone at the top management is an important part of this analysis since any organization is influenced by its senior executives. What this implies for Elanda Inc. is that management will be the base of every action, goal and mission of the business. All decisions of Elanda Inc. are decided by management; therefore, it is so essential to identify the type of algorithmic pathway that is implemented to determine management's goals and their action to achieve them. Hence, an examination of two different scenarios regarding the tone of the top is guided by the Throughput Model Analytical Algorithmic Pathway. The Analytical Algorithmic Pathway (I→J→D) defines relevant and reliable information is the assurance of good decision choices. When implementing this algorithmic pathway, information will directly influence the judgment stage before a decision choice is made. If possible, the information is predetermined and is weighted by other sources, without biases [5 - 7].

As indicated in Fig. (**6.1**), the typical decision-making process for the Analytical Algorithmic Pathway includes "specifying the problem, identifying all factors, weighting factors, identifying all alternatives, rating alternatives on each factor, and choosing the optimal alternative" [1]. The advantage of using this pathway is, of course, accuracy; information is reliable and relevant and personal preference will not influence our judgment. We only decide based on the analysis of precise and complete information; therefore, the choice we make is the most useful alternative. However, since information is rarely complete and the environment is constantly changing, if we cannot ensure that we have relevant and reliable information to begin with, the use of I→J→D will lead to an ill-informed, useless decision.

Fraud analysis utilizes the elements previously mentioned as well as the risks that are inherent in Elanda, Inc. The intent is to create a more appropriate analysis, and to be more efficient preventing and detecting fraud. This analysis of fraud elements is directed at the inventory/purchasing (part of the expenditure cycle) and the conversion cycles that focuses on the main risks that these two cycles present. The analysis also contains a solution or recommendation of how to prevent or reduce the risk of fraud, which is focused on the application of biometrics. In other words, biometric verification is how an individual can be distinctively identified by evaluating one or more distinguishing biological traits. This definition implies that a person is born with unique characteristics in their bodies which can identify them. Further, biometrics can be implemented to increase the internal controls of an organization and to achieve the reduction of fraud.

## Inventory and Purchasing Cycle

The inventory and the purchasing cycles are an essential part of Elanda Inc. since its' main assets are stored and received in this step of the business process. Pharmaceutical laboratories or companies have to be aware of the risks that this department is related to, especially because of the fragility and importance of the control of the substances that this department receives and stores. In the pharmaceutical industry the existence of laws controlling the types of chemicals that can be used, inventory control, drug storage and control are common. One of the organizations that control this issue in the United States is the Office of Diversion Controls and the title 21 Section 1304.11, which establishes the inventory requirements for this type of businesses. There are two main focuses that are related to this cycle: First creating the requisition of inventory and the second is the receipt of inventory and its control (Fig. **6.9**).

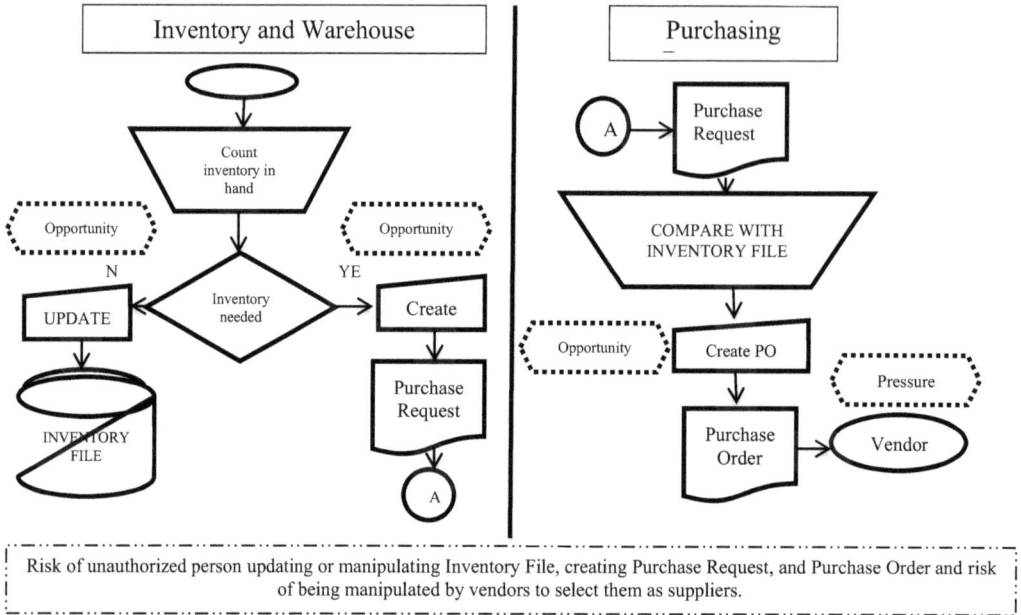

**Fig. (6.9).** Inventory requisition. Source: Partially produced by students and author.

The inventory requisition is basically the process that employees have to go through to order inventory. Fig. **(6.9)** reflects how the process of requisition of inventory functions on Elanda Inc., it also illustrates the types of risks and elements of the fraud triangle that create these risks. In the process inventory is counted and analyzed, then a purchase request is created and sent to the purchasing department for authorization, to finalize with the creation of the purchasing order. In this part of the inventory/purchasing cycle it is essential to detect and prevent risks to avoid higher issues as the process continues. In this section of the cycle there are four risks identified that can be divided in: misrepresentation of Inventory and the selection of vendors.

### *Misrepresentation of Inventory and Falsification of Documents*

The risk of misrepresentation of inventory balances can create the opportunity of fraud in different ways. The main issue for this risk is that the misrepresentation of drugs will create not only an issue of unaccounted assets and losses, but also regulations and laws that control the management of chemicals can be broken. This can create not only losses in higher inventory costs, but also costs related to legal issues. There are two main components of the misrepresentation of inventory that are the update of the inventory file, the falsification of purchase requisition and purchase orders.

The first risk is the manipulation of the inventory file, which is protected using a username and password. This type of control can be easily manipulated, stolen, and hacked; thereby, leaving the file unprotected and easy to access. This risk creates the opportunity to employees to manipulate the file to obtain a gain by recording fewer inventory balances and stealing the unreported chemicals or drugs. This opportunity is a temptation to employees and can open the door to huge losses that can arise from inventory theft and fines created by this uncontrolled asset. As previously mentioned, an appropriate "opportunity" control feature would be a sufficient way to address and minimize this risk. Therefore, using an appropriate biometric tool in this situation can address the problem. A beneficial recommendation pertaining to the issue is the use of voice recognition to log into the system as a verification process (see Fig. **6.10**). This type of system records the voice of an authorized personal, it uses the saved record to identify and give access to the person. Even though this system is not as secure of other biometric control tools it will assist in reducing risk, creating low costs and low effect on personal morale. This recommendation will work fittingly with the Analytical Algorithmic Pathway to be implemented in Elanda, Inc. One of the main reasons is that it has a low cost, assist in the reduction of risks, and since the tool is touchless, it will not affect employees in any way. This type of system will be effective in the requirements of Elanda Inc. preventing unauthorized changes in the inventory files.

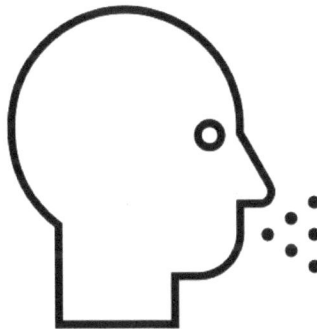

**Fig. (6.10).** Voice recognition. Source: Author created.

The second risk in the falsification of documents, which are closely related to the manipulation of the inventory file. This risk relates to the opportunity of employees to access the system and create falsified purchase requisitions and purchase orders. This opportunity can create a liability to the business since unauthorized people can be requesting inventory and stealing the inventory for their own benefits. The inadequate use or control of the files previously mentioned (*i.e.*, purchase request and purchase order), can create higher risks related to theft, fraud, or legal problems. A suitable recommendation for the creations of these files is the usage of the keystroke dynamics biometric system, which is a low-cost system that saves the movements or characteristics of how a person types to identify him as a unique individual. This type of system can trace access to the system by any individual, history of creation of documents, and verification of authorized users.

## *Vendor Selection*

Employees can send vendors the purchase orders, which means that they can select the vendors from an approved list. The procedure that the employee must use to select the correct vendor is by identifying best prices in of the products needed, by comparing the authorized vendors. Since the employee creates this decision there is the risk of manipulation from the vendor, which can be created by either a pressure, creating opportunity and even rationalization. The employee might be facing financial problems that vendors might use to convince the employee by paying him to select them as the vendor. This type of deals between employee and vendor would create for the employee an opportunity to obtain extra cash and he can rationalize the issue by thinking that he is not harming anyone by accepting this type of collusion. The risks on Elanda Inc. may seem small since it is an authorized vendor; however, if the company was going to save 50 cents for every pound of product by using another vendor, and buys one million pounds, then the loss would be material ($500,000). This type of risk can create losses related to overpaying for inventory, and even the implementation of low-quality products because of the relationship employee-vendor. To minimize this collusion, risk the recommendation would be to use strong supervision and the approval of purchase orders by the supervisor by using a dynamic signature verification, which would be used by the employee who creates the order and the person who approves it (Fig. **6.11**).

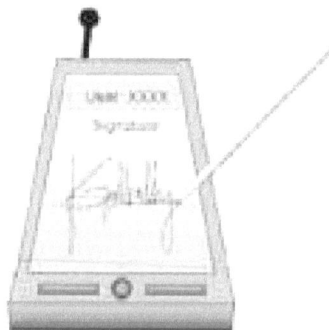

**Fig. (6.11).** Dynamic signature verification. Source: from Rodgers [3].

The receipt of inventory and control starts when the entity obtains the goods from the vendor (Fig. **6.12**). This process starts at the receiving department in which employees from Elanda, Inc. receive the drugs from suppliers and analyze and revise them for correct amounts and quality. After the appropriate tests are implemented, the goods are transferred to the inventory department where they are safeguard and the inventory file is updated.

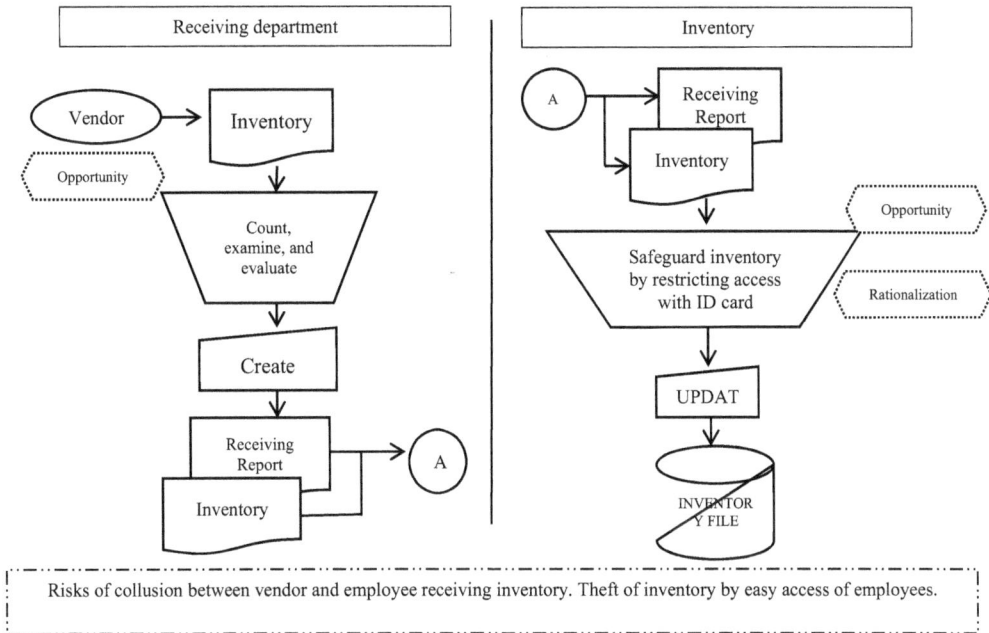

**Fig. (6.12).** Receiving and inventory department. Source: Partially produced by students.

## Safeguard of Drugs and Chemical Components and Theft of Inventory

The safeguard of drugs and chemical components received from vendors and the management of inventory are part of the purchasing/inventory cycle. The basic movement of assets on the purchasing department comes from vendors to Elanda Inc., receiving department, and the main assets received are the different chemical components used to produce the drugs that Elanda Inc. offers to the public. The chemicals that are received by the department must be analyzed, measured and accounted correctly to avoid any incorrect receiving reports related to quantity or quality. This transaction can bring many risks to Elanda Inc. including the collusion of vendors with any employee from the receiving department, the misuse low quality components to lower costs even though quality of the product can suffer and the risk of inventory theft.

For the first risk, the avoidance of collusion between vendors and employees the analysis is based on the opportunity reduction to commit fraud by collusion. Employees from the receiving department may make a deal with vendors to report more quantity or quality for chemicals; and they can be presented with the opportunity by only requiring one person to create the reports. The best solution for this issue is to segregate the responsibilities related to the assets. First by using biometric signature verification at the point of receiving from vendor and transferring to the examiners of inventory, with the implementation of at least two employees. The biometric signature verification uses a signature to identify a person as the correct user, not only by signature but also by how a person writes. That is, the correct signature is based upon the correct pressure, speed, and sequence. For the examination of the chemicals, two people can make the reports and using the fingerprint biometric to approve the data, which would be done by both individuals (Fig. **6.13**). The Analytical Algorithmic Pathway will generate the need for management to decide on the quality and the vendors that provide the best products for their own goods, creating high quality drugs and that will help the largest number of people and still create a good profit for Elanda Inc.

**Fig. (6.13).** Fingerprint biometrics. Source: Futuristic fingerprint scanning device biometric security system. Innovation concept. 3D Rendering. https://www.romaniajournal.ro/society-people/study-reveals-exten--of-biometric-data-collection-in-romania/

The second risk is related to inventory theft, which is a common problem especially in the pharmaceutical industry. As a result of the nature of the industry of drugs and medication, Elanda Inc. could be open for attacks due to a weakness in the system (*i.e.*, "opportunity" in the Fraud Triangle). That is, employees could present a problem by having easy access to the inventory, which is a risk that should be prevented by improving security and control measures. The pharmaceutical industry tends to have a high problem regarding this issue since the "rationalization" of some employees regarding stealing drugs. Some employees may tend to rationalize their actions by thinking that it will a small quantity, which will not make a difference to the company, or by stealing it to create a greater good for other people to which they give the medicines. The employees may also face different "pressures" (*i.e.*, motivations or incentives) to commit this type of aggression towards Elanda Inc. This transgression may be related to drug addiction to economic problems that can be solved by employees selling the drugs. The preeminent way to lower this risk is by creating a security system that prevents unauthorized users to have access to the inventory; thereby, making the authorized employees liable for loss of inventory by tracking access. A noteworthy biometric tool for this control would be using a palm print reader (Fig. **6.3**) or vein pattern biometric (Fig. **6.14**) for inventory room access which give access to authorized employees in a fast way tracking access, so Elanda Inc. can track their inventory movements relating them to an employee.

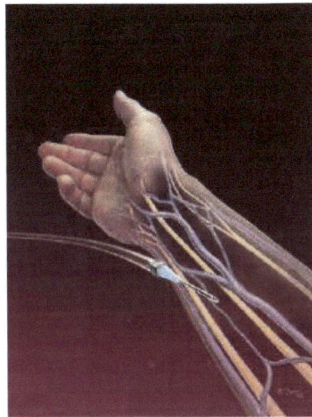

**Fig. (6.14).**  Vein patterns. Source: from Rodgers [3].

These types of scanners are more costly that fingerprint scanners, but they also provide more security, they are less costly and less invasive than other biometrics which could prevent employees of feeling attacked or harassed. The tone of top management emphasized Analytical Algorithmic Pathway will not create a distinction in this risk since they will be able to control their employees using the vein pattern scanner (see Fig. **6.14**) creating lower costs by controlling theft, the implementation of this technology is low invasive and the costs of the process of verification is low; so Elanda Inc. will be able to reduce costs and prevent employees from feeling attacked or invade the internal control systems.

The conversion cycle is defined by the process of converting the different chemicals and substances into the finish goods, which are medicines or drugs. Fig. (**6.15**) illustrates how the conversion system flows for Elanda Inc., identifying the highest risks on the cycle and including what category of the fraud triangle is presented. The flow chart in Fig. (**6.15**) shows how employees produces finished products. Personnel use several different formulas that are essential intangible assets for its success. The formulas are stored in a database, which is protected by the use of passwords. Even though these passwords are changed constantly (*i.e.*, every two months) there is still a high risk of unauthorized personnel to gain access to the formulas and steal them to use for personal gain such as selling to other pharmaceutical laboratories or manipulating them. Another important part of the conversion cycle is the research and development, which has to do with the creation and innovation of new drugs to improve products and increase satisfaction from customers. This side of the token has to do with "tone at the top" management, since it is their responsibility to accept and revise products, to prove that these products have the can be marketed by Elanda Inc. Implementing the Analytical Algorithmic Pathway can offer a means for management to explore for higher profits by claiming "extraordinary results" from medicines or drugs.

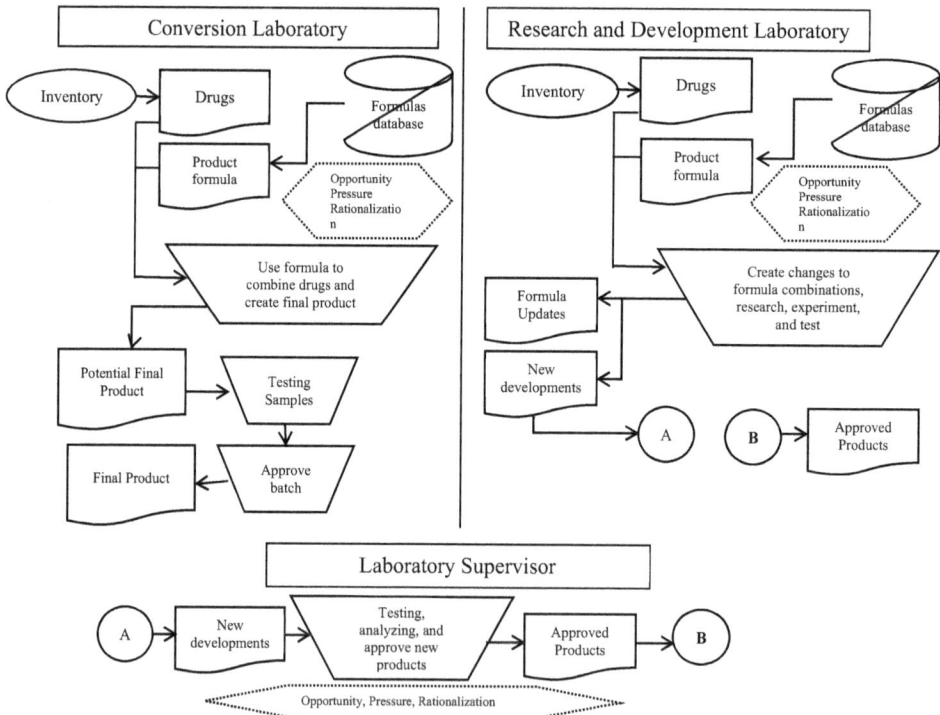

**Fig. (6.15).** Conversion cycle. Source: Partially produced by students.

One of the many concerns for this cycle that is the protection of Elanda Inc.'s intangible assets. These assets are stored in databases for the use of laboratory employees. Therefore, exploration should be considered for all three elements of the Fraud Triangle. In addition, external employees may try to access the computers using a stolen user identification and password. Hence, this type of fraud can not only originate from laboratory employees but also from external sources. In examining the "opportunity" component of the Fraud Triangle, the employees may observe that the access to the formulas have very low security controls; therefore, they may believe there is a chance to obtain a monetary gain by taking and selling the firm's assets. In examining the Fraud Triangle "rationalization" component, some employees may be unhappy working for Elanda Inc. This discontent may occur because of resentment or some type of disagreement, which may influence employees to take the formula to generic drug producers. In other words, they can sell the formulas in the open market at lower costs thereby causing harm to Elanda Inc. Employees may also think that selling the formulas will create a greater good to the people and that they are "heroes" for saving the world in this way. Finally, the Fraud Triangle component depicting "pressure" can contribute to wrongdoing by employees. For example, sometimes other pharmaceutical businesses will pay large amount of money to people who can sell this type of intangible assets to them, and employees that are facing financial problems may be tempted to do so. One way to reduce this element of the Fraud Triangle is to implement facial recognition for employees to log into the formula system. This procedure would be complemented by supervision of the laboratory management system when copies or prints of the formulas are made. The approval of prints and copies will be done electronically by using the biometric signature verification. The facial recognition biometric will create a database of individuals that are allowed to have formula access. Hence, this system can provide tracking the accesses with the employees' allowing Elanda Inc. to protect their intangible assets.

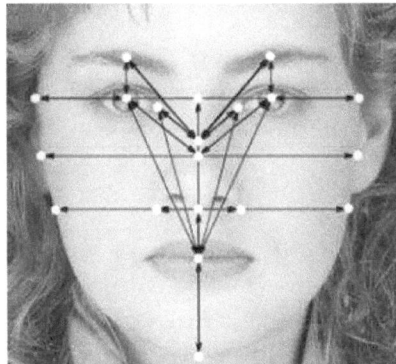

**Fig. (6.16).** Facial recognition. Source: from Rodgers [3].

The second concern pertains to pharmaceutical wrongdoing, which is a claim that a product has different results than what they have or not disclose the secondary effects. Since all Elanda Inc.'s products have to pass different tests for the approval of selling from the laboratory to management this issue is more related to them. A good way to avoid false claims of products is to have several approvals from different individuals in management. This approval process can be highly controlled by using biometric tools that display good results. For this reason, three types of biometrics will be introduced, which are: vein pattern scanner, biometric signature verification, complementing by a retina biometric scanner (see Fig. **6.6**). This combination will increase security to a large degree. The first step of approval would start with the signature of the laboratory supervisor, who will test the drug and analyze the results extensively (Fig. **6.11**). She/he will then send the prospective drug test results to the production manager, who will approve the drug by using a vein pattern scanner as a verification.

Finally, the production manager will send a summarized document to senior management for the last approval using a retina biometric scanner, resulting in the approval of the drug as a Elanda Inc. product or change in formula. The importance of Analytical Algorithmic Pathway is essential, since using this perspective will be suitable to eliminate or minimize risk. In the long run the implementation of the biometric systems will allow the company to be profitable in the future protecting its assets and preventing legal costs that can have a negative effect not only in profits but also in their clients' perspective. With the issuance of ineffective or harmful drugs, Elanda Inc. will be at risk of losing reputation, client loyalty, decreasing profit and economic stability.

Table **6.1** provides a summary for the classification of each biometric, identifying them individually to have a better understanding of the recommendation and its effects of the company.

**Table 6.1. Summary of biometrics tools.**

| Risk Concerns | Biometric Recommended | Classification | Control Activity |
|---|---|---|---|
| Manipulation of Inventory | Voice Recognition | Behavioral | Prevention |
| Falsification of documents | Keystroke Dynamic | Behavioral | Prevention & detection |
| Vendor Selection | Dynamic Signature | Behavioral | Prevention |
| Collusion employee-Vendor (inventory quantity and quality) | Dynamic Signature | Behavioral | Prevention |
| Inventory theft | Vein Pattern recognition | Physiological | Prevention & detection |
| Protection of Intangibles | Facial Recognition | Physiological | Prevention & detection |
|  | Dynamic Signature | Behavioral | Prevention |

*(Table 6.1) cont.....*

| Risk Concerns | Biometric Recommended | Classification | Control Activity |
|---|---|---|---|
| Pharmaceutical wrongdoing | Dynamic Signature | Behavioral | Prevention |
| | Vein Pattern scanner | Physiological | Prevention |
| | Retina Scanner | Physiological | Prevention |

Source: Adopted partially from Rodgers [2,3].

## Benefits of Biometrics

Benefits that will arise from the biometrics recommended for Elanda Inc. are related to the biometrics as a system and not as a single unit. Biometrics in general is more concerned on identifying a person based on personal characteristics. This type of systems is not only a great advance for the implementation of technology in internal systems they also reduce, at a great scale, theft of vital information and assets in an organization. In the case of Elanda Inc. it is very important to protect not only information, but also tangible assets, intangibles, and patents that may be beneficial to competitors.

Once an organization has established a secure environment for individuals will allow for a more trusting environment. Security includes building security, intangible assets security, and legal problems avoidance. Biometrics, in the case of Elanda Inc. will allow the company to prevent theft, increase their effectiveness, prevent losses and prevent high legal costs. Elanda Inc. management may have doubts arising from the costs of this system. The only answer to the question is that in the short run the investment may appear large, but the expense of the new biometrics system will pay for itself in the long run.

### Awareness of Bill of Rights

The application of biometrics can have several legal implications which are related to the Bill of Rights from the United States Constitution. The most important Bill of Rights is the first, third, fifth, and ninth amendment. Elanda Inc. must be aware of these amendments to avoid legal implications related to the violations that can occur with the application of biometrics.

The First amendment is related to the right of individuals to their freedom of speech. In case of the recommended biometrics the voice recognition biometric and the typing dynamics are the most important related to the right. The best way to avoid any repercussions related to violation of the right is to create a policy that must be signed by the employees that will be subject to the biometric system specifying the function of the systems and how they would be use. This type of policy will be a protection to the enterprise showing the rights and obligations that the business has related to voice and keystroke dynamic recognition. Under this policy Elanda Inc. should specify the uses and intention of the systems, it should also use the system as it is specified and avoid using these biometrics to obtain other types of information.

The Third Amendment protects an individual against unreasonable searches and seizures. As in the previous amendment a policy should be implemented regarding the uses of biometrics, specifying an agreement between employees and employers to the allowable uses and prohibitions of each system. This right basically prohibits Elanda Inc. from using any information obtained as an internal security in other purposes. For example, the retina data obtained from employees should only be used with the intend of verification and allowing access for employee, if this type of data shows any type of illness or problem Elanda Inc. would not be allowed to use that information to fire the employee or to take other actions that can affect the individual in a negative matter.

The Fifth Amendment is related to self-incrimination; this amendment gives individual the right to not be witness against themselves. This is an important issue that has to be clear to all employees that will be using the biometric systems. The policy should specify that if the biometrics of an individual can prove a wrongdoing, he or she will be liable. This will protect Elanda Inc. against suits that are based on this right, since the employee will have an agreement in which he specifies that any proof obtained with his biometrics would be useful evidence in any court of law.

Finally, the ninth amendment is related to any rights that are not specified under the bill of rights but that an individual should have. This opened right is the hardest one to protect from since it is difficult to predict the creativity of individuals. The best recommendation here is to create the biometric policy agreement as clear and specific as possible trying to cover as much territory related to rights as it is possible. The key for a good protection against employee legal actions is the clear understanding of the mentioned policy.

## CONCLUSION

The $I \rightarrow J \rightarrow D$ analytical pathway implies that available information sources ($I$) have a direct impact on our analysis ($J$) before a decision is made. This is a more analytical pathway in the perceptual framing ($P$) is played down or it is just not part of the decision-making course of action. The information sources ($I$) have been weighted in terms of their analysis function impact ($J$). The information sources use is to be reliable and programmable, however, changes in the environment can happen but the information sources used by a person typically do not change.

## Classification of Recommended Biometrics

Biometrics are grouped either by type of by classification. On the first category which is type, biometrics are categorized depending on the function that they fulfill: identification or verification. The first biometric type (identification) has to do with a larger or undefined group of individuals. These types or biometric are commonly used in government in and require a huge databank. Identification biometrics matches the information that is presented to the system to a databank that contains millions of records. Verification in the other side, recognizes a record of a database, and instead of matching the information it only revises that the data provided is correct and that the person is really who claims. The recommendations previously mentioned all fall into the second type of biometric which is Verification. This is because the information provided to the system only revises the data and matches the information in a 1:1 record.

Biometrics systems can also be classified as behavioral and physiological, depending on the biometric information used. Basically, the difference between the two depends on the change over time. The behavioral systems relate to movement, characteristics, and personal details that even though they are unique for each individual they can change over time. For example, voice recognition will fall under this category; the voice of an individual changes because of different events of a person's life including sickness, time passing, and other external circumstances that affect this characteristic of an individual. The classification as physiological biometric systems is related to individual characteristics that never change even with the effect of time or other natural events on a person's life. An example of this classification of biometrics is facial recognition, which uses facial traits or complex points in the face of an individual to identify him as a unique person. Our recommendation counts with both classifications of biometrics to improve the effectiveness and the benefits of the use of the system.

Finally, biometrics that was recommended in this study has the function of acting as internal controls and as such they should be classified as either preventive or detective controls. Preventive controls are the controls that reduce the risk of happening and detective controls identify where issues are arising so correction can be made. Between the different systems recommended the prevention controls are the ones that verify authorized users and prevent unauthorized users to access information and assets. By the application of these controls Elanda Inc. will be able to control access, manipulation, reporting and other parts of the business that might be presented with risks. For the detection controls that are recommended, their basic function can trace and record accesses. Moreover, misstatements, thefts or frauds can be traced to a specific individual, which will allow organizations to detect, eliminate and correct fraud issues.

# REFERENCES

[1]  W. Rodgers, *Process Thinking: Six pathways to successful decision making* iUniverse, Inc: NY, 2006.

[2]  W. Rodgers, *Biometric and Auditing Issues Addressed in a Throughput Model.* Information Age Publishing, Inc.: Charlotte, NC, 2012.

[3]  W. Rodgers, *E-commerce and biometric issues addressed in a Throughput Model.* Nova Publication: Hauppauge, NY, 2010.

[4]  W. Rodgers, A. Söderbom, and A. Guiral, "Corporate Social Responsibility Enhanced Control Systems reducing the Likelihood of Fraud", *J. Bus. Ethics,* vol. 91, suppl. Suppl. 1, pp. 151-166, 2014.

[5]  W. Rodgers, A. Guiral, and J.A. Gonzalo, "Different Pathways that Suggest Whether Auditors' Going Concern Opinions are Ethically Based", *J. Bus. Ethics,* vol. 86, no. 3, pp. 347-361, 2009. [http://dx.doi.org/10.1007/s10551-008-9851-8]

[6]  A. Guiral, W. Rodgers, E. Ruiz-Barbadillo, and J.A. Gonzalo, "Ethical Dilemmas in Auditing: Dishonesty or Unintentional Bias?", *J. Bus. Ethics,* vol. 91, no. S1, suppl. Suppl. 1, pp. 151-166, 2010. [http://dx.doi.org/10.1007/s10551-010-0573-3]

[7]  W. Rodgers, and T. McFarlin, *Decision Making for Personal Investments: Real Estate Financing, Foreclosures and Other Issues.* Palgrave Macmillan: London, 2017. [http://dx.doi.org/10.1007/978-3-319-47849-4]

# CHAPTER 7

# The Revisionist Algorithmic Pathway

Everything that civilisation has to offer is a product of human intelligence; we cannot predict what we might achieve when this intelligence is magnified by the tools that AI may provide, but the eradication of war, disease, and poverty would be high on anyone's list. Success in creating AI would be the biggest event in human history. Unfortunately, it might also be the last.

---Stephen Hawking

In case you are sitting here pondering this question thinking that AI will never eliminate human intelligence because humans still have to program and train them, that isn't entirely true. Right now, there are of course still researchers, programmers, and engineers who train robots and rudimentary AI systems. However, more and more code -- much of it in relation to AI -- is actually being written by AI programs already. Programmers today no longer have to write long complex codes for AI telling the robot to do this or that. They simply have to write code that tells a program to write code telling the AI to do this or that.

---Trevor English

One could argue that an AI system would not only imitate human intelligence, but also "correct" it, and would also scale to arbitrarily large problems. But we are now in the realm of science fiction.

---Michael Jordan

**Abstract**

The Revisionist Algorithmic Pathway (I→P→D) focusses on an unstructured environment whereby people or organizations may use all available information to influence their perception before rendering a decision. In this situation, the information can be complete or incomplete. Nonetheless, due to the vagueness of the event it becomes challenging for individuals or organizations to model the data according to rating, ranking, or ordering. Hence, the use of this algorithmic pathway is highly dependent on information changing resulting in a alteration of how individuals or organizations perceive a situation.

**Keywords:** 4th Industrial Revolution, Algorithm, Biometrics, Decision choice, Deep learning, Facial recognition, Fraud triangle, Identification, Information, Machine learning, Neural networks, Opportunity, Perception, Pressure, Rationalization, Revisionist algorithmic pathway, Supervised Learning, Throughput Model, Unsupervised Learning, Verification, Voice recognition.

## INTRODUCTION

The I→P→D algorithmic pathway is known as the "revision pathway" because information can influence an individual's perception of looking at things. When individuals use this pathway, they must trust the information is accurate. When there is time pressure or an unstable environment this pathway can force an individual to use it because they may not have time to analyze the situation. The I→P→D pathway can be divided into two parts given a stable or unstable environment, which could result in different decision choices.

The Revisionist Algorithmic Pathway (I→P→D) is based on Information to Perception to Decision Choice. This pathway suggests that available sources of information will influence the perception of the problem and therefore, will guide the decision. This pathway relies on information to revise our perception. This pathway suggests that information will be used to shape our perception even if it is incomplete, unreliable, or wrong, as long as the person making the decision believes the information to be true. This pathway serves well in unstable environments and is used when time is not sensitive in solving the problem (Fig. **7.1**).

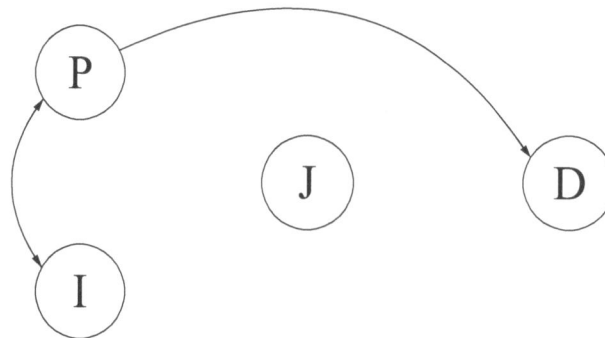

**Fig. (7.1).** I→P→D The algorithmic decision pathway consists of information to perception to decision choice. Source: Rodgers [1].

The Revisionist Pathway (I→P→D) is similar to the Expedient Pathway (P→D), with the exception that information revises the perception of an individual. An example about this would be when an audit firm gets a new client. Before accepting a new engagement with a new client, auditors have the responsibility of contacting the prior year auditor's and get the necessary information to get started on the audit. Since the auditor does not know the client, the information received from the prior auditors helps shape the auditor's perception of the client. This is a very important and mandatory step in the process. If the auditor is unable to obtain information from the prior auditors, the auditor must Fig. out a way to replace that step. In this case, the decision would be whether to accept the client or not. AI that would help the auditor with this step, would be if the prior auditors had some sort of compatible software, where the new auditors could easily transfer the required information.

The information can be considered as the starting point, since new information provides the necessary signals to improve our shape or the way we are understanding the situation and it helps before any action is taken. This process is like a symbolic neural network function that updates an entity's perception (*i.e.*, I→P), which reflects a Bayesian model (Rodgers, 2020).

Furthermore, in this pathway information is effectively used even if it may be incomplete, or with interpretational problems. In other words, this pathway may also indicate individuals making decisions based on information they are given, whether it is accurate or not. If the information confirms their framing or belief structure with what they have already perceived, an individual may go ahead and continue to make a decision choice based on it. An important example is when some individuals may decide to attend graduate school and pursue a postsecondary education because they believe that will prepare them better for the workforce and they will get paid more as compared to someone who does not attend graduate school.

## EXAMPLE 1: REVISIONIST PATHWAY (I→P→D) FOR PAY CARD SYSTEMS

Driven by the 4th Industrial Revolution, technology has completely infiltrated our world and there is no going turning back. AI and the concepts surrounding it may still seem to the layperson, as distant ideas that do not lay within our homes but that would be incorrect. Our everyday lives are filled with computers and the advancements that tech giants have created. This is even more apparent in the business world. There are fewer and fewer organizations that do not rely on technology and AI to help stabilize and grow their business. As a result of this, there are more opportunities' for not only fraud prevention, but also for misstatements and flaws that can wreak havoc on any organization. As technology and the businesses that utilize them advance it is vital that auditors and forensics advance and understand these models as well. Understanding algorithms, natural language processing, machine learning, and deep learning is becoming more and more important in the lives of people as they are faced with reviewing these models.

As technology has advanced and the use of machines and computers increased, the amount of data has massively increased. Today organizations can have data sets that are so large that it is impossible to interpret them without the help of computers and programs to assist in mining the information. Algorithms help with the understanding of big data and can adapt to the growth of big data. There are six main types of algorithms that are used today. Algorithms as described in the Throughput Model use different structures of perception, information, judgement to determine the decision choice as follow:

1. **The Expedient Pathway P→D**
2. **The Ruling Guide Pathway P→J→D**
3. **The Analytical Pathway I→J→D**
4. **The Revisionist Pathway I→P→D**
5. **The Value Driven Pathway P→I→J→D**
6. **The Global Perspective Pathway I→P→J→D**

The first algorithm described in the model is related to quick and uncomplicated decision paths described as the Expedient Pathway (P→D). This model focuses plainly on what is the need of the user. The second algorithm is related to the Ruling Guide Pathway (P→J→D), which depicts guidelines and procedures. The third algorithm is the Analytical Pathway, which embraces the use of relevant and reliable information for decision-making process. The major difference that sets this pathway apart from the previous two pathways is the importance of information. The fourth algorithm is the Revisionist Pathway, which can alter the Expedient Pathway depending on the information input into the system. That is, the Revisionist Pathway implies that the available information sources (**I**) can influence individuals' framing (**P**) of the problem before arriving at a decision (**D**) [1].

Next, we have the Value-Driven Pathway, which views the perception first then reviews the information before making a judgment and a decision. The Value-Driven Pathway (P→I→J→D) builds on the Analytical Pathway (I→J→D) by adding individuals' perception to modify the information a decision-maker uses in their analysis. With this particular pathway, although the decision maker uses relevant and reliable information in his analysis process, the very information used is sculpted by perceptual framing.

Finally, the last algorithm is the Global Perspective Pathway. This algorithm scrutinizes the information and then at the perspective of the person or thing before making judgments and the final decision choice. Further, the Global

Perspective Pathway (I→P→J→D) includes a framing aspect of "P" that influences the Ruling Guide Pathway process (P→J→D) of procedures and guidelines.

Understanding these algorithms and how to apply them can make not only problem solving in organizations easier but can increase efficiency and improve internal control systems. This algorithmic structure can help policy makers, medical professionals, legal experts, auditors, forensics specialists, and others to understand how computers are making decisions and that factors that can alter those decisions. Big data can be applied to the I or information of the Throughput model.

## Machine Learning Implemented with the Revisionist Pathway (I→P→D)

Machine learning works well in the Revisionist Pathway, since it allows computers and other machines to learn information and essentially make predications on incoming information. Technologists have applied the ideas of the way that humans learn to the way that they teach machines to learn. There are 2 main forms of machine learning: supervised and unsupervised learning.

## Supervised Learning

Supervised learning is a model that assigns labels or categories to a set of data to allow the machine to understand what the expected output should be based on the inputs. A coin machine, such as the common Coin Star machines, can quickly calculate how much money is deposited by summing and identifying the various coins within the deposit. These machines operate by pouring one's coins into a kiosk (stand-alone booth typically used in high-traffic areas). When all the coins have been counted, a person will receive a paper voucher for cash, or an eGift Card, which has a unique code printed at the top.

An AI machine learning supervised model could be implemented to teach the machine that coins of different weights have different values. A quarter would weigh about .2 ounces and have a diameter of about .955 inches whereas, a penny would have a weight of .08 ounces and has a diameter of about .75 inches. The machine would understand that coins that came in with a quarter's dimensions should be given a value of .25 while those that came in with a value of a penny should be given a value of .01. The machine has used a supervised model to calculate the amounts because the machine was provided labels or categories of a data set to help it understand what output it should provide.

## Unsupervised Learning

Unsupervised learning is when labels are not provided to the machine, so other techniques need to be utilized to attain the desired output. In contrast to supervised learning, there is not technically any incorrect outputs since there are no specified categories. This system works quite well in a Revisionist Algorithmic Pathway (I→P→D) setting. An appropriate example of this would be a system that helped assign coupons based on customer habits. The system would use a cluster of the customers data points to determine different characteristics about the customers. The machine may be able to indicate what customers order frequently, but only one pizza at a time. Further, the machine could determine which customers order less frequently but order many pizzas at a time. This information and systems that are unsupervised can produce different types of information that can be useful to analyze and evaluate the data in much more manageable groups.

## Deep Learning

Deep learning is another concept related to machine learning; however, benefits more from neural networks. The most significant differences from basic machine learning to deep learning is that deep learning machines can learn and apply its methods and learned information to data that is new to the system. Additionally, deep learning is usually identified by technologists as a system that has many hidden internal layers and levels as opposed to the simple network that has one, as shown in Fig. (**7.2**).

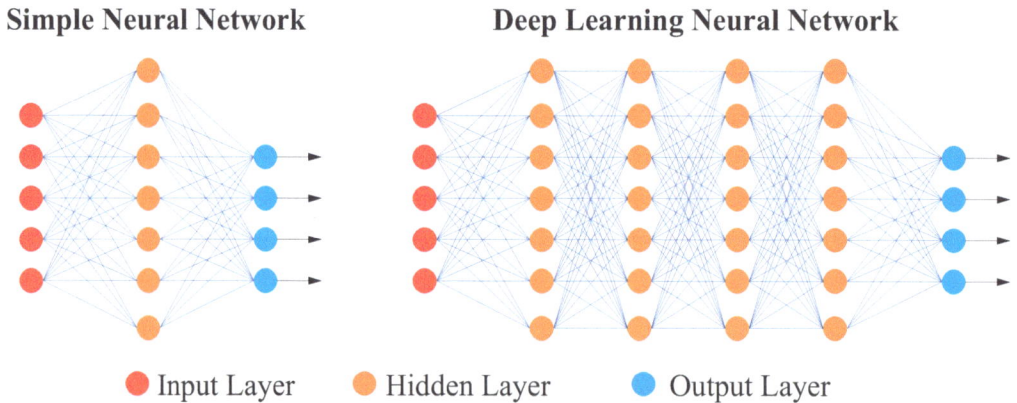

**Simple Neural Network**                    **Deep Learning Neural Network**

● Input Layer      ● Hidden Layer      ● Output Layer

**Fig. (7.2).** Neural networks. Source: Partially adopted from Rodgers [2].

The implementation of multiple layers expands the capabilities of the networks and allows the system to go even further and interpret information that basic machine learning systems cannot perform. A deep learning system would be able to receive unknown input and continuously learn to become more and more accurate. For example, a system can be shown hundreds of different flowers and eventually be able to receive new pictures of flowers and correctly label their genus. These systems can achieve this by making millions of micro calculations with the given data. This technique is called neural networks. Deep learning systems can become extremely advanced and have the capability of making decisions that we once thought were only possible with humans. These types of deep learning machines are more and more present in our everyday lives such as in our vehicles. That is, today it's very common to find a vehicle that offers lane assistance and safety stopping options. The engineers of these features have utilized deep learning machines that can interpret the lane lines, walls, or other objects and make quick decisions to make corrective actions and keep the driver safe.

## Application for Accountants, Auditors and Forensic Accountants

Understanding these concepts is essential for managers and auditors since these tools are used with an ever-increasing number of organizations in today's world. Managers and auditors ought to understand these concepts and how these tools leave organizations open to fraud based off the way someone could try to manipulate these systems. Additional fraud prevention and deterrence can be enhanced by using some of the mentioned techniques. Even staff accountants can use these techniques to help improve internal controls. For example, internal controls can be enhanced by using biometrics to control who is able to view or work with certain information or even to verify who is working on what task. Auditors can use machine learning to categorize transactions to help determine what kinds of test and samples need to be provided. An unsupervised system could possibly categorize transactions or accounts that have higher dollar amounts that are not consistent with what was expected. Although seemingly complicated, artificial intelligence is a growing reality in the world of accounting that should be embraced and enhanced to grow the profession.

## Biometrics Enhancing the Revisionist Algorithmic Pathway

For more reliable and precise systems, machine learning and deep learning techniques can be applied to biometrics and their application areas [3]. These novel powerful algorithms are superb candidates for solving the challenging biometrics problems. Organizations experiencing major data breaches are seriously looking for better methods to increase their access control and security systems as well as stay one step ahead of data hackers.

Biometrics denotes any reliable method that tell apart one person from another using measurable qualities that may be physiological (*e.g.*, fingerprints, hand geometry, retinas, iris, facial image) or behavioral (signature, voice, keystroke dynamics). Biometrics is a notable tool for identifying the "who' aspect in internal control systems. Biometrics unlike other measures, do not test what you know such as a password or login but rather test what you are. A fingerprint scan can either be a low grade or a higher-grade sensor or sonar. Facial recognition uses an algorithm to identify key points on a frame of the objects face (usually between the lower forehead and upper lip area). A palm scan just as with a fingerprint scan can vary in intensity and accuracy depending on the level of security needed. Moreover, there are new methods of biometrics emerging, that are extremely accurate. There is a system that monitors who a person is by their walking strides (*i.e.*, gait biometrics), yet another tool, which identifies typing methods and strokes (*i.e.*, typing dynamics). Furthermore, there has been continual advancements every few years regarding a biometric tool that identifies people by sense of smell [4]. The system attempts to mimic a canine's acute sense of smell to help identify individuals or traits of the individuals. This system although highly accurate is incredibly expensive to implement.

The most common biometrics used today are fingerprint scans, palm scans, iris scans, and facial recognition. The level of protection provided by biometrics is generally weighed against the value that a particular object has. For example, the common fingerprint sensor on most cell phones today is a lower grade scan that protect the contents of the phone for the owner. This is a lower-level security measure. Compare that with the security of a bank vault where there might be multiple measure of biometric scans or a dual system. These types of higher security might use a high-grade sonar to scan a fingerprint in addition to an iris scan or facial recognition.

More secure systems generally use a dual system of either 1 or multiple levels of biometric reads along with what the person knows. This level of protection is ideal for high value items or top-secret information.

Although, biometrics have great potential in increasing security measure for organizations they have also open the doors for ethical questioning of the apparatuses. Many have come to question how ethical it is to hold records of this nature on people and what can this information be used towards or sold for. There are serious privacy concerns when looking at the growing biometric world because individuals cannot be certain what this information will be used for or who has access to it or what it can be used for. For example, the United States 4th amendment protects citizens from unreasonable searches and seizures. This implies that police must have permission or a valid warrant to conduct a search, however this area becomes grey with the use of biometrics. For example, in a case that sparked controversy, during a Superbowl game a face recognition scan was run over the audience. The local police then accessed this information to find individuals with warrants on them and promptly went to the game to arrest them. These types of actions bring serious concern over the use of biometrics in large scales and what this could mean for privacy.

## Fraud and Artificial Intelligence

One of the greatest uses in the business world of AI is the use to detect and prevent acts of fraud. The fraud triangle provides a visual for characteristics of those that commit fraudulent activities. The fraud triangle areas are pressure, rationalization, and opportunity (Fig. **7.3**).

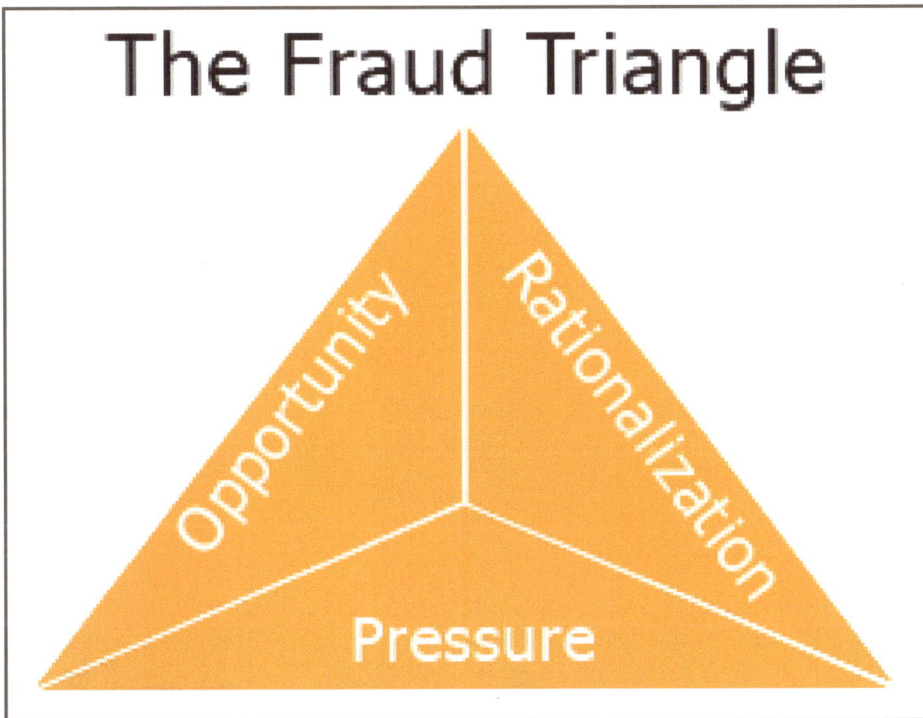

**Fig. (7.3).** Fraud triangle. Source: Rodgers, Söderbom, and Guiral [6].

With the use of biometrics and AI there is the capability of making the opportunity of committing fraud more difficult.

## Decision Trees

Decision trees are great tools to help create a pathway for how the Revisionist Algorithmic Pathway (I→P→D) algorithm will operate. Decision trees use branches, nodes, and roots to show different alternative for a given situation. They are based on if then statements. They can be very simple or extremely complex. Although there are many positive associated with decision trees, there are a few negatives. Decision trees are only as good the potential branches created within them. If certain scenarios are not played out correctly or if a situation arises that the decision tree has not foreseen than an issue can occur. To combat the idea of open forest has been created, which is a highly advanced form of decision trees that work in conjunction with each other to combat these situations. In addition, it is essential when creating a decision tree to identify what type of errors the system should lean to for implementation.

## Type 1 and Type 2 Errors

Type 1 errors are those in which the correct person is prevented from entering into the system. Most Type 1 systems are created for very protected items such as access to high amount of cash or protected trade secrets. These systems would rather inconvenient a user that should be in the system than to allow someone in that should not be in the system. On the contrary, Type 2 systems are those that admit a person into the system that should not be admitted. Type 2 systems are more common in operations settings where the cost of hindering this information. An example of this would be a line at Disneyland, there are scanners, and the guards are checking that no outside food or drink enter and that only people with tickets enter the park. Nonetheless, it would greatly slow down the line and affect profits if each person where thoroughly searched and tickets were biometrically verified.

## Pay Card Access System

Pay cards are options for employees that do not have direct deposit information of prefer to have their funds deposited on a pay card rather than traditional forms of payment. Pay cards act as cash or pre-paid cash cards, where funds can be instantly removed from the cards. Pay card systems are generally linked the companies banking institution and once access is granted payroll processors can deposit funds to pay cards. The processor also can set up a new card and activate them in the system. Payroll fraud can be achieved by running a duplicate payroll for a particular employee and subsequently have the funds deposited onto a pay card. Infuriately, systems such as this have been subject to fraud, and it has become necessary to identify ways to deter fraudulent activity. Apparently, perhaps an AI program utilizing a decision tree would be effective in cultivating this process.

The advantage of this proposed system is that there will be a greater sense of control over the access into the Pay Card system. The system would provide management greater visibility of activities that are occurring int the system. The system would be able to identify any duplications made in the system so that users can address and improve the process. The disadvantages of the system are that it poses the opportunity that production could be slowed if information is not properly adjudicated. Finally, this system is somewhat more costly. Nonetheless, when comparing the potential loss in assets to the cost of the system it seems clear that implementing a system like this would be overall beneficial.

## EXAMPLE 2: REVISIONIST PATHWAY (I→P→D)

AI software provides organizations and individuals to use and analyze data by making it possible for machines to learn from experience, but most importantly to perform human-like tasks, such as analyzing, decision-making, as well as problem solving. Some of the AI examples are self-driving cars, Apple's Siri and Amazon's Alexa, flying drones and many more. These AI robots reply heavily on deep learning and natural language processing. By utilizing these technologies, computers can be trained to achieve specific tasks by processing large amounts of data and recognizing patterns in the data set. AI is a field that requires knowledge in many subjects, such as computer science, linguistics, biology, and philosophy.

This section discusses the implementation of AI technology involving machine learning, deep learning, algorithms, and big data to the relationship with the Throughput Model. That is, the Throughput Model algorithms are discussed in relationship of AI powered biometrics addressing fraud concerns. In addition, the biometrics technologies are associated with the process of decision making. These technological tools are important for organizations since they help in preventing fraud. The implementation of the security system employing biometrics improves efficiency by freeing up employees to concentrate on areas where human judgment is required for other problem-solving issues. In addition, a decision tree is presented on airport security systems and the relationship to biometrics technologies.

### AI Technologies Employed in Airports

During the previous two decades, airports globally have considerably ramped up security in response to developing threats. In the intervening time, rising passenger expectations have placed pressure on major transport hubs to augment throughput, cut queues and make the journey from entrance to departure gate as seamless as possible.

For example, the US Transportation Security Administration has instituted a novel computed tomography (CT) scanners, which use AI to help target threats, at Los Angeles International Airport, John F. Kennedy and Phoenix airports (see https://www.airport-technology.com/features/ai-at-airports-security/). In addition, Hartsfield-Jackson Airport has launched its first biometric terminal in the United States. Willing participants can utilize facial recognition scanners at self-service kiosks, TSA checkpoints and boarding gates. Fingerprinting, facial recognition and retinal scans undoubtedly will become progressively used for security purposes at airports.

A biometric computerized tomography (CT) scan merges a series of X-ray images taken from distinct angles around a person's body and utilizes computer processing to create cross-sectional images (slices) of the bones, blood vessels and soft tissues inside the person's body. CT scan images provide more-detailed information than plain X-rays do. Moreover, AI technologies are emerging across the entire aviation spectrum, from self-service check-in robots to facial recognition checks at customs.

AI systems improve as more and more information is nursed into them. In the case of airport security, machine learning can be used to analyze data and identify threats quicker than a human could perform. Items that heretofore required to be scanned separately, such as laptops, can be kept in passenger luggage as they pass through security checkpoints.

In addition to checkpoints, AI can refine security at the landside area of airports. The Evolv Edge system (https://www.htds.fr/en/security/body-scanners-a-d-thermal-cameras/evolv-edge-mass-people-screening-solution/) implements a combination of camera, facial recognition, and millimeter-wave technologies to scan people walking through a portable security gate. Machine learning techniques are utilized to automatically analyze data for threats, including explosives and firearms, while ignoring non-dangerous items such as keys and belt buckles users may be carrying on themselves. Evolv Technology provides security screening by combining advanced sensors and AI to protect visitors at a wide variety of events and venues from concealed weapons and public health threats.

In airports, machine learning utilizes to apply AI techniques in which a machine "learns" patterns in a dataset by itself without being guided by any human. In other words, the systems can change actions and responses depending on the situations as they are exposed to more data. In addition, machine learning, which is a branch of AI, is based on the notion that systems can learn from data and experience, identifying patterns and make decisions with minimal human intervention. These capabilities will enhance the judgments that management must make for decision-making process and ultimately providing better, and more effective airport security. The advancement of technologies is increasing very quickly in today's world, to where AI has the power to understand data by applying algorithms to it and ultimately making predictions on the outcome that is still "unknown". Machine learning brings many possibilities of extending automated decision-making processes, allowing a greater range and depth of decision-making without human input, which is truly crucial in many organizations.

## Deep Learning

Deep learning, also powered by neural networks and goes further than machine learning in terms of the output that a machine produces as applied to AI. The strength of machine learning is that it performs very well in situation like "known but new" information. However, when it comes to "unknown and new," machine learning lacks in performance. Whereas deep learning is design to learn from internal data and apply it to external data. Deep learning uses neural networks, which are a set of algorithms and works like a human brain to recognize patterns and to make human-like judgement. By using this biometrics, deep learning can look at an image, text or sounds and determine what it represents, whether it is a human eye, face, flower, landscape, car, or building. Deep learning is a key technology behind all the technologies that are becoming popular, such as driverless cars. Further, it recognizes the traffic sign, and distinguish a pedestrian when crossing the street. Moreover, some cities have driverless train, which can always operate automatically, including door closing, detecting obstacle, people and emergency situations.

## Big Data in Relationship to the Throughput Model

To perform high-quality audit, several keys must be taken into considerations before a decision is made. This will make to improve the design, develop, and implement biometrics into an internal control security system. Thus, the *Throughput Model* is introduced since it separates the decision-making process into its four main parts. Fig. **(7.4)** represents the *Throughput Model*, where it contains, "P" for *perception*, "I" for *information*, "J" for *judgment* and "D" for *decision choice*.

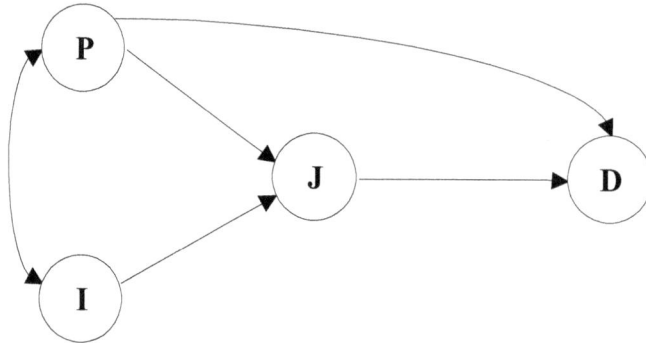

**Fig. (7.4).** Throughput modelling diagram. Source: Rodgers [1].

In this *Throughput Model,* to make a sound decision, several process must be followed and evaluated. (1) First, perception provides a screening, which is a special case of sorting and categorizing information. This is evaluated by classifying kind of similarities and dissimilarities to standards. (2) Second, information in this model, perception and information are interdependent or any other words mimics a neural network (*i.e.*, P←—→I). For instance, before making any judgment or decision choice, a person develops a representation for the problems, ultimately affecting the information and *vice versa.* In addition, "big data" is also related to the component of information. Having a large amount of information, provides individuals and organizations the resources to make better informed decisions. (3) In this stage, "judgment" is influenced by an individual's perception and information sources when evaluating or predicting events when deciding choice. (4) Finally, decision choice depicts the summary of decision-making in the use of perception, information sources such as AI enhanced biometrics defined as information-processing function, and judgments of cognitive, economic, political, and social processes for final outcomes.

## Algorithms

AI enables us to train the computer in ways that we could not before. Organizations can feed a great deal of data in the AI system and use that data to train a model to recognize objects or signals of interest.

With all the technology resources available in the world, most companies are becoming data-driven, then never. Investing money into technology enables the organizations to transform into a greater productivity and a high output, as well as better decision making. Therefore, the application of algorithms is truly crucial for future component of every business. In other words, the secret source behind of all of these technologies that we normally use in a daily life, are 'algorithms', since it is everywhere in our everyday lives. Algorithms as depicted by the

Throughput Model are unambiguous specification of how to solve a class of problems. These algorithms can be implemented to perform calculation, data processing, and other related computer and mathematical operations.

The Revisionist Algorithmic Pathway (I→P→D) can be employed to find the maximum number ("I") in a list of numbers of random order. Therefore, finding the solution requires looking at every number in the list. Some of the examples that algorithms are depicted in the *Throughput Model*. This model is the process of making choices by identifying a decision (*i.e.*, perception), gathering information ("I"), assessing alternative resolutions (*i.e.*, judgment) before rendering a decision choice (see Fig. **7.1**).

## The Relationship of Biometrics and Fraud

Biometrics can be viewed as a special type of AI technology that uses metrics, such as measurements that are directly linked to human biology, for instance, physical characteristics or behavioral trait. Since no one has the exact same genetic information, it's possible to use biometrics for security purposes. Lately, biometrics tools are used increasingly to protect from identity thief problems and safeguarding of assets. Some of the examples that uses biometrics in the financial world are, banks and credit card issuers since they authenticate transactions by matching users' biometrics with information stored on file. Therefore, biometrics increases productivity and reduces costs by minimizing possible fraud. Thus, in business internal control biometrics system-based financial fraud includes scam e-mails, identity theft, and fraudulent transactions, which can help in preventing and detecting in advance. Most biometric application fall into several categories, including financial and investment service such as ATM. In the field of auditing, this biometric system is very important, because it implements not only at a data-stored facility, but also in laptop access. Commonly used example is fingerprints, which scans and recognizes individual information to prevent forgery. Frauds and misappropriation of asset is hard to eliminate. Although, biometrics control can be put in place to minimize these risks from happening.

According to Rodgers [4] 2010, the term "Biometric" refers to measuring biological and behavioral characteristics, which describes the art and science of capturing an individual's characteristic information, feature, and personal trait. In other words, biometric is used in a wide range for automated human identification and recognition.

Automated methods of recognizing a person based on biological or behavioral characteristics is the basic assumption underlying biometrics. To run this system without errors, it requires two additional data: (1) a representation of a person's identity, such as a username to retrieve one's biometric template developed in a database and (2) one's biometric information. Table **7.1** illustrates the different treatment on recognizing individual identification *versus* individual's verification.

**Table 7.1. Identification *versus* Verification.**

| Identification | Verification |
|---|---|
| Who is this INDIVIDUAL? | Is this INDIVIDUAL who she says She or he is? |
| 1:N | 1:1 |
| Databank with linked personal information | No Databank |
| Overt or Covert | Overt |

Source: Partially adopted from Rodgers [4, 5].

Chiefly, identification is on a higher demand by organizations and society than verification since it involves "1: N" matching users comparing to only "1:1" matching. The reason why identification is more complicated to solve in terms of analyzing the personal data is because when asking the question for instance, "Who is this individual," the system must go through all the personal documents to find and recognize from a list of N users within the database. On the other hand, in verification process, when asking the question, "Is this Individual who she says she or he is," the system only must check the person's identity and check whether to accept or reject the person.

The innovative AI induced biometrics tool can be broken down into two major categories, which are (1) physiological biometric, and (2) behavioral biometric [4, 5].

1. Physiological biometric includes, fingerprint, palm print, hand geometry, vein patterns, DNA, Retina scan, iris san, face recognition, face thermography, ear recognition, and body odor recognition.
2. Behavioral biometrics includes, speaker recognition, gait, dynamic signature, keystroke dynamics, and data mining, such as google, yahoo and any other search engine.

Biometric technology provides a stronger protection in identification, access control, and verification system. A well-developed security system can implement three different types of authentications. One of the strengths of AI based biometric technology is that it applies biometric matching in detecting fraud from identity databases. To better grasp the concept of biometric system and its potential of technology, below are some examples.

**1. Something you know** – This authentication depends on something you know, in other words, information that it is difficult to guess from others. When logging in to a website or an application, the system asks our username and password. This type of security system falls into this category by requiring the users to put an answer, such as password, or PIN. In addition, in cases, the systems ask us to put an answer to a piece of personal questions, such as "what is your mother's maiden name?" or "what is color was your first automobile?" All these are related to what we know, so that others cannot easily access our information.

**2. Something you have** – This authentication is like a card key, smart card, or token. This is considered one of the powerful authentication systems for security purposes. The implementation of electronic cards, such as, ATM cards makes it efficient in using challenge-response or time-based encryption depending on the situation. Another example is the use of one-time passwords system as push notification by sending an directly to a mobile device a text message that contains a temporary password.

**3. Something you are** – This biometric authentication is a system that works based on an individual's physical data information. Many kinds of biometric systems are being utilized in a variety of range, and perhaps, still in the process of developing since they test such a diverse personal characteristic, including a person's face, voice, eyes, fingerprints, signature, as swell as typing patterns. Mobile device industry is one of the examples that utilizes this type of biometrics. When the smart phone first came out, the security method of unlocking the phone was just by putting a password or 4-digit PIN. However, by the implementation of the biometric technology, this now have shifted from a password to a face recognition or fingerprint when unlocking the phone.

Among all these different types of security authentication, a biometric is the most secure and convenient authentication tool, since it is extremely hard to borrow, stole, or to forget our personal traits and information. Most importantly, authentication or verification biometrics is the key in making sure you are who you claim to be and not somebody else.

Biometrics are widely used as part of an internal control systems of recognizing an individual centered on physiological or behavioral characteristics. The strength of the biometric system is that it is very accurate, and it guarantees in securing access to sensitive information, such as personal, governmental as well as financial information. Since the incident of 9/11, the airport security process changed completely by the creation of Transpiration Security Administration (TSA), and by integrating biometric system. There are many biometrics and deep learning apparatuses involved in the process of protecting who gets into the airplane.

According to the Transportation Security Administration (TSA) website, they announced that TSA are planning to expand the use of biometric technology as part of its continued effort on enhancing security to deliver a positive experience for all travelers. Currently, TSA and airline companies checks the traveler identity but matching the individual's biographic data and inspecting physical identity, in addition to travel documents, such as passport or a valid ID. However, the use of biometric will not only increase the effectiveness in terms of security, but also it will minimize the waiting time when passing through all the airport screenings and checkpoints.

The roadmap that TSA released in achieving the goal of implementing the biometrics' securing system is as the followings: 1) partnering with U.S. Customs and Border Protection (CBP) on biometrics for international travelers, 2) using biometrics provided by TSA Pre members to enhance the travel experience, 3) expanding biometrics to additional domestic travelers, 4) developing the infrastructure for biometric technology. As a result, in 2017, TSA has already begun testing biometrics for TSA Pre-check travelers by using both Fig. print and facial recognition.

There are many frequent travelers since business is conducted around the globe. Recently there has been many changes of the security system, especially in the past decade with the development of AI based biometric technologies. For example, the Los Angeles International Airport (LAX), implements facial recognition when arriving from international flights. Also, in Narita International Airport (Tokyo), they use the fingerprint of both hands when entering to the country to have information about each traveler. As a matter of fact, many airports outside the United States are also starting to experiment these technologies as part of the inspection process.

1. Fingerprint Technology

According to the TSA website, fingerprint technology can be used to verify identity, allowing a traveler's fingerprints to serve as both a boarding pass and as an identity document (see Fig. **7.5**). The technology matches passenger finger-prints provided at the checkpoint to those that were provided to TSA by travelers when they first enrolled in the TSA Pre-check application program.

**Fig. (7.5).** Fingerprint biometrics. Source: Futuristic fingerprint scanning device biometric security system. Innovation concept. 3D Rendering. https://www.romaniajournal.ro/society-people/study-reveals-exten--of-biometric-data-collection-in-romania/

## 2. Facial Recognition

TSA is evaluating facial recognition technology to automate the identity and boarding pass verification process (see Fig. **7.6**). After the traveler scans their boarding pass and their passport, the system takes a photo of the passenger and verifies that the name on the boarding pass and their passport matches. It also confirms that the person on passport photo matches the photo taken by the camera to make sure it's the same person. This was tested in Los Angeles International Airport (LAX).

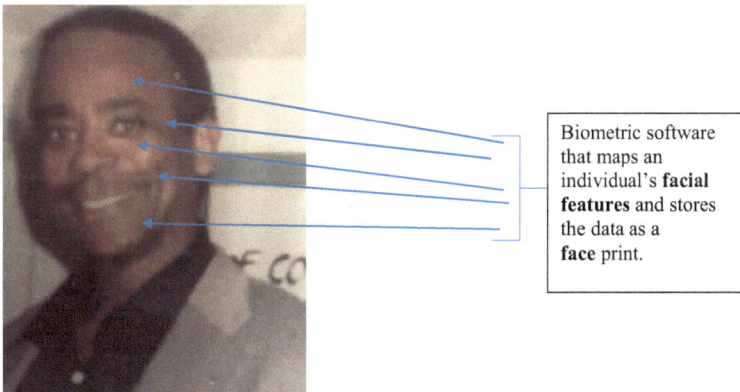

Biometric software that maps an individual's **facial features** and stores the data as a **face** print.

**Fig. (7.6).** Facial recognition. Features identified by machine intelligence, Source: Generated by author.

Fig. (**7.7**) above illustrates the relationship between the passenger and the security system, which are as the following: 1) reservation, 2) check in the date of departure, 3) bag drop, 4) check point screening, 5) boarding, and 6) departure. The biometric technology is involved in each of the stage.

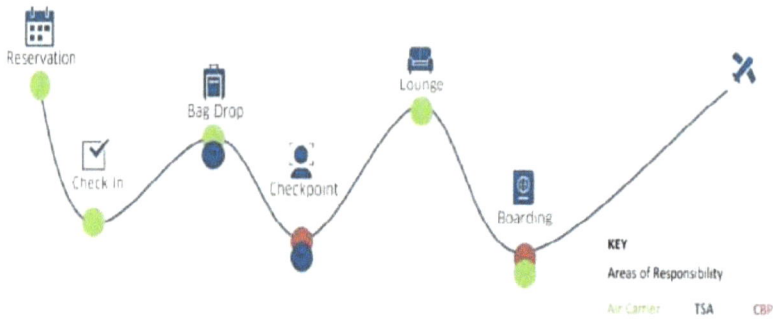

FIGURE 4 Notional Biometric Passenger Experience Stakeholder Roles and Responsibilities

**Fig. (7.7).** Reservation system. Source: TSA website.

## Reservation

The reservation is when one book a flight through online or through a travel agent. The image below explains how TSA assess each passenger and categorizes in three risk categories, which are high, unknown, and low by developing a "watch list". This implies that, risk categories are assigned to each individual passenger when purchasing the ticket. All passengers managing an airline reservation must provide personal information, such as their full name, date of birth, and gender. With this information, TSA matches against the Terrorist Screening Database (TSDB), then transmits the results back to the airline companies so that they can decided whether to issue or deny passenger boarding passes. According to the United States Government Accountability Office (GAO), the passenger pre-screening process are summarized in Fig. (**7.8**).

At the airport checkpoints, those passengers that were identified as "high risk" receives an intense screening, passenger identified as "low risk" are eligible for expedited screening, and for those passengers identified as "unknown" goes through the standard screening process. However, passenger matched to the "No Fly List" or "Do Not Board List," including individuals who has significant health risk that can affect to others are not allowed to fly.

## Check-in

Unless a person is categorized as "high risk" passenger, you are allowed to buy the airplane ticket and proceeds to the next process, which is the check-in stage at the date of the departure. The security system used in this stage involves, showing your passport or a valid ID, as well as the boarding pass to make sure the information matches with the correct individual.

**Figure 3: Transportation Security Administration (TSA) Passenger Prescreening Process**

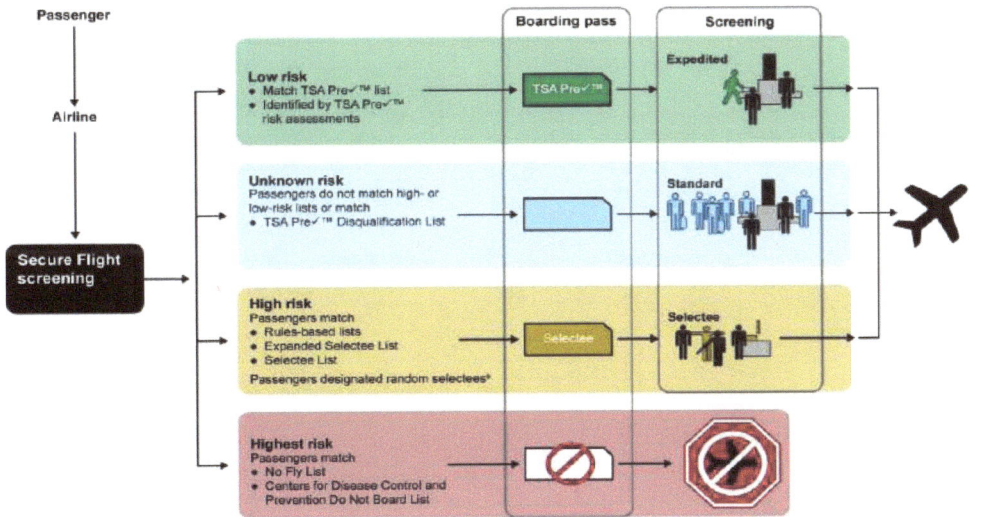

Source: GAO analysis of TSA information | GAO 17-794

*These individuals are identified for enhanced screening at random, not because they are included on government watch lists

**Fig. (7.8).** TSA passenger prescreening process. Source: TSA website.

## Checkpoint Screening

TSA ensures that all individuals and their personal carry-on bags are inspected as part of its checkpoint screening process to detect and prevent weapons, bombs, any explosive items that are prohibited to board an aircraft or carry to the airport area. To detect these dangerous items, many biometrics machines are used. Some of the examples includes, walk-though metal detector, advanced imaging technology (AIT) and X-ray scanner. In case the traveler, or the traveler's carry-on property fails these inspections, the person who works as manual reaches and explosives trace detection (ETD) will come and check to make sure there are not any prohibited items. Fig. (**7.9**) represents the decision tree associated with the check-point screening process.

Nonetheless, there may be Type I error, which is an error that occurs in a statistical test when a true claim is incorrectly rejected. Also Type II error, which occurs in a statistical test when a false claim is incorrectly not rejected. For example, if the machine detects women's neckless as a suspicious object, but it is not a prohibited item, this is a Type I error.

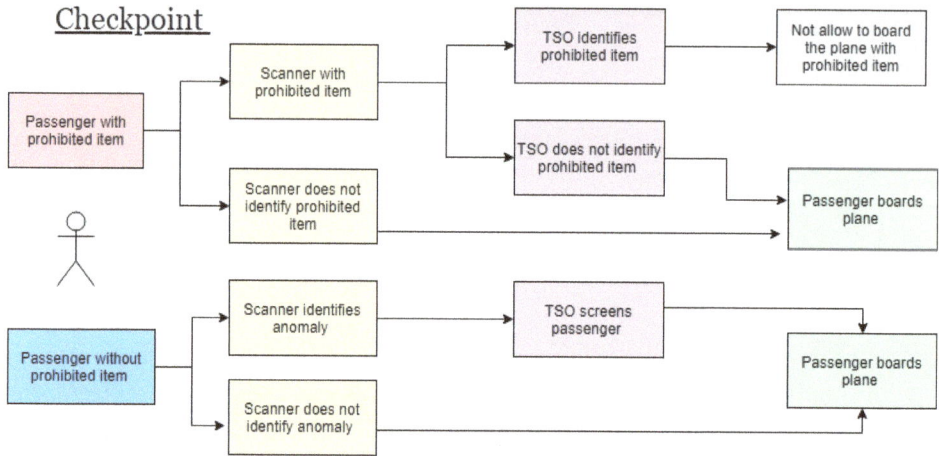

**Fig. (7.9).** TSa check-point screening process. Source: TSA website.

## CONCLUSION

The **IPD** algorithmic pathway suggests that available information sources (**I**) can influence the framing (**P**) the problem before arriving to the decision (**D**). We must understand that in this pathway, available information complements to the stage as it informs our perception (**P**) in route to a decision. It is crucial to understand information is very important and should not be ignored. When we receive more information, we are basically updating our memories, which are used for a more detailed analysis (**J**) due to time pressures, experiences, or an unstable environment.

Aside from the convenience of using these biometric technologies, the individuals' privacy issues have also in risen. Privacy advocates are calling on lawmakers to create legal safeguards to prevent the abuse of these kinds of databases. Nonetheless, biometrics technologies are advancing more and more in a variety of industries. It is becoming part of our daily operations and these technologies will be able to improve the quality of the security system.

AI driven biometrics as a security and productivity innovation has the potential to not only authenticate users based on their physiological characteristics, but also on contextual cues from behavioral biometrics as well. Behavior biometrics measure and classify human activities. Things like voice inflection, keystroke dynamics, error patterns, stance and gait among many others.

Technology has completely infiltrated our world and there is no going backwards. As technology and the organizations that utilize them advance it is essential that individuals advance and understand these models as well. Understanding AI and the components of algorithms, machine learning, deep learning, and natural language processing is becoming more and more important in world. Using AI driven biometrics and decision trees can be applied to assist the overall outcomes of business activity. The world will continue to advance, and we must embrace and move forward.

## REFERENCES

[1]     W. Rodgers, *Process Thinking: Six pathways to successful decision making* iUniverse, Inc: NY, 2006.

[2]     W. Rodgers, *Artificial Intelligence in a Throughput Model: Some Major Algorithms?* Science Publications (CRC Press: Taylor and Francis Group): Florida, 2020.

[3]     W. Rodgers, F. Yeung, C. Olindo, and W.Y. Degbey, "Artificial intelligence-driven music biometrics influencing customers' retail buying behavior", *J. Bus. Res.,* vol. 126, pp. 401-414, 2021.
[http://dx.doi.org/10.1016/j.jbusres.2020.12.039]

[4]     W. Rodgers, *Biometric and Auditing Issues Addressed in a Throughput Model.* Information Age Publishing, Inc.: Charlotte, NC, 2012.

[5]     W. Rodgers, *E-commerce and biometric issues addressed in a Throughput Model.* Nova Publication: Hauppauge, NY, 2010.

[6]     W. Rodgers, A. Söderbom, and A. Guiral, "Corporate Social Responsibility Enhanced Control Systems reducing the Likelihood of Fraud", *J. Bus. Ethics,* vol. 91, suppl. Suppl. 1, pp. 151-166, 2014.

# CHAPTER 8

# The Value-driven Algorithmic Pathway

I'm hoping the reader can see that artificial intelligence is better understood as a belief system than as a technology.

---Jaron Lanier

In a way, AI is both closer and farther off than we imagine. AI is closer to being able to do more powerful things than most people expect -- driving cars, curing diseases, discovering planets, understanding media. Those will each have a great impact on the world, but we're still figuring out what real intelligence is.

---Mark Zuckerberg

The implications of AI are still being worked out as technology advances at a dizzying speed. Christians, like everyone else, are asking questions about what this means. But one thing people of faith want to affirm most strongly is that technology has to serve the good of humanity -- all of it, not just the privileged few. Intelligence -- whether artificial or not -- which is divorced from a vision of the flourishing of all humankind is contrary to God's vision for humanity. We have the opportunity to create machines that can learn to do things without us, but we also have the opportunity to shape that learning in a way that blesses the world rather than harms it.

---Mark Woods

**Abstract**

The Value Driven Algorithmic Pathway (P→I→J→D) designates how people or organizational perceptual framing assists in guiding and selecting types of information utilized in the judgmental stage. This algorithmic pathway is motivated by information processing limitations, complexity, and coherence between perception and the available information. Therefore, to take this algorithmic pathway, a person or organization's perception is modified and selected as the information that will be analyzed for a decision choice.

**Keywords:** Algorithms, Artificial intelligence, Big data, Categorical variables, Continuous variables, Decision choice, Decision tree, Deep learning, Entropy,

Information, Judgment, Learning, Machine learning, Perception, Problem solving, Reasoning, Retina Scan Image, Throughput Model, Type 1 and type 2 errors, Value-Driven Algorithmic Pathway.

## INTRODUCTION

The Value-Driven Algorithmic Pathway (**P→I→J→D**) indicates that perception (**P**) guides the different types of information sources (**I**) is used in the analysis (**J**) enroute to make a decision choice (**D**). Perceptual framing (**P**) has an influence on a variety of information (**I**) that will be selected and used in the analysis process (**J**) (see Fig. **8.1**). It is crucial to understand that our handling of a situation is strongly influenced by the education, training, and experience of individuals. This pathway is also known as the "value driven," since our perception tend to change or how we interpret the information that we have available or have share with us. Further, the information in this pathway is weighted based on how we frame each situation [1].

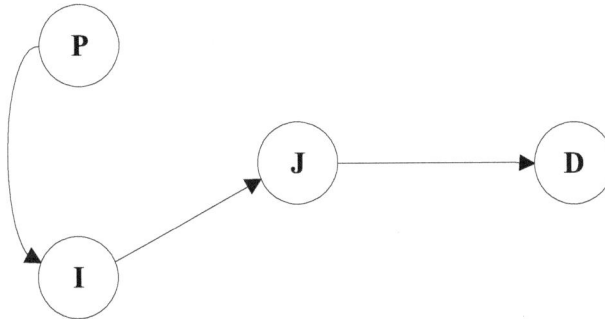

**Fig. (8.1).** Value-driven algorithmic pathway (P→I→J→D). The decision path consists of perception to information to judgment to decision choice. Source: Rodgers [2].

Yet another aspect of the Value Driven Pathway is that it embodies the Analytical Pathway (**I→J→D**). Or another way of describing this embodiment is to view the perceptual frame (**P**) as a conditioning influence on an analytical and programmatic way of reaching a decision. The highlight of the Value Driven Algorithmic Pathway is that it can modify or discard informational sources used in analysis (**J**).

Moreover, in the use of this pathway, we must make sure we take extra case to acknowledge that certain strategies may be a part of our perceptions, which will impact on the available information. In addition, this is an appropriate pathway to use when an individual has the knowledge or can consider himself/herself and expert in the situation. Nonetheless, this pathway should not be also under extreme time pressure that may limit the use of relevant and reliable information [1].

The Value Driven Pathway is one of the two pathways that include all of the elements in the Throughput Model: perception, information, and judgment to arrive to a decision. The Value Driven Pathway suggests that perception shapes the types of information that will be used in the analysis. This means that the person making the decision will look for sources based on his/her perception of the situation. This limits the amount of information that comes into play and some useful and relevant information sources may be ignored. This pathway is especially useful when the person is an expert on the situation, there is no time pressure, and the information acquired is relevant and reliable.

The Value Driven Algorithmic Pathway is used by expert auditors when there are no time pressures, and the information is reliable. Suppose you are working on an audit for a client that had a few findings last year, and it was hard to get appropriate documentation from them. The auditor already has the perception of the client that it will be a complicated audit and therefore asks for additional information than usual because the client has made material misstatements in the past. The auditor will try to find the same material misstatements as last year, because it is likely for a repeat finding to happen. Suppose the client had several material misstatements in the financial statements, and net income is overstated, expenses are understated. This year, the auditor will perform additional procedures and request more information, to ensure that the same mistakes are not made again. This process is lengthier because it requires the auditors to go over a lot more information and perform a deeper analysis. If the same material misstatements exist, there will be repeat findings, and possibly a qualified opinion. If the company improved their internal controls, and avoided the same mistakes, the opinion will be unmodified. AI technology can be suggested by the auditors to help the client implement more efficient internal controls, such as better software more tailored to the company's size and industry.

## DECISION TREES

Machine learning is part of AI. It can provide new ways of solving problems. AI inspired machine learning can learn, predict, and decide. In this way this type of technology analyzes the data in new ways, recognize, like facial recognition, automated car recognition and make decision choices. There are different kinds of machine learning. Supervised learning where you have the data and answers. In this case, you already have the data as to who can make the payments and who cannot from the people who have already applied for the loan. This process helps predict on the next person if they are going to make the loan or not. The second learning is unsupervised learning groups the like kind of data like it would categorize all houses in one group, all trees in one group without knowing what they are. The third type of learning is reinforcement learning. Here you don't have to data prior to getting started. You get data one line at a time. This way you make a good or bad decision, and you learn from that. There are problems in machine learning. One is classification problem where the solutions fall under yes or no, true or false, 1 or zero. Then there are regression problems where you need continuous values to predict like product prices and profit. Last, is clustering wherein the data need to be organized to find specific patterns like in the case of product recommendation. There are four tools used in classification. Naïve Bayes, logistic regression, decision tree and random forest. Naïve Bay and logistic regression are for simpler data. If data is not too complex these two helps. It gets complicated when decision tree comes into play.

What is a decision tree? A decision tree is a tree shaped diagram used to determine a course of action. Each branch of the tree represents a possible decision, occurrence, or reaction. For example, if you are purchasing a vegetable and you don't know what it is, how do you decide as to what kind of vegetable it is (see Fig. **8.2**).

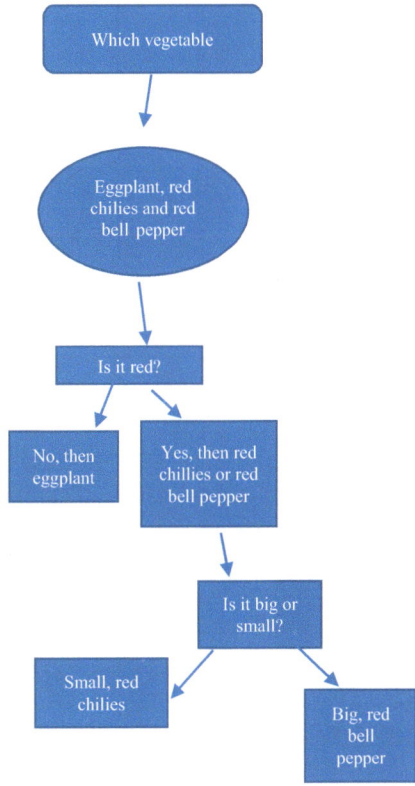

**Fig. (8.2).** Flowchart for selecting vegetables. Source: Produced by Students and author.

# Different Kinds of Decision Tree Models

Decision tree models can be implemented to solve problems depending upon the kind of data that requires prediction. They fall into the following categories:

**1.** Prediction of continuous variables

**2.** Prediction of categorical variables

## Prediction of Continuous Variables

The prediction of continuous variables rests on one or more predictors. For example, the prices of homes in a region may be contingent on many factors such as an address, availability of amenities such as a swimming pool, number of rooms, *etc*. In this situation, the decision tree will predict a home's price grounded on a variety of factors. The predicted value will also be a factor to determine the home's value.

The decision tree model utilized to determine such values is described as a continuous variable decision tree. Continuous various decision trees elucidate regression-type problems. In such situations, labeled datasets are implemented to predict a continuous, variable, and numbered output.

## Prediction of Categorical Variables

The prediction of categorical variables is also established on other categorical or continuous variables. Nevertheless, in place of predicting a value, this division of decision trees pertains to classifying a new dataset into the available groups of datasets. For example, examining a comment on Facebook to classify text as negative or supportive. Accomplishing a diagnosis for an ailment centered on a patient's symptoms is also an example of a categorical variable decision tree model. Categorical variable decision trees solve classification-type problems where the output is a class instead of a value.

Decision tree can help solve problems. There are two different categories: Classification and regression. In classification, a classification tree will determine a set of logical if-then conditions to classify problems. For example, discriminating between three types of flowers based on certain features. In regression, a regression tree is used when the target variable is numerical or continuous in nature. A regression model can be fitted to the target variable using each of the independent variables. Each split is made based on the sum of squared error. There are advantages of decision tree. It is simple to understand, interpret and visualize. Very little effort is required for the data preparation. There is no special scaling required. It can handle both numerical and non-numerical data. Non-linear parameters don't affect its performance. Even if the data don't fit the curve graph, we can still use it. There are also disadvantages of decision tree. Overfitting occurs when the algorithm captures noise in the data. That means you are solving for one specific instance than a common solution. High variance – the model can get unstable due to small variation in data. Last, is a low biased tree. It is a highly complicated decision tree. It tends to have a low bias which makes it difficult for the model to work with new data.

The following are some important terms of a decision tree:

**Entropy**

Entropy is the measure of randomness or unpredictability in the dataset. Data should be divided into different subgroups.

**Information Gain**

It is a measure of decrease in entropy after the data set is divided. In this manner, once the subgroups are produced then it is easier to identify the data. This diminishes the entropy less and less.

**Leaf Node**

It carries the groupings or the decision. Leaf node has two or more branches.

**Root Node**

The uppermost decision node is known as the root node.

Consequently, a *decision tree* or a *classification tree* is a tree whereby each internal (non-leaf) node is labeled with an input feature. The arcs coming from a node labeled with a feature are labeled with each of the possible values of the feature. Each leaf of the tree is labeled with a class or a probability distribution over the classes.

How does a decision tree work? – For example, let's take a group of animals based on their features using decision tree. The data set is looking quite messy, and the entropy is very high as you have animals of different color, height, and labels. First, we must split the data. We must frame the conditions that split the data in such a way that the information gain is the highest. Gain is the measure of decrease in entropy after splitting. Once the data set is entered in the program it will calculate the entropy of the dataset similarly after every split to calculate the gain. Gain can be calculated by finding the difference of the subsequent entropy values after split. We can now choose a condition that gives us the highest gain. To do that, we split the data using each condition and checking the gain that we get out of them. The condition that gives us the highest gain will be used to make the first split.

## How Decision Trees in AI Are Developed

As the name suggests, the decision tree algorithm is in the form of a tree-like structure. Thus, it is inverted. A decision tree starts from the root or the top decision node that classifies data sets based on the values of carefully selected attributes.

The root node represents the entire dataset. This is where the first step in the algorithm selects the best predictor variable. It makes it a decision node. It also groups the whole dataset into various classes or smaller datasets.

Deciding whether a given picture is that of a cat or a dog is a typical example of classification. Therefore, the features or attributes could be the presence of claws or paws, length of ears, type of tongue, *etc*. The dataset will be split further into smaller classes based on these input variables until the result is obtained.

## EXAMPLE 1: THE VALUE-DRIVEN ALGORITHMIC PATHWAY APPLIED TO HEALTHCARE SYSTEMS

This section focuses on how the Value-Driven Algorithmic Pathway (P→I→J→D) can assist in constructing better management tools in the healthcare industry. According to the U.S. Centers for Medicare & Medicaid Services [3] healthcare costs represent one of the top expenditures in the United States, accounting for 17.7% of the Gross Domestic Product (GDP) in 2019.

During the present decade, Medicare setting rules and regulations for this industry, has relied heavily on AI to measure healthcare industry's efficiencies by creating "Value Based Models" such as the Medicare Access and CHIP Reauthorization Act (MACRA) and the Merit-based Incentive Payment System (MIPS) in order to substitute its current "fee for service" payment system with a "quality" payment structure [3] and in order to prevent fraudulent billing. This initiative is forcing hospitals and private practices to have a metric system that focuses not only on quality figures but also is vigilant on cost efficiencies (*i.e.*, hospital admission rates, office visit frequencies) across the board. Not complying with this initiative signed by President Obama on April 16, 2015, can lead to fines and/or payment sequestration for services provided. Current state of healthcare application of AI, the challenges it faces and the future of AI in healthcare relies on healthcare policy and the constant need to bring down the cost of healthcare in the United States [4]. Topics like, current problems faced by hospitals and private practices during hospital or office visits, surgical procedures or major trauma surgeries and how AI, can be useful in the decision-making process will be discussed throughout this section.

According to Rodgers [5], AI is where computers perform tasks that are usually assumed to require human intelligence, is currently being discussed in nearly every domain of science and engineering. AI is the investigation and foundation of computer systems that can perceive, reason and act. AI's primary purpose is to develop intelligent machines. Its intelligence can correlate primarily on its learning (machine and biometrics) followed by its algorithms, and its data.

Machine learning refers to the theory that systems can change outputs and be more efficient as they are exposed with more data. Machine learning can be supervised when technological tools infer functions from known inputs to known outputs, or it can be unsupervised when it works with inputs only transforming or finding patterns, thus, is a task-oriented application of statistical transformation.

Biometrics as part of "deep learning" methods is designed to learn from input data and apply results or the same input with other data. Biometrics uses neural networks, which require their own deeper dive another post. Major scientific companies are providing evidence where computers can achieve human-like competence in image recognition [2]. AI has also enabled significant progress in speech recognition, transactional trends and fraud prevention among others [5]. All of these create interest on how such capabilities can support human decision-making in the healthcare industry, whether applicable to operational efficiencies or to managerial improvement. AI focused on operational efficiencies is less prone to trial and error like all other fields of an economy; a single error due to technological malfunctioning could cost a human life, thus, technological transition procedure in the field of healthcare needs to go as slowly and precisely as possible.

The Throughput Model is defined by four components that guide our decisions, which are perception, information, judgment, and decision choice (Fig. **8.3**). Perception is defined as the process in which individual frames and views a problem. Information is defined as information used by a decision maker for problem-solving purposes, this information could be biometrics characteristics, big data, an image, *etc*. Judgment is defined as the process individuals implement to analyze information and well as the perception. Decision choice is the action an individual organization execute to completion.

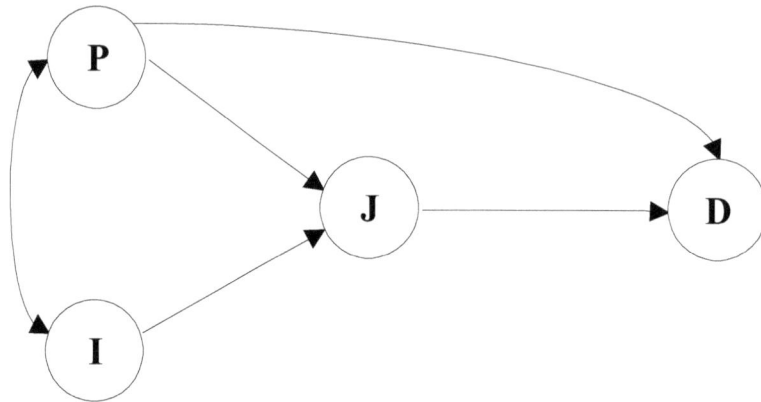

**Fig. (8.3).** Decision makers' processes diagram. (Source: Rodgers [10]).

*Where P = perception, I = information, J = judgment, and D = decision choice.*

1. **The Expedient Pathway P→D**
2. **The Ruling Guide Pathway P→J→D**
3. **The Analytical Pathway I→J→D**
4. **The Revisionist Pathway I→P→D**
5. **The Value Driven Pathway P→I→J→D**
6. **The Global Perspective Pathway I→P→J→D**

Algorithms are unambiguous specifications used for problem solving. These can perform calculations, data processing, and automated reasoning tasks. Algorithms play a crucial role in the decision-making process as involves four elements: perception (P), information (I), and judgment (J) and decision choice (D). Fig. (**1**) represents some paths than can be referenced as algorithms. They are a limited set of guidelines that instruct a computer system how to solve a problem [2]. Machines often use a relationship between information data and perception to learn by detection, thus through a type of algorithm that learns from experience in order to decide, this is also known as neural network. With exposure and experience, machine gathers all learned information, which is known as deep learning. This process is more complex and requires excessive amounts of data known as big data. Deep leaning requires metrics to process big data in an efficient way. A combination of six algorithms below can be reflected in the Throughput Model as shown on Fig. (**8.3**).

The promise of AI is tightly coupled to the availability of relevant data [6]. Although, in the healthcare domains, there is a plenty of data, the quality and accessibility of these resources remain a crucial challenge. First, healthcare data has privacy protection issues associated with it which makes the collection and sharing process of health data hard in comparison to other types of data. Moreover, data collection is not as accessible as it appears, especially in long-term studies and clinical trials. With the evolution of digital capacity, more and more data are produced and stored in the digital space every second. The amount of available digital data is growing rapidly, doubling every two years. In 2013, it encompassed 4.4 zettabytes, however it is expected by 2020 the digital universe – the data we create and copy annually – will reach 44 zettabytes, or 44 trillion gigabytes. Therefore, AI will redesign healthcare). With the data so huge we will need AI to be able to keep track of it.

A gigabyte represents a unit of data storage capacity that is roughly equivalent to 1 billion bytes. It is also equal to two to the 30th power or 1,073,741,824 in decimal notation. Giga derives from a Greek word meaning giant.

In addition, gigabytes have been replaced by terabytes, petabytes, exabytes, zettabytes, and eventually yottabytes. A terabyte is just over 1,000 gigabytes, which is a label most of us are familiar with from our home computers [6]. A petabyte is just over 1,000 terabytes. Moreover, Google was said to process around 20 petabytes of data a day (Google will not release information on how much data it processes on a daily basis). To put that in context, if you took all of the information from all US academic research libraries and lumped it all together, it would add up to 2 petabytes [6].

To obtain a better understanding of the shear amount of data that is increasing daily, the International System of Units (SI) denotes "exa" as a multiplication by the sixth power of 1000 or ($10^{18}$). In other words, 1 exabyte (EB) = $10^{18}$ bytes = $1,000^6$ bytes = 1000000000000000000 bytes = 1,000 petabytes = 1 million terabytes = 1 billion gigabytes.

A zettabyte represents a digital unit of measurement. One zettabyte is equal to one sextillion bytes or $10^{21}$ (1,000,000,000,000,000,000,000) bytes, or one zettabyte is equal to a trillion gigabytes.

Soon, a yottabyte is a septillion byte, which is so huge that no one has yet coined a term for the next higher magnitude. Moreover, this pertains to the fact that a yottabyte is the largest storage term we have, not that septillion is the highest numerical descriptor for a large Fig. in existence. Now, to place everything in proper perspective, the most rudimentary smartphone comes with approximately 30GB of data storage, while a top-of-the-line iPhone has more than 500GB!

Although, the world of information technology has not reached the state of "real" AI, narrow versions of it are already in our smartphones, web searches, social media advertising and in many other devices and software. Apple's Siri,

Microsoft's Cortana, Google's Assistant, and Amazon's Alexa can already do a limited set of things, like getting directions, indicating temperature outside, performing a web search, playing music *etc.* using speech recognition technology. In terms of physical biometrics, different types of systems have been already established mainly with the purpose of nation security, some pros and cons are established in Fig. (**8.4**). Nonetheless, the majority of these tools have yet not been implemented in the healthcare industry.

| Type | Pros | Cons |
|---|---|---|
| Fingerprints | Fingerprints are unique<br>Easy to use<br>Cheap/Low power<br>Non-intrusive | Patterns can be affected by cuts, dirt, wear and tear<br>High quaility image challenge<br>Not able to identify picture from real finger print |
| Iris/retina scans | Highly accurate<br>Hygienic<br>Capacity to discriminate between indivuduals | User must hold still while the scan is taking place Image can be used to bypass security |
| Plam Vein | Not susceptible to minor trauma<br>Difficult to forge<br>Contactless<br>Highly accurate | Expensive<br>High maintenance involved |
| Facial Patterns | Not intrusive | More suited for authenticatin than identification<br>User perceptions/civil liberty |

**Fig. (8.4).** Pros and cons of biometrics systems. Source: Produced by Students and author.

There are some limited versions of AI used in hospitals to detect diseases, such as cancer, more accurately and in their early stages using image recognition and early deep learning technology. According to the American Cancer Society, a high proportion of mammograms yield false results, leading to 1 in 2 healthy women being told they have cancer. The use of AI is enabling review and translation of mammograms 30 times faster with 99% accuracy, reducing the need for unnecessary biopsies [7]. There are also data platforms that are currently being built by federal agencies that will promote operational and financial trends in the healthcare industry that not only will serve as quality indicator when establishing a payment system but will also serve as a fraud protection tool for practice overbilling.

**MACRA and its Correlation with AI**

On April 14, 2015, a bipartisan majority in Congress passed the Medicare Access and CHIP Reauthorization Act of 2015 (MACRA). The MACRA will make comprehensive changes to how Medicare pays for physician services with the help of data collection through AI. Changes to the current payment structure are:

a. Prevents the use of Sustainable Growth Rate (SGR) as a formula for determining Medicare payments for health care providers.
b. Creates a new platform that contains a rewarding system based on quality of care.
c. Combines existing quality-reporting programs into one new system.

The MACRA supersedes the SGR with annual 0.5% payment increases for each of the next five years and gives providers two payment track options which are: Merit-Based Incentive Payment System (MIPS) and an Alternative Payment Models (APM's).

The MIPS combines three existing quality initiatives—Meaningful Use (MU), the Physician Quality Reporting System (PQRS), and the Value-Based Payment Modifier (VBPM)—into a single program. Under the MIPS, CMS will calculate a cumulative assessment score for physicians to determine reimbursement increases or decreases. The score will be based on four categories:

- Quality
- Resource use
- Meaningful use of certified electronic health records (EHR) technology
- Clinical practice improvement activities

APM participants will receive a 5% lump sum incentive payment from 2019 to 2024. Starting in 2026, participating providers will receive 0.75% fee schedule update while other providers will receive a 0.25% update.

The MACRA requires CMS to establish "care episode groups" and "patient condition groups" through Electronic Health Records (EHR). The creation of these groups is intended to help CMS measure resource use more effectively. These groups will also play a part in determining payments to providers (under the MACRA, care episode groups will account for at least 50% of expenditures under Medicare Parts A and B). Fig. (**8.5**) represents the MACRA timeline for both payment model options, APM and MIPS.

The MACRA payment system can be considered implementing machine learning to scrutinize patient outcomes and quality trends. Nevertheless, sometimes AI based machine learning applications fails to collect correct data. Instead, AI based machine learning changes the use of received data. Since AI systems are just a software, just like any other computer software, AI is vulnerable to bugs and more so, misinterpretation. Infection of bugs or poor patient documentation from the provider may manipulate the outcome of machine learning. Besides, AI depends greatly on individuals' data. Any inaccurate data derived from its initial sources such as data analytics and online users can influence the integrity of the outcomes produced by AI system and machine learning. Sometime, errors may occur in AI systems [8]. Overreliance of these bias outcomes produces by AI can expose people to severe risks.

**Fig. (8.5).** MACRA timeline. Source: https://www.aafp.org/dam/AAFP/documents/practice_management/payment/MACRATimeline.pdf

While today's society is living in a world with no regulations or ethical guidelines regarding the nature of data collected by AI machine learning, it is crucial to minimize collection of sensitive information of individuals. Decision-making based on the algorithm could produce bias and discriminatory outcomes particularly where the dataset is incomplete.

For purposes of the decision tree employed (see Fig. **8.6**), the Throughput Model encapsulating the MACRA discipline is the Value-Driven Algorithmic Pathway (P→I→J→D). This algorithm representing P→I→J→D illustrates the cases when healthcare providers observe the health patterns in society first and collect data based on those observations. In this process, the data collection is more efficient and may lead to more efficient judgement making and eventually, the decision choices are made.

Further, Medicare is actively seeking to replace a fee for service reimbursement for a quality-based incentive system that forces healthcare practices to submit patient data through their electronic health record (EHR) system. There are some organizations that have not implemented an EHR system; however, they are subject to penalties through payment sequestration. The Value-Driven

Algorithmic Pathway (P→I→J→D) suggests that "individual values" (*i.e.*, "P") can override utilitarianism based on collective "economic egoism" (*i.e.*, I→J→D). The judgment ("J") is based on information ("I") and the information conditions the decision ("D"). The Value-Driven Algorithmic Pathway suggests that individuals' values drive the algorithmic process as well as influences the structural part of the utilitarian segment of the algorithm.

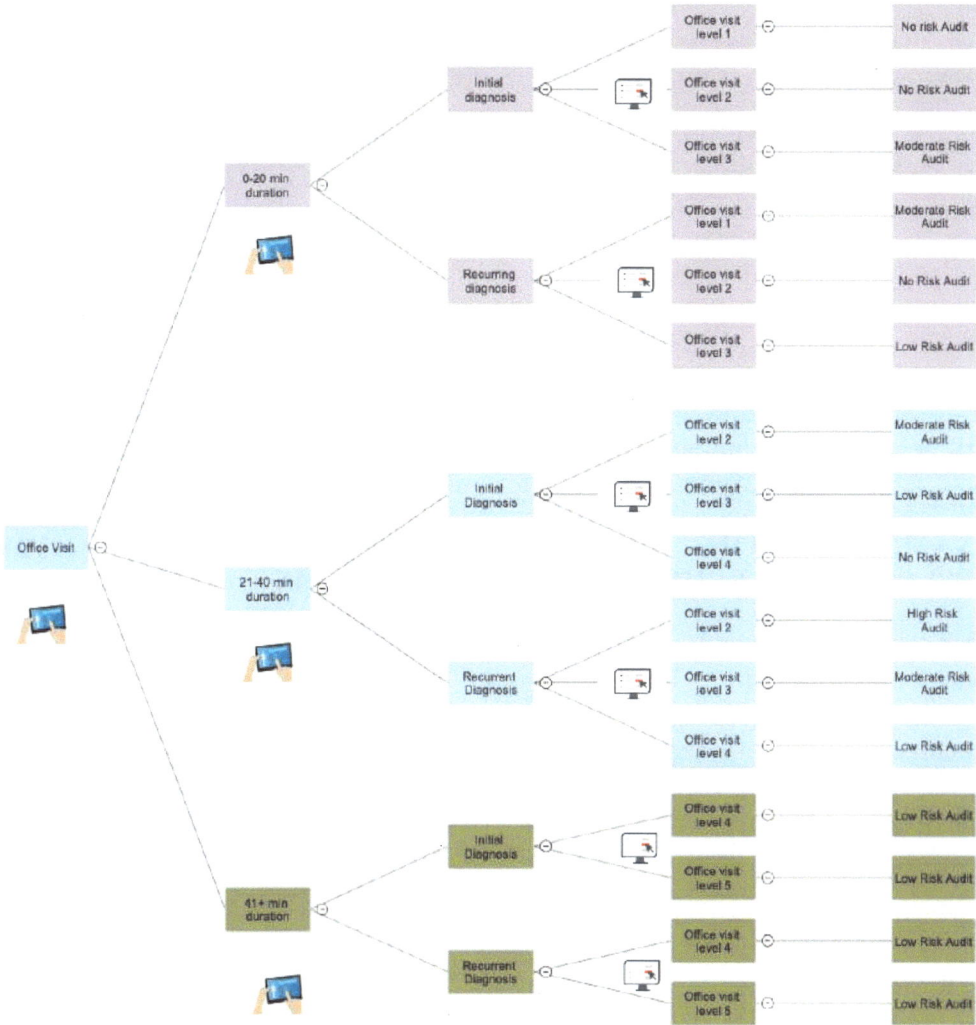

**Fig. (8.6).** Decision tree private practice. Source: Student generated.

With the introduction of MACRA, Medicare's main goal is to measure healthcare cost with patient quality outcomes that potentially benefits the elderly population, however this initiative has risen overhead costs significantly to hospitals and private practices with the introduction of AI (*i.e.*, electronic health records). This new era of patient documentation has raised ongoing concerns that are mostly affecting private practices. A considerable amount of infrastructure has now been invested in hospitals and private practices that helps develop AI through data input. Unfortunately, several small practices unable to cope with additional AI costs have closed doors and have joined established multispecialty groups or hospitals in order to comply with this discipline.

Fig. (**8.6**) represents a Value-Driven Algorithmic Pathway decision tree for a private practice where an office visit is measured by its time and by its diagnosis; certain biometrics are currently used for ensuring patient arrival but still the diagnosis is done manually using a trust factor. For the most part visits in the timeframe of more than 41 minutes are subject to review by CMS.

In sum, although MACRA is a new discipline in the healthcare industry, introduction of AI to this market has raised several questions regarding privacy of health information and has introduced various gadgets (I-watch) that eventually will help governmental agencies such as Medicare to evaluate health trends a to have better control of reimbursement for hospitals and private practices.

## EXAMPLE 2: THE VALUE-DRIVEN ALGORITHMIC PATHWAY APPLIED TO WAREHOUSE SECURITY SYSTEMS

This section discusses how AI and its related technologies of deep learning and machine learning play a role on warehouse security systems. Further, the Throughput Model provides a grounded foundation in the understanding of machine learning and deep learning functionality. Furthermore, the Throughput Model algorithms also assist in the overview of the role of biometrics to verify individuals. Finally, a discussion is provided for a decision tree relating to warehouse security access and the related type I and type II errors.

### Background

A highly secured warehouse is known for its rigorous security system. The core business entail storing and securing customers' assets. This classification of assets can vary, for example some of the assets that are stored are collectibles, highly valued inventory, or other assets that require high security. Due to technological advances the company was able to implement a more reliable security system, which requires biometric verification to unlock the access door. The system will require a two-factor verification method, which will be different for customers and employees. Customers will use a generated code and a retina scan as part of the verification, and employees will use a retina and voice recognition scan to gain access to the warehouse.

AI play a huge role in today's world. AI technology allows for computer systems to perform activities that would usually require a human to perform. AI is defined as using computers to perform tasks that would require human intelligence. For AI to function properly, the computer system must have to ability to learn, process big data, be able to problem solve, and can reason. In addition, once the system has been set up properly, artificial intelligence has the capability to perform tasks better than a human. Fig. (**8.7**) illustrates the characteristics needed for AI to function properly.

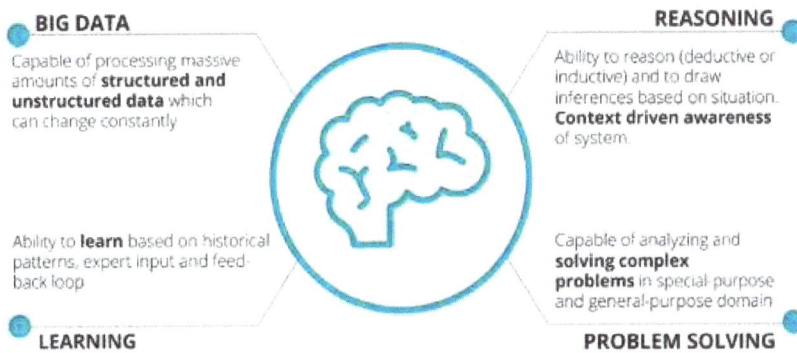

**BIG DATA**

Capable of processing massive amounts of **structured and unstructured data** which can change constantly

**REASONING**

Ability to reason (deductive or inductive) and to draw inferences based on situation. **Context driven awareness** of system.

Ability to **learn** based on historical patterns, expert input and feed-back loop

Capable of analyzing and **solving complex problems** in special-purpose and general-purpose domain

**LEARNING**

**PROBLEM SOLVING**

**Fig. (8.7).** Characteristics for AI to function properly. Source: Web sources.

Due to advancements in AI, companies have been able to implement more efficient security systems into their companies. These systems often require biometrical verification in order to authorize certain users into specific locations or provide access to a company's technological systems. Due to this, companies have been able to safeguard their assets and minimize the potential of fraud. The warehouse security system installed in the warehouse facility would rely on AI to provide access to registered users and deny access to unauthorize users.

## Algorithms

The Throughput Model is based on an algorithm. An algorithm is defined as mathematical instructions to reach a calculation. You can program a computer to reach an outcome by teaching a computer a step-by-step process. For the Throughput Model to function properly, the components of the Throughput Model must follow a certain algorithm. Fig. (**8.3**) shows a diagram of the Throughput Model as well as the different algorithms that can be withdrawn from the model.

The warehouse security system being used by the warehouse will implement the throughput model by following the following algorithm: P→I→J→D. The perception that will be programmed into the system will be to detect certain characteristics in the biometric being analyzed. The information will be the biometrical feature the individual is presenting to the system. Based on the biometric characteristic (Information) being presented, the system will determine if the characteristic matches with the data stored on the system and a judgment will be created. Lastly, the decision choice will be whether to give or deny access to the warehouse.

## Biometrics

Biometrics are defined as behavioral or physical characteristics that can be used to identify individuals. This can include facial recognition, eye scans, fingerprint mapping, movement, voice recognition, *etc.* Biometric security is more reliable and convenient than other systems such as identification cards. Table **8.1** below lists different types of physiological and behavioral characteristics.

**Table 8.1. Physiological and behavioral characteristics.**

| Risk Concerns | Biometric Recommended | Classification | Control Activity |
|---|---|---|---|
| Manipulation of Inventory | Voice Recognition | Behavioral | Prevention |
| Falsification of documents | Keystroke Dynamic | Behavioral | Prevention & detection |
| Vendor Selection | Dynamic Signature | Behavioral | Prevention |
| Collusion employee-Vendor (inventory quantity and quality) | Dynamic Signature | Behavioral | Prevention |
| Inventory theft | Finger vein recognition | Physiological | Prevention & detection |
| Protection of Intangibles | Facial Recognition | Physiological | Prevention & detection |
| | Dynamic Signature | Behavioral | Prevention |
| Pharmaceutical wrong doing | Dynamic Signature | Behavioral | Prevention |
| | Finger Vein scanner | Physiological | Prevention |
| | Retina Scanner | Physiological | Prevention |

Biometrics are one of the most reliable ways of identifying an individual since each person has different biometrical characteristics that make it almost impossible to replicate. Due to the effectiveness of using biometrics to verify an individual, the warehouse security system will use biometrics to verify individuals who want to access the warehouse. The types of biometrics implemented in the warehouse are retina scan and voice recognition.

## Machine Learning

Machine learning is defined as the part of AI that allows computers to learn and act as humans do. By feeding the system data and information you allow the machine to improve their learning over time. There are two main types of machine learning methods, supervised learning and unsupervised learning. Supervised training algorithms are accomplished by using an input where the desired output is known. Unsupervised learning is used in contradiction of data that has no right answer, the system attempts to find structure within the data.

Unsupervised machine learning will be incorporated into the warehouse security system as one of the forms of verification of customers. A six-digit code will be sent to the customer *via* email, the code is to be inputted into the system's keypad. The security system will verify the code by comparing the data being inputted *vs.* the data file, and if the code is verified, the customer may proceed.

## Deep Learning

Deep learning is a more sophisticated method of machine learning. A machine is trained to perform human like tasks like identifying images, recognizing speech, or making predictions. The system sets up parameters about the data and trains the machine to learn by its own by recognizing information. Deep learning is the process in which a machine learns by doing and can acquire new skills without human intervention. Deep learning use algorithms, neural networks, and sets of big data to learn. Therefore, machines, which are implementing deep learning, learn from experience *via* neural networks.

Sometimes the characteristics of the biometric that are analyzed has slight changes when the warehouse security system uses AI based biometrics to verify employees and customers. For example, an individual's voice can be raspier due to having a cold or the pupils can dilate due to allergies. The system should be able to recognize these changes; however, still identify main components of the biometric being analyzed. Deep learning allows to system adjust for these changes without failing to provide access to authorize users.

### Decision Tree Applied to the Warehouse

A decision tree has been created to determine who can access the warehouse. Since the assets stored in the warehouse are of high value, only registered employees and customers are allowed to enter into the warehouse. In order to maximize security, the system requires a two-factor verification, requirements for employees and customer varies.

Before an employee can use the system, the employee must be registered by a manager into the system. To be registered, the employee must first pass a background check. In addition, the employee biometrics will be recorded into the system. These biometrics will be used to verify the employee and grant access to the warehouse. The biometrics that will be used will be retina scans and voice recognition systems.

For customers to access the warehouse, first, they must have a valid contract with the company. Once a contract has been initiated, and second, the customer must provide a valid email address and a retina scan (see Fig. **8.8**). These two factors will be recorded into the security system.

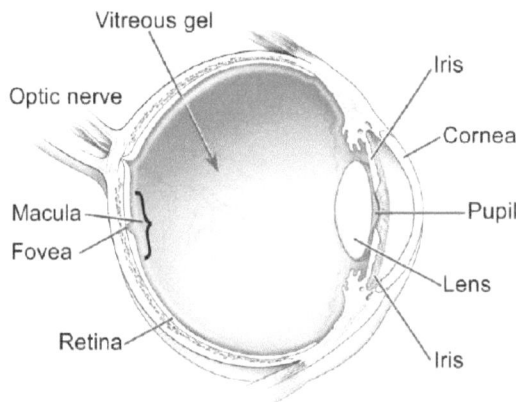

**Fig. (8.8).** Retina scan image. Source: from Rodgers [9].

Beginning in the 1980's, retinal scans are one of the most well know AI based biometric tools. However, it is one of the least deployed. A retinal scan is performed by a low-powered infrared beam being shot at a person eye as they look into the machine. The beam of light traces a standardized path on the retina. Then the unique blood vessel pattern from the eye is put into a template. This process can take a long period of time for the need of multiple pictures to be taken until one is sufficient. Retinal scans require high-quality cameras and will not work if picture in not clear.

For registered employees, to unlock the warehouse door, they must allow the system to scan their retina, by using the retina eye scanner (Fig. **8.9**). The security system will analyze certain characteristics of the retina and compare them to the data file. If the scan is verified, the system will allow for the employee to proceed to the next step. If the does not recognize the retina, access will be denied.

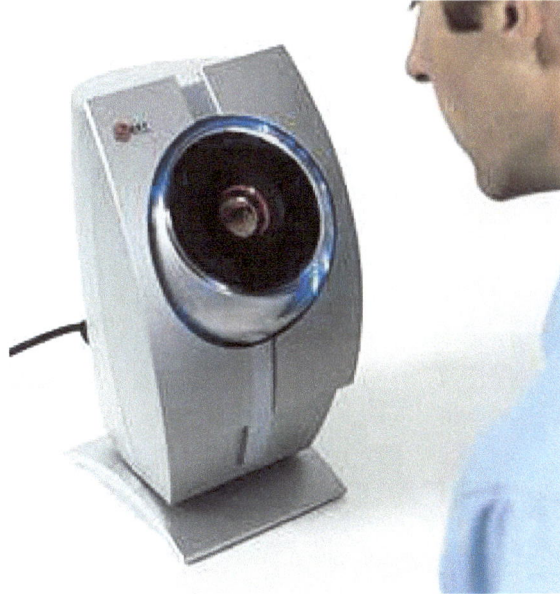

**Fig. (8.9).** Retina scan machine. https://sites.google.com/a/jeffcoschools.us/biometric-dolan-chorny-sm-th-desgarennes/home/retinal-scans.

The AI based retina scan characteristics for positives and negatives aspects.

**Positives:**

 -Very accurate
 -No two people have same retina
 -Fast results once done

**Negatives:**

 -Very expensive
 -Takes long time for correct picture
 -Can be affected by disease

The second part of the verification process will be a voice recognition (Fig. **8.10**). The employee must say their full name into the system's speaker, the system will analyze the pitch of the voice as well as the name being said. If the system recognizes the voice and name, access will be granted. If the does not recognize the voice or the name, access will be denied.

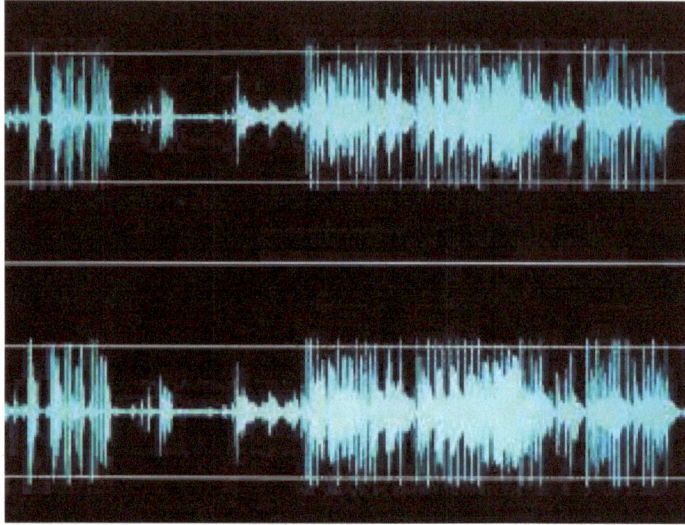

**Fig. (8.10).** Voice (or speaker) recognition. Source: from Rodgers [9].

AI supported voice recognition system characteristics regarding positives and negatives aspects.

**Positives:**

-Easy to use
-Hands free
-Only works when a certain voice is detected
-Every voice is unique

**Negatives:**

-May not pick up on what user says

-Recording of certain individual's voice can be used to access system without them being there

-Background noise might interfere

For customers, the verification process is different. First, the employee must notify the warehouse ahead of time that they will be requiring access to the warehouse. Once notify, the system will generate a 6-digit code and send the code *via* email to the customer. Once the customer is ready to access the warehouse, they will use the 6-digit code and enter it into the keypad. If the code is recognized by the system, the system will allow the customer to proceed to the second part of the verification. If the code is not recognized, access will be denied. The second part of the verification is for the customer to allow the system to perform a retina scan. If the retina is verified, the system will grant access to the employee, otherwise access will be denied (Fig. **8.11**).

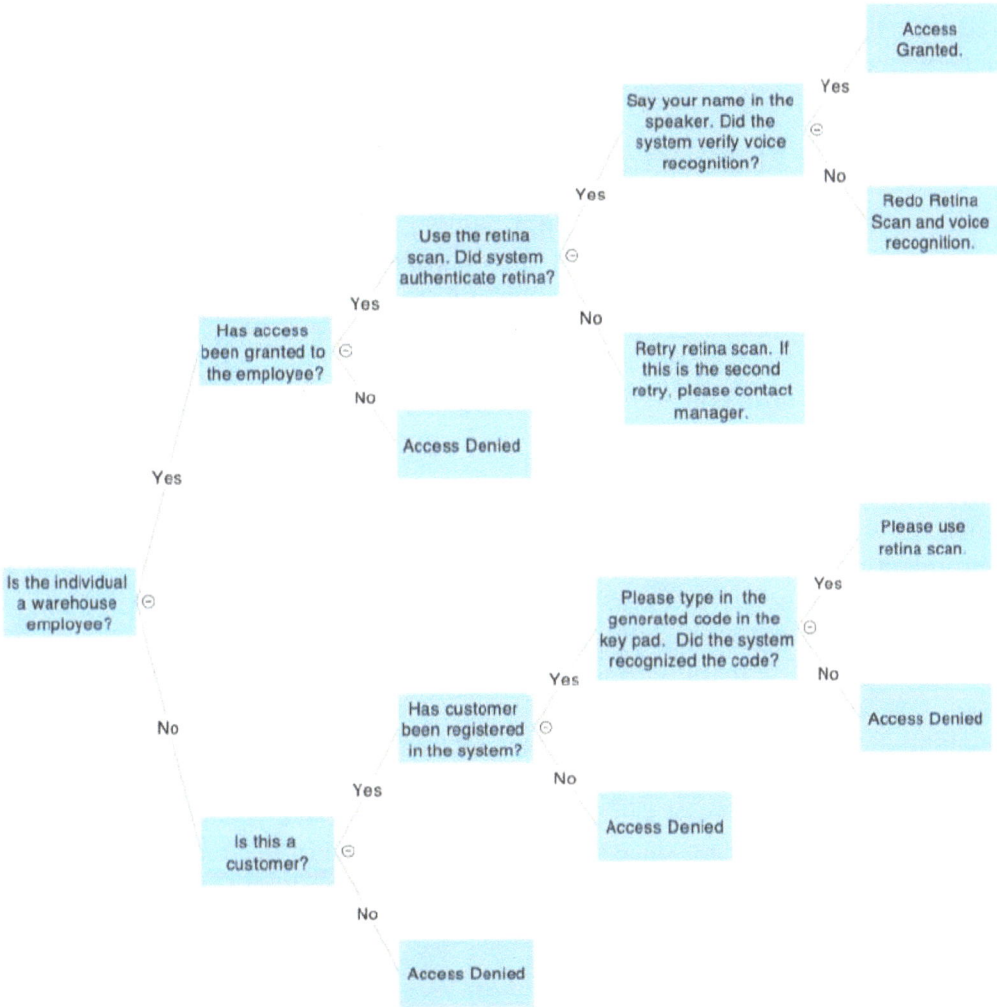

**Fig. (8.11).** Flowchart for warehouse retina scan and voice recognition systems. Source: Generated by students.

## Type I and Type II Errors

Type I errors are defined as incorrectly rejecting a true null hypothesis. In other words, generating a "False Positive." A type II error is when the system rejects a false null hypothesis. This will lead to a "False Negative" [8].

Type II errors can cause the largest problems in the warehouse system, because this implies that the system will grant access to a person who should have been rejected. Since the warehouse stores valuable inventory for customers, then to reduce the potential risk a two-factor authentication system will be implemented reduce risks. A type I error is not as risky as a type II error. If the system denies access to an approved employee, the employee will simply have to wait a minute for the system restart and retry.

## Aadhaar Use of Biometrics

Aadhaar number is a 12-digit random number issued by the UIDAI [11] to the residents of India after satisfying the verification process laid down by the Authority. Aadhaar is the world's largest biometric Identification. This system is one of the most sophisticated Identification programs in the world. This system allows one to be considered a proof of residence and not a proof of citizenship. Hence, Aadhaar does not itself grant any rights to domicile in India.

Any individual, irrespective of age and gender, who is a resident of India, may voluntarily enroll to obtain Aadhaar number (Fig. **8.12**). Person willing to enroll must provide minimal demographic and biometric information during the enrolment process which is totally free of cost. An individual need to enroll for Aadhaar only once and after de-duplication only one Aadhaar shall be generated, as the uniqueness is achieved through the process of demographic and biometric de-duplication. The main purpose to obtain the Aadhaar card is to eliminate fake identities, reduce corruption and give access to people to certain facility like banking. It does not profile people based on caste, religion, or income. The way it works is a person must give all ten fingerprints, iris scan and a photograph to obtain the card. You can obtain the card once you are five years old. You do need to get fingerprinted again once you turn fifteen as the ridges on your finger have developed and will remain the same for the rest of your life. The Aadhar program is by far the largest biometrics-based identification system in the world.

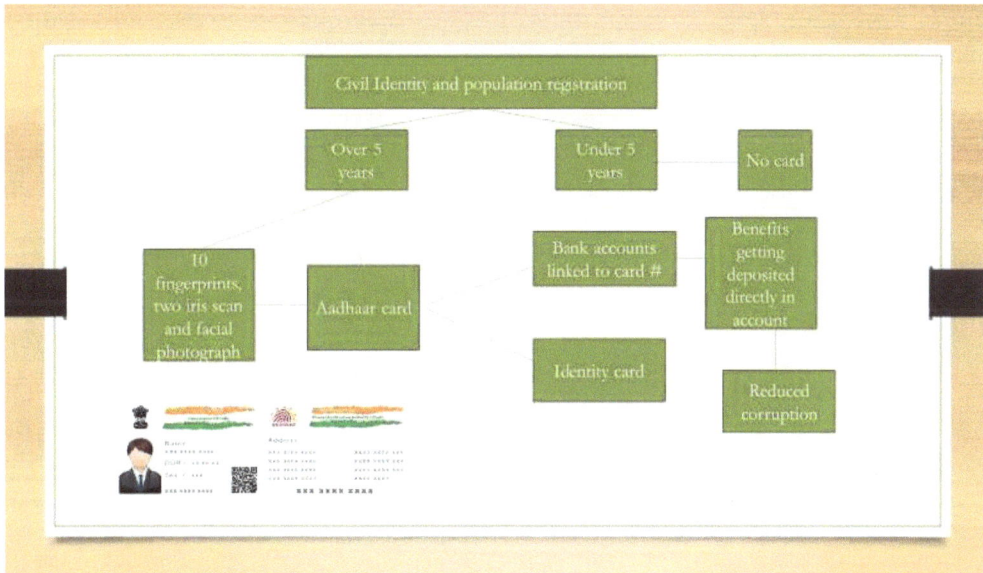

**Fig. (8.12).** Flowchart for warehouse retina scan and voice recognition systems. Source: Generated by students.

## CONCLUSION

The Value Driven Algorithmic Pathway symbolizes the Analytical Algorithmic Pathway ($\mathbf{I}{\rightarrow}\mathbf{J}{\rightarrow}\mathbf{D}$). Simply put, describing this embodiment is to consider the perceptual frame ($\mathbf{P}$) as a conditioning impact on an analytical and programmatic way of reaching a decision. The focus of the Value Driven Analytical Pathway is that it can amend or discard informational sources used in analysis ($\mathbf{J}$). In today's world machine learning is growing rapidly. In biometrics world, machine learning, deep learning and AI go hand in hand in powering the Value Driven Algorithmic Pathway.

While behavioral biometrics identifies how people interact with devices and online applications the physical biometrics are static like a device, token, fingerprint, iris scan. Due to advances in field of science it has become possible to process large data which drives machine learning and more deep learning. With continuous learning, advancements, and adoption the AI will continue to drive more capabilities of the technology. And with more refinement and advancement the system will get better and cheaper to be used in a very large scale.

A Decision tree is the explicit representation of a decision-making process. Further, decision trees in AI are utilized to arrive at conclusions based on the data available from decisions made in the past. Moreover, these conclusions are assigned values, deployed to predict the course of action likely to be taken in the future. Therefore, decision tree models are support tools for supervised learning in machine learning.

Decision trees are statistical, algorithmic models of machine learning that infer and learn responses from a variety of problems and their possible results. Accordingly, decision trees understand the rules of decision-making in precise situations grounded on the available data. The learning process is continuous and based on feedback. This advances the outcome of learning over time. This type of learning is called supervised learning. Therefore, decision tree models are support tools for supervised learning.

Decision trees are classic and natural learning models. They are based on the fundamental concept of divide and conquer. In the universe of AI, decision trees are utilized to develop learning machines by teaching them how to determine success and failure. These learning machines then analyze incoming data and store it.

Then, they make innumerable decisions constructed on previous learning experiences. These decisions form the basis for predictive modeling that helps to predict outcomes for problems. In business, organizations use these techniques to make innumerable small and big business decisions leading to giant gains or losses.

Consequently, the Throughput Model framework employing the Value Driven Algorithmic Pathway enhanced with decision trees offers a scientific decision-making process based on facts and values rather than intuition. Organizations can use this process to make significant decisions choices.

## REFERENCES

[1] W. Rodgers, and T. McFarlin, *Decision Making for Personal Investments: Real Estate Financing, Foreclosures and Other Issues.* Palgrave Macmillan: London, 2017.
[http://dx.doi.org/10.1007/978-3-319-47849-4]

[2] W. Rodgers, *Artificial Intelligence in a Throughput Model: Some Major Algorithms?* Science Publications (CRC Press: Taylor and Francis Group): Florida, 2020.

[3] CMS, "U.S. Centers for Medicare & Medicaid Services", *National Health Expenditure Data,* 2021.https://www.cms.gov/Research-Statistics-Data-and-Systems/Statistics-Tren-s-and-Reports/NationalHealthExpendData/NHE-Fact-Sheet

[4] Health System Tracker, *How does health spending in the U.S. compare to other countries?,* 2020.https://www.healthsystemtracker.org/chart-collection/health-spending-u-s-co-pare-countries/#item-start

[5] W. Rodgers, *Biometric and auditing issues addressed in a Throughput Model.* Information Age Publishing Inc.: Charlotte, NC, 2012.

[6] B. Marr, *How Much Data Is There in The World?,* 2021. https://www.bernardmarr.com/default.asp?contentID=1846

[7]     A. Wired, *Artificial Intelligence: How Algorithms Make Systems Smart,* 2019. https://www.wired.com/insights/2014/09/artificial-intelligence-algorithms-2/

[8]     W. Rodgers, R. Attah-Boakye, and K. Adams, "The application of algorithmic cognitive decision trust modelling for cybersecurity within organisations", *IEEE Trans. Eng. Manage.,* 2020. [http://dx.doi.org/10.1109/TEM.2020.3019218]

[9]     W. Rodgers, *E-commerce and biometric issues addressed in a Throughput Model.* Nova Publication: Hauppauge, NY, 2010.

[10]    W. Rodgers, *Process Thinking: Six pathways to successful decision making.* iUniverse, Inc: NY, 2006.

[11]    UIDAI, https://uidai.gov.in/about-uidai.html

**CHAPTER 9**

# The Global Perspective Algorithmic Pathway

The story of evolution unfolds with increasing levels of abstraction.

---Ray Kurzweil

Any kind of artificial intelligence clearly needs to possess great knowledge. But if we are going to deploy AI agents widely in society at large -- on our highways, in our nursing homes and schools, in our businesses and governments -- we will need machines to be wise as well as smart.

---Gillian Hadfield

Although we don't know much about how the human brain works, we know a bit more about how it got to this state: natural selection. So some people are trying to artificially replicate natural selection with machines -- although it won't take millions of years, because it's less random. It's called evolutionary computation, or genetic algorithms, and it sets up machines to do certain tasks; when one is successful through trial and error, it's combined with other machines that are successful. But it's an iterative process, which presents a problem: We don't know how long it will take to create intelligence equal to our own.

---Vasco Pedro

**Abstract**

The Global Perspective Algorithmic Pathway (**I→P→J→D**) takes into deliberation all types of information sources. This algorithmic pathway requests for an open-minded approach in which all possible information sources will be considered that can assist to update and modify a person or organization's perceptual frame. This process begins with information revising perception, followed by judgment to the decision choice. This algorithmic pathway is most ideal when there are no time pressures that will bound the time it takes to assemble the information and analyze the problem.

**Keywords:** Artificial intelligence, Decision choice, Facial Recognition, Fraud, Fraud triangle, Global perspective algorithmic pathway, Information, Iris recognition, Judgment, Keystroke dynamics, Opportunity, Perception, Pressure,

Rationalization, Risk of Material Misstatement (RMM), Type I "False Positive," Type II "False Negative," Retina Scan, Vein Recognition, Voice (Speaker) Recognition.

## INTRODUCTION

Algorithms are not characteristically biased, algorithmic decisions are contingent on several factors, including but not limited to how the software is employed, and the quality and representativeness of the underlying data. The Throughput Model ensure that data transparency, review and remediation is considered during its algorithmic engineering processes. The Throughput Model has several important aspects regarding its algorithmic pathways.

*First*, input: it provides a set of defined input (*i.e.*, perception and information).

*Second*, output: it produces results as output pertaining to problem solving or decision-making tasks.

*Third*, finiteness: the algorithmic pathways have a finite number of instructions.

*Fourth*, generality: the algorithmic pathways apply to a set of defined inputs.

Similar to the Value Driven Algorithmic Pathway, the Global Perspective Algorithmic Pathway also includes all the concepts, but in a different order of importance: information, perception, and judgment (see Fig. **9.1**). The Global Perspective Pathway suggests that information sources provide us to modify our perceptions and biases before the analysis gets to a decision. In the Value Driven Pathway, perceptions, or framing of the problem, influenced the information sources used in the analysis. In the Global Perspective Pathway, information sources are more extensive and varied, and they shape the person's perception or problem framing. This modified perception drives the analysis performed and therefore, the final decision choice. This algorithmic pathway has a much more elaborate process to gather information. The person (or for that matter a machine software program) making the decision must find information that is useful and identify and eliminate the biases and errors in it. This pathway considers incoming information sources in the framing of the perception that influences judgment (*i.e.*, analysis). This pathway is the most time consuming; therefore, it is not useful when time is very sensitive. For this pathway to result in the superior decision, the information must be reliable and relevant.

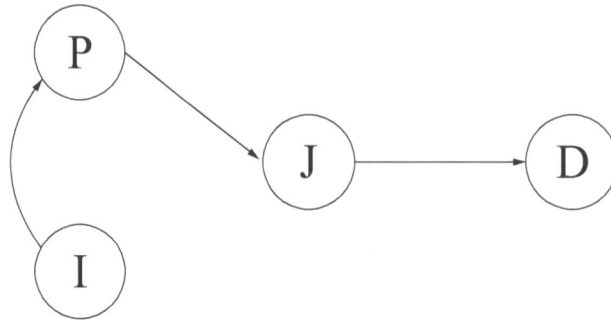

**Fig. (9.1).** I→P→J→D The decision path consists of Information to Perception to Judgement. Source: Rodgers [1].

For example, an auditor's perception can be shaped by the information received. Suppose an auditor is analyzing a client's inventory and obtains new information that the client just introduced robots that organize all the inventory. The only ones allowed to move inventory are the robots, and the orders must be approved by customer's online orders or by several people in management. This new information helps the auditor determine that internal controls related to inventory are strong and not a lot of procedures are necessary. The auditor analyses how the robots work, and the segregation of duties in the approvals, and decides the procedures that will be used in the audit.

The pathway represents a challenge for individuals perceptual framing **(P)** to devise a system to process information **(I).** This process contributes to the following dimensions: (1) to recognize the use of information and how we can identify biases and error in it; (2) to establish a system that helps/alerts for changing information; and last (3) provide a system that is similar or matches incoming information with our frame.

Nonetheless, it is important to mention one of the situations we may face with this pathway will be that can be immensely weakened by time pressure situations. In every situation time pressure may affect our decisions not just in projects but also in life. It can cause an individual to hurry to make a decision and it can end up on not making the right one. This will be because of missing information or trustable information. Time pressure can be seen as an unstable environment since it brings many stresses to individuals.

## EXAMPLE 1: GLOBAL PERSPECTIVE ALGORITHMIC PATHWAY

When it comes to new advances in technology, one of the most important innovations is AI and the different aspects of it that help it become more useful for individuals, organizations, and society. This example illustrates how machine learning, deep learning, algorithms, and big data can contribute to enhancements to algorithms as depicted by the Throughput Model.

As discussed previously, machine learning models are a mathematical representation of a real-world process. These machines work in a manner that requires training data input into them so that they can learn from it and this way, they identify patterns and are able to make decisions with very minimal human intervention or no intervention at all. Moreover, machine learning models are categorized as *supervised* or *unsupervised*. The main difference between these two is that with supervised models, the machines have more information, and it has known inputs and outputs, whereas unsupervised models work without knowing inputs and the results they get are usually unknown or unexpected [1].

Another important aspect of AI is the implementation of deep learning. This technique consists of machines that mimic human behavior in the way by which they learn through example. With this, we have been able to have driverless cars and other electronic devices that are taught to recognize certain patterns and perform tasks by themselves. If done correctly, with deep learning machines can exceed human-level performances, as the chances for error would be minimal.

Algorithms are key components of AI. Based on the Throughput Model (Fig. **9.2**), algorithms can assist in the creation and expansion of AI technology. Algorithms are be depicted as instructions or pathways that tell computers and machines what to do through codes and mathematics. The Throughput Model is conformed of six algorithms which are:

$$P \rightarrow D \tag{1}$$

$$P \rightarrow J \rightarrow D \tag{2}$$

$$I \rightarrow J \rightarrow D \tag{3}$$

$$I \rightarrow P \rightarrow D \tag{4}$$

$$P \rightarrow I \rightarrow J \rightarrow D \tag{5}$$

$$I \rightarrow P \rightarrow J \rightarrow D \tag{6}$$

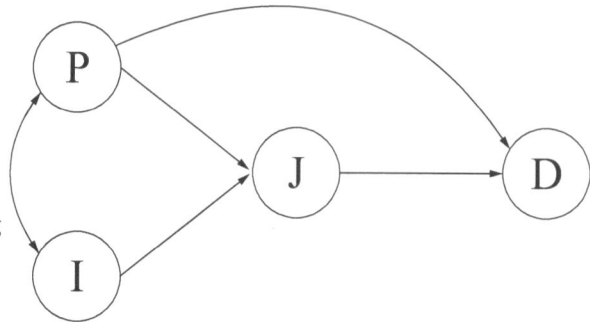

In the case of P ↔ I, neural networks work to make little calculations to obtain information about the data instead of following an algorithm.

**Fig. (9.2).** Throughput model. Source: Rodgers [2].

*where P = perception, I = information, J = judgment, and D = decision choice.*

The Throughput Model can assist AI when it comes to handling large amounts of data. As technology advances, data sets become bigger and more complex, and with the help of this feature of artificial intelligence, it is possible to process all the data adequately. Big Data makes this possible to us, as it helps to discover all the information that it is possible to get, through the guidance of the Throughput Model.

As previously discussed, the global environment use of AI technology is magnifying every day when it comes to improvements in the technology. Therefore, to maintain this growth rate, the data that is used in these processes must improve as well. This is what is known as Big Data, which can be described as the body of technology representing algorithms, programming systems, and hardware, that stress our abilities to handle the data. Efforts to take the most advantage of all this new information and new data are made every day to collect, store and work with as much data as it is possible to us.

When it comes to advances in technology, new ways to make things easier for humans are constantly being implemented, but at the same time it can be a door for criminals to find new ways to commit crimes. For this reason, the implementation of biometrics is useful when searching for different approaches in which AI becomes more resilient to fraud and can deter, eliminate, and prevent unethical acts from rooting itself in organizations and society.

Implementing biometrics tools requires three types of authentication factors: "Something you know", which is something that is a secret, such a password or a secret question; "Something you have", for example a credit card, which only the person who possesses it can use it, and "Something you are"; which are personal characteristics such as face, voice, fingerprints, *etc*. As with everything, biometrics are subject to errors, and this can be Type I or Type II. Errors Type I, which are also known as a "false positive" are those that reject a null hypothesis when it is true. Errors Type II, on the other hand, are known as a "false negative", as they do not reject a null hypothesis when the alternative hypothesis is the true state of nature [3].

An example of the implementation of biometrics to decrease the risks of fraud are through biometric payments. The most important factor that AI has when it comes to preventing fraud in this area is the authentication factor. There are three main authentication factors, which are: (1) *ownership,* which is something that the user possesses; (2) *knowledge,* something the user knows, and (3) *inherence,* something that the user intrinsically part of the process.

From the above-mentioned factors, the one that is the easiest to break is ownership, as a physical object can be easily taken from one person or be duplicated, such a credit card. Knowledge is not as easy to get but it can be obtained from a person, as fraudsters can find ways to get sensitive or important information from one person through different techniques. Therefore, with biometric payments the inherence factor would be the most secure way to protect a person's possessions. It would be more difficult for a fraudster to get access to someone's fingerprint, for example, as it would be to their credit card.

This is just an example of how biometrics are helping into making it more difficult for people to commit fraud in the technology area, but the application of these techniques that help protect people's possessions are implemented in a variety of aspects of our everyday life. Unfortunately, in the same breath, as mentioned before, advances in technology can help criminals hide their identities or obtain more access to private information, so the efforts to fight this must be constant.

In sum, AI has provided new opportunities and developments to humanity through its algorithms and the ways that they improve every day. In the following, different aspects of AI are related to the Fraud Triangle. Furthermore, more detail is provided on how biometrics tools interact with the Throughout Model depiction of algorithms utilized in organizational transactions.

The Fraud Triangle triangulates Incentives/Pressures, Opportunities, and Attitudes/ Rationalization, in describing the reasons behind people committing fraud [4]. Incentives/Pressures refer to the motivation behind the crime committed and it can be in the form of personal or financial motivation, such as a personal debt or workplace debt problems. Opportunities refer to how the individual will commit the fraud in the organization; most of the time it is a result from people abusing the power that they have by having a position of influence in the organization. Finally, Attitudes/Rationalization is the final step in the fraud triangle and it during this stage, the fraudster must be able to justify the crime in a way that is acceptable to his or her values and moral compass.

Moreover, the Association of Certified Fraud Examiners [5] has a similar definition of the Fraud Triangle, which is a model for explaining the factors that cause someone to commit occupational fraud. Fig. (9.3) illustrates how the Fraud Triangle components can be explained by the Throughput Model algorithms [6].

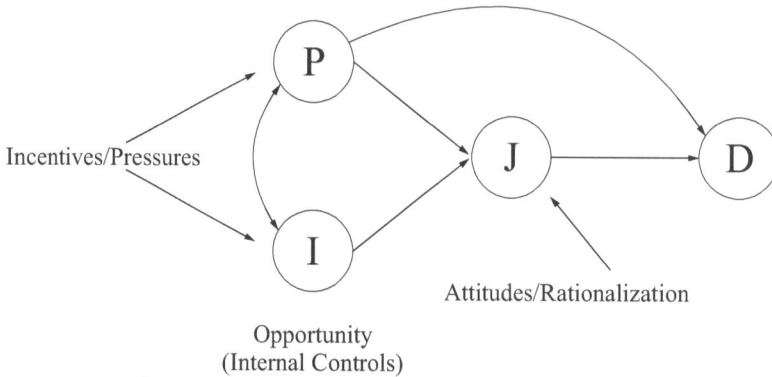

**Fig. (9.3).** Fraud triangle components in the throughput model. Source: Rodgers, Söderbom, and Guiral [6].

The AI technology and biometrics tools such as iris and facial recognition have been useful to practitioners and researchers to analyze the issues that individuals and organizations may encounter when confronted with fraudulent acts. Biometrics can be used through the Global Perspective Algorithmic Pathway (I→P→J→D), as they must first get the information and determine how it is perceived in order to make a judgment about it and eventually a decision choice.

The role of biometrics can play a major role in the situations that organizations may encounter to prevent or deter fraud. Examples of biometrics that have been implemented into our everyday lives include iris scan, voice recognition, facial recognition, and the scan of fingerprints. According to the Throughput Model, this mainly affects the areas of "setting up" or framing the problem (*i.e.*, perception) and information aspects of it, as it allows fraudsters to use these algorithms to access important information.

Along with biometrics tools come the issues of ethics that may affect individuals when it comes to their privacy and/or lack of it. In other words, individuals' notion that biometrics will assault their privacy is one of the foremost impediments to the wider acceptance of these technologies. With the development of this new technology, it is easier for a person to access his or her personal information without the need of any physical objects, but at the same time, if someone hacks or duplicate these characteristics, the fraudster will have more access to a person's personal and private information, which may lead to a substantial invasion of a person's privacy and access to her/his possessions and valuable information.

Furthermore, one of the main issues concerning personal privacy, is the conflict with one's beliefs and values and the collection, protection, and utilization of personal biometric data. Therefore, it is very pertinent for organizations to continually establish new forms of security and to establish limits to respect people's privacy. At the same time, organizations must work unswervingly to ensure that the information that is handled with Biometrics technology cannot be corrupted or accessed by hackers and fraudsters.

There are many activists who claim that Biometrics will have a limited future in our society, and as these technologies proliferate the harder will be for people to keep their privacy. In essence, biometrics can make a serious impact on personal freedom and democratic rights. Nonetheless, due to other societal threats such as terrorism, identity theft and fraud, illegal immigration, has made it necessary to have the capability to obtain individuals' identity for later identification and verification. Therefore, biometrics, if implemented with good security regulations can help decrease these threats upon society.

The biometrics tools advances in technology have an impact on enhancing goals results by increasing everyday satisfaction of living, productivity, and the smooth running of a society. At the same time, it is important for the management of biometric tools for organizations to grow. This is achieved by what is known as the Global Perspective Algorithmic Pathway and it implies that individuals should constantly formulate and implement processes that would lead to satisfy their needs in order to achieve the long-term success of any entity. For example, biometrics can play a big role into this approach as it can accelerate the growth of the firm by increasing security and providing to its employees the most sophisticated instruments to perform their job.

Next, a decision tree is presented that incorporates biometric technology. A decision tree is a graphical representation of possible solutions to a decision based on certain conditions.

Organizations implement these tools in the working environment because through them, it is easy to understand data and make interpretations.

An example of a decision tree involving iris and voice biometrics is now presented below (see Figs. **9.4** and **9.5**).

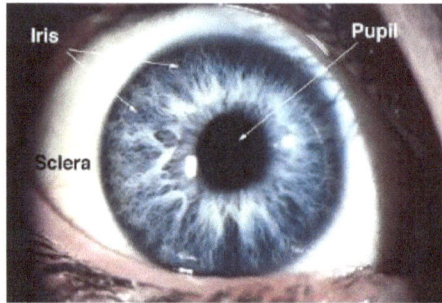

**Fig. (9.4).** Iris recognition technology. http://webvision.med.utah.edu/imageswv/pupil.jpeg.

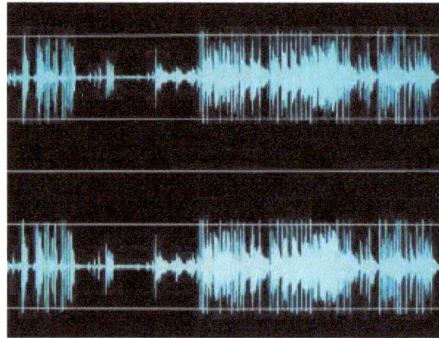

**Fig. (9.5).** Voice (speaker) recognition technology. See Rodgers [7].

A firm has a system that works with iris and voice recognition.

1. Through iris scan, system records employees' clock-ins and clock-outs.
2. Employees access their offices through iris scan and can turn on their computers through voice recognition.
3. System records the time each employee takes to finish an assigned task.
4. System automatically records when an employee starts working overtime hours.
5. No receptionist, system receives phone calls.

A senior accountant of a firm asks partners to give him one week of paid off time (*i.e.*, POT) at the beginning of the year, without having any days accrued for that year. The classification rules are as follows (Fig. **9.6**):

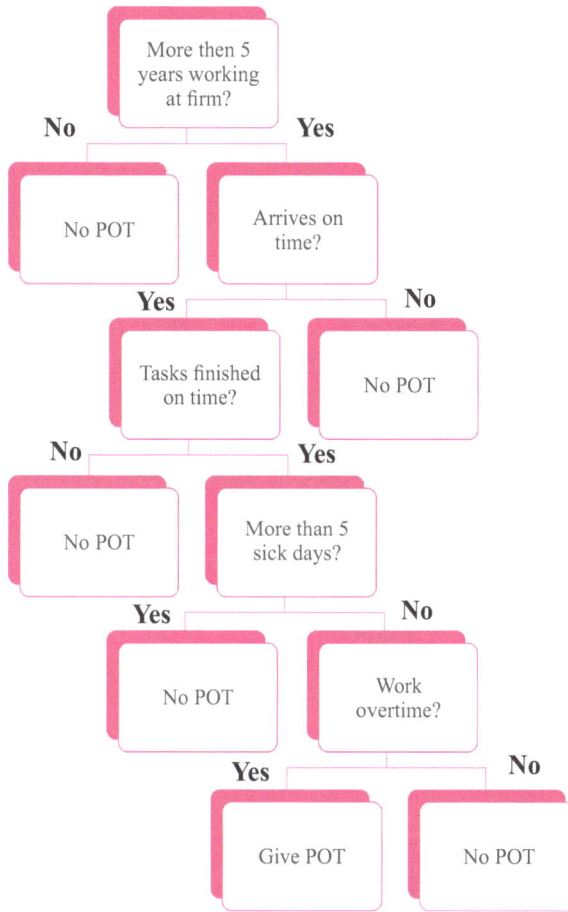

**Fig. (9.6).** Decision tree using biometrics technology. Source: Students and author 7generated.

1. Employee has been working in the firm for more than 3 years → Give POT

2. Employee arrives to work on time → Give POT

3. Employee performs tasks assigned on time → Give POT

4. Employee has called in sick more than 5 times during the previous year → Don't give POT

5. Employee works overtime hours if it is needed → Give POT

Examples of Type I and Type II errors that could occur are:

Type I "False Positive":

1. System does not recognize the voice of the employer
2. System does not approve POT when it is deserved

Type II "False Negative":

1. System does not record sick days taken by employee
2. System approves POT when it is not deserved

In summary, AI has made major improvements in our everyday lives, and it consists of different factors that help it grow and improve. Machine learning models, along with deep learning, train computers into mirroring human behavior as they learn by example and can perform tasks without the need of human supervision. Algorithms are codes that tell a computer what to do, and when it comes to artificial intelligence, the Throughput Model is conformed of six algorithms. Biometrics have made implementations to prevent fraud from happening, but at the same time, it opens more doors for fraudsters to commit fraud and get access to people's information, so the efforts to fight this must be constant and new protection techniques must be constantly implemented.

Biometrics can be very beneficial to our society if implemented with good security measures. It can be related to the Fraud Triangle, as with new advances in technology fraudsters have more opportunity to commit fraud. Finally, ethical issues are constantly raised when it comes to Biometrics, with both parties having their argument points.

## EXAMPLE 2: GLOBAL PERSPECTIVE ALGORITHMIC PATHWAY DECREASING FRAUD

We live in a fast-paced world on account of technology. Our instant communication, whether *via* cellphone, email, text, or online posts, has accelerated all aspects of business including globalization. The accumulation of data and the complexity of transactions in the economy have increased as well, and our society needs a standardized financial language that we can trust to participate in it. Auditors fulfill this need in the public sector. Auditors ensure that all managerial assessments presented in the company's financial statements are reasonably accurate and truthful, in addition, auditors also reasonably assure that the company's operations are working as intended in the time frame reviewed. With the aid of AI tools, auditors can accomplish this task in a much more efficient and expediated manner.

To put big data to advantageous use, organizations create algorithms such as the Global Perspective Algorithmic Pathway. An algorithm is a set of rules for the machine to follow. An algorithm is what enables a machine to quickly process vast amounts of data that a human cannot judiciously process, or even comprehend. The performance and exactness of algorithms is very essential. Algorithms in this book flows from the Throughput Model. Nonetheless, in some of the Throughput Model algorithms, human error, and biases (both intentional and unintentional) can impact the performance of the algorithm. Faulty inputs into the algorithms can produce minor undesirable glitches in an organization's operations, or major catastrophic outcomes.

The $I{\rightarrow}P{\rightarrow}J{\rightarrow}D,$ which is the Global Perspective Algorithmic Pathway provides information to change auditors' perception before analyzing and making a final decision. As mentioned previously, this can weaken a decision if there are time pressures happening since the individual may rush into trying to make the right decision. Nonetheless, if unreliable information and time pressures do not limit this pathway, then there is a high probability of the best decision being made. The $I{\rightarrow}P{\rightarrow}J{\rightarrow}D$ pathway can be divided into two parts given a stable or unstable environment, which could result in different decision choices.

AI has provided a higher speed of data processing, reduction of human fatigue errors and the costs related to them, helping not only the Auditors but the business managers to make the right decisions, putting more time in their hands becoming more efficient by accomplishing more. In this paper we will see how the implementation of AI tools can enhance inventory business processes through computer software algorithms in the accounting systems and biometrics reducing the Risk of Material Misstatement (RMM).

Algorithms, a step-by-step process, are found in the internal control systems of a company and are interconnected with the company's governance culture. To better understand this relationship, this section examines the Throughput Model and the Fraud triangle to handle fraudulent situations [6]. And on the other hand, we will be discussing AI biometrics, which are body measurements and calculations related to human characteristics used in computer science as a form of identification and access control. These biometrics are implemented in organizations to authorize data access for confidential data, approval process, and security clearance, all to safeguard assets and some of them are: Voice recognition, Keystroke dynamics, Dynamic signature, Finger vein recognition, Facial recognition and, Retina biometrics [7].

Fraud is an intentionally deceptive action designed to provide the perpetrator with an unlawful gain or to deny a right to a victim. The Fraud triangle depicts that for fraud to occur, each of three conditions must be present: perceived pressure, perceived opportunity, and rationalization, depicted below [6].

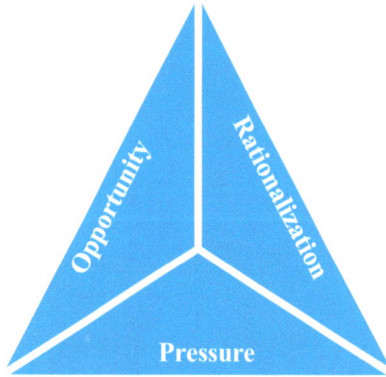

- Perceived pressure from a non-sharable financial problem produces the motive or incentive for the crime.

- Perceived opportunity is the perception that a control weakness is present, and the probability of being caught is remote.

- Rationalization is an attempt to diminish the cognitive dissonance within the person.

**Fig. (9.7).** Fraud triangle. Adopted from Rodgers.

It is very difficult to eliminate all negative aspects of the human nature of individuals that work within an organization. Financial problems, addictions, gambling can be identified as elements of "pressure" for an individual, that goes hand in hand with the element of "rationalization" to justify their actions of fraud, by trying to survive a difficult situation in their lives. Thus, by setting strong management control systems we can decrease the element of "opportunity" for fraud and protect the company's assets [8] (Rodgers, Al Fayi, Al-Refiay, and Murray, 2020).

Management Culture comes from the tone at the top governing body and will direct every action, pursuing the same goal and mission of the business. The Global Perspective Algorithmic Pathway (I→P→J→D) suggests that the information available influences the decision maker's perception before an evaluation analysis in route to making a decision choice. In this pathway, informational sources influence a non-consequential ruling guide process (P→J→D). In other words, decision makers may substitute a standard procedure or rule base process, if information sources are very persuasive for modifying a "ruling guide process". In these circumstances, the information assessable by the decision maker either would positively or negatively guide the frame (perception) regarding the current situation.

Since AI is powered by algorithms, the Global Perspective Algorithmic Pathway (I→P→J→D) can be fueled by big data. Therefore, before an organization embarks on employing AI systems, they should have a strong foundation in subjecting the algorithms to big data. Further, audits can be enhanced by addressing AI when it has a strong foundation in big data [6].

Big data implies more than just considerable amounts of data. Moreover, big data indicates data to be formulated into information that organizations undertake at high levels of volume, variety, velocity, and variability. In addition, organizations invest in system architectures, tools, and practices particularly intended to handle the data. Much of this data may be produced by the organization itself, while other data may be publicly available or purchased from external sources.

When we combine the organization's Global Perspective Algorithmic Pathway (*i.e.*, that fits with the managerial decision-making tone at the top), with the fraud triangle; we can significantly impact fraudulent behavior. By making employees more aware of what behavior is acceptable or unacceptable and suggest what to do if they encounter improper behavior, through continual education, a written code of conduct, or oral communication in staff meetings when dealing with day-to-day activities. Annual reviews can measure whether all employees acknowledge understanding of the Global Perspective Algorithmic Pathway to be implemented in certain tasks [6]. This algorithmic position should provide management with guidance on documentation, how often to intervene or investigate in case of a deviation from the established managerial positions to prevent any future occurrence.

To prevent or detect and correct any Risk of Material Misstatement (RMM), "opportunity for fraudulent activity," a discussion is required to investigate potential weaknesses in the company's internal control system. The auditor must understand the internal control components and documents generated in the business transactions to make a control risk assessment (RMM) depicted in Fig. **(9.8)**.

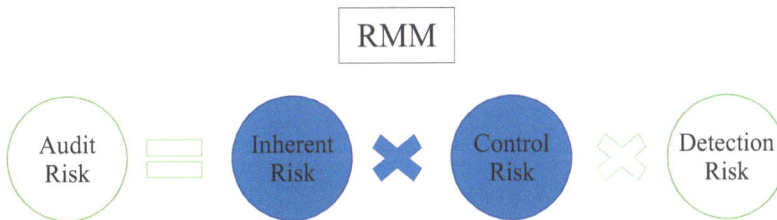

**Fig. (9.8).** Risk of Material Misstatement (RMM). Source: Partially adapted from: Rodgers, Söderbom, and Guiral [6].

Where Inherent Risk is in the business nature itself with no related control; Control Risk is found in the company's internal control system; and Detection risk is the capacity to detect potential risks in time to correct the material wrongdoing. When the auditor finds a moderate to high Control Risk; the Detection risk is low, signaling a red flag to the auditor for an opportunity of a material misstatement. The auditor then, performs more analytical procedures (rigorous substantive tests) gathering more evidence to prove any error or fraud that can lead to material misstatements in the management assertions [9].

Later a literature review section and flowchart (decision tree) are presented for the inventory audit of a company to have a picture of how AI tools can help in the auditor process. Finally, this example continues with an analysis section and concludes with the importance of the AI in today's auditing process.

The inventory cycle is one of the most comprehensive cycles of an organization. That is, that it includes the purchasing, payroll, and revenue cycles, which means "cradle to grave" components. This presents major auditing risks, which can have a tremendous impact on a company's profitability. The next flowchart depicts the decision processes in these three departments, and it helps the auditor visualize the core of the business itself to be emerged into their operations.

Some of the documents and records included in the inventory management process (Fig. **9.9**) are: Production Schedule, Receiving Report, Materials Requisition, Inventory Mater file, Production data information, Cost accumulation and variance report, Inventory status report, and Shipping order. These documents are used as evidence of transactions, to test management's financial assertions of occurrence, authorization, completeness, accuracy, cutoff, and classification [9].

*Occurrence*: By the inspection of these records, the auditor can test if the transaction or event recorded have in fact occurred.

A common internal control process implemented in the system is the prenumbered documents to handle the receipt, transfer, and withdrawal of inventory to prevent fictitious inventory in the accounting record. In other words, the misrepresentation of inventory is the falsification of purchase requisition and purchase orders.

By observation, the auditor can evaluate if one individual is responsible for both controlling and accounting for inventory, opening the opportunity of unauthorized purchases to be made or theft of inventory goods. The segregation of duties as a control activity, can nowadays be enhanced with the implementation of AI generated "keystroke dynamics" biometrics (Fig. **9.10**).

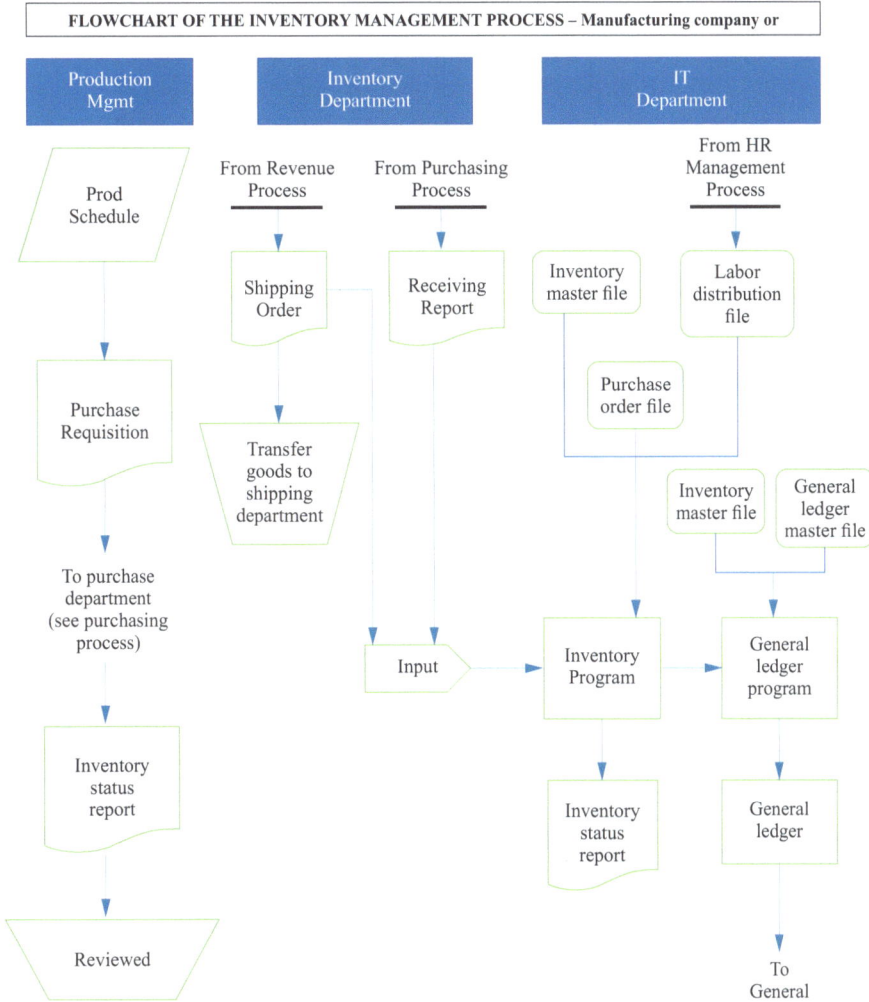

Fig. (9.9). Risk of Material Misstatement (RMM). Source: Partially adapted by: Rodgers, Al Fayi, Al-Refiay, Murray [8].

**Fig. (9.10).** Keystroke dynamics. Source: from Rodgers [7].

Keystroke dynamics (or typing biometrics) pertains to the detailed timing information which describes exactly when each key was pressed and when it was released as an individual is typing at a computer keyboard. The behavioral biometric of keystroke dynamics utilizes the manner and rhythm whereby a person types characters on a keyboard or keypad. The keystroke rhythms of a user are measured to develop a unique biometric template of the user's typing pattern for future authentication. Moreover, this AI tool, gauges the characteristics of a person's typing pattern, including the time spacing of words, identifying the individual within the company who is generating the document and give access or deny it.

*Authorization*: All transactions and events need to be properly authorized.

In the example described above, we can see how the implementation of the "keystrokes dynamics" ensured proper authorization by signature biometrics making this auditor test much easier.

*Completeness*: When a transaction took place, such as the receipt of purchased inventory in the warehouse, it needs to be recorded in the system for the transaction to be complete.

By reviewing the entity's procedures, accounting for the numerical sequence of purchase orders, receiving reports and vouchers, the auditor will determine the control risk within the information technology department processes. By tracing a sample of receiving reports to their respective vendor invoices and vouchers, the auditor can see if the receiving report matches the vendor invoice and if it was entered in the purchase journal for the transaction to be complete.

*Accuracy*: The assertion is that the full amounts/quantities of all transactions were recorded, without error.

The inspection of tangible assets against inventory records in the system, will give the auditor the opportunity to observe the physical safeguards over this company assets. Even after the segregation of duties, for the authorized personnel to have access to the warehouse where the inventory is kept, the risk of password theft, key card theft or hacking is present, leading to inventory shortages. This manipulation of the inventory file by altering the inventory quantities, can be prevented with the implementation of an AI control tool. Some examples of these tools are voice recognition (see Fig. **9.11**), vein recognition (see Fig. **9.12**), facial recognition (see Fig. **9.13**) or retina biometrics (see Fig. **9.14**), to log into the system as a verification process of the authorized personnel. Voice recognition is utilized to determine an unknown speaker's identity based on patterns of voice pitch and speech style. Finger vein recognition is utilized to identify people and verify their identity by matching the vascular patter in a person's finger to previously obtained data. Facial recognition uses algorithms to analyze features, including position/size/shape of the eyes, nose, cheekbones, and jaw line. Retina biometrics is a means for identifying individuals by the pattern of blood vessels on the retina. The Retina scanner about the size of a shoebox can map the distinctive pattern of blood vessels on the retina [8].

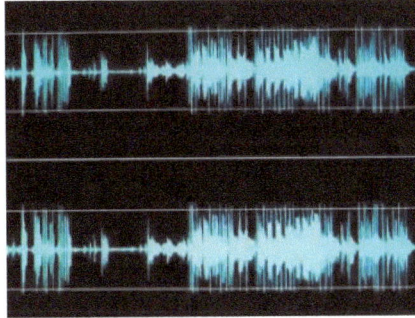

**Fig. (9.11).** Voice (speaker) recognition. Source: from Rodgers [7].

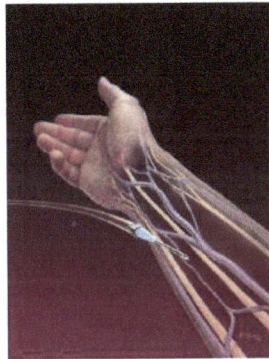

**Fig. (9.12).** Vein recognition. Source: from Rodgers [7].

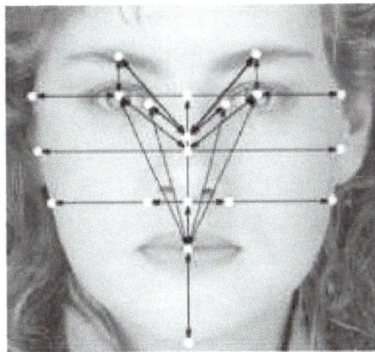

**Fig. (9.13).** Facial recognition. Source: from Rodgers [7].

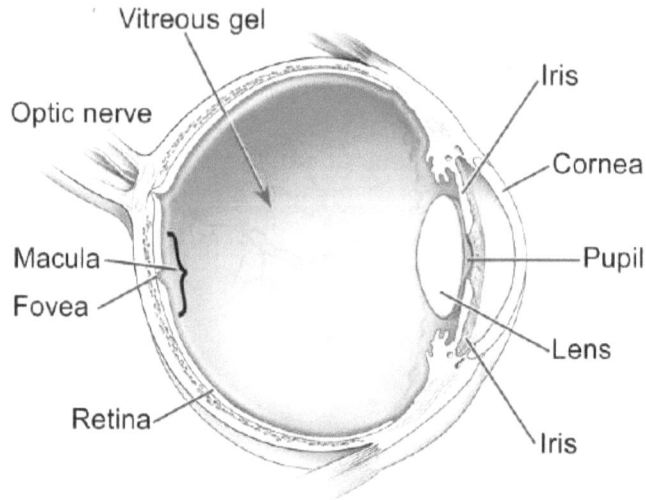

**Fig. (9.14).**  Retina scan. Source: from Rodgers [7].

*Cutoff*: Events and transactions have been recorded in the correct accounting period.

The company control activity in the IT department is to record all receiving reports and all shipping documents processed daily into the perpetual inventory. With this internal control in place, the auditor can then review and test these procedures to assess if the receiving reports and the shipping documents against the perpetual inventory report pertain to the appropriate accounting period.

*Classification*: In the inventory cycle, classification assurance pertains to the proper classification of transactions into raw materials, work in process and finish goods accounts.

The company's internal control activity involves the materials requisitions and production data forms used to process goods through manufacturing. The auditor reviews this procedures and forms used to classify inventory into their accounts.

In the Purchase/Inventory cycle we will encounter the Vendor selection risk. The employee in the purchasing department oversees identifying best prices for the products needed by the company. The vendor selection risk is when the vendor offers incentives such as gifts or monetary compensation to manipulate the employee decision to choose him as a supplier over his competitors. This kind of "pressure" to the employee can be very attractive, since the decision is his, among the already authorized vendors. Consequently, the employee could be overlooking the quality of the material offered that can financially harm the company. The

Vendor approval control is an effective employee protection mechanism. This mechanism includes the stroke dynamic signature for purchase orders approvals and a strong supervision of the purchaser [8].

With data volumes growing across industries, there is a high demand among public accounting firms using AI to improve human performance and formulate risk strategies to assess their client data to ensure faithful representation of financial reporting. In addition, companies' CFOs are using AI data analytics to provide investors with guidance on future financial positions. Some of the benefits are increased business insight, transparency and automatization. The fear of AI lacking human professional judgement or replacement of human jobs, quickly disappears when the right technologies are placed in the hands of people that care, turning today's ideas into tomorrow's solutions driving the right outcomes. Currently, PwC accounting firm is delivering an audit that is smart and streamlined. PwC platform, Aura, seamlessly and securely ingest the company's data one time, so they can use it throughout the audit, saving time and rework. PwC data analytics, Halo, will deliver insights of a billion processed records in each instance for journals applications to improve risk assessment, analysis and testing, and insight. AI technology makes it easy to stay in the same page 24/7 with streamlined and real-time situations promoting efficiency (PwC online publication 2017). In this analysis we have found that AI can only improve the audit performance and its capabilities are growing exponentially as we speak.

In sum, the different situations presented in this example indicates a close relationship among decision-making, internal control systems and fraud in any type of business. Biometrics are a powerful technology that can be applied in management control systems. Also, AI enhanced biometrics systems can aide in the reduction of information theft and other assets in an organization. The investment cost consideration for the implementation of biometrics systems can appear expensive in the short run; however, the knowledge-based recommendation has displayed positive results. The expense in new AI system investments will pay for itself by eliminating the costs that the entity is occurring from weak controls risks or lawsuits in the long run [8]. At the end of the day, AI enhanced auditing procedure are growing at an exponentially. These results make it more evident how human professional judgment in the audit process with the combination of AI can prevent financial loss with risk control management.

## CONCLUSION

One of the most recognizable examples of an algorithm is a recipe. It represents a determinate list of instructions employed to execute a task. For example, to follow the algorithm to produce brownies from a box mix, a person would follow the three to five step processes written on the back of the box. Throughput Modelling decision-making is the process of deciding by automated means without any human involvement. These decisions can be based on factual data, as well as on digitally created profiles or inferred data. While not all mistakes can be prevented, automated decision-making can streamline the process of identifying and addressing issues, providing prompt detection, automated correction attempts and more time for operator recovery when it is indispensable.

The I→P→J→D algorithmic pathway stipulates that information sources **(I)** enable individuals to update or modify the person's perception **(P)** before analysis **(J)** begins in route to decide choice **(D)**. This will assist for providing an open-minded viewpoint of a person to consider the various types of information sources that will influence his or her perceptions.

This pathway starts with having information in an influential impact on perception, it allows a person to focus on different informational sources. To add, as we view information as conditioned data that has properties of relevance and reliability. It also crucial and it must be understanding that the information relates to past, present, and/or future events; reliability is associated with having things correct, the reproduction, and confirmation of information sources.

The algorithmic characteristics of the Throughput Model provides the following:

1. Finiteness. An algorithm must always terminate after a finite number of steps.
2. Definiteness. Each step of an algorithm must be precisely defined; the actions to be carried out must be rigorously and unambiguously specified for each case.
3. Input concepts or variables.
4. Output, prediction, prescription, or description, and
5. Effectiveness in problem solving or decision-making chores.

In research and practice areas, the use of the global perspective algorithmic pathway in AI can be implemented to analyze data, to gain insight and to subsequently make a prediction or create a determination with it. Instead of manually coding software with a specific instruction set, the computer can be trained at machine learning, deep learning, or natural language processing.

Further, the global perspective algorithmic pathway has the potential to eliminate biases or discrimination. Nonetheless, this depends on how the software is deployed, and the quality and representativeness of the underlying data used by the algorithm.

Global perspective algorithmic pathway can use data and statistical analyses to classify issues or events for the purpose of assessing their effectiveness as it pertains to decision making. This pathway can be used in the public sector, including for the delivery of government services, and in the justice system. For example, medical algorithms assist in standardizing selection and application of treatment regimens. Supplementary, algorithm automation can reduce the potential of errors.

In addition, this algorithmic pathway can be an especially valuable tools for novice nurses who may lack experience and confidence in their decision making. The global perspective algorithmic pathway can create more efficiency in care planning, cue nurses to follow up on critical monitoring, and help maximize confidence in the decisions they make.

In sum, algorithms are essential to the way computers process data. Algorithms can assist people to manage information overload and can filter searches. The global perspective algorithmic pathway provides the detail specific instructions a computer should perform in a specific order to carry out a specified task, such as gauging environmental issues pertaining to locating a factory in a new area.

Finally, AI techniques are progressively expanding and enriching decision support through such means as coordinating data delivery, analyzing data trends, providing forecasts, developing data consistency, quantifying uncertainty, anticipating the user's data needs, providing information to the user in problem solving or decision-making tasks. Foregoing a design algorithm such as the global perspective algorithmic pathway may increase complexity, lack of transparency around algorithm design, inappropriate use of algorithms, and weak governance. The lack of a design are specific reasons why algorithms are subject to such risks as biases, errors, and malicious acts.

## REFERENCES

[1]    W. Rodgers, *Artificial Intelligence in a Throughput Model: Some Major Algorithms.* Science Publications, Taylor & Francis: Florida, 2020.

[2]    W. Rodgers, *Process Thinking: Six pathways to successful decision making.* iUniverse, Inc: NY, 2006.

[3]    W. Rodgers, *Biometric and auditing issues addressed in a Throughput Model.* Information Age Publishing Inc.: Charlotte, NC, 2012.

[4]    D.R. Cressy, *Other people's money: The social psychology of embezzlement.* The Free Press: New York, 1953.

[5]    Association of Certified Fraud Examiners (ACFE), *The Fraud Triangle.,* 2021.https://www.acfe.com/fraud-triangle.aspx

[6]    W. Rodgers, A. Söderbom, and A. Guiral, "Corporate Social Responsibility Enhanced Control Systems reducing the Likelihood of Fraud", *J. Bus. Ethics,* vol. 91, suppl. Suppl. 1, pp. 151-166, 2014.

[7]    W. Rodgers, *E-commerce and biometric issues addressed in a Throughput Model.* Nova Publication: Hauppauge, NY, 2010.

[8]    Al Fayi Rodgers, "Artificial Intelligence Algorithms Implemented for Ethical Issues in Management Accounting, China Management", *Account. Rev.,* vol. 11, no. 1, pp. 116-131, 2020.

[9]    W.F. Messier, S. Glover, and D. Prawitt, *Auditing and Assurance Services: A Systematic Approach.* 11th ed. Irwin-McGraw-Hill, Inc.: New York, 2019.

# CHAPTER 10

# Moving Forward with Throughput Modelling and Advancing Technologies

*"The pace of progress in artificial intelligence (I'm not referring to narrow AI) is incredibly fast. Unless you have direct exposure to groups like Deepmind, you have no idea how fast—it is growing at a pace close to exponential. The risk of something seriously dangerous happening is in the five-year timeframe. 10 years at most."* —Elon Musk wrote in a comment on Edge.org

*It is difficult to think of a major industry that AI will not transform. This includes healthcare, education, transportation, retail, communications, and agriculture. There are surprisingly clear paths for AI to make a big difference in all of these industries.* ---Andrew Ng

Artificial intelligence may well help solve the most complex problems humankind faces, like curing cancer and climate change -- but in the near term, it is also likely to empower surveillance, erode privacy and turbocharge telemarketers.

---Jeff Goodell

**Abstract**

AI and related digital technologies have practically weaved its way through everything the 21st Century is tied to for performance and productivity. It provides individuals and organizations with a better, closer, more holistic view of solutions as never before. For most organizations, speed is essential on today's landscape. Furthermore, AI, machine learning, deep learning, natural language processing, big data, and other digital technologies assist individuals and organizations to collaborate with others in real time and connect processes and data to rapidly build trust and confidence.

**Keywords:** 5G, As-a-Service (aaS), Augmented reality, Automation, Blockchains, Cyber security, DARQ, Extended reality, Fifth dimension, First dimension, Fourth dimension, Human enhancement (HE), Internet of Behavior (IoB), Internet of Things (IoT), Parallelism, Quantum computing, Quantum qubits, Second dimension, Six dominant algorithmic pathways, Third dimension, Throughput Model, Virtuality reality.

**Waymond Rodgers**

**INTRODUCTION**

Today computers are in practically everything humans are involved with daily. Previously, the image of computers was depicted as rectangular objects either on a desk, or during contemporary times in our pockets. However, computers are in automobiles, thermostats, refrigerators, *etc.* More and more computers are no longer objects at all, but they permeate fabric and practically every other material. Some scholars predict that the influence of AI will be as worldwide transformative on economic and social structures as steam engines, railroads, electricity, electronics, and the Internet [1, 2]. In essence, the future of computing is going to impact individuals and organizations on an everyday basis.

Some of the exciting technological breakthroughs can be pictured by the Throughput Model in capturing the first, second, third, and fourth dimensions (Fig. **10.1**). For example,

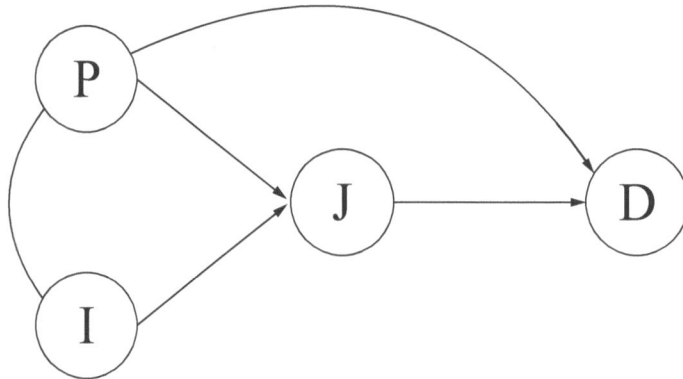

**Fig. (10.1).** Throughput modelling diagram. Source: Rodgers [7, 8].

*Where P= perception, I= information, J= judgment, and D= decision choice.*

DeepMind teams, a subsidiary of Google, work on leading-edge computer science, neuroscience, ethics, and public policy to responsibly pioneer AI systems. This research is very instrumental in clarifying ethical considerations and its importance between human and AI tools interaction (Rodgers and Gago [3 - 6]. Research scientists and engineers work together throughout DeepMind and with partners to produce systems that can advance all parts of society.

The Throughput Model's six dominant algorithmic pathways are motivated by different branches of learning such as psychology, behavioral economics, human-centered design, and ethics (Rodgers [7 - 10]. The Throughput Model postulates diverse stages as well as algorithmic pathways that depict the patterns in data use.

1. **The Expedient Algorithmic Pathway P→D**
2. **The Ruling Guide Algorithmic Pathway P→J→D**
3. **The Analytical Algorithmic Pathway I→J→D**
4. **The Revisionist Algorithmic Pathway I→P→D**
5. **The Value Driven Algorithmic Pathway P→I→J→D**
6. **The Global Perspective Algorithmic Pathway I→P→J→D**

Research implies that the dimensions are states of consciousness, and the higher dimensions are closest to the source energy and others say that they are different densities [11]. AI neural networks attempts to mimic the human brain to provide faster, more efficient, and more effective problem solving in arriving at better decision choices (see Fig. **10.2**).

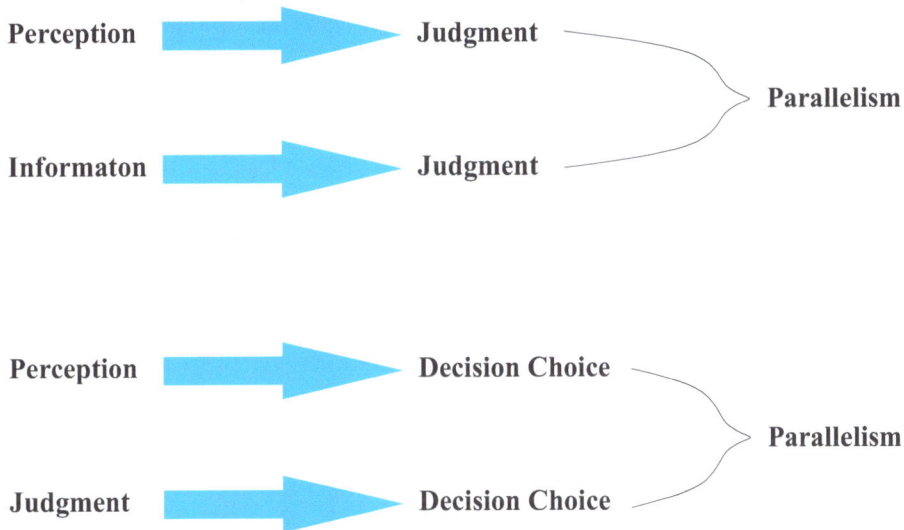

**Fig. (10.2).** Fifth dimension showing parallelism in the throughput model. Source: author.

The first dimension is a single point. For example, the constructs of perception, information, judgment, or decision choice. The second dimension contains two axis, x & y. For example, the two axes in the Throughput Model represents the following:

1. P→J

2. P→D

3. I→J

4. J→D

The second dimension has height and width, but not depth. However, the third dimension, represents all three, that is height, width, and depth. The third dimension has three axes: x, y, and z, or height, width, and depth. Out of these come emergent properties like density and volume. Volume refers to the measurement of the amount of three-dimensional space occupied by an object. Unlike mass, volume changes according to the external conditions. Density refers to the mass contained in a substance for a given volume. It explains the relationship between mass and volume.

The relationship of P←—→I depict the third-dimension properties of density and volume. Previous research has confirmed that the comparative volume of visible space can indicate the comparative perceived density and volume [12]. That is, research has suggested that three-dimensional (3D) structure-from-motion (SFM) perception in humans involves several motion-sensitive occipital and parietal brain areas. Moreover, research on human density has indicated that how individuals perceive a high-density situation strongly guides their behavior, and that density itself rarely has a direct unmediated effect on human behavior [27]. Humans, and all matter, are three dimensional; however, we exist within the fourth dimension.

The 4th dimension comprises "time," and what that implies is uncertainty. Our perspective of time is relative, and that "time" is more likely nonlinear. Further, "time" is conceivably transpiring all at once, and we, as three-dimension beings can only perceive a single slice of the 4th dimension, the present. If that is the case, then the 4th dimension would be a static collection of all possible probabilistic outcomes from the event that was the birth of our universe.

The Throughput Model relationship of P←—→I represent the 4th dimension encapsulating "time." In the P←—→I relationship, individuals do not only perceive events ("I") only, but also their temporal relations. For example, just as it is natural to depict that people perceive spatial distances and other relations between objects (*e.g.*, I see the butterfly as floating above the surface of the water), it appears natural to discuss perceiving one event following another (*e.g.*, the thunderclap as following the flash of lightning).

The study of time perception is an area within psychology, cognitive linguistics and neuroscience that denotes the subjective experience, or sense, of time, which is measured by a person's perception ("P") of the duration of the indefinite and unfolding of events (captured by "I").

When we perceive B as coming after A, we have, surely, ceased to perceive A. In which case, A is merely an item in our memory. Now if we wanted to construe 'perceive' narrowly, excluding any element of memory, then we would have to say that we do not, after all, perceive B as following A.

Pöppel [13] argued that 'elementary time experiences,' or fundamental aspects of our experience of time represent the following: (1) duration, (2) non-simultaneity, (3) order, (4) past and present, and (5) change, including the passage of time. Experience of non-simultaneity is not the same as experience of time order. That is, when two events occur very close together in time, we can be aware that they occur at different times without being able to say which one came first [14]. Further, the perception of order is itself understandable in terms of our experience of the distinction between past and present. Finally, the links between the "perception of time order" and the "perception of motion" makes sense if the latter simply involves perception of the order of the different spatial positions of an object.

Einstein' special theory of relativity postulates that the laws of physics are consistent for non-accelerating observers, no matter where in space they are, as absolute frames of reference do not exist [15]. First, Einstein's theory stated that an entity's velocity, or its momentum, is only measurable in relation to something else. Second, the speed of light is a constant in a vacuum, regardless of the individual measuring it and the speed at which the person travels. Third, nothing can travel faster than light in contrast to Newton's gravitational laws. Fourth, Einstein introduced the fourth dimension described as space-time. He expressed his theory utilizing the equation $E=mc^2$.

Advancing from the 4th dimension, the 5th dimension is depicted as a vastness and complexity of time that could be perceived as the 2nd dimension is perceived in the 3rd. Brownian motion is a good analogy. The only way we are aware of this dimension for now is in quantum measurements which perceive the individual fluctuations that are always occurring in that dimension. These are not averaging but measurements of randomness.

The 5th dimension is in statistical equilibrium (*i.e.*, entropy is constant) with a "temperature" such that it clarifies quantum uncertainty (this is a temperature of Planck's reduced constant). Planck's constant is the amount of energy enclosed in any single cycle of an electromagnetic wave, irrespective of the wavelength. The Planck's constant is an essential physical constant denoted "h" and is of fundamental significance in quantum mechanics. A photon's energy is equal to its frequency multiplied by the Planck constant [16]. This implies that any single electromagnetic wave, no matter how long or short contains 6.63X10-34 Joules of energy at a minimum [17].

The quantum qubits cannot be disturbed whatsoever during the processing. If they are unintentionally collided into by nearby particles they will "collapse" from representing all points to just one point and thus ruin the parallelism. Second, the algorithm must be very ingenious. Near the end, the qubits simultaneously embodied all the low points, when there is a measurement of the qubits, there is a probability of getting a low point that is not the lowest point. The Throughput Model's parallel pathways represent a design for quantum computers to handle complex problems [18, 19] (Fig. **10.2**).

As quantum computers and the quantum information science field mature, more algorithms and strategies will emerge that leverage quantum parallelism to solve imperative problems faster than any supercomputer ever could.

The idea of construction a computer that utilizes light rather than electricity goes back more than half a century. "Optical computing" has long promised faster functioning while using much less energy than standard electronic computers. Enormous breakthroughs are developing in creating a way for all objects to communicate whereby, telephones may communicate to your refrigerator that may communicate to the light bulb. Soon, the light bulb may itself become a computer, projecting information instead of light. That is, an underlying silicon chip devises the operation of the photonic part and supports temporary memory storage [20].

Moreover, a conventional computer banks on electronic circuits that change one another on and off in a manner prudently designed to match the multiplication of two numbers. On the other hand, optical computing shadows a similar notion; however, in its place of streams of electrons, the calculations are accomplished by beams of photons that cooperate with one another and with directing mechanisms such as lenses and bean splitters. Contrasting to electrons, which must flow through changes of circuitry against a wave of resistance, photons have no mass, travel at light-speed and obtain no extra power once produced.

A foremost novel change is possible with the implementation of quantum computers. Instead of binary bits, which are the classic elementary unit of information, quantum computing exercises qubits (quantum bits), attained by the superposition of binary states. This would permit them to process a much greater amount of information thousands of times quicker than classical computers.

Researchers such as Brodnik, *et al.* [21] proposed that light-based computing would be especially helpful to enhancing deep learning, a technique fundamental to many of the contemporary enhancements in AI. Deep learning necessitates a massive amount of computation. That is, it requires supplying substantial data sets into sizeable networks of simulated artificial "neurons" constructed roughly on the neural structure of the human brain. Each artificial neuron takes in an array of numbers, achieves a simple calculation on those inputs and guides the result to the next layer of neurons. By adjusting the calculation each neuron accomplishes, an artificial neural network can learn to perform tasks as varied as recognizing dogs or driving an automobile.

Other developments in computing are driving the transformation of entire systems of production, management, and governance. Advancing technologies include the following:

1. blockchains,
2. quantum computing,
3. 5G,
4. Internet of Things (IoT),
5. augmented, virtuality, and extended reality,
6. cyber security,
7. DARQ,
8. As-a-Service (aaS),
9. Internet of Behavior (IoB),
10. Human enhancement (HE), and
11. automation (*i.e.*, robotics) appear to be way forward.

## *1. Blockchain*

Blockchain is also denoted to as Distributed Ledger Technology (DLT). Blockchain is a distributed database of records of all transactions or digital events that have been apportioned among participating entities. Every user authenticating that the database is precise and thwarting unauthorized transactions from being fulfilled. For valuable and sensitive data to protect, blockchain may be the essential to ensure its integrity.

## *2. Quantum Computing*

Q.C is a form of computer science that benefits from quantum phenomena such as superposition and quantum entanglement. Quantum computing is also involved in preventing the spread of Coronavirus and developing potential vaccines. It can easily query, monitor, analyze and act on data regardless of the source.

Both the classical computers and quantum computers solves the problem for us. The only difference is, how they manipulate the data. In classical computing, computer chips use bits, that can be off or on, corresponding to the states 0 and 1. In quantum computing these terms are electrons, 0 and 1 simply correspond to states like the lower and upper energy levels.

Superposition is a "complex linear combination" that represents a real number plus an imaginary number. Therefore, "linear combination" implies adding together different multiples of states. Accordingly, a qubit is a bit that has a complex number called an amplitude attached to the possibility that it is 0, and a different amplitude ascribed to the possibility that it is 1. These amplitudes are closely related to probabilities, in that the further some outcome's amplitude is from zero, the larger the probability of realizing that outcome. In other words, the probability equals the distance squared (Fig. **10.3**).

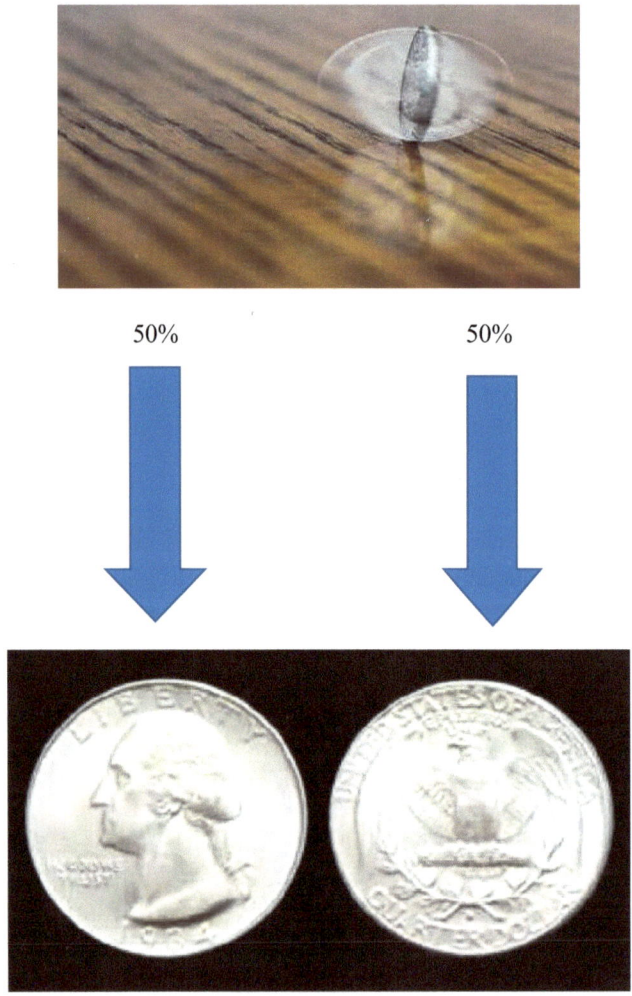

50%          50%

**Fig. (10.3).**  Is a spinning coin heads, tails or both. Source: Partially adopted by web sources and author.

Today's computers use billions upon billions of 0's and 1's called bits to operate. Superposition is comparable to a spinning coin. While a coin is spinning, is it heads (0) or tails (1)? Over a period of trials, the coin will give heads (0) 50% of the time and tails (1) the other 50%. Given that the spinning coin can give a head (0) and tails (1) result, the spinning coin is, theoretically speaking, both heads and tails at the same time! Correspondingly, a qubit in superposition is both 0 and 1; however, when measured, the qubit will read either 0 or 1.

Quantum qubits, like coins, once "measured," become just one or the other (0 or 1, analogous to "heads" or "tails") until they are "spun" again.

Therefore, quantum computers use of qubits can characterize all possible points simultaneously. The quantum computer processes these qubits whereby all the points go downwards simultaneously, and consequently it finds all the low points in one computation!

For high-frequency trading and fraud detection, quantum computers are now thousands of times faster than regular computers. As a result, tech companies are going large in a microscopic way, dispensing millions of dollars into a novel form of computing, which is quantum computing. Quantum computers will revolutionize drug research, material discovery, and artificial intelligence by solving complex problems in a new way. Organizations such as AWS, Google, Microsoft, and many more are providing innovations in the field of quantum computing.

Further, one of the advantages is called quantum parallelism since the quantum computer elucidates for each point in parallel (*i.e.*, at the same time) as every other point. Fundamentally, quantum computing permits the evaluation many potential answers simultaneously, which is something parallel computers also perform. Conversely, parallel computers demand a tremendous quantity of hardware proportional to the number of things being simultaneously evaluated (N), while the number of qbits required by a quantum computer is only proportional to $\log(N)$.

Thus, what are these qubits, and why do they let a quantum computer solve this problem in parallel instead of one point at a time? The fifth dimension represents a dimension unseen by people whereby the forces of gravity and electromagnetism unite to create a simple but graceful theory of the fundamental forces. Today, scientists employ 10 dimensions and string theory to explain where gravity and light from the electromagnetic spectrum meet [22] (Figs. **10.4** and **10.5**).

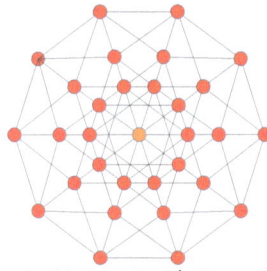

**Fig. (10.4).** Quantum computing embedded in the 5$^{th}$ dimension. A 2D orthogonal projection of a 5-cube. Source: Adopted from web sources.

**Fig. (10.5).** What is the 5th dimension? Source: Adopted from web sources.

## 3. 5G Technology

5G provides a novel type of network that is intended to connect practically everyone and everything jointly, which includes machines, objects, and devices. 5G is planned to offer ultra-low latency, more reliability, network capacity, and a comfortable experience to users (Fig. **10.6**).

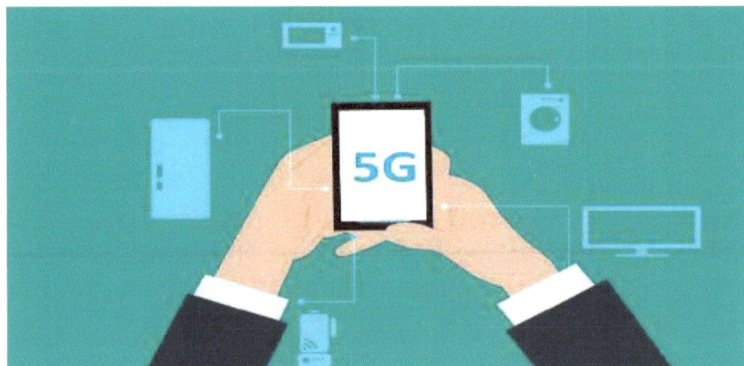

**Fig. (10.6).** 5G. Source: Adopted from web sources.

5G speeds up the services on the cloud while AI scrutinizes and learns from the same data faster. Previous networks such as 3G and 4G created an easier way to browse the Internet, utilize data-driven services, enhance bandwidth for streaming on online audio and video platforms. In a similar manner,

## 4. Internet of Things (IoT)

The Internet of Things (IoT) depicts a system of Internet-interrelated computing devices, mechanical and digital machines, objects, animals, or people that are provided with unique identifiers (UIDs) and the ability to transfer and share data over a wireless network without requiring human-to-human or human-t- -computer interaction. IoT mechanisms encompass sensors and mini-computer processors that act on the data collected by the sensors *via* machine learning or deep learning software.

Six leading types of IoT wireless technology include the following:

1. Low Power Wide Area Networks (LPWANs),

2. Cellular (3G/4G/5G),

3. Zigbee and other Mesh Protocols,

4. Bluetooth and Bluetooth Low Energy (BLE),

5. Wi-Fi, and

6. Radio-Frequency Identification (RFID).

Zigbee is a wireless technology developed as an open global standard to address the unique needs of low-cost, low-power wireless IoT networks. A mesh network is a cluster of tools that act as a single Wi-Fi network. Hence, there are multiple sources of Wi-Fi around a person's home, instead of just a single router. If they are within range, they can communicate with one another wirelessly without the need for a router or switch. Zigbee requires a low bandwidth but greater than Bluetooth's bandwidth most of time. The radio signal range of ZigBee is ten to hundred meters.

RFID is a technique of data collection that comprises automatically identifying objects through low-power radio waves. Data is sent and received with a system consisting of RFID tags, an antenna, an RFID reader, and a transceiver.

IoT is growing into the intelligence of things as more and more devices become AI-enabled. IoT enabled devices can have applications like clinical decision-making, thermal image recognition, surgical assistance, smart clinics, and telemedicine centers. AI technologies such as speech recognition and computer vision can assist in extracting insight from data that is implemented to necessitate human review. AI applications for IoT enable organizations to circumvent unplanned downtime, increase operating efficiency, spawn new products and services, and enhance risk management.

Further, AI is undertaken to perform smart tasks such as language translation, voice recognition, decision making, *etc*. without human intervention. Moreover, AI can immensely assist to accumulate the vastness of data that is processed by the IoT gadgets. In other words, AI can evaluate the data and make sense of it (Fig. **10.7**).

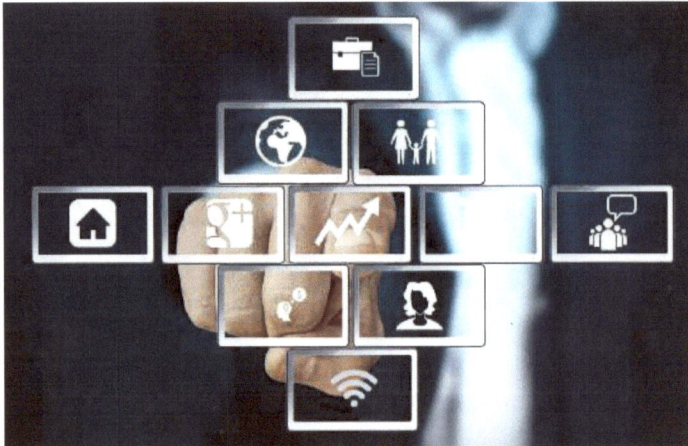

**Fig. (10.7).** Internet of Things (IoT). Source: Adopted from web sources.

The infusion of IoT is assisting individuals to perform a variety of jobs with just a click. Technologies are helping such as smartphones and advancements in Internet connectivity around the world, which is connecting more and more people to the Internet and to everything and everyone around us. Organizations like Huawei, Cisco are currently working on making all new IoT applications.

### 5. Enhancing augmented reality (AR), virtual reality (VR), and mixed reality (MR)

5G is empowering services that rely on advanced technologies like augmented reality (AR) and virtual reality (VR). AR implements a real-world venue while VR is completely virtual.

Augmented reality (AR) is an interactive experience of a real-world environment whereby the objects that inhabit in the real world are enhanced by computer-generated perceptual information, every so often across multiple sensory modalities, comprising visual, auditory, haptic, somatosensory, and olfactory. AR can be delineated as a system that integrates three basic features. First, a combination of real and virtual worlds, second, real-time interaction, and third, precise 3D registration of virtual and real objects. The superimposed sensory information can be fruitful (*i.e.*, complement to the natural environment), or harmful (*i.e.*, concealing of the natural environment). This experience is flawlessly intertwined with the physical world such that it is perceived as an immersive element of the real environment. In this manner, augmented reality modifies a person continuing perception of a real-world environment, while virtual reality entirely replaces the user's real-world environment with a simulated one. Augmented reality is related to two basically synonymous terms: extended reality and computer-mediated reality.

Further, VR involves a headset device; however, AR can be retrieved with a smartphone. Therefore, AR enriches both the virtual and real world while VR only enhances a fictional reality. Science and technology are advancing incalculably from computers being capable of interacting on their own. For example, the merger of AR with AI provides the Instagram user app to deliver filters, while Facebook users benefit from enhanced facial recognition when it comes to tagging photographs.

Moreover, the military implements AR technology that provides its soldiers with an improved awareness of the battlefield around them utilizing technology, which is fashioned by mobile game developers (https://steantycip.com/blogs/top-10--r-ar-trends/).

Giant sporting organizations and events are reaching out to a broader audience, as the technology permits sports fans to be at the game, even though they are physically on the other side of the globe. In addition, while stadiums and events have a specific capacity, enhanced VR technology provides sporting events to be broadcast across the globe, with fans able to become closer to the action than they ever could in real life.

Retail organizations are beginning to apply AR and VR to afford novel consumer experiences in a market, which is presently overshadowed by online sales. To keep customers using retail outlets and shops, AR and VR can provide unique experiences, such as allowing customers to be influenced by music and try on clothes without attempting them on physically [23].

AR and VR technologies have been around for years and originate from concepts that date back centuries. Nevertheless, it is only in contemporary times that the technology has achieved a level whereby it is capable to become prevalent globally. 5G is expected to be used for traffic management, smart grid control. Finally, major telecommunication organizations are working on producing 5G applications.

*Extended reality* or mixed reality (XR) is novel and refers to all real-and-virtual combined environments and human-machine interactions generated by computer technology and wearables. For the future, one of the significant advancements in the XR domain is the CAVE (Cave Automatic Virtual Environment). A VR CAVE is a small room or cubicle whereby at least three or more walls appear as large display monitors (Cruz-Neira, Sandin, DeFanti, Kenyon, and Hart, 1992). People using the CAVE can see objects seemingly floating in the air, and can walk around them, getting a proper view of what they would look like in reality. Users can also move around in the CAVE system without being tethered to a computer, wearing a pair of funky VR Goggle that are like 3D glasses. Finally, unlike VR, Holograms are those which creates some three-dimensional objects in our "own reality" (Fig. **10.8**). Microsoft HoloLens is a union of AR and VR technologies. That is, the HoloLens can create realistic three-dimensional images and place those images in the world around a person [24]. Microsoft, AT&T, and Nexus are some of the major companies working towards AR and VR.

**Fig. (10.8).** Augmented Reality (AR), Virtual Reality (VR) and Extended Reality (ER). Source: Adopted from web sources.

Extended reality generates jointly real world and digital elements. In mixed reality, a person intermingles with and employ both physical and virtual items and environments, exploiting next generation sensing and imaging technologies. Mixed Reality permits a person to view and engage oneself in the world around her or him even as interacting with a virtual environment utilizing her or his own hands. This is also performed without ever removing the headset. It imparts the capability to have one foot (or hand) in the real world, and the other in an imaginary place, breaking down fundamental concepts between real and imaginary, proffering an encounter that can change the way people work today.

**Employing Virtual Reality Technologies**

In sum, the benefits for Virtual Reality, Augmented Reality, and Extended Reality are expanding in the arenas of gaming, movies, and medicine in the following manner.

a. **Healthcare**—For training, such as for surgical simulations,
b. **Film and TV**—For movies and shows to produce distinctive experiences,
c. **Virtual travel**—For virtual trips to an art museum or another planet, which can occur from home,
d. **Professional sports**—For training programs to assist professional and amateur athletes, and
e. **Gaming**—For over 1,000 games at present accessible, from first-person shooters to strategy games to role-playing adventures.

For example, several organizations provide practice with VR training software converts to real-world performance, with outcomes that can be measured through distinctive data and insights.

VR is an astonishing experience also termed computer simulation reality. It is similar to viewing something in front of your eyes corresponding the real world; however, it is not there. Undoubtedly, VR is anticipated to play a gigantic role in the province of healthcare by delivering training simulations to support medical professionals.

## 6. Cyber Security

Represents the prevention of damage to, protection of, and renovation of computers, electronic communications systems, electronic communications services, wire communication, and electronic communication, comprising of information contained within, to safeguard its availability, integrity, authentication, confidentiality, and nonrepudiation. Cybersecurity also denotes to the measures taken to maintain electronic information private and safe from damage or theft. It is also employed to assure that electronic devices and data are not misappropriated. Cybersecurity pertains to both software and hardware, as well as information on the Internet, and can be exercised to safeguard everything from personal information to complex organizational systems (Fig. **10.9**).

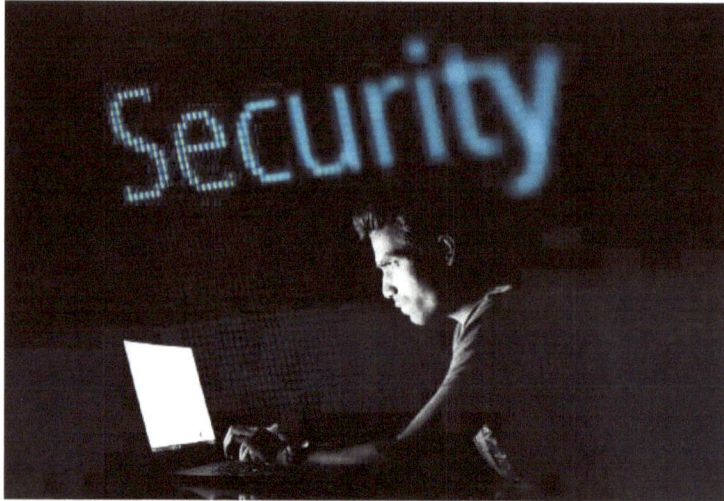

**Fig. (10.9).** Cyber security. Source: Adopted from web sources.

The essential three elements of cybersecurity commence with a strong cybersecurity program that embrace:

1. Assessing an organization's current cybersecurity program and its prioritization,

2. Remedying endpoints at scale, taking them into compliance with security best practices, and

3. Executing cybersecurity policies and monitoring them to stay in compliance.

### 7. DARQ Technology

DARQ is fundamentally an abbreviation for **D**istributed Ledger technology (D). **A**rtificial Intelligence (AI), Extended **R**eality (R), and **Q**uantum Computing (Q). In the post-digital era, DARQ becomes the new SMAC (**S**ocial, **M**obile, **A**nalytics, **C**loud). It is a set of the most advanced and emerging technologies that are bound to conquer the technical industry in the future (Fig. **10.10**). Individually these technologies are influencing the transformation across industries today. DARQ is now primarily geared towards the healthcare industry to reduce the cost of care, improve labor productivity, as well as contribute to enhance experiences for consumers.

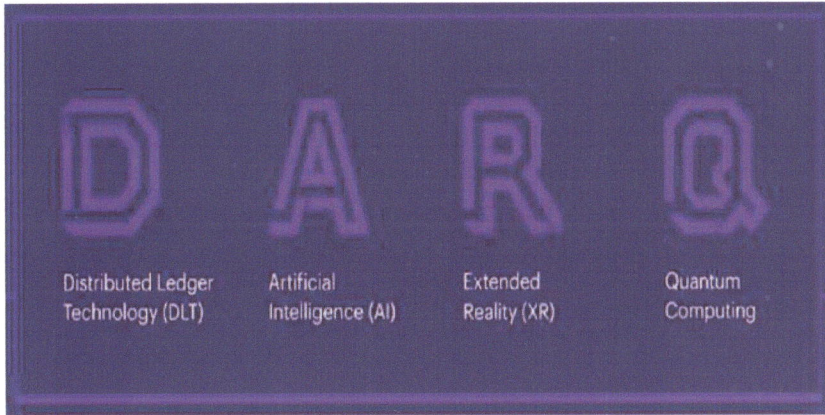

**Fig. (10.10).** DARQ. Source: Adopted from web sources.

Some of the related technology to DARQ includes:

a. AI related components of machine learning, deep learning, NLP
b. 5G and enhanced connectivity,
c. Edge computing,
d. Internet of behaviors (IoB),
e. Quantum computing,
f. Blockchain,
g. Cybersecurity, and
h. Human augmentation.

## 8. As-a-Service

Aas is an acronym for as-a-service. Aas can mean just about anything delivered by subscription or even just a plain old, outsourced service, whether the cloud is involved or not. As a Service, or XaaS (Anything as a Service) offerings furnish endpoints for customers to interface with which are typically API driven. Nonetheless, Aas technology can normally be controlled *via* a web console in a user's web browser. Some Aas models are an industry classification, and some are proprietary to a single company.

## 9. IoB

Internet of Behavior (IoB) depicts a process whereby user-controlled data is analyzed through a cognitive psychology perspective. From the results of a cognitive psychology analysis, it informs novel ways to constructing a user experience, search experience optimization, as well as offer products and services to individuals and organizations.

IoB is utilized to link a person digitally to their actions. This data mining associates data analytics and behavioral science. Devices related to location, facial recognition, iris recognition, and other biometrics that can essentially act as guides to mapping customer behavior (Fig. **10.11**).

**Fig. (10.11).** Internet of Behavior (IoB). Source: Adopted from web sources.

Therefore, the purpose of the IoB is to capture, analyze, comprehend, and respond to all kinds of human behaviors in a way that permits tracking and interpreting those behaviors of individuals implementing emerging technological innovations and developments in machine learning and deep learning algorithms. Individuals' behaviors are scrutinized, and incentives or disincentives are directed to influence them to perform towards a desired set of operational parameters. What is relevant about IoB is that it is not only descriptive (analyzing behavior), but also proactive (detecting which psychological variables to influence to bring about a certain outcome) [9, 25, 26].

The IoB influences consumer choice, but it also redesigns the value chain. While some users are wary of providing their data, many others are happy to do so if it adds value – data-driven value. For companies, this implies being able to change their image, market products more effectively to their customers or improve the customer experience of a product or service. Hypothetically, information can be collected on all facets of a user's life, with the goal of improving efficiency and quality.

IoB working through big data, can accessed information from multiple points of contact. This makes it possible to explore this technology platform from start to finish, to know where the customer's interest in a product begins, their journey to purchase and the procedure exploited to make the purchase. Further, this endows the capability to produce more touch points to positively participate with the consumer. This personalization is instrumental to the adeptness of a service. The more adept a service is, the more the user will remain to interact and even modify their behavior as a result.

The benefits of IoB are:

a. Analyze customer purchasing habits across all platforms.
b. Study heretofore unreachable data on how users interrelate with devices and products.
c. Acquire more particularized information concerning where a customer is in the purchasing process.
d. Provide real-time point of sale notifications and targeting.
e. Settle problems promptly to close sales and keep customers' content.

Nevertheless, may be challenged with the adversity of how data is collected, stored, and utilized. This portrays considerable legal and security risks to privacy rights, which also fluctuate between jurisdictions globally.

Moreover, behavioral data can permit cybercriminals to have a gateway to sensitive data that uncovers customer patterns, collect, and sell property access codes, delivery routes and even banking codes. These cybercriminals may take phishing to another level by engendering more advanced scams, personalized to the habits of individual users, and thereby amplifying the probability that users will be scammed.

Through Big Data, information can be accessed from multiple points of contact. This makes it possible to explore the CX from start to finish, to know where the customer's interest in a product begins, their journey to purchase and the methodology used to make the purchase. This provides the ability to create more touch points to positively engage with the consumer. This personalization is key to the efficiency of a service. The more efficient a service is, the more the user will continue to interact and even alter their behavior as a result.

The specific benefits of IoB are:

• Analyze customer buying habits across all platforms.
• Examined previously unattainable data on how users interrelate with devices and products.

- Acquire more particularized information about where a customer is in the buying process.
- Provide real-time POS notifications and targeting.
- Resolve problems quickly to close sales and keep customers satisfied.

The problem that can occur with this technology is not of a technical nature. The IoB is confronted with the adversity of how data is collected, stored, and used. Its level of access is difficult to control and therefore all companies need to be aware of the liability of IoB use. Google, Facebook or Amazon continue to acquire software that potentially brings the user from a single app to their entire online ecosystem, without their permission. This presents significant legal and security risks to privacy rights, which also vary between jurisdictions around the world.

Behavioral data can allow cybercriminals to access sensitive data that reveals customer patterns, collect, and sell property access codes, delivery routes and even banking codes. These cybercriminals could take phishing to another level by generating more advanced scams, tailored to the habits of individual users, and thus maximizing the likelihood that users will be scammed. It is therefore important to have a secure platform, storage, and execution of data with the use of tools such as Confidential Computing, E2E encryption or SDP tools.

## 10. Human Enhancement (HE)

Human enhancement (HE) can be described as the natural, artificial, or technological alteration of the human body to enhance physical or mental capabilities (Fig. **10.12**). The field of human augmentation spotlights on crafting cognitive and physical enhancements as an integral component of the human body. An example is utilizing active control systems to construct limb prosthetics with characteristics that can outstrip the peak natural human performance.

**Fig. (10.12).** Human enhancement. Source: Adopted from web sources.

Service cloud services are expected to offer more services that allow the technology like AI and robotics accessible to every organization. Resources have been plowed in this area by companies such as Google, Microsoft, Amazon as well as several startups and innovators. Aas affords users the chance to work on the core product without functioning and managing the servers. Further, Aas growth in part is due to its speed ease of control and security options.

## 11. Automation and Robotics

Automation is the process of utilizing physical machines, computer software, and other technologies to accomplish chores that are typically performed by people. Robotics is the process of designing, inventing, and implementing robots to perform a particular task (Fig. **10.13**).

**Fig. (10.13).** Automation and robotics. Source: Adopted from web sources.

With an increasing number of potential cases, initiatives towards self-driving vehicles is a priority for civic authorities and many other organizations across the globe. This make certain that the cost of human labor is lessened and manages customer demand. Eventually, there will also be an augment in the inclusion of robots in the care and assisted living sectors.

Moreover, robotic process automation (RPA) is a software technology that makes it easy to build, deploy, and manage software robots that emulate individuals' actions interacting with digital systems and software. Like people, software robots can do things like understand what is on a screen, complete the right keystrokes, navigate systems, identify, and extract data, and perform a wide range of defined actions. Software robots' advantage is that it can perform faster and more consistently than people, without the need to get up and str*etc*h or take a coffee break.

Organizations are beginning to turn their attention to RPA to streamline operations and reduce costs. With RPA, organizations can automate mundane rules-based business processes, permitting users to devote more time to serving customers or other higher-value work. Other organizations view RPA to intelligent automation through machine learning, deep learning, and other AI tools, which can be trained to make analysis regarding future outputs.

RPA is an application of technology, administered by reason and structured inputs, directed at automating business processes. Exercising RPA tools, an organization can conFig. software, or a "robot," to capture and interpret applications for processing a transaction, manipulating data, generating responses, and communicating with other digital systems. RPA situations str*etc*h from something as simple as producing an automatic response to an email to implementing thousands of bots, each programmed to automate functions. Bots are chatbots that simulate human conversation by responding to certain phrases with programmed responses

In addition, robotic devices are also expected to deliver companionship to elderly people. Drones are also expected to be integrated for the delivery of medicine, groceries, and other indispensable goods. Some of the companies in the field of automation are Siemens, Honeywell, and Mitsubishi.

## CONCLUSION

Machine learning and deep learning, a sub-discipline of AI, has guided the function of Internet searches, e-commerce sites, goods and services recommender systems, image and speech recognition, sensor technologies, robotic devices, and cognitive decision support systems. AI leverages computers and machines to mirror the problem-solving and decision-making competences of the human mind. Technologies that are affected by AI apparatus includes, but is not limited to the following:

1. blockchains,
2. quantum computing,
3. 5G,
4. Internet of Things (IoT),
5. augmented, virtuality, and extended reality,

6. cyber security,
7. DARQ,
8. As-a-Service (aaS),
9. Internet of Behavior (IoB),
10. Human enhancement (HE), and
11. automation (*i.e.*, robotics).

AI is a field that is expected to see the most amount of growth in the coming years. AI can help interpret and understand the enormous amount of content produced. Machine learning and deep learning algorithms will continually become better informed and perform much more sophisticated operations. AI is expected to be used to analyze interactions to determine underlying connections and insights to help predict demand for services like hospitals and enable authorities to make better decisions about resource utilization (Fig. **10.14**).

**Fig. (10.14).** AI and related apparatuses. Source: Adopted from web sources.

Furthermore, when blockchain, is combined with AI, the best of both worlds can be leveraged for a scale of resources. AI can provide for the isolation of processing without the downside of aggregate knowledge sharing. That is, AI can enable the user to process information independently, among varying computing apparatuses or devices. Therefore, an individual or organization can accomplish different results and then analyze the knowledge, creating new solutions to a problem.

Moreover, AI facilitates many projects and administrations that assist individuals and organizations with performing ordinary things. For example, associating with companions, utilizing an email program, or utilizing a ride-share administration are areas that AI is beginning to dominate. Machine learning and deep learning have a titanic future in several industries such as the animation industry. Animators are intense about creativity but now it appears like that their art is on the edge of an extreme alteration.

AI in education makes a laudable contribution to individuals. That is, a multifaceted problem is solved by dividing the problem into subcomponents and unearthing the solution to each subcomponent. The subcomponents may be a system or individual attempting to locate a solution to the problem. The proposed theory exhibits that cognitive science in education cultivated a tutor by programming a computer and that tutor would observe the students problem-solving skills. Now the tutor will direct students and advises them in each step of their solution by averting them before they are ensnared into a corner. This method provides students learn a lesson about the problem and be more cognitive in the future.

AI technology in spell corrector and spell checker is improving every year. This AI tool acts as a proofreader by checking spellings and grammatical mistakes and provides all the possible suggestion to enhance the document. The AI tools in the automation industry is widely implemented in the manufacturing process. It saves the labor cost, diminishes errors and offers a maximum output in minimum time since the robot does not need a lunchtime or break hour. On the other hand, an individual worker can take hour to complete a pain taking task whereby the robot does in a fraction of minutes.

Needlessly to say, AI and related technologies such as robotics, drones and driverless vehicles may supplant many jobs previously performed by individuals; however, it will also generate numerous additional jobs as productivity and real incomes rise and new and better products are developed for implementation.

AI will be used by organizations to detect the changing patterns of customer behavior and for detecting the various ways. Further, AI can assist the global community in education, healthcare, manufacturing, and many other areas. Global spending will continue supporting cognitive and AI systems in the future.

# REFERENCES

[1]  J. Manyika, and J. Bughin, "The Promise and Challenge of the age of artificial intelligence", *The McKinsey Global Institute,* 2018. https://www.mckinsey.com/featured-insights/artificia--intelligence/thepromise-and-challenge-of-the-age-of-artificial-intelligence

[2]  D.M. West, and J.R. Allen, *How Artificial Intelligence is Transforming the World.* Brookings: Washington, DC, 2018. https://www.brookings.edu/research/how-artificial-intelligence-is-transforming-the-world/

[3]  W. Rodgers, and S. Gago, "Cultural and ethical effects on managerial decisions: Examined in a Throughput Model", *J. Bus. Ethics,* vol. 31, pp. 355-367, 2001.
[http://dx.doi.org/10.1023/A:1010777917540]

[4]  W. Rodgers, and S. Gago, "A model capturing ethics and executive compensation", *J. Bus. Ethics,* vol. 48, pp. 189-202, 2003.
[http://dx.doi.org/10.1023/B:BUSI.0000004589.34756.8a]

[5]  W. Rodgers, and S. Gago, "Stakeholder influence on corporate strategies over time", *J. Bus. Ethics,* vol. 52, pp. 349-363, 2004.
[http://dx.doi.org/10.1007/s10551-004-1534-5]

[6]  W. Rodgers, and S. Gago, "Biblical Scriptures Underlying Six Ethical Models Influencing Organizational Practices", *J. Bus. Ethics,* vol. 64, pp. 125-136, 2006.
[http://dx.doi.org/10.1007/s10551-005-0657-7]

[7]  W. Rodgers, *Throughput Modeling: Financial Information Used by Decision Makers.* JAI Press: Greenwich, CT, 1997.

[8]  W. Rodgers, *Process Thinking: Six pathways to successful decision making.* iUniverse, Inc: NY, 2006.

[9]  W. Rodgers, *Ethical Beginnings: Preferences, rules, and principles influencing decision making.* iUniverse, Inc: NY, 2009.

[10]  W. Rodgers, *Trust Throughput Modeling Pathways.* Nova Publication: Hauppauge, NY, 2019.

[11]  W. Rodgers, *Artificial Intelligence in a Throughput Model: Some Major Algorithms.* Taylor and Francis publication: Florida, 2020.

[12]  A.L. Beer, T. Watanabe, R. Ni, Y. Sasaki, and G.J. Andersen, "3D surface perception from motion involves a temporal-parietal network", *Eur. J. Neurosci.,* vol. 30, no. 4, pp. 703-713, 2009.
[http://dx.doi.org/10.1111/j.1460-9568.2009.06857.x] [PMID: 19674088]

[13]  E. Pöppel, Time Perception.Handbook of Sensory Physiology

[14]  I.J. Hirsh, and C.E. Sherrick Jr, "Perceived order in different sense modalities", *J. Exp. Psychol.,* vol. 62, pp. 423-432, 1961.
[http://dx.doi.org/10.1037/h0045283] [PMID: 13907740]

[15]  A. Einstein, and P. Bergmann, "On A Generalization of Kaluza's Theory of Electricity", *Annals of Mathematics,* vol. 39, no. 3, pp. 683-701, 1938.
[http://dx.doi.org/10.2307/1968642]

[16]  J.C. Mohr, and W.D. Phillips, "Dimensionless Units in the SI", *Metrologia,* vol. 52, no. 1, pp. 40-47, 2015.
[http://dx.doi.org/10.1088/0026-1394/52/1/40]

[17]  *International Bureau of Weights and Measures* 9th edition. The International System of Units (SI): SI Brochure, 2019, p. 131.

[18]  W. Rodgers, "The effects of accounting information on individuals' perceptual processes", *J. Account. Audit. Financ.,* vol. 7, pp. 67-96, 1992.
[http://dx.doi.org/10.1177/0148558X9200700107]

[19]    W. Rodgers, and T. Housel, "The role of componential learning in accounting education", *Account. Finance,* vol. 32, pp. 73-86, 1992.
[http://dx.doi.org/10.1111/j.1467-629X.1992.tb00179.x]

[20]    J. Dunietz, "Light-Powered Computers Brighten AI's Future", *Scientific America.,* 2017. http://www.scientificamerican.com/article/light-powered-computers-brighten-ai-rsquo-s-future

[21]    G.M. Brodnik, M.W. Harrington, J.H. Dallyn, D. Bose, W. Zhang, L. Stern, P.A. Morton, R.O. Behunin, S.B. Papp, and D.J. Blumenthal, "Optically synchronized fibre links using spectrally pure chip-scale lasers", *Nature Photonics,* 2021.https://www.nature.com/articles/s41566-021-00831-w
[http://dx.doi.org/10.1038/s41566-021-00831-w]

[22]    I. Klebanov, and J. Maldacena, Solving Quantum Field Theories *via* Curved Spacetimes, *Phys. Today,* vol. 62, no. 1, pp. 28-33, 2009.
[http://dx.doi.org/10.1063/1.3074260]

[23]    W. Rodgers, F. Yeung, C. Odindo, and W. Degbey, "Artificial Intelligence-Driven Music Biometrics Influencing Customers' Retail Buying Behavior", *J. Bus. Res.,* vol. 126, pp. 401-414, 2021.
[http://dx.doi.org/10.1016/j.jbusres.2020.12.039]

[24]    K. Essmiller, T.I. Asino, A. Ibukun, F. Alvarado-Albertorio, S. Chaivisit, T. Do, and Y. Kim, "Exploring mixed reality based on self-efficacy and motivation of users", *Res. Learn. Technol.,* vol. 28, 2020.
[http://dx.doi.org/10.25304/rlt.v28.2331]

[25]    W. Rodgers, "How do loan officers make their decisions about credit risks? A study of Parallel Distributed Processing (PDP)", *J. Econ. Psychol.,* vol. 12, pp. 243-265, 1991.
[http://dx.doi.org/10.1016/0167-4870(91)90015-L]

[26]    W. Rodgers, "The influences of conflicting information on novices' and loan officers' actions", *J. Econ. Psychol.,* vol. 20, pp. 123-145, 1999.
[http://dx.doi.org/10.1016/S0167-4870(99)00002-1]

[27]    P.C. Cozby, "Effects of density, activity and personality on environmental preferences", *J. Res. Pers.,* vol. 7, pp. 45-60, 1973.
[http://dx.doi.org/10.1016/0092-6566(73)90031-7]

**CHAPTER 11**

# The Coming Era of Artificial Intelligence will Provide Prosperity and Peace

**Abstract: Abstract**

*"The coming era of Artificial Intelligence will not be the era of war, but be the era of deep compassion, non-violence, and love".*

---Amit Ray, Pioneer of Compassionate AI Movement.

*Deep-learning will transform every single industry. Healthcare and transportation will be transformed by deep-learning. I want to live in an AI-powered society. When anyone goes to see a doctor, I want AI to help that doctor provide higher quality and lower cost medical service. I want every five-year-old to have a personalised tutor. ---Andrew Ng*

The coming of computers with true humanlike reasoning remains decades in the future, but when the moment of "artificial general intelligence" arrives, the pause will be brief. Once artificial minds achieve the equivalence of the average human IQ of 100, the next step will be machines with an IQ of 500, and then 5,000. We don't have the vaguest idea what an IQ of 5,000 would mean. And in time, we will build such machines--which will be unlikely to see much difference between humans and houseplants.

---David Gelernter

*Computers already undergird our financial system, and our civil infrastructure of energy, water, and transportation. Computers are at home in our hospitals, cars, and appliances. Many of these computers, such as those running buy-sell algorithms on Wall Street, work autonomously with no human guidance. The price of all the labor-saving conveniences and diversions computers provide is dependency. We get more dependent every day. So far it's been painless. But artificial intelligence brings computers to life and turns them into something else. If it's inevitable that machines will make our decisions, then when will the machines get this power, and will they get it with our compliance?.... Some scientists argue that the takeover will be friendly and collaborative--a handover rather than a takeover. It will happen incrementally, so only troublemakers will balk, while the rest of us won't question the improvements to life that will come from having something immeasurably more intelligent decide what's best for us. Also, the superintelligent AI or AIs that ultimately gain control might be one or more augmented humans, or a human's downloaded, supercharged brain, and not cold, inhuman robots. So their authority will be easier to swallow. The handover to machines described by some scientists is virtually indistinguishable from the one you and I are taking part in right now--gradual, painless, fun.*

James Barrat

**Abstract**

All around the planet, individuals and organizations have had to suddenly re-evaluate their plans. The necessity to innovate and transform organizations to the new frontier is upon us now. AI and its related digital technologies have taken over the traditional computing methods, changing how many individuals and organizations perform their day-to-day operations. From research and manufacturing to modernizing finance and healthcare streams, leading AI has transformed the entire tapestry in economic, political, and social endeavors in a relatively short amount of time. Moreover, the Throughput Model algorithmic processes can assist in the digital transformation and adoption of AI and related digital technologies by organizations by providing essential algorithms to solve and optimize many core challenges in the world today. These algorithms can be applied directly to assist programmers when it comes to designing software systems, detecting, and overcoming software bugs, as well as when it comes to writing code. By utilizing the Throughput Model algorithmic pathways may assist the structure of the code, which can provide the AI system with useful suggestions, not only improving the overall productivity but also assist in reducing wasteful time, confusion as well as ethical dilemmas.

**Keywords:** Algorithms, Analytical algorithmic pathway, Artificial intelligence, Big data, Biometric technology, Cloud computing, Decision choice, Deep learning, Ethics, Expedient algorithmic pathway, Global perspective algorithmic pathway, Information, Internet of Things, Judgment, Machine learning, Natural language processing, Perception, Revisionist algorithmic pathway, Ruling guide algorithmic pathway, Six dominant algorithmic pathways, Throughput Model, Value driven algorithmic pathway.

## INTRODUCTION

AI is a computing concept that involves the creation of an independent non-human agent to carry out tasks. Originally conceived by Alan Turing in the 1950's, artificial intelligence now surrounds us at every turn. All industries utilize some form of artificial intelligence, whether it be through software suites in offices or physical robots in warehouses. While AI is the driving force behind recent economic and technological advancements, there are some ethical concerns worth considering. Privacy, accuracy, and equity are all problems that must be addressed using an ethical framework.

Decades of AI research have confirmed that the difficult tasks, those that require conscious attention, are easier to automate. It is the easy tasks, the things that we take for granted, that are challenging to automate. The things that individuals perform without much thought such as looking out in the world and making sense of what we view, carrying on a conversation, walking down a jam-packed sidewalk without bumping into anyone appears to be the toughest challenges for machines. While machines can outperform people on particular tasks, AI systems are a bit away from matching the more general human abilities we associate with ordinary tasks. For example, the most advanced language models still struggle with understanding basic concepts that most humans learn at a very young age without being instructed.

That is, today's AI systems can accomplish complex tasks in a variety of areas, such as mathematics, games, and photorealistic image generation. Moreover, some of the early goals of AI like housekeeper robots and self-driving cars continue to fade as we approach them. The speedy stride of development in AI and autonomy around the world drives new developments and in initiatives announced almost daily. As this body of work demonstrates, it is critical that individuals, organizations, nations and policymakers consider prioritize investing in and capitalizing on developments in AI and autonomy. That is to say, that AI is an evolving game changing technology that is been employed in various areas around the globe. Just as the wealthy Italian cities and merchants funded that country's Renaissance, AI has stimulated a renaissance of its own.

Algorithms, machine learning, deep learning, natural language processing, and big data are subsets of AI that focuses on the utilization of data and algorithms mimicking the way people learn. The machines are programmed to use an iterative approach to learn from the analyzed data, making the learning automated and continuous, to enhance explanations, predictions and prescriptions.

Algorithms are an unknown specification that enables a solution to a problem. Algorithms are able to process data, calculations, and even automated reasoning tasks. In short, an algorithm is a sequence of riles that specifies how to solve a problem. You could write a code and the code could technically be considered an algorithm. The advantage of algorithms in general are that they tell you step by step on how to solve a problem. People use algorithms in their everyday lives, for example, every time we brush our teeth, we first water the toothbrush, put tooth paste on the brush, brush our teeth, and then floss. In general, algorithms can be as simple and effective as brushing your teeth. One advantage in algorithms is that you can easily tweak the algorithm for improvement and overall create a more effective procedure.

Machine learning is a study of algorithms and statistical models that computer systems use to complete task without delegating specific instructions. Rather than telling the computer system exactly what to do the computer system relies on patterns instead. Machine learning algorithms create a mathematical model of sample data to make certain decisions without being instructed to do so. A common example of machine learning algorithms that mostly every has utilize is the application of email filtering. Another fascinating factor is that data mining plays a role with machine learning because it uses the data to make predictions that ultimately can be referred as predictive analytics and several businesses can use predictive analytics to obtain a competitive advantage.

Overall, machine learning is based on the concept that the computer system can learn by analyzing patterns. Nevertheless, machine learning can be very helpful not only for businesses to obtain a competitive advantage but also enables them to detect fraud. For example, when you go online shopping machine learning uses the data and makes recommendation based on the items you have searched or bought and websites like Amazon or eBay.

On the other hand, deep learning goes a bit further as compared to machine learning. Deep learning is designed to learn from the data it has processed and then apply it to other data advantageously. Deep learning is an algorithm that learns from a large amount of data that makes a decision based on the data acquired, similarly to the throughput model with information. Just how humans learn from experience, which may be compared to the perception (*i.e.*, "P") in the Throughput Model, a deep learning algorithm does so as well, but each time it improves the outcome. Due to the fact that deep learning requires a ton of data to learn from it helps to promote data creation which is why deep learning has evolved over the years and become more popular. Deep learning improves each outcome and enhances the decision choice each time. For example, deep learning as depicted by image identification, such as for example with a new mobile phone, as the phone unlocks itself with facial recognition it provides security and privacy so that only the owner can ultimately access the phone and prevent fraud. Deep learning distinguishes images by learning thousands or even millions of images to be able correctly identify the images it has processed, such as an animal or car it stores the memory just like with the throughput model. Another example of deep learning are driver-less cars that use sensors and analytics to recognize obstacles that allow the car to prevent accidents.

Deep learning is one of the driving forces of AI and is perhaps one of the most sensational technologies of the decade. Presently, it has made inroads in fields such as recognizing speech or detecting cancer, domains that beforehand were padlocked or hardly accessible to traditional software models.

Natural language processing is a branch of linguistics, computer science, and AI involved with the interfaces between computers and human language. Moreover, natural language processing software is how to program computers to process and analyze large amounts of language data. Further, it allows machines to analyze and interpret human language. In addition, natural language processing is at the center of tools utilize every day. These tools are from translation software, chatbots, spam filters, and search engines, to grammar correction software, voice assistants, and social media monitoring tools.

By implementing text vectorization, natural language processing tools convert text into something a machine can understand. Text vectorization is the procedure of transforming text into numerical representation.

Next, machine learning or deep learning algorithms are fed training data and expected outputs (tags) to train machines to make connections between a particular input and its corresponding output. Machines then use statistical analysis techniques to construct their own "knowledge bank" and discriminate, which aspects best embody the texts, before making predictions for unseen data (new texts).

Big data is a self-explanatory term as it refers to a large volume of data and can ultimately be compared to one of the phases of the Throughput Model, that is "information" (I). Big data is used to provide insights that could potentially lead to better decisions or even strategic business initiatives. Moreover, just like information provided in the Throughput Model, big data analysis allows for the examination of patterns and trends of an entity. Further, big data analysis like what is depicted in the Throughput Model is a tool that can assist in fraud. Overall big data is used to arrive at decision choices that are based on the perception, information, and judgment. Big data encompasses three main components, volume, velocity, and variety. Organizations collect data from various sources that consist of large amounts of data. Velocity is another factor of big data as organizations are dependent of real time data or near-real time data to use to their advantage. Finally, the third factor of big data represents "variety," as data is derived in all types of formats such as in numbers, text, video, audio, or financial transactions. Big data is important if an organization understands how to use it to their advantage. For example, an organization may be able to reduce cost, time, or optimize existing products as well as produce new products with the information that has been gathered for an insightful purpose. An important factor that big data can also be implemented for is the detecting or preventing fraudulent behavior. This concept is related to "information" ("I") in the Throughput Model, whereby entities can use fingerprinting, facial recognition, iris scans, *etc.* to place restrictions and help prevent fraud rather than just detect problems.

There are several relationships between biometrics and fraud with the Throughput Model. The relationships arise with the four inputs of the model, perception, information, judgement, and decision choice. The Throughput Model allows for the understanding, explaining (*i.e.*, descriptive modeling), and forecasting (*i.e.*, predictive, and prescriptive modeling) of decisions choice. Further, the Throughput Modeling enables individuals and organizations to examine information and cognitive processes in various stages before reaching a conclusion. The model provides analysis of multiple stages that could potentially affect the decisions. With this model individuals and organizations may be able to increase our knowledge on the learning behavior, problem solving, and decision making that they take before arriving at a decision choice. By using a combination of either of the four concepts of the Throughput Model assisted with AI based biometrics technology, fraud can easily be mitigated by the appropriate algorithmic pathway used to solve the problem.

AI based biometrics technology are utilized to mitigate and prevent fraud from occurring by inserting it into organizations' internal control systems. A biometric internal control system is basically a pattern recognition system that recognizes an individual by comparing the binary code of a distinctively specific biological or physical characteristic. For example, quite a few banks require users to authenticate a transaction by matching the consumer or users' biometrics with the information that the bank had stored. The most common type of biometric data that is used are fingerprints, iris recognition, and facial patterns. Implementation of these and other biometrics can have a huge impact on preventing fraud. An algorithm such as the ones presented in the Throughput Model can assist in the prevention of fraud by using biometric information. As part of the Throughput Model, the algorithmic pathways can utilize big data and then depending on the algorithm it could use the process of perception and/or judgment to arrive at a decision choice that can prevent fraud or detect fraud.

Biometric technology is now being used more and more such as with apps like Apple pay, which requires facial recognition or fingerprints before the authorization of a payment. Biometric data should be implemented in organization since it allows the organization to have enhanced internal control systems. Further, AI based biometrics can help resolve the problem of being able to detect and/or prevent fraud in an organization. Biometrics can help in the safeguarding of assets such as creating obstacles that only allow certain users to be able to access the organizational assets through, for example, fingerprinting or face recognition. Lastly, biometrics could also assist with private information by also having certain restrictions and biometric verification methods that would only allow certain users to access the information biometrics.

## THROUGHPUT MODELLING

The Throughput Model is a key element in implementing biometrics into an internal control system. The Throughput Model is broken down in four parts: perception, information, judgment, and decision choice (Fig. **10.1**). "Perception" is a phase of framing which is part of the screening process which is based on the presentation of an item that is subjectively tailored to a person's expectancies. The second factor of the Throughput Model is the information. Information is tied to perception because individuals construct a perception based on the information being presented to them. In other words, perception and information are interdependent (*i.e.*, P←→I). Information also affects the types of judgments and decision choice that individuals execute. Information can affect judgment by the information stored in the individual's memory.

The third factor of the model is "judgment" in this phase the information is evaluated. Judgment is based on the individual's perception and information. Judgment is a phase can be conceptual or analytical as it relates to an analysis of a person, place, or thing. Overall, perception and judgment can affect the decision choice of an individual. The last factor of the model is decision choice which is also affected by perception and judgment because in decision choice. In sum, the four concepts of the Throughput Model represent:

*Perception* involves the process individuals use to frame their problem-solving set or view of the world. Further, perception is when the main issue is acknowledged or framed, which influences latter stage processing. A person observes a situation and forms a categorization or classification regarding the issue, even though it may not always be the case. This step goes hand in hand with information that can influence judgment.

*Information* includes the set of available information to a decision maker for problem solving purposes. Generally, we hope that information is both reliable and relevant.

*Judgment* contains the process that individuals implement to analyze incoming information as well as the influences from the perception function. From these sources, rules are implemented to weigh, sort, and classify knowledge and information for problem solving or decision-making purposes. Judgment provides an analysis of the perception and information acquired in the process. In addition, the judgmental process can involve a compensatory and/or non-compensatory strategy in forming rankings, ratings, or comparisons when utilizing significant variables.

*Decision choice* represents an action taken or not taken. That is, the individual or organization exercise the responsibility to decide what action is to be taken.

The Throughput Model describes the process that people experience when performing a task. It also focuses can focus on decision-making issues [1], social corporate responsibility [2], ethical considerations [3], and trust and democratic issues [4] that individuals or organizations must firmly carry to effectively produce the appropriate decision choices when using expertise and/or information. Further, this model suggests algorithmic pathways that individuals follow. Moreover, it simulates dominate algorithms since it shows the flow of how actions can be followed (*i.e.*, opening the black box) to arrive to a final decision.

Each algorithmic pathway contains two or more of the concepts of perception, information, judgment, and decision choice. Basically, the Throughput Model can influence machine learning or deep learning apparatuses, which can be viewed as a technological improvement. It enhances AI algorithm and other automated features. There are six different algorithmic pathways that always begins with either with perception or information.

Below are the six algorithms that are extracted from the Throughput Model.

1. **The Expedient Pathway P→D**
2. **The Ruling Guide Pathway P→J→D**
3. **The Analytical Pathway I→J→D**
4. **The Revisionist Pathway I→P→D**
5. **The Value Driven Pathway P→I→J→D**
6. **The Global Perspective Pathway I→P→J→D**

In Fig. (**11.1**), the following relationships apply to the model.

(**1**) **P→D** characterizes the expedient algorithmic pathway, whereby an individual with a certain level of expertise or knowledge plans without the benefit of information.

(**2**) **P→J→D** illustrates the ruling guide algorithmic pathway that accentuates an individual's perceived understanding of rules irrespective of if the present information may be contradictory.

(**3**) **I→J→D** underlines the analytical algorithmic pathway that embraces a systematic and programmatic approach in using information.

**(4) I→P→D** mirrors the revisionist algorithmic pathway, which is abundantly dependent on changing information.

**(5) P→I→J→D** accentuates the value driven algorithmic pathway that denotes how a person's perception helps channel and choose certain kinds of information.

**(6) I→P→J→D** symbolizes the global perspective algorithmic pathway that undertakes that the available information influences a person's perception.

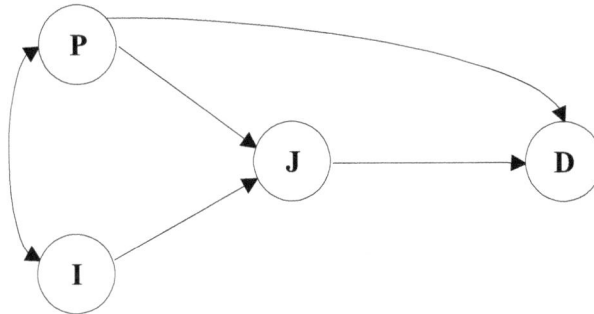

**Fig. (11.1).** Decision makers' processes diagram. Source: Rodgers [5, 6].

*where P = perception, I = information, J = judgment, and D = decision choice.*

## AI BASED BIOMETRICS TECHNOLOGY AND THE FRAUD TRIANGLE

Biometrics are the measurement and analysis of personal physical characteristics. These characteristics vary from vocal recognition to fingerprints to even the color and shape of the user's iris. Height, weight, and posture are also technically biometrics. While it may seem like science-fiction, many of these biometrics are being used in newly emerging technologies. Biometrics are typically gathered from information-technology systems through some sort of sensory apparatus as a part of the perception portion of the Throughput Model's decision-making process [7, 8].

Biometric technologies are like an individual's perceptual process in that its pattern recognition systems use either image acquisitions devices, such as scanners or cameras in the case of fingerprint or iris recognition technologies; For example, sound or movement acquisition devices collect biometric patterns or characteristics. Regarding the Throughput Model, there are six algorithmic pathways that can be implemented with biometric technology to prevent fraud [6].

Overall biometrics technology provides a higher level of assurance of security and protection that is implemented through for example providing access control, ID, or any other sort of verification problem. Security systems enable the implementation of different types of authentications such as requiring users to create either a password, pin or security questions that are usually personal to the users. There are also tangible security measures such as card keys or a token. Also, identification and verification as stated may work hand in hand. For example, identification determines who the individual is while verification confirms if the individual is who he or she claims he/she is. The identification process contains a databank that links the personal information and is how an individual may be identified. In addition, organizations could start developing and analyzing algorithms that may essentially assist management. The algorithms can be used to analyzing fraudulent activity by also relating algorithms to the Fraud Triangle. First and foremost, an algorithm assist management in solving certain types of problems by performing calculations, data processing and even automated reasoning tasks.

The Fraud Triangle is composed of three factors: opportunity, rationalization, and incentive.

Moreover, there are several physiological biometrics that may assist entities in preventing fraudulent activity both externally and internally. First, fingerprint technology can be used for the verification. More specifically, electronic fingerprint matching can used through two procedures by simply identifying and verifying the individual's information.

## ARTIFICIAL INTELLIGENCE RE-SHAPING THE WORLD

With technological tools taking over many duties and tasks in the fourth industrial revolution, AI introduces flexibility into traditional working patterns, permitting people to rethink what work-life balance should look like and transforming both the weekday routine and retirement thresholds. With more freedom and time in such a new social contract, individuals will be unshackled to follow their passions, creativity, and talents, and to allow that personal exploration inform their careers as never before.

Furthermore, painters, sculptors and photographers can implement AI technologies to compose, experiment, enumerate and refine their artwork. Novelists, journalists, and poets can utilize novel tools to take their writing in heretofore unthought-of directions. Educators, freed from the drudgery of grading and paperwork, can now release their energy to design lessons that embolden curiosity, critical thinking, and creativity. AI programs can benefit in clarifying facts and figures, whereby teachers can spend more time developing students' emotional intelligence (Fig. **11.2**).

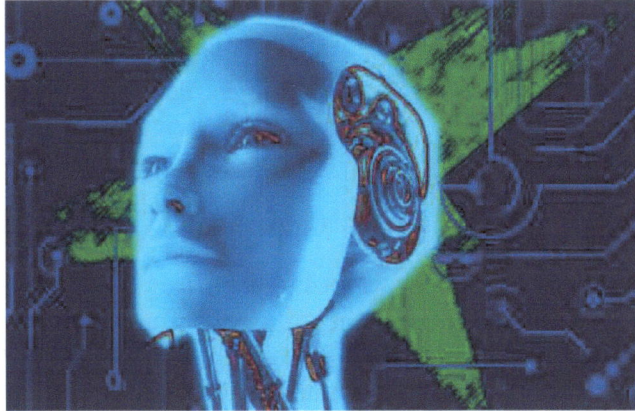

**Fig. (11.2).** AI impact on the world. Adopted from: The Difference Between Artificial Intelligence, Machine Learning, and Deep Learning | by Calum McClelland | IoT For All | Medium.

While, in the past, AI may have been thought to be a product of science fiction, in today's world the adoption of smart technology is actively changing workplaces. There are applications of AI throughout nearly every profession and industry, and human resources careers are no exception. Moreover, organizations will need to retrain a massive number of displaced workers. Governments are motivated to raise an enormous amount of money and redistribute it to fund this transition. Schools are beginning to reinvent education to produce creative, social, and multidisciplinary graduates. In the aggregate, people, places, and things are being redefined. This includes the work ethic of society, entitlements for citizens, responsibilities for corporations and the role of governments.

In all of this, the role of AI technologies is crucial. If performed properly, AI will free us to encapsulate not only our creativity and compassion for one another, but also our humanity. While individuals, organizations, and nations are adopting AI into their infrastructures, machines, and human resources processes at varying rates, it is abundantly clear to that the technology will have a lasting impact as it becomes more widely accepted. For this reason, it is important that individuals, organizations, and nations prepare themselves for these changes by understanding what the technology is and how it is applied across various functions.

On a practical level, these information systems use biometrics for security purposes. Broadly speaking there are two aspects of this security function, identification and verification. Identification is being able to determine *who* a user is, while verification is the judgement of whether or not a particular user has the right to access certain data information.

Compared to traditional password methods, which usually rely on memorized alphanumeric codes, biometrics are quicker and more sophisticated. Additionally, passwords can be easily forgotten or misremembered, while biometric information is an integral part of a person's body that is not easily altered or lost (barring medical reasons). Already iPhones have fingerprint lock-screens that exclusively open for the user based on their own unique fingerprint. Technology of this magnitude is the result of two other factors; algorithms and deep learning.

## THROUGHPUT MODELING AND ALGORITHMS

Algorithms are mathematical formulas used to aid with complex computation. Using the Throughput Model, they process and draw judgements from data provided by their environment. They accomplish everyday tasks such as sorting, searching, and analyzing massive amounts of data. Google uses algorithms in its search engine in our to make sense of the millions of search results it generates. By ranking the relevancy of hyper-linked websites, the Google search algorithm can provide websites that not only have the same title as the search query, but also contain relevant content. New inputs are on the horizon; however, with AI infused biometrics combined with a decision-making discourse such as the Throughput Model. Algorithms typically use biometric data to identify users and to grant them appropriate access. Nonetheless, no computer is ever invulnerable to fraud or abuse. Even a closed-network system can be compromised by inside actors.

Experts like computer scientist Avi Marciano are cautious about giving international algorithms access to our biometric information for this reason. That is, when we provide personal information such as fingerprints or even health information to an Internet algorithm, we lose control of it. From that point onward the algorithm could easily be ransacked by malware [16]. Further, privacy concerns have always been important; however, in the 4th industrial revolution so much can be shared so quickly. Ethical quandaries are never solved with simplistic answers, especially when the technology is so rapidly advancing. The rapid advancement is the result of a process called "deep learning".

Over time, these algorithms will natural improve themselves through an iterative process of deep learning. By re-incorporating the information, it receives from user interactions, the algorithms can evolve to become more sophisticated. The American game show *Jeopardy* hosted a contest between IBM's AI "Watson" and two other previous *Jeopardy* champions [15]. Since IBM's Watson had "played" thousands of previous *Jeopardy* games through a computer simulation, it had amassed general knowledge and developed an understanding of the game's rules and advantageous strategies. This raw data combined with advanced processing speeds allowed Watson to outperform the previous champions on nearly every single question [15]. Essentially deep learning allows algorithms to maximize the Throughput Model by exercising itself and remembering past results.

Deep learning can also occur when information systems encounter biometric information, adapting and predicting correlations between various physical characteristics. For example, an algorithm using deep learning to commutate biometric information could easily generate possible correlations and links between different biometric factors. Perhaps different speech patterns correlate with certain psychological predispositions, and an algorithm could make that connection and display it to the user [14]. Applications are numerous, though we must be cautious and considerate before pursuing too grand of a goal.

All this new and exciting technology appears to be a boon, promising faster and more efficient transfers of data by using newer methods of user identification and verification. However, with speed comes increased sensitivity to hacking attempts from bad actors. For example, if fingerprints are submitted to government agencies for security clearance while crossing a border, then they will forever exist on a public-sector server. No server is ever completely safe from hacking or fraud. For example, a government insider can leak that information and then others would take it and use it to perform fraudulent transactions in the name of another individual.

Possible solutions to this dilemma include legal and civil protections for individuals from their national governments. Perhaps firms ought that use this technology ought to follow a set of federally standardized security protocols. This would help to ensure a basic level of competency that would protect the public and provide reasonable assurance to them that their data is protected.

When viewing AI-based biometrics, it is apparent that more time is needed to understand the interplay between biometrics, algorithms, and deep learning. Overall biometrics are highly personal information that can be utilized to custom tailor user experiences. But with that comes significant drawbacks regarding privacy and fraud [16]. Further, ethical considerations and the various ethical positions should be considered and discussed for adoption when employing AI technology [9-12].

We live in a globalized society, in the so called "Internet Age" we share more than ever. Facebook, Twitter, and Instagram are exploited by billions of people. Many people impart their entire life story on these sites, but at a hidden cost. Every time we exercise a search-engine we feed our preferences to an AI that employs complicated algorithms to categorize and monetize our behavior. The AI then proceeds to organize and sell this information to advertising agencies employing machine learning. This is a process of exponential growth in the quantity of knowledge. These advertising agencies then purchase advertising space from websites and furnish the advertisements to our peculiar preferences. If a person is contemplating purchasing a new automobile and search for listings, she or he is more likely to come across advertisements for new automobiles. Therefore, this advances an ethical issue of privacy that must be considered for individuals and organizations. Fraud risks are elevated when a great deal of confidential data is inclined to hacking. Biometric information such as medical records, family photos and speech patterns could all be targets for an attack. Internet organizations must be more transparent about what data is being accumulated and in what time period. Today, organizations have created a tap for consent between them and the user.

## THE ROLE OF CLOUD COMPUTING ON THE INTERNET OF THINGS

Cloud computing works to enhance the efficiency of daily tasks in conjunction with the Internet of Things. Cloud computing is about providing a path for data to reach its destination while the IoT generates a huge amount of data.

There are at least four benefits of cloud computing:

1. No need to conjecture infrastructure capacity needs,

2. Saves money, since there is only a requirement to pay for those resources, that are utilize, the larger the scale, the more savings,

3. In a few minutes, platforms can be deployed around the globe, and

4. Elasticity and speed in offering resources to developers.

Therefore, the role of cloud computing in IoT is to work together to store IoT data, providing easy access when require. Further, to assist in modeling, such as using the Throughput Model, cloud computing is a simpler way to shift large data packets across the Internet produced by the IoT.

As AI improves and becomes progressively sophisticated, firms are willing to place more and more accountability in their hands. This reduces waste, time, and overall cost. Nevertheless, this is a double-edged sword. AI can make mistakes just like human intelligence. If the program's parameters are not properly calibrated, or if the AI is nourished with unreliable and irrelevant data, then mistakes can happen. The seriousness of these mistakes can fluctuate from small misstatements in reports to spectacular workplace accidents. For example, in 2018 an Amazon robot in New Jersey accidentally punctured a canister of bear repellant, which released a potent pepper spray and sent 24 employees to the hospital [13]. Leaving dangerous tasks at the dispense of machines is not something to take lightly. The benefits come with inherent risks that must be accounted for individuals and organizations.

Managers should be cautious when relegating responsibility to an AI program and always provide proper professional oversight. Human observers can catch errors and arbitrate before calamitous events can occur.

A system of ethics based on values is the best way to safeguard consistent positive decision making no matter the conditions [3]. As technology progresses and the magnitude of these machines grows, more and more of the human experience will be impacted by them [9 - 12, 17]. Fewer inputs will be able to need to produce tremendous results. Already we have expert-systems that can analyze millions of data-points and provide detailed reports to organizational users within minutes. The concentration of information and power is something quite revolutionary, and organizations and nations need innovative solutions to manage this rapid development. The global community must be ready to face a future where the exponential development of AI through machine learning, deep learning, and natural language processing is a fact of life, rather than science fiction.

## CONCLUSION

AI represents machines and tools that performs the cognitive functions typically connected with humans, embracing perceiving, reasoning, learning, interacting, etc. In addition, AI is an enveloping economic, societal, and organizational expression of human ingenuity. Examples of AI technologies encompass robotics and autonomous vehicles, facial recognition, iris recognition, natural language processing, neural networks, virtual agents, deep learning and machine learning, which are being implemented in a assortment of problem domains extending from cybersecurity to fintech to education to healthcare. Technologies embracing AI provide fathomless possibilities for elevating people's lives in an collection of areas consisting of their homes, healthcare, education, employment, entertainment, safety, and transportation.

Furthermore, AI provides individuals and organizations with unparalleled opportunities for blueprinting intelligent products, devising novel service offerings, and inventing new business models and organizational forms. Nonetheless, AI is not a technological panacea. Ensuant to the skyline of potentials are a multitude of emerging and complex challenges around business strategies, people–AI interfaces, data, privacy, security, ethics, trust, labor, human rights, and national security. Currently supervisors ought to deal with both possibilities and challenges that complement the pervasive use of AI.

The application of AI algorithms to all manner of processes can significantly affect peoples' lives at work, at home and as they travel around the world. Machine-learning systems, deep learning systems, neural networks, predictive analytics, speech recognition, natural-language understanding, and other instruments is principally depicted as AI are presently governing the global arena. Moreover, research is progressing speedily, media focus is at a record high, and organizations are more and more applying AI solutions in the pursuit of automation-driven efficiencies.

AI systems are also implemented more regularly in critical sectors like healthcare and defense to make decisions and augment efficiency. In terms of sustainability issues, AI is systematically transforming the social, economic, political, and security environments. AI systems have a widespread assortment of uses from automobiles undertaking of driving on their own to algorithms that can calculate through huge quantities of data in seconds. And algorithms, as discussed in this book via the Throughput Model, is one of the main factors underlying the AI performance and guiding its ethical considerations.

Moreover, without AI, today's global environment would appear a great deal differently. Further, AI has already had a gargantuan influence on basically every attribute of the digital world and will continually flourish into our normal operations for years to come.

Nevertheless, AI algorithms are typically operating in a non-transparent mode. Although these algorithms are proficient of making very precise decisions at a high rate, researchers and practitioners do not really understand how they operate especially in the case of deep learning use of neural networks. In other words, AI algorithms are depicted in a "black box," which makes it very difficult to uncover the reasoning behind its decisions built upon this apparatus.

Further, the machineries of the many detail AI algorithms are not open to examination due to the proprietary nature of being assets of an organization or since they are opaque by their very design nature. That is, designers of AI algorithms generally do not leave a pathway describing a procedural manual of understanding of an algorithmic code. Hence, there is no interpretation of what is transpiring line-by-line, which could lead to cognitive biases inserted into the system. This problem is exacerbated due to designers turning to the so-called "black box approach" when developing AI systems. Perhaps the Throughput Model is a first step in revealing the underline mechanisms from a design perspective of AI machinery.

## REFERENCES

[1]     W. Rodgers, *Decision Making for Personal Investments: Real Estate Financing, Foreclosures and Other Issues*, 2017.
        [http://dx.doi.org/10.1007/978-3-319-47849-4]

[2]     W. Rodgers, *Knowledge Creation: Going Beyond Published Financial Information.* Nova Publication: Hauppauge, NY, 2016.

[3]   W. Rodgers, *Ethical Beginnings: Preferences, rules, and principles influencing decision making.* iUniverse, Inc: NY, 2009.

[4]   W. Rodgers, *Trust Throughput Modeling Pathways.* Nova Publication: Hauppauge, NY, 2019.

[5]   W. Rodgers, *Throughput Modeling: Financial Information Used by Decision Makers.* JAI Press: Greenwich, CT, 1997.

[6]   W. Rodgers, *Process Thinking: Six pathways to successful decision making.* iUniverse, Inc: NY, 2006.

[7]   W. Rodgers, *E-commerce and biometric issues addressed in a Throughput Model.* Nova Publication: Hauppauge, NY, 2010.

[8]   W. Rodgers, *Biometric and auditing issues addressed in a Throughput Model.* Information Age Publishing Inc.: Charlotte, NC, 2012.

[9]   W. Rodgers, and S. Gago, "Cultural and ethical effects on managerial decisions: Examined in a Throughput Model", *J. Bus. Ethics,* vol. 31, no. 4, pp. 355-367, 2001.
[http://dx.doi.org/10.1023/A:1010777917540]

[10]  W. Rodgers, and S. Gago, "A model capturing ethics and executive compensation", *J. Bus. Ethics,* vol. 48, no. 2, pp. 189-202, 2003.
[http://dx.doi.org/10.1023/B:BUSI.0000004589.34756.8a]

[11]  W. Rodgers, and S. Gago, "Stakeholder influence on corporate strategies over time", *J. Bus. Ethics,* vol. 52, no. 4, pp. 349-363, 2004.
[http://dx.doi.org/10.1007/s10551-004-1534-5]

[12]  W. Rodgers, and S. Gago, "Biblical Scriptures Underlying Six Ethical Models Influencing Organizational Practices", *J. Bus. Ethics,* vol. 64, no. 2, pp. 125-136, 2006.
[http://dx.doi.org/10.1007/s10551-005-0657-7]

[13]  J. Jolly, *Amazon robot sets off bear repellant, putting 24 workers in hospital.,* 2018.https://www.theguardian.com/technology/2018/dec/06/24-us-amaz-n-workers-hospitalised-after-robot-sets-off-bear-repellent

[14]  J. Dilson, *The Abacus.* St. Martin's Press: New York, 2007.

[15]  J. Markoff, "Computer Wins on 'Jeopardy!': Trivial, It's Not", Available from: https://www.nytimes.com/2011/02/17/science/17jeopardy-watson.html

[16]  A. Marciano, "Reframing biometric surveillance: From a means of inspection to a form of control", *Ethics Inf. Technol.,* 2018.
[http://dx.doi.org/10.1007/s10676-018-9493-1]

[17]  W. Rodgers, *Artificial Intelligence in a Throughput Model: Some Major Algorithms.* Taylor and Francis publication: Florida, 2020.

# SUBJECT INDEX

## A

Aas technology 278
Accountability 10, 12, 30, 41, 73, 74, 79, 92, 301
  algorithmic 10, 12, 30, 73
Accounting 143, 144, 146
  environment 146
  errors 146
  functions 143
  software 144
Accounting firms 19, 20, 100, 143, 144, 145, 147, 258
  public 258
Adoption of deep learning 150
ADP system 167
Age 43, 61, 63, 105, 153, 154, 235
  high-tech digital 105
Agencies 31, 40, 77, 223, 227, 300
  advertising 300
  federal 223
  governmental 227
  human services 77
Agent 10, 22, 84, 209, 239, 289, 302
  independent non-human 289
  virtual 302
Agreements, biometric policy 187
AI-based algorithms 70, 79, 86, 87, 94
  transfers 94
AI-based biometrics 152, 300
AI-powered techniques 150
Airport 206, 207
  screenings 207
  security process 206
Alexa program 100
Algorithms 3, 16, 61, 80, 118, 239, 260
  automation 260
  branch 80
  design 260
  functions 3
  genetic 239
  implementing machine-learning 118

  medical 260
  quantum 61
  synopsis 80
  voice recognition 16
Algorithmic 2, 10, 11, 12, 13, 23, 77, 84, 226, 240, 289
  architect 2
  decision-making routes 13
  engineering processes 10, 240
  methods 77
  processes 23, 84, 226, 289
  techniques 11
  transparency 12
Algorithmic pathways 2, 14, 24, 31, 51, 80, 83, 84, 88, 182, 263
  decision-making 31
  dominant 2, 14, 24, 51, 80, 83, 84, 88, 263
  emphasized Analytical 182
American institute of public accountants (AICPA) 148, 161
Amplitudes, outcome's 269
Analytic pathway decision tree 160
Anthropology 70, 93
Applications 2, 6, 7, 8, 17, 18, 25, 30, 31, 39, 41, 42, 43, 62, 63, 144, 224, 273, 283
  autonomous military 2
  based machine learning 224
  cloud-based 144
  commercial 17
  web-based 25
AR technology 274
Artificial intelligence 103, 126, 131, 134, 297
  algorithms 103
  modeling 126
  models 126
  re-shaping 297
  technologies 131
  technology 134
Artificial neural networks (ANNs) 4, 33, 37, 114, 126, 128
Audio, transcribing 16

www.ingramcontent.com/pod-product-compliance
Lightning Source LLC
Chambersburg PA
CBHW050809220326
41598CB00006B/158